SINDHI

An Introductory Course for English Speakers

Hubert F. Addleton
Pauline A. Brown

Doorlight Publications
South Hadley, Massachusetts

©2010 by Hubert F. Addleton and Pauline A. Brown
The right of Hubert F. Addleton and Pauline A. Brown
to be identified as the Authors of this
Work has been asserted in accordance with
US and UK copyright laws.
All rights reserved. No part of this publication may be reproduced,
stored in a retrieval system, or transmitted, in any form or by any
means, electronic, mechanical, photocopying, recording or
otherwise, except as permitted by US or UK copyright laws, without
the prior permission of Doorlight Publications or the authors.

First published 1984 by the Indus Christian Fellowship
Original title: Functional Sindhi

Published 2010 by Doorlight Publications.
ISBN 978-0-9778372-8-1

Printed and bound in the United States of America

For further information contact Doorlight Publications at
P.O. Box 718
South Hadley, MA 01075
www.doorlightpubs.com

Dedicated to
the Reverend Richard A. Carson,
for many years a missionary
with the New Zealand
Church Missionary Society
in Sindh, Pakistan,
a man of God, humble scholar,
and lover of the Sindhi language.

PREFACE

I am indebted to Norman Zide of the University of Chicago for his encouragement and guidance when I began writing this course in 1976. I am also indebted to Eugene Glassman of the United Bible Societies for his excellent course, <u>Spoken Urdu</u>, a pioneer work published by Nirali Kitaben, Lahore, Pakistan the year I began to develop the present Sindhi Course. With his consent I have transferred many of his language learning concepts into this work.

I am grateful to the Conservative Baptist Foreign Mission Society of Wheaton, Illinois for freeing me of other missionary activities in 1976-77 so that I could pursue the writing of the course at the University of Chicago under Dr. Zide's tutorship. I am also grateful to Duane Sorenson of Sarasota, Florida, and to churches across the USA for funding this study program during that academic year.

Circumstances prevented my return to Pakistan to put my efforts to the test in actual language-learning situations. Therefore much of the credit for this course goes to Pauline Brown. She took my incomplete manuscript back to Pakistan in 1978. She has used it in teaching newcomers to Sindh and has brought it into the shape you now have in hand. I personally feel deeply gratefully to her. All students using this course will share this gratitude.

Hubert Addleton
Cochran, Georgia
1981

Hubert and Bettie Addleton came to Sindh in 1956 about a year and a half after my husband Ralph Brown and I arrived here. We lived together and studied Sindhi in Ratodero, Larkana District from 1956-59. We share with them a deep love for the Sindhi people and their language.

We had long felt the need for a basic language course for students of Sindhi. We were happy to know that Hubert had started this course. When they were unable to return to Pakistan in 1978, I was asked to continue the project. This was not because I have superior academic qualifications, but because of being one of very few foreigners conversant in Sindhi. My principle qualification is a love for the Sindhi language, and having lived in Sindh for many years. I am grateful for early linguistic training at SIL in Norman, Oklahoma. I have tried to keep abreast of modern trends in language learning through reading. I appreciate the encouragement of my colleagues with the Conservative Baptist Foreign Mission Society here in Pakistan, and of the administrative staff of the mission. The mission has also made funding available for the completion of the course.

My husband Ralph E. Brown, although more than busy with his own work, has been a constant support to me. He has also spent substantial time in checking of sentences and grammar notes, and has supervised the writing of the Sindhi calligraphy. This fine work was done by Muhammad Alam Samejo, M.A. Eco; M.A. Eng; B. Ed. of Shikarpur, Sindh.

An incentive to get on with the project was having Anne Pollock Noble, the first student to study the course, living and studying in our home in 1979. Recognition should also be given to Miss Rizvana Mangi of Shikarpur, who was the first to teach it. Their suggestions and corrections, as well as those of other teachers and students have been invaluable. Thus, the course has been tested on students while it has been in the process of preparation. Eloise Roub gave a great many hours of help in the typing of the final draft. I am most grateful to each one who has made any contribution toward the completion of this work.

It is my hope that FUNCTIONAL SINDHI will prove to be a help to those who desire to learn the Sindhi language.

Pauline A. Brown
Shikarpur, Sindh
Pakistan
1981

As we revise this textbook and prepare it for composition on the computer, we need to say thanks to our many teachers who have labored over the years to correct the book and make suggestions for alternate words. Our thanks also go to all of those students who faithfully and fastidiously made notes on confusing sentences and difficult words, or made suggestions for revisions. Thanks go to friends like Q.K. Chandio and Aziz Panhwar who read through the book in its entirety and caught numerous composition errors and spelling mistakes in Sindhi and English, as well as making suggestions for revised grammar explanations and new vocabulary.

Over the years since this book was first published, there have been many new advances made in language learning. While we have incorporated many such changes to our own curriculum, we feel that this book remains unique in its place as a tool to help English-speaking foreigners learn the Sindhi language. Hu and Polly, we are so grateful for your hard work!

Rod Black
Hyderabad, Sindh
Pakistan
2009

TABLE OF CONTENTS

Preface	i
Table of Contents	iii
General Introduction About the Course	xi
To the Student	xi
To the Supervisor	xiii
Introducing Sindhi	xv
Ancestry	
Development	
Script	
Phonology	
Grammar	
Lexicography	
Dialects	
Literature	
Bible Translation	

Lesson 1 — 1

The Sounds of Sindhi – Consonants	1
Voicing	1
Places of Articulation	2
Manner of Articulation	3
Implosives	6
Aspiration	7
Description of Consonants	8
Chart of Consonants	11

Lesson 2 — 12

The Sounds of Sindhi --- Vowels	12
Chart of Vowels	13
Description of Vowels	13

Lesson 3 — 16

Differential Drills	16

Lesson 4 — 28

A.	Pronunciation Drill /r/&/R/ /k/&/K/	28
B.	Cardinal Numbers 1 to 5	29
C.	Plural Forms of Masculine Nouns	29
D.	Masc. Demonstrative Pronouns: (Hua $\tilde{R}^u$ (to be))	30

E.	Question Words, chA (what) and kEr^u (who)	31
F.	"Yes" and "No" Questions with chA	33
G.	Vocabulary	34
H.	Conversational Review	35

Lesson 5 — 37

A.	Pronunciation Drill /b/&/bb/ / n/&/R̃/	37
B.	Plural Form of Feminine Nouns	37
C.	Feminine Demonstrative Pronouns	38
D.	Vocabulary	41
E.	Conversational Review	42

Lesson 6 — 43

A.	Pronunciation Drill /c/& /ch/ /T/&/ Th/	43
B.	Cardinal Numbers 6-10	43
C.	Personal Pronouns as Subjects	44
D.	Present Tense of HuaR̃^{u} (to be)	45
E.	Statements, Questions and Negatives in the Present Tense of HuaR̃^{u}	45
F.	Introducing Adjectives	47
G.	Vocabulary	48
H.	Conversational Review	49

Lesson 7 — 51

A.	Pronunciation Drill /dh/ & /Dh//t/ & /E/	51
B.	The Postposition jO (of;) Inflection of Nouns	51
C.	Demonstrative Adjectives	55
D.	Oblique Forms of Demonstratives and of Question Words kEr^u and kaHiRO	57
E.	Inflected Personal Pronouns	59
F.	Vocabulary	63
G.	Conversational Review	63

Lesson 8 — 66

A.	Pronunciation Drill /d/&/dh/ /R/&/R̃/	66
B.	Location Shown by the Words kithE (where), HutE (there, and HitE (here)	66
C.	Postposition mE (in, at) and tE (on, at)	68
D.	Some Uses of the Word kO	70
E.	Some Postpositions with jE	72
F.	Vocabulary	73
G.	Conversational Review	75

Review One	**77**

Lesson 9	**81**
A. Pronunciation Drill /D/&/Dh/ /p/&/b/	81
B. The Cardinal Numbers 1-16	81
C. Other Uses of the Question Word kaHiRO	82
D. Greetings and Courtesies	83
E. The Question Word kEtrO, How many? and ghaR̃O, How much?	84
F. The Use of Postpositions vaT^i and khE with the verb HuaR̃^{u} to express "to have"	86
G. Vocabulary	89
H. Conversational Review	90
I. Introduction to the Sindhi Writing system I	92

Lesson 10	**99**
A. Pronunciation Drill /th/ & /Th/ /ph/ & /bh/	99
B. The Formation of the Simple Imperative	99
C. The postposition khE as the Sign of the Object	102
D. The Formation of the Present Tense	104
E. Statements, Questions, and Negatives in the Present Tense	105
F. The Reflexive Pronouns: pAR̃^{a} and sandus^u	108
G. Vocabulary	109
H. Conversational Review	112
I. Introduction to the Sindhi Writing system II	114

Lesson 11	**118**
A. Pronunciation Drill /p/&/ph/ /A/&/a/	118
B. The Cardinal Numbers 17-20	118
C. The Oblique form of Cardinal Numbers	119
D. The Comparison and Superlative of Adjectives	120
E. Compound Verbs	122
F. The Formation of the Subjective Tense	124
G. Some Uses of the Subjective	124
H. Vocabulary	126
I. Conversational Review	128
J. Introduction to the Sindhi Writing System III	130

Lesson 12	**137**
A. Pronunciation Drill /O/&/ao/ /b/&/bh/	137
B. Cardinal Numbers in "tens"	137
C. The Formation of the Present Habitual Tense	138
D. Statements, Questions, and Negatives in the Present Habitual Tense	139

E.	The Use of the Vocative	142
F.	The Word khapE (needed) in Impersonal Constructions	143
G.	The use of Ordinal Numbers	145
H.	Vocabulary	147
I.	Conversational Review	149

Lesson 13 — 152

A.	Pronunciation Drill /U/&/u/ /g/&/gh/	152
B.	Cardinal Numbers by "fives"	152
C.	Asking the Cost of Something	153
D.	Fractions	156
E.	The Past Tense of Hua R̃ᵘ	160
F.	Statements, Questions and Negatives with the Past Tense of Hua R̃ᵘ	160
G.	Vocabulary	161
H.	Conversational Review	163

Lesson 14 — 166

A.	Pronunciation Drill /I/&/Ĭ/ /t/&/d/	166
B.	Cardinal Numbers by "ones"	166
C.	The Formation of the Simple Future Tense	167
D.	Statements, Questions and Negatives in the Simple Future Tense	167
E.	The Formation of the Past Habitual Tense	170
F.	Statements, Questions and Negatives in the Past Habitual Tense	170
G.	Other Forms of the Imperative	172
H.	Vocabulary	174
I.	Conversational Review	175

Lesson 15 — 178

A.	Pronunciation Drill /O/&/U/ /D/&/dd/	178
B.	The Cardinal Numbers by "twos"	178
C.	The Days of the Week	179
D.	More Postpositions	180
E.	Infinitives used as Nouns	181
F.	The Infinitive with –vArO to indicate the Doer of an Action	182
G.	The Use of the Infinitive with vArO to Indicate Imminent Action	183
H.	The Use of tE with the Infinitive to Indicate Imminent Action	184
I.	The use of the Infinitive with ghurjE to Express Obligation	184
J.	The Long Form of the Infinitive to show Necessity, Compulsion, obligation	186
K.	Vocabulary	188
L.	Conversational Review	190

Lesson 16		193
A. Pronunciation Drill	/A/&/Ã/ /g/&/gg/	193
B. The use of the Conjunctive Participle		193
C. The Formation of the Present Continuous Tense		196
D. Statements Questions and Negatives in the Present Continuous Tense		198
E. The use of saghaR̃ᵘ (to be able)		200
F. Vocabulary		201
G. Conversational Review		202

Review 2	204

Lesson 17		212
A. Pronunciation Drill	/d/&/D/ /O/&/Õ/	212
B. Cardinal Numbers by "threes"		212
C. The Simple Past Tense of Intransitive Verbs		213
D. Statements, Questions, and Negatives in the Simple Past Tense of Intransitive Verbs.		214
E. The Simple Past Tense of Transitive Verbs		217
F. Statements, Questions, and Negatives in the Simple Past Tense of Transitive Verbs		218
G. Compound Verbs in the Past Tense		220
H. Vocabulary		220
I. Conversational Review		221

Lesson 18		223
A. Pronunciation Drill	/E/&/Ẽ/ /K/ and /G/	223
B. Cardinal Numbers by "fours"		223
C. More Postpositions with jE		224
D. Common Conjunctions		225
E. The present Perfect Tense of Intransitive Verbs		227
F. The Present Perfect Tense of Transitive Verbs		227
G. Statements, Questions and Negatives in the Present Perfect Tense		228
H. Vocabulary		229
I. Conversational Review		230

Lesson 19		232
A. Pronunciation Drill	/k/, /kh/&/K/ /g/, /gh/&/G/	232
B. Cardinal Numbers by "sixes"		233
C. The Past Continuous Tense of Transitive & Intransitive Verbs		233
D. Sentences Illustrating the Past Continuous Tense		235
E. Causal Verbs		236

F. Sentences Illustrating Causal Verbs	238
G. Telling Time	238
H. Mentioning Time in Statements and Questions	240
I. Vocabulary	242
J. Conversational Review	243

Lesson 20 — 245

A. Pronunciation Drill /D/&/dd/ /R/&/D/	245
B. Cardinal Number by "Sevens"	245
C. Pronominal Suffixes as used with Postpositions	246
D. Pronominal suffixes as used with Nouns of Relationship	247
E. Pronominal suffixes as used with the verb Huja$\tilde{R}^u$ (to be)	248
F. Relative and Co-relative Words and their use in Compound Sentences	249
G. Vocabulary	255
H. Conversational Review	256

Lesson 21 — 259

A. Pronunciation Drill /jh/&/j/+/H/ /c/&/j/	259
B. Compound Postpositions with khÃ	259
C. The Formation of the Past Perfect Tense	261
D. Statements, Questions, and Negatives in the Past Perfect Tense	262
E. Intensifying Verbs	264
F. Vocabulary	266
G. Conversational Review	267

Lesson 22 — 269

A. Pronunciation Drill /$\tilde{g}$/&/n/+/g/ /H/&/K/	269
B. Cardinal Numbers by "eights"	269
C. The Infinitive with ddia$\tilde{R}^u$ (to give) to Indicate Permission	270
D. More postpositions	271
E. Reported Speech	272
F. The Infinitive plus lAi (for) with cava$\tilde{R}^u$ to give an order	273
G. Vocabulary	273
H. Conversational Review	274

Review 3 — 275

Lesson 23 — 280

A. Pronunciation Drill	280
B. Expressing Probability of Presumption	280
C. Expressing Probability of Doubt/Uncertainty	283

D. Completion as shown by cukaR̃ᵘ	285
E. Vocabulary	286
F. Conversational Review	287

Lesson 24 — 288

A. Pronunciation Drill	288
B. Cardinal Numbers by "nines"	288
C. Ages of People and Things	288
D. More Postpositions	290
E. Fulfillable Conditions	292
F. Unfulfilled Conditions in the Past	294
G. Vocabulary	295
H. Conversational Review	296

Lesson 25 — 297

A. Pronunciation Drill	297
B. Some uses of the Imperfect Participle	297
C. The Infinitive with caHaR̃ᵘ to show Desired State or Action	300
D. The Infinitive with jjAR̃aR̃ᵘ/acaR̃ᵘ to Express Knowing how	301
E. The Infinitive with sikhaR̃ᵘ to Express Learning how	303
F. Vocabulary	303
G. Conversational Review	304

Lesson 26 — 306

A. Pronunciation Drill	306
B. The Imperfect participle Used with raHaR̃ᵘ to express continuation	306
C. Showing Progression by the use of vaÑaR̃ᵘ and acaR̃ᵘ	307
D. Expressing Necessity by the use of zarUrI, zarUrat, zarUr	308
E. Repetition of words	309
F. The Use of the Perfect participle as an Adjective	311
G. Vocabulary	311
H. Conversational Review	312

Lesson 27 — 314

A. Pronunciation Drill	314
B. The Use of Pronominal Suffixes with Verbs	314
C. Sentences Illustrating the use of Pronominal Suffixes as Subjects of Verbs	315
D. Pronominal Suffixes used with Verbs in the Present Perfect and Past Perfect Tenses as Subjects and Objects	316
E. Sentences Illustrating Double Pronominal Suffixes	317

F.	Inherently Passive Forms of Verbs	319
G.	Derived Passive Forms of Verbs	321
H.	Vocabulary	324
I.	Conversational Review	324

Lesson 28 — 326

A.	Pronunciation Drill	326
B.	The Infinitive with laggaR̃ᵘ to mean "to begin"	326
C.	Some Idiomatic uses of laggaR̃ᵘ	327
D.	More Relative Words with their Co-relatives	328
E.	The Use of vaR̃aR̃ᵘ (to like); Odharⁱ vaThaR̃ᵘ & ddIaR̃ᵘ (to borrow and lend); laHaR̃aR̃ᵘ (to have due)	329
F.	The use of vaThaR̃ᵘ as an Intensifier	331
G.	Some Prefixes and Suffixes	331
H.	Vocabulary	332
I.	Conversational Review	333

Review 4 — 335

Appendix 1 – Summary of Verb Forms — 340

Appendix 2 – Verb Tense Paradigms — 344

Appendix 3 – Combined Vocab List — 352

Appendix 4 – Subject Index — 370

GENERAL INTRODUCTION

ABOUT THE COURSE

FUNCTIONAL SINDHI, as described by the sub-title, is "a Basic course for English Speakers." It has been prepared for those who wish to learn Sindhi in order to live and work in Sindh. It is a basic course in idiomatic, every-day Sindhi. All the structures necessary to daily living are included within a limited vocabulary. The script is taught after Lesson 8 for the benefit of those who wish to read and write. Following this introduction, the student is expected to begin reading from available government school primers and books, and later from other literature. However, a person who expects to spend only a short time in Sindh can also study the course as an oral course. The phonetic script is included throughout for the benefit of such students[1]. This script is the same as that developed by Eugene Glassman for his Spoken Urdu course, with the addition of symbols for Sindhi sounds not found in Urdu.

The Sindhi script has been included throughout the course, too, since many who will teach the course may not be trained in the use of phonetic script. This also benefits the student after s/he begins to read.

The basic method used in this course is that of pattern or model sentences. Each new structure is presented in the form of sentences. Each pattern is to be mastered through repetition and drill. It is not possible to do too much of this type of drill. The grammatical explanations included with each set of sentences usually follow, but occasionally precede them. These are given with a minimum of technical terms, and are not to be "learned" as so many rules. However, the information in these sections is useful and the student will find it helpful to his/her understanding of Sindhi. It should be remembered that no amount of knowledge about the language can substitute for really knowing it.

TO THE STUDENTS

You are anxious to get on with learning Sindhi, but you will find it profitable to take the time to read this introductory material. Very few, if any, students of Sindhi will have the opportunity to study in a group situation in a language school. If you have had opportunity to learn something about direct methods of language study, these principles will be of help to you. Try to incorporate them into your structured study as you go along. Your language teacher or helper probably will not be trained in teaching his language to a foreigner. It is not necessary, even at the beginning, for him/her to be fluent in English, or even to know English. While this may prove frustrating at times, especially in the early stages, it will be an advantage in the long run. With this in mind, suggestions are included in the course to help you in directing your teacher. It is also helpful if a supervisor who has learned Sindhi is available to counsel with the student.

1. Sounds   Since sounds are absolutely basic to speaking and understanding Sindhi, they must take precedence. The first three lessons introduce the sounds of Sindhi, first in isolated words, and then in differential drills. It is important that adequate time be spent in active listening in the first few weeks. From Lesson 4 on each lesson begins with a pronunciation drill. You should

---

[1] Students who have opted for reading and writing will find that the script is not included after lesson 16.

begin each session with your teacher by drilling these words and phrases. There are a number of sounds in Sindhi which can present problems to the student. Mastering these will require real work on the part of most beginners. The conscientious, persistent correction of the student by his/her teacher is vital, not only at this stage, but later, too. At the beginning you will only be able to manage a few minutes of intensive pronunciation drill. Make a note, and ask your teacher to note the difficult sounds/words. After a few unsuccessful attempts it is better to leave it for something else, and return to it later for more drill.

2. Structure The pattern sentence method has already been mentioned. Words have to be put into sentences to be meaningful. It is possible to learn a word such as amb^u (mango) and, with sign language, convey the idea that you want to buy some mangoes. But this is not really effective communication! As sounds are meaningful only in words, so the words need to be combined into larger units, i.e., sentences. The sentence patterns in each lesson must be mastered. The pattern practice method of teaching and learning is basic to this course. Each new pattern or structure is taught through the introduction of models. They are clearly presented, and they must be mastered to the point where they can be repeated at proper speed and with correct pronunciation and intonation. This can only be done through much repetition and drill, both with the teacher and using an audio recorder for extra listening. After mastering a pattern it should be practiced with a variety of substitutions. This will fix it firmly in your mind, and will also help to adapt it to your unstructured conversational needs. The substitutions should not ignore or depart from the basic pattern, but should reinforce it.

The "Conversational Review" at the end of each lesson, from lesson 4 on, contains exercises and suggestions as to how the patterns may be varied. Keen students and teachers will be able to think of many other variations to use the structures in meaningful real life situations, suited to the individual needs of the student. Depending on time available and the difficulty and usefulness of the structure, you can practice a great number of alternate but related sentences. By this time the pattern should be firmly fixed in your mind even if you have not made a conscious effort to memorize it. Our emphasis is not on rote memory, but if the patterns are to be used and useful, they have to be learned. You may find it helpful to pick one or more patterns in each section and consciously commit them to memory. Other sentences in the same pattern would be drilled as substitutions.

The exercises in the conversational review sections are given only in Sindhi with no reference to English meanings. After several days on a lesson you should be able to understand and to "think" these sentences in Sindhi. Since this is our aim, no time is spent in the course on translating English ideas into Sindhi. You will learn far more through seeing or hearing a correct pattern and filling in or changing one part of it.

They ultimate goal is that you should be able to converse, not recite random sentences. So it is important that as each new structure is learned through a group of models, you and your teacher try to imagine real-life situations in which the model or a variation of it can be used. Some suggestions for real-life conversation practice are included in the conversational review sections. Within the structures and the vocabulary of any given stage, no amount of substitution can be too much.

3. Vocabulary The vocabulary of a basic course is necessarily limited. Words are introduced in sentences, and you should learn any new word in such a context. The vocabulary list at the conclusion of the lesson is a summary, and is for reference and review, not to be memorized as a list of words. You, as a learner of Sindhi, will find a need for words each day which may not be included in the lessons. Your teacher will help you to use these words and sentences correctly. Take some time with your teacher to prepare for those situations which you are involved in and where you need to talk. Write down words you hear, and learn to use them in context. Keep a notebook for such vocabulary, and make a habit now which you will find helpful as long as you live in Sindh.

4. Speed/fluency The culture of any people is closely related to their language. You will find as you inquire from your teacher how to say something that "You can't say that", or "You can't say it that way." Habits, customs, beliefs, taboos, etc., are all transmitted through language, not only through what is said, but what is not said, and the way in which things are said. In this course reference is made from time to time to such linguistic-cultural situations. No amount of textbook material can substitute for what you will learn through living among Sindhis, and relating to them in your daily life. Be sensitive; ask questions of your teacher and a few close friends whom you can trust.

TO THE SUPERVISOR

The suggestions in this section are based on the author's personal experience and observations over a period of years, as well as considerable reading on the subject of language learning. There are certain factors helpful and/or necessary to the successful learning of a second language. I have separated these into two categories: those which relate to the individual and those which relate to his/her language learning situation.

1. The Individual The factors most helpful to success are motivation, willingness to adjust to living in another culture, natural linguistic ability, and some linguistic training. Of these the first two are absolutely essential. A student with a great deal of ability, and even linguistic training, but without a high level of motivation and willingness to adjust to the culture will almost surely fail.

Linguistic training may be helpful but not necessary. It can be a hindrance if the training has led the student to think that s/he can learn the language better and more easily on his/her own without the help of a supervisor or language course. Very few students are so motivated and disciplined as to be able to stick it out when things get rough. There is no easy, painless way to learn a difficult language like Sindhi.

2. The Language Learning Situation The following are the important factors relating to the situation in which the student will learn Sindhi: an opportunity to hear and use Sindhi daily, a competent teacher, close supervision, an adequate course.

Hearing Sindhi and practicing everyday what one is learning is absolutely essential. It is not enough to talk with the teacher, to drill and to listen to tapes. Effort and self-discipline are required to go out and talk with people when one is hardly able to communicate the simplest things. It is not quite so hard for a man in the man's world of Sindh. He can go to the bazaar, the tea shops and chat with his neighbors outside in the evening. But for a woman in the smaller cities of Sindh this can be a very real problem. I would recommend a Sindhi woman to help in the house if this is possible. Then a woman should try to meet at least a few neighbors. A married woman can arrange to meet the wives of some of her husband's friends. A woman student should have a woman as a teacher. This is much more culturally acceptable, and will open up many social contacts as well.

The teacher need not be fluent in English. If the student is forced to communicate with his/her teacher in Sindhi from the beginning, it can even be an advantage. The teacher should be educated in Sindhi, and have a genuine interest in teaching his/her language. It is a very demanding job to teach one's language to a foreigner, who may often seem to have dull ears and a stiff tongue! The supervisor can be very helpful in keeping up the enthusiasm of the teacher as time goes on.

Ideally the language supervisor should be one who has already learned Sindhi, and who has adjusted to living and working in Sindh. S/he should be sympathetic to the problems of the newcomer both in learning Sindhi and in his/her cultural adjustments, since his/her encouragement and counsel may be a key factor to the student who may be of average ability or who is having some cultural adjustment problems. The supervisor should be able to sit in on language lessons with the teacher, and to make suggestions both to the teacher and student. S/he should be available to the student both for counsel and to advice on any difficulties with the language.

A structured but not rigid course is also very important. It is my hope that this course will fill this need for language students desiring to learn Sindhi.

EVALUATION OF PROGRESS

Not all students will progress at the same rate. In a language school situation there is pressure to keep up to a schedule. This is helpful to some students, but discouraging to others. When students are following an independent course of study, each one should be helped to set realistic goals. A progress test or evaluation is recommended to follow each of the four review lessons, with a final comprehensive examination following the completion of the course. These should test or evaluate the student's progress in comprehension and his ability to use what he has been studying.

No timetable of study is included here, but an average student should plan to study 6-8 hours a day, five days a week. His/her time could be divided as follows: 2-3 hours with his/her teacher in drilling, pattern practice and conversation; 2 hours listening to material s/he has recorded from the lessons; 2-3 hours conversing and listening to Sindhis other than the teacher. With such a schedule, the student could expect to take the first progress test after 6-8 weeks, and the others at 3 month intervals. The comprehensive examination would take place about one year after study of Sindhi has begun. This would include evaluation of reading and writing skills also. A student studying the course orally without learning to read and write might complete it in 6-8 months, or sooner.

Pauline A. Brown
Shikarpur, Sindh
Pakistan
1981 (rev. 2009)

INTRODUCING SINDHI

Sindhi is spoken by approximately twenty to twenty-five million people in Pakistan[2], most of whom live in the province of Sindh. An estimated eight million Sindhi-speaking people live in India. They also may be found in the great metropolitan centers of Southeast Asia, East Africa, Great Britain, North America, and many other countries of the world.

Ancestry

Sindhi belongs to the northwestern group of Indo-Aryan languages. Most scholars agree that it evolved from Sanskrit, the oldest known member of the Aryan language family. The 19th century German scholar, Ernest Trumpp, declared that

> "Sindhi is a pure Sanskritic language, more free from foreign elements than any other of the North Indian vernaculars… It is much more closely related to the old Prakrit[3] than the Marathi, Punjabi and Bengali of our days and it has preserved an exuberance of grammatical forms for which all its sisters may well envy it."[4]

However, a few scholars have attempted to connect its origin to other language families more ancient than Sanskrit. Nabi Bux Baloch states that

> "Sindhi probably (has) its origin in a pre-Sanskrit Indo-Iranian Indus Valley language… (it), in particular, may have imbibed some of the influence of the ancient language of Moenjodaro civilization having affinities with the Sumerian and Babylonian tongues."[5]

Development

Whatever may have been its origin, the Sindhi language developed down the centuries by freely absorbing elements of various other languages. The Sindh Province was one of the major gateways from the northwest into South Asia, making it an oft-used invasion route drawing Greeks, Arabs, Persians, Turks and other peoples across its territory. Thus, if Sindhi had its origin in Sanskrit, it owes its continued development to the influence of these invading peoples' languages upon it. Because of the strong Muslim influence since the eighth century, the Sindhi vocabulary and grammar are saturated with Arabic and Persian elements. Indeed, the script itself is a result of that influence. Sindhi even absorbed many English words during the century of British rule.

Script

When the British began to rule in Sindh in 1843 Sindhi was the common language but Persian was used in education and administration. Use of Sindhi was restricted to trade and some religious writings, both Muslim and Hindu. British policy, however, was to run their administration in the common languages of the people. This gave Sindhi a higher status, edging out Persian altogether.

Initiating this policy the British were faced with several problems, the first of which was adopting a uniform Sindhi script. In the mid-19th century Sindhi was written in a variety of

---

[2] The total number of Sindhis is very unclear as there has not been a reliable census since the early 80's.
[3] A general name for those popular languages or dialects of northern and central India which existed alongside or grew out of Sanskrit.
[4] Trumpp, Ernest, Grammar, 1872, p.1
[5] Baloch, Nabi Bux, Dictionary, 1960, Preface, p.9

Devanagari, Gurmukhi, Arabic, and Persian scripts. Choosing one script to be the official one was a sensitive issue because there were wide differences of opinion about the choice. Pressure from Muslims and Persian-oriented Hindu scholars led the British to accept the Perso-Arabic script devised by Ellis and some Sindhi scholars. Although this script has undergone some modifications it is basically the same script in use today. However, you will still find the Gurmukhi script used among some Hindu groups. Many Sindhi Hindus in India are using the Devanagari script although the Perso-Arabic script is still dominant there.

Phonology

European scholars were the first to attempt a phonological and grammatical analysis of Sindhi. Their attention was drawn especially to the implosive stops which is a unique characteristic of Sindhi and a few other Indo-Aryan languages. The four implosive stops in Sindhi were first described by George Stack in 1853. From that time to the present linguists have, with varying degrees of clarity, attempted to describe these sounds. However, two contemporary linguists, John Bordie[6] and L.M. Khubchandani,[7] have applied modern linguistic methods in their analysis and description of Sindhi sounds.

Grammar

Beginning as early as 1835 various European and Sindhi scholars attempted to write the grammar of Sindhi. However, the first detailed grammar was written by Ernest Trumpp in 1872. His Grammar is a scholarly work written in English with Sindhi terms in the Devanagari script. Even today scholars hold this work in high respect. Several other grammars appeared later, usually written as teaching manuals for Europeans. Shahani's Sindhi Instructor was published in 1906 and C.W. Haskell's Grammar in 1942. As Sindhi gained status and as literacy spread, Sindhi scholars began writing grammars for native Sindhis to give them a deeper understanding of their own language. Recently Sindhi grammar has been taught via Urdu television for the benefit of people living in Sindh (sometimes called "New Sindhis") who do not yet speak Sindhi.

Lexicography

Captain Stack, Deputy Collector of Hyderabad, compiled the first two bilingual dictionaries - English-Sindhi and Sindhi-English - , published in 1849 and 1855 respectively. In these works the Sindhi terms were given in the Devanagari script. The first English-Sindhi dictionary using the Perso-Arabic script was published in 1868 by L.V. Parajpye. In 1879, a Sindhi-English dictionary using the Perso-Arabic script was prepared by Rev. George Shirt and Oodharam Thanvardas. Permanand Mewa Ram's Sindhi-English dictionary published in 1910 is still a standard for today[8]. The Sindhi Adabi Board of Hyderabad published Sindhi-Urdu and Urdu-Sindhi dictionaries in 1959-60. Dr. Nabi Bux Baloch has edited a massive 5 volume Sindhi-English dictionary from the Sindh Adabi Board, and a one-volume abridged version was later produced. Shahani's bilingual dictionaries are still in use and recently companies such as Roshni, Sindhica and Oxford have published English-Sindhi dictionaries. The advent of computers has

---

[6] Bordie, John, The Phonology of Sindhi, PhD. Thesis, University of Texas, 1958.
[7] Khubchandani, L.M., The Phonology and Morphonemics of Sindhi M.A. Thesis, University of Pennsylvania, 1961.
[8] His English-Sindhi dictionary was published in 1933.

made dictionary production much easier and so legal, medical, scientific and newspaper English-Sindhi dictionaries are also on the market.

Dialects

Griersen, in his monumental work, Linguistic Survey of India published in 1911, states that Sindhi may be divided into six major dialects:
- (1) Siro or Siraiki, spoken in the northern part of Sindh
- (2) Vicholi, spoken in the central part of Sindh
- (3) Lari, spoken in the southern part of Sindh
- (4) Lasi, spoken in Las Bela and the Khirtar Range on the western border of Sindh
- (5) Thari or Thareli, spoken in the eastern part of Sindh and the Sindh-Rajastan border areas.
- (6) Kacchi, spoken in the Kutch region of Gujrat on the southern brother of Sindh

The Sindhi most used in publication and in this course is the Vicholi dialect spoken in central Sindh around Dist. Nawabshah. Literate Sindhis throughout Sindh understand this dialect. The writer of this course has lived in northern Sindh and has found it rather easy to adapt to the Siro dialect after learning Vicholi. Some of the differences between these two dialects will be pointed out in this course. The writer is not familiar with the other four dialects and thus cannot make comparisons between them and Vicholi.

Literature

Because of the late emergence of Sindhi as a vehicle of literary expression Sindhi does not possess as great a volume of old literature as one might expect from an ancient language. Until the middle 19th century learned Sindhis expressed themselves in Arabic and Persian. One notable exception is Shah Abdul Latif, sometimes referred to as the Shakespeare of Sindhi literature. Born in 1689 in southern Sindh, he became a powerful poet, expressing in his own language ideas that reflected the current thought of his time. The Sindhi language student should acquaint himself with this powerful figure. Because his poetry was written mostly in the Lari dialect few Sindhi students will be able to read Shah Abdul Latif's writings with understanding. However, the student can learn much about him and his writings by reading H.T. Sorely's Shah Abdul Latif of Bhit; His poetry, Life and Times, published by the Pakistan Branch of the Oxford University Press. A more recent work discussing Shah Abdul Latif is A. Schimmel's Pain and Grace, published by Sang-i-Meel Publications in Lahore.

The best known Sindhi prose writer is Mirza Qaleech Beg who wrote during the first part of 20th century. His novels and other writings are found in most literate Sindhi homes today and he is held in high esteem.

The Sindh Adabi Board, located on the Sindh University campus in Jamshoro, promotes Sindhi literature by reprinting old Sindhi titles and by encouraging new Sindhi writers. The board publishes a scholarly journal quarterly. The Institute of Sindhology located on the Sindh University campus is also encouraging new Sindhi writings and publishing books on the Sindhi language. In this regard the most active in publishing and promoting Sindhi literature is the Sindh Language Authority in Hyderabad, Sindh.

Bible Translation

The first translation of the New Testament into Sindhi was completed in Hyderabad in 1878 by Rev. George Shirt of the Church Missionary Society of London. It was done in the Perso-Arabic script and published in London in 1890. In 1930 another translation was published. It was the work of Sindhi clergyman Bhagtani and New Zealand Church Missionary Society workers. The famous Sindhi writer, Mirza Qaleech Beg, also assisted. This translation was later revised by another Sindhi clergyman, Chandu Ray, assisted by CMS clergyman, Richard Carson. This revision was published in 1961.

The Pakistan Bible Society sponsored a third translation which was begun in 1974 by Hubert Addleton of the Conservative Baptist Foreign Mission Society with Ghulam Ali Roshan and Ghulam Sarwar. It was continued by Ralph E. Brown (CBFMS) and Ghulam Nabi, and completed in the 80's. It has continued to go through revisions until the present edition of 2008. A similar new translation for Hindu Sindhi readers whose religious vocabulary is different was begun in 1979 by Fred Stock of the United Presbyterian Church (USA) with Karam John and Kesar Lal. A new translation for Hindu Sindhi readers is being prepared for publication in 2008.

The translation and printing of the complete Old Testament experienced much slower progress. Rev. George Shirt did portions of it in the 1870's, Rev. Bhagtani continued it in the 1920's and Rev. Chandu Ray brought it to completion and through the press in 1955 with the help of New Zealand CMS personnel Richard Carson, Charles Haskell, and Alice Ward. A new translation was sponsored by the Bible Society and thanks to the efforts of G.M. Ansari, Mark Naylor and others, this work was published in 2009.

LESSON ONE

The sounds of Sindhi - Consonants

We begin learning Sindhi not with the alphabet, but with the Sindhi sounds, or "phonemes" as linguists call them. After you have become familiar with these sounds you will see how they are represented in the letters of the Sindhi alphabet.

This course distinguishes 63 meaningful units of sound. They include 43 consonant sounds, 18 vowel sounds and 2 diphthong sounds. The 20 vowels and diphthong sounds are actually 10 pairs - 1 regular and 1 nasalized, and they will be described in the next lesson. This lesson will describe the 43 consonant sounds.

In this course we have used the available keyboard English symbols to represent the Sindhi sounds. Students who have studied at the Murree Language School will be familiar with most of those symbols because they are employed in the teaching of Urdu. In addition to these, however, a few more will have to be introduced to represent those sounds that are peculiar to Sindhi. After lesson eight the student will be introduced to the Sindhi script. Because many Sindhi teachers may not have experience and training in the use of a phonetic script, the Sindhi script is also used throughout the course. A student's version with the phonetic (Roman) script not used after lesson 16 is available.

Remember that no written symbol can teach you the correct pronunciation of a language until that symbol is associated with the sound to be learned. This is to be taught face to face with a Sindhi person. Once you have heard the correct sound as made by your teacher and learned to imitate it, the symbol attached to it will serve as a useful guide to pronunciation. But in the beginning it can mean nothing until you hear the sound made by your teacher and connect the sound with the symbol. For example, the /t/ in this lesson, although it is a kind of "t" described by linguists, is not the "t" which is used in English. Therefore, correct pronunciation will have to be acquired by listening to your teacher.

The articulatory explanation of the sounds given on the following pages must necessarily contain some technical linguistic terms. For students not already familiar with them there follows a summary of those terms which are relevant in describing the sounds of Sindhi.

Voicing

Try saying the "v" sound: vvvvv. Now compare this with the long "f" sound: fffff, saying each of them alternately: fffffvvvvvfffff. Both sounds are said the same way in the mouth. The difference is found in the position of the vocal cords. When saying the "v" sound the vocal cords are partially closed. The airstream coming out of the lungs is forced through the vocal cords' narrow passageway causing the cords to vibrate. You can hear the vibration and, by placing your hand on your throat, can feel them. But when saying an "f" sound you can hear and feel no vibrations of the vocal cords because they are apart and the airstream is not obstructed as it passes through them. Sounds produced when the vocal cords are vibrating are said to be voiced. Those produced when the vocal cords are apart are said to be voiceless.

Places of articulation

In order to articulate the consonants the airstream must be obstructed in same way as it passes through the vocal tract. Consonants can therefore be classified according to the place and manner of this obstruction. The principal terms for these particular types of obstruction, all of which are required in Sindhi, follow:

1. **Bilabial** (Made with both lips) Say the words "pie," "by," "my," and note how the lips come together for the first sound in each of these words.
2. **Labiodentals** (Lower lip and front teeth) When saying such words as "five" and "vie" most people raise the lower lip until it nearly touches the upper front teeth.
3. **Dental** (Tongue tip or blade and upper front teeth) Say the words "thigh" and "thy". Some people have the tip of the tongue protruding below the upper front teeth while others have it close behind the front teeth. This latter tongue position is common in several Sindhi sounds.
4. **Alveolar** (Tongue tip or blade on the alveolar ridge, located just behind the upper front teeth) When pronouncing words such as "tie," "die," "nigh," "sigh," do you place the tip of your tongue on this ridge?
5. **Retroflex** (Tip of the tongue on the back side of the alveolar ridge) Retroflex sounds do not occur in most forms of English. However, you can hear it when a Pakistani is speaking English. Notice that when he says "t" in "tea," "ten," "take," he curls the tip of his tongue back so that the underside touches the back part of the alveolar ridge.
6. **Palato-Alveolar** (Tongue blade and back of alveolar ridge) say words such as "shy," "she," "show." During the consonants the tip of your tongue will be near the alveolar ridge, and the blade of the tongue is always close to the alveolar ridge. You can feel the place of articulation more distinctly if you hold the position while taking a breath through the mouth. The incoming air cools the blade of the tongue and the back part of the alveolar ridge.
7. **Palatal** (Front of the tongue and the hard palate) Say the word "new," very slowly so that you can isolate the consonant at the beginning. You should be able to feel that the front of the tongue is raised toward the hard palate. The "n" sound in the Spanish word, "Señor," is another example of this sound.
8. **Velar** (Back of the tongue and the velum, or soft palate) Say "hack," "hag," "hang." The consonants that occur at the end of these words are produced as the back of the tongue is raised to touch the velum.
9. **Uvular** (Back of the tongue raised toward the uvula) This sound does not occur in English. It is produced by saying the "k" sound with the tongue raised as far back as possible toward the end of the soft palate. Try to swallow and say "k" at the same time.
10. **Glottal** (Vocal cords held tightly together) This sound is produced in English but is not phonemic (i.e., meaningful). Americans produce it at the beginning of the second syllable in such words as "button (but-'n)" and "bitten (bit-'n)."

Way or Manner of Articulation

Besides knowing the place of the air obstruction to articulate consonants it is also necessary to know how the articulation is accomplished. For example, is the air at any point completely cut off or only partially so? For convenience of explanation the consonants of Sindhi may be classified as follows:

1. **Stop**   This is a complete closure of the articulators involved so that the airstream cannot escape. There are two types of stops: **(1) Nasal stop:** If the airstream is stopped in the oral cavity but the velum, or soft palate, is down so that the air can go through the nasal tract, the sound produced is called a nasal stop. Sounds of this kind occur at the beginning of the words, "me" (bilabial stop) and "nigh" (alveolar stop), in the middle of the word, "union" (palatal stop), and at the end of the word, "sang" (velar stop). All four of these are found in Sindhi, namely /m/, /n/, /Ñ/, and /g̃/. In addition to these there is a nasal flap, /R̃/. **(2) Oral stop:** If, in addition to the articulatory closure in the mouth, the velum, or soft palate, is raised so that the nasal tract is blocked off, then the airstream will be completely obstructed. Pressure in the mouth will build up and an oral stop will be formed. When the articulators suddenly come apart, the airstream will be released in a small burst of sound. This kind of sound occurs in the consonants of the words, "pie," "buy" (bilabial stops), and "Kay," "gay" (velar stops). Apart from the presence of velic closure there is no difference between the oral stop in "buy" and the nasal stop in "my". Although both the nasal stop and the oral stop may be classified as stops, we will use the term stop by itself to indicate oral stop only, and the term nasal to indicate a nasal stop. For example, the consonants in the words, "Pa" and "Ma," would be called bilabial stop and bilabial nasal respectively. There are 18 such stops in Sindhi, namely, /p/, /b/, /ph/, /bh/, /t/, /d/, /th/, /dh/, /T/, /D/, /Th/, /Dh/, /k/, /g/, /q/, /kh/, /gh/, and /'/.
2. **Fricative**   Unlike a stop, a fricative is not a complete closure of the two articulators involved, but a partial closure, causing friction or turbulence as the airstream passes through them. We have included seven Sindhi sounds in this category, namely, /f/, /v/, /K/, /G/, /s/, /z/, and /S/.
3. **Affricate**   Say the word, "chat," and think how you made the first sound. At the beginning the tongue comes up to make contact with the alveolar ridge to form a stop. Then the stop suddenly opens so that a fricative sound is produced in the same place as the stop. An affricate then is a combination of a stop and a fricative. We have listed four in Sindhi, namely, /c/, /j/, /ch/ and /jh/.
4. **Approximant**   This is the approach of one articulator toward another without coming so close together as to make a fricative sound. Notice the "y" sound in "yacht" and "mayor." The front of the tongue is raised toward the plate but it does not come close enough to cause friction as the airstream passes through. The one approximant we have listed is the /y/.
5. **Lateral**   This sound is an obstruction of the airstream at a point along the center of the oral tract with the incomplete closure between one or both sides of the tongue and the roof of the mouth. This is represented in Sindhi by /l/ and is similar to the English "l" in "lip."
6. **Trill**   The tongue is held loosely on the alveolar ridge and the flow of air between these two articulators sets the tongue tip in motion. The trill may be very short with only a single contact of the tongue tip with the alveolar ridge. This is represented in Sindhi by /r/.

7. **Flap** The tongue is placed in the retroflex position, then is flapped down suddenly against the back of the alveolar ridge. There are two flaps in Sindhi: the oral flap, /R/ and the nasal flap, /R̃/ already mentioned under nasal stops.

The air passages within the head above the larynx are known as the vocal tract.

The diagram below gives the location and names of the principal parts of the vocal tract.

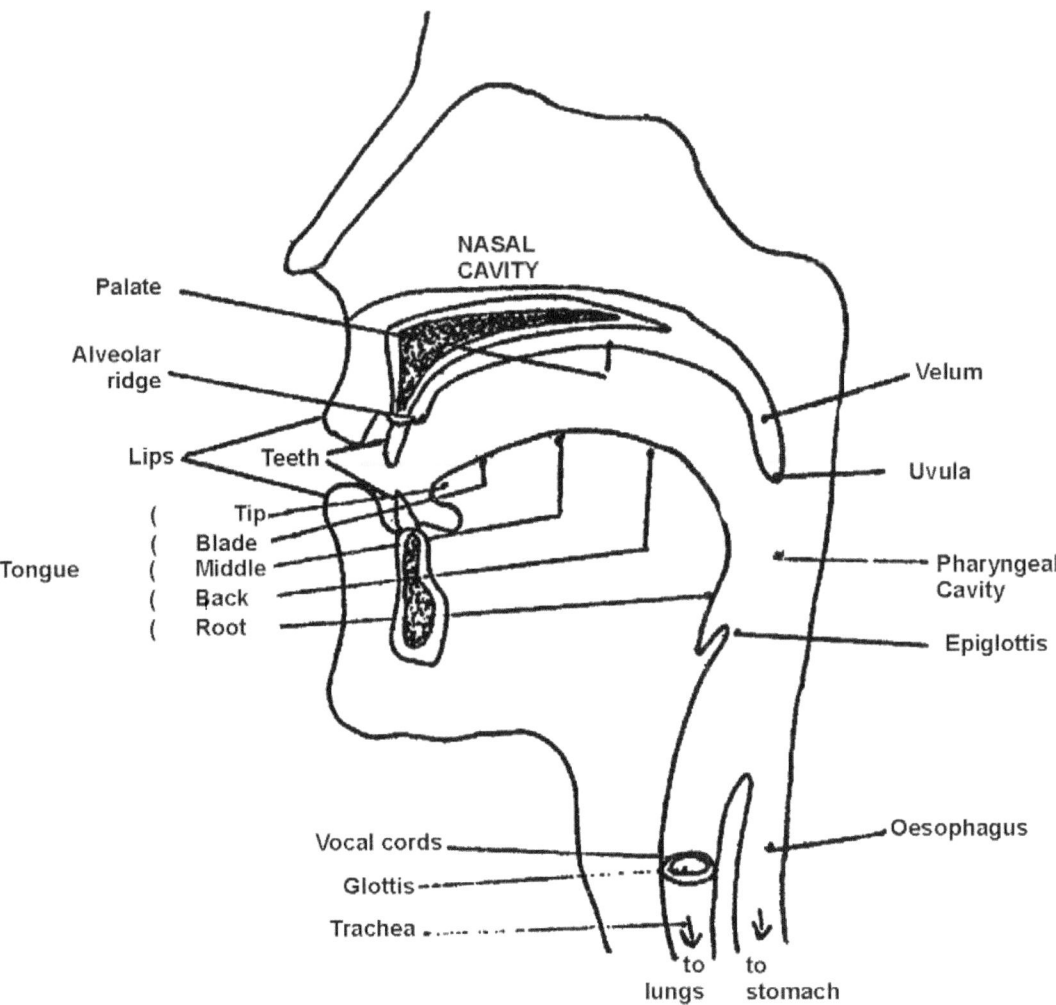

Figure 1

This diagram shows the principal places of articulation important in describing Sindhi consonants.

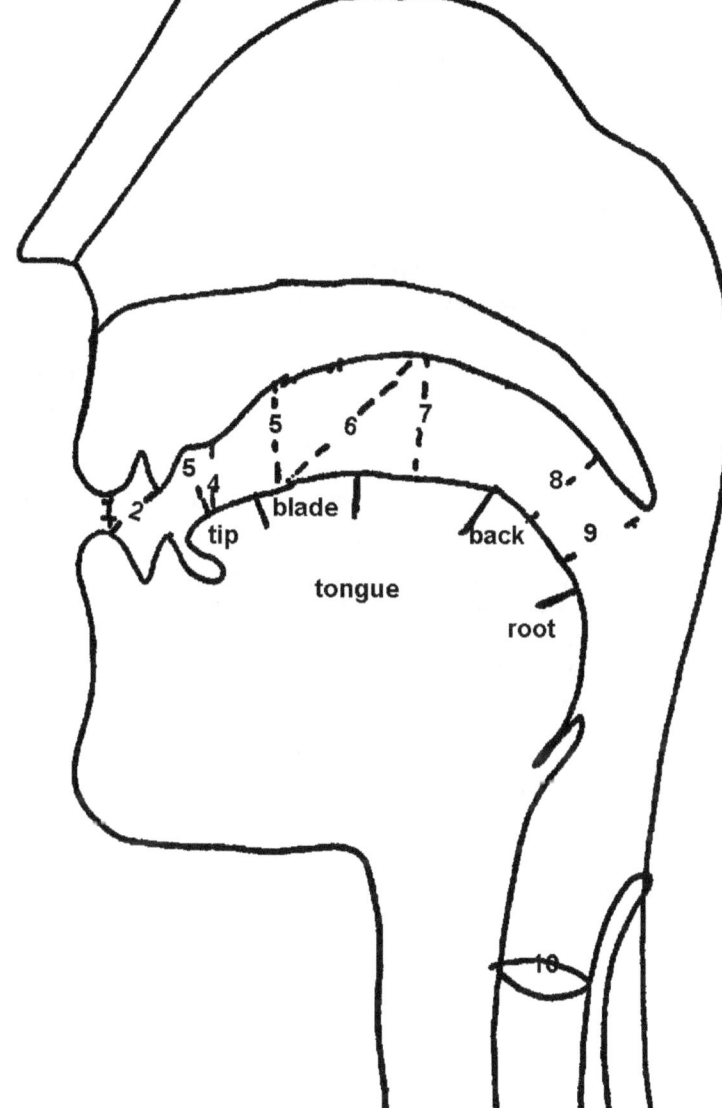

1. bilabial
2. labio-dental
3. dental
4. alveolar
5. palato-alveolar
6. retroflex
7. palatal
8. velar
9. uvular
10. glottal

Figure 2

Implosives

We take it for granted in speaking English that when articulating consonants the airstream is moving outward through the vocal tract. Stops that use an outward or egressive airstream are called "plosives." All English stops are plosives. But there are languages that produce sounds with an inward-moving or ingressive airstream. Sindhi has four ingressive consonant sounds and we call them "implosive stops." We have represented them as /bb/, /dd/, /jj/, and /gg/.

Peter Ladefoged in his book, A Course in Phonetics[1], describes these sounds in this way:

"In some languages sounds are produced by moving different bodies of air. If you make a glottal stop so that the air in the lungs is contained below the glottis then the air in the vocal tract itself will form a body of air that can be moved. An upward movement of the closed glottis will move this air out of the mouth. A downward movement of the closed glottis will cause air to be sucked into the mouth. When either of these actions occurs there is said to be a glottalic airstream mechanism…."

"Stops made with an ingressive glottalic airstream mechanism are called 'implosives.' In the production of implosives the downward moving of the larynx is not usually completely closed. The air in the lungs is still being pushed out and some of it passes between the vocal cords, keeping them in motion so that the sound is voiced. (The chart which follows) shows the movements in a voiced bilabial implosive of a kind that occurs in Sindhi…."

"In all implosives that I have measured, the articulatory closures — in this case the lips coming together — occurs first. The downward movement of the glottis, which occurs next, is like a piston that would cause a reduction of the pressure in the oral tract. But it is a leaky piston in that the air in the lungs continues to flow through the glottis. As a result, the pressure of the air in the oral tract is not affected much. (In an ordinary plosive /b/ there is, of course, an increase in the pressure of the air in the vocal tract.) When the articulatory closure is released there is neither an explosive nor, in the literal sense, an implosive action. Instead, the peculiar quality of the sound arises from the complex changes in the shape of the vocal tract and in the vibratory pattern of the vocal cords."

Figure 3 on the next page gives the estimated sequences of events in a Sindhi bilabial implosive /bb/.

---

[1] Peter Ladefoged, A Course in Phonetics (Harcourt Brace Javanovich, Inc. 1975), pp. 114-117.

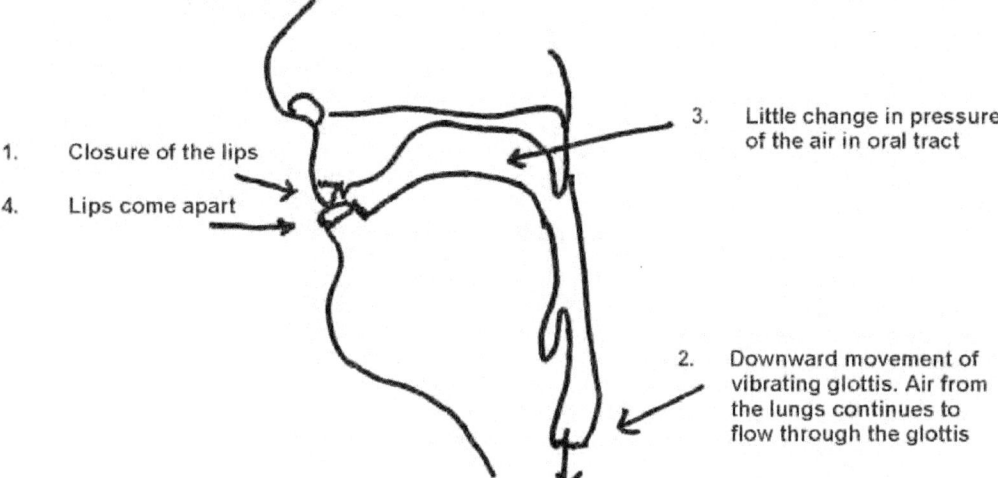

Figure 3

Breathing or Aspiration

This is a special feature of stops and affricates in Sindhi, and is extremely important. English speakers are not aware of the fact that there is a difference between the /p/ in "pie" and the /p/ in "spy." This is because the difference is not phonemic in English. That is, you can pronounce the /p/ either way in each word and still be understood. When pronouncing "pie" a rather strong puff of air, called "aspiration," can be seen by holding a thin strip of paper in front of the mouth. However, such a puff of air is lacking when pronouncing "spy." Although this difference in the "p" sound is unimportant in English it is absolutely essential in Sindhi. The release of a puff of air (aspiration) in the wrong place, or the failure to release it in the right place, can make the difference between comprehension and misunderstanding. So, in Sindhi pal (without aspiration on the /p/ sound) refers to a minute of time, while phal (with aspiration) refers to fruit. Likewise, bAlO means "an upper room" while bhAlO means "spear."

It is important to note that the puff of air is not released as an afterthought; that is, it is not added to the consonant as a separate item (as if it were /b/ /h/), but rather the mouth is already full of air before the opening of the stop and the puff of breath is released along with the consonant sound as an essential part of it (thus, /bh/).

With these linguistic terms we are ready to describe the consonant sounds of Sindhi.

			Sindhi examples[1]	
1.	m	Voiced bilabial nasal, as in "man," "dim".	mAp[a2] ماپُ	malUm[a] مَعلومَ
2.	n	Voiced dental nasal, somewhat similar to the English "n," but the tip of the tongue is behind the upper teeth, not on the alveolar ridge as in English.	namak[u] نَمَكُ	panO پَنو
3.	Ñ	Voiced palatal nasal, as in the Spanish word, "Señor".	vaÑO وَڃو	suÑ[a] سُڃَ
4.	g̃	Voiced velar nasal. This is one consonantal sound, not two as in bingo (bing-go)." It is similar to the sounds in "singing." Think of the sound as a velar /n/.	cag̃O چڱو	sig̃[u] سڱُ
5.	R̃	Voiced retroflex nasal flap. Curl the tip of the tongue up to the back of the alveolar ridge, and make an "n" sound as you flap the tongue against the back of the ridge as it returns to its position behind the lower front teeth.	vaR̃[u] وَڻُ	kaR̃ik[a] ڪَڻڪَ
6.	p	Voiceless unaspirated bilabial step, as in "spin," "spot."	pEr[u] پيرُ	kap[u] ڪَپُ
7.	b	Voiced unaspirated bilabial step, as in "baby," "boy."	bAb[u] بابُ	jabal[u] جَبلُ
8.	bb	Voiced bilabial implosive stop.	bbI ٻي	kabbaT[u] ڪَٻَٽُ
9.	ph	Voiceless aspirated bilabial stop, as in "pin," "pie."	phEr[u] ڦيرُ	phikO ڦِڪو
10.	bh	Voiced aspirated bilabial stop.	bhalO ڀَلو	sabh[u] سَڀُ
11.	t	Voiceless unaspirated dental stop; not the English "t" sound, which is alveolar.	tArO تارو	SitArO سِتارو
12.	d	Voiceless unaspirated dental stop; not the English "d" sound, which is alveolar.	dAl[i] دالِ	madad[a] مَدَدَ

---

[1] The Sindhi examples are given in the Sindhi script also for the benefit of the teacher. The meanings of the words are irrelevant at this point.

[2] Most Sindhi words end in a vowel. If the ending vowel is "short" it is always of very brief duration and is never stressed. Take special notice of how your teacher handles these final vowels in a sentence. S/he may overemphasize them in isolated words.

13.	dd	Voiced alveolar <u>implosive</u> stop.	ddis^u ڏِسُ	vaddO وَڏو
14.	th	Voiceless aspirated dental stop.	thuk^u ٿُڪُ	mathO مَٿو
15.	dh	Voiced aspirated dental stop.	dhak^u ڌَڪُ	vadhIk^a وَڌيڪَ
16.	T	Voiceless unaspirated retroflex stop. Speakers native to Upper Sindh trill this stop in many words.	TapAl^a ٽپالَ	puT^u پُٽُ
17.	D	Voiced unaspirated retroflex stop. Speakers native to Upper Sindh trill this stop in many words.	DighO ڊِگهو	khanD^u کَنڊُ
18.	Th	Voiceless aspirated retroflex stop.	ThIk^u ٺيڪُ	vaThO وَٺو
19.	Dh	Voiced aspirated retroflex stop.	DhAl^a ڍالَ	vaDh^u وَڍُ
20.	jj	Voiced palatal <u>implosive</u> stop.	ajj^u اَڄُ	jjAtO ڄاتو
21.	k	voiceless unaspirated velar stop, as in "school," "skin."	kalAm^u ڪَلامُ	nak^u نَڪُ
22.	g	Voiced unaspirated velar stop as in "go," "gum."	gAh^u گاهُ	magarⁱ مَگَرِ
23.	gg	Voiced velar <u>implosive</u> stop.	ggOTh^u ڳوٺُ	ruggO رُڳو
24.	q	Voiceless unaspirated uvular stop. This is the "qui" of Classical Arabic and in Sindhi it occurs in loan words from Arabic. In ordinary Sindhi pronunciation it becomes /k/.	qalam^u قَلَمُ	'aqul^u عَقُلُ
25.	kh	Voiceless aspirated velar stop, as in "<u>c</u>ool" and "<u>k</u>in."	khap^u کَپُ	likhO لِکو
26.	gh	Voiced aspirated velar stop.	ghar^u گهَرُ	paghAr^a پگهارَ
27.	'	Glottal stop. This is the "ain" of classical Arabic and in Sindhi it occurs in loan words from Arabic. It is not emphatically pronounced as a glottal stop in Sindhi. In fact, it is usually not pronounced at all. Notice how your teacher pronounces the examples.	'aqul^u عَقُلُ	in'Am^u اِنعامُ

28.	c	Voiceless unaspirated palato-alveolar affricate, similar to the sound in "cheese," if pronounced without aspiration.	cAr[i] چارِ	sacO سَچو
29.	j	Voiced unaspirated palato-alveolar affricate, as in "joy," "major."	jang[i] جَنگِ	bAjO باجو
30.	ch	Voiceless aspirated palato-alveolar affricate, as in "choo-choo."	chO چو	chanchar[u] چَنچَرُ
31.	jh	Voiced aspirated palato-alveolar affricate, as in "age," "judge."	jhang[u] جھَنگُ	jhajhO جھَجھو
32.	f	Voiceless labiodental fricative, as in "fish," "fifty.	fasal[u] فَصَلُ	SafA شفا
33.	v	Voiced labiodental fricative, similar to the sound in "vine," but the friction is weaker. It is somewhat between the "v" in "vine" and the "w" in "wine."	vArO وارو	cavE چَوي
34.	K	Voiceless velar fricative, similar to the German "ach" and the Scottish "loch."	Kas[u] خاصُ	taKt[u] تَختُ
35.	G	Voiced velar fricative; same as 34; plus voicing.	Gam[u] غَمُ	bAG[u] باغُ
36.	s	Voiceless alveolar fricative, as in "city," "see."	sabh[u] سَپُ	nasal[u] نَسَلُ
37.	z	Voiceless alveolar fricative, as in "zebra," "rose."	zabar[a] زَبَر	sazA سَزا
38.	S	Voiceless palato-alveolar fricative, as in "sheep," "nation."	SEr[u] شيرُ	kOSiS[a] کوشِش
39.	y	Voiced palatal approximant, as in "yes," "union."	yAr[u] يارُ	mayat[u] مَيَتُ
40.	l	Voiced dental lateral; similar to the sound of "l" in "lean," "feel" when the tongue is behind the upper front teeth.	lasI لَسِي	dil[i] دِلِ
41.	H	A stream of air passed through the vocal cords. Position of the tongue is determined by the vowel that follows it.	HU هُو	rAH[a] راهَ
42.	r	Voiced alveolar trill or flap; similar to the Spanish trilled "r".	rAt[i] راتِ	darI دَرِي
43.	R	Voiced retroflex flap.	pARO پاڙو	kurARI کُراڙي

Chart of Sindhi Consonants

	Bilabial	Labio-dental	Dental	Alveolar	Palato-Alveolar	Retroflex	Palatal	Velar	Uvular	Glottal
Nasal (Stop)	m		n			R̃	Ñ	g̃		
Plosive (Stop)	p b ph bh		t d th dh			T D Th Dh		k g kh gh	(q)	(˙)
Implosive (Stop)	bb			dd			jj	gg		
Affricate					c j ch jh					
Fricative		f v		s z	S			G K		
Approximant							y			
Lateral				l						
Trill				r						
Flap						R				

Whenever there are pairs of symbols within a cell, the one on the left represents a voiceless sound. All other symbols represent voiced sounds. The consonant /H/ does not appear on the chart. This sound acts like a consonant, but from an articulatory point of view it is simply the voiceless counterpart of the following vowel. The sounds /q/ and /'/ are in parentheses because they are found only in words originating from Arabic and are not really pronounced as indicated above in ordinary Sindhi speaking.

LESSON TWO

The sounds of Sindhi – Vowels and Diphthongs

Vowels in any languages are more difficult than consonants to describe because they vary from person to person. In addition to the differences of vocabulary and grammatical usage, the difference in the vowels, too distinguishes what most people think of as "dialects." Americans can see this easily by comparing what are known as "Southern" and "New England" dialects.

Overlooking minor variations, then, it is possible to distinguish eight vowels and one diphthong. Because each of these nine sounds can be nasalized, we thus have eighteen contrasting vowel and diphthong sounds.

Apart from the diphthong all vowels are "pure," that is <u>level</u> in their quality. The tongue does not change its position throughout the sounding of the vowel. In making English vowels the tongue usually glides up or down, resulting in a vowel that is actually a diphthong, or "double sounds." So an English word like "beat," when transcribed phonetically sounds like (biyt), and the word "boat," actually sounds like (bowt). In these two examples /y/ and /w/, sometimes known as semi-vowels, combine with /i/ and /o/ respectively to give the impression of a diphthong or gliding sound. The student of Sindhi therefore, must make considerable effort to keep his tongue still while making vowel sounds so that his vowels will be level, or unglided.

However, a glide is necessary to produce the one Sindhi diphthong which only appears in its nasal form. This diphthong is /āõ/ and it is produced by a quick glide of the tongue from the position for /a/ to the position for /O/. Until recently Sindhi grammarians had classified /ai/ also as an unglided vowel. Linguist L. M. Khubchandani declares that /ai/ is "one simple vowel" and /ao/ is the one "falling diphthong."[1] Very rarely you may hear Sindhis use the /ai/ and /ao/ glides such as in the words "paisa" or "qaidI," and "maolvI" or "aorat." These glides seem to have largely disappeared from everyday speech. However, if your teacher does pronounce them, learn them as they are taught. Be sure to also keep listening carefully for how they are pronounced by others in your area.

Vowels are distinguished from each other by the position of the tongue. The Sindhi vowels range from the tongue high in the front of the mouth for /I/ to the tongue high in the back of the mouth for /U/, with the other vowels falling somewhere in between and lower. Linguists sometimes plot the location of these vowels on a chart. As they are pronounced in the order of /I/, /i/, /E/, /a/, /A/, /ao/, /O/, /u/, and /U/, you will notice that the jaw is almost closed for /I/, that it opens as we move down the chart to /E/; then it opens more as we move down the chart to /A/;

---

[1] Khubchandani, L.M., <u>The Phonology and Morphophonemics of Sindhi</u>, A thesis presented to the faculty of the Graduate School of the University of Pennsylvania, 1961, p.23.

then it closes again as we move up to /U/. The tongue, too, drops progressively lower from a high front position at the beginning until it reaches a mid-position, then rises progressively at the back. The following chart describes this movement of the jaw and tongue as Sindhi vowels are formed:

	Front	Central	Back
High	I		U
Lower-high	i		u
Higher-mid	E		o
Mid		a	
Lower-mid			ao
Low		A	

The vowels /I/, /E/, /A/, /O/ and /U/ differ in duration as well as quality from the vowels /i/, /a/, and /u/, being approximately twice as long, i.e. taking twice as long to say. These latter vowels, plus the diphthong /ao/ may be classified as "short." This is extremely important for English-speaking students to remember because the vowels are especially meaningful at the end of Sindhi words, distinguishing gender, number, tense, etc. The student will not be understood if s/he shortens the vowel when it should be long or lengthens it when it should be short.

The vowel sounds mentioned thus far are oral. In pronouncing them the velum is closed and all of the air used in the production of the sounds passes out through them mouth. None is allowed to escape through the nasal tract. But these sounds may also occur with component nasalization; that is, the velum is open and some of the air passes out through the nasal tract. The symbol for nasalization in these beginning lessons is a tilde (~) placed above whatever vowel or diphthong is to be nasalized.

Since nasal and oral vowels and diphthongs contrast in Sindhi, the student must be careful to make the distinction in his own pronunciation. Many westerners tend to nasalize vowels in speaking English. In speaking Sindhi this must be carefully controlled.

Beginning where we left off the description of the consonant sounds we are now ready to describe the Sindhi vowels sounds.

Sindhi Examples

44.	I	High, front, long; velum is closed so that the air escapes only through the mouth; similar to "heed" and "bead" but without the off-glide as in these English words.	ca g Ĩ چَڱِي	bIThO بيٺو
45.	Ĩ	Same as 44, plus nasalization; thus the velum is open so that air escapes through both nose and mouth.	S Ĩ h ũ شِينهُن	AH Ĩ آهين
46.	i	Lower-high, front, short, velum closed; as in "hid" and "kid" if pronounced without an off-glide.	ddinO ڏِنو	akh[1] اِکِ

47.	ĩ	Same as 46, plus nasalization; velum open.	H ĩ arᵃ هِينئَرَ	ga ĩ گانءِ
48.	E	Higher-mid, front, long, velum closed; as in "fate" and "sake" but without the y-like off-glide.	pETᵘ پيٽُ	mErO ميرو
49.	Ẽ	Same as 48, plus nasalization; velum open.	mẼ مِ	kAẼ كائين
50.	ai	Lower-mid, front, long, velum closed; similar to "hat" and "sad" if pronounced without the "y-like" off-glide. Some grammarians call this a diphthong. **However, in ordinary conversation it becomes a pure vowel.**	qaidI قئيدي qEdI قئيدي	paisO پئيسو pEsO, pasO پئسو
51.	ã ĩ	Same as 50, plus nasalization; velum open. **In ordinary conversation it becomes a pure vowel.**	b ã ĩ sirI بَينسري	m ã ĩ Hⁱ مَينهِن
52.	a	Mid, central, short, velum, closed; similar to "but" and "above."	jaldI جلدي	madadᵃ مددَ
53.	ã	Same as 52, plus nasalization; velum open.	H ã yO هَنيو	p ã HinjO پَنهنجو
54.	ao	Lower-mid, back, long; a glide or diphthong from /a/ (52) to /o/ (59); shorter than similar sound in "house" and "now;" velum closed. **In ordinary conversation it becomes a pure vowel (O).**	naokarᵘ نوڪرُ nOkarᵘ	raonakᵃ رَونق rOnakᵃ
55.	ã õ	Same as 54, plus nasalization; velum open.	Dh ã õ g̃ ڏَوڱ	s ã õ pᵃ سَونپَ
56.	A	Low, central, long, velum closed; similar to standard Midwestern American pronunciation of "father," "cot," "bother."	Abᵘ آبُ	SAbAs شاباس
57.	Ã	Same as 56, plus nasalization; velum open.	tavHÃ توهان	bÃ sᵃ بائس
58.	O	Higher-mid, back, long; velum closed lacks the "w-like" off-glide of the similar sound in "go" and "boat."	kOThI كوني	mazO مزو
59.	Õ	Same as 58, plus nasalization; velum open.	dŨHÕ دُونهون	sAmHÕ سامهون

60.	u	Lower-high, back, short, velum closed; similar to the sound in "pull," "put," "foot," but with no of-glide.	uTh^u اُٺُ	pI^u پيُ
61.	ũ	Same as 60, plus nasalization; velum open.	mũHũ مُنھُن	tũHinjO تُنھنجو
62.	U	High, back, long, velum closed; similar to the sound in "shoe," "boot," but without the "w-like" diphthongal off-glide.	khUH^u ڪوھُ	mAR̃HU ماٺھُو
63.	Ũ	Same as 62, plus nasalization; velum open.	AŨ آءُ	dŨHÕ دُونھون

Note: Page 11, note 3 points out the special character of Sindhi short vowels when they are in word-final position. In the phonetic script, these final short vowels are slightly raised to help the student to remember that in this position in the word the vowel is of very brief duration, and very nearly voiceless.

LESSON THREE

In lessons one and two you have been introduced to the sounds of Sindhi in separate words. The purpose of this lesson is that the student may be able to distinguish these sounds when they are found in words which are very similar. In some cases there will be only the one difference in the two words being compared. Since minimal pairs are not always possible or practical, the words chosen are as close as it is possible to find.

These drills are for ear and tongue practice. The phonetic script is given only as an <u>aid to listening</u>. At this point in his/her language learning, the student should be doing much more listening than speaking. Until the ear is trained to <u>hear</u> the difference between sounds, the tongue will not be able to imitate or mimic what is heard. When drilling with a teacher, the student should have the book closed. The teacher should repeat the pair of words several times before the student tries to mimic. The student should <u>never</u> at this stage, try to pronounce unless s/he has a Sindhi speaker to repeat the word first. If the student finds it impossible to hear the difference, s/he may refer to the phonetic script in order to know just what he is listening for. The drills should be put onto tapes for extra listening practice. When listening to the tapes, it will be helpful to refer to the phonetic script. The student should <u>never</u> try to "read" from the phonetic script.

The meaning of the words is not given, since the student is not intended to be learning them as words. However, they are all real Sindhi words. No nonsense syllables are used.

3-A Differential Drills – Vowels

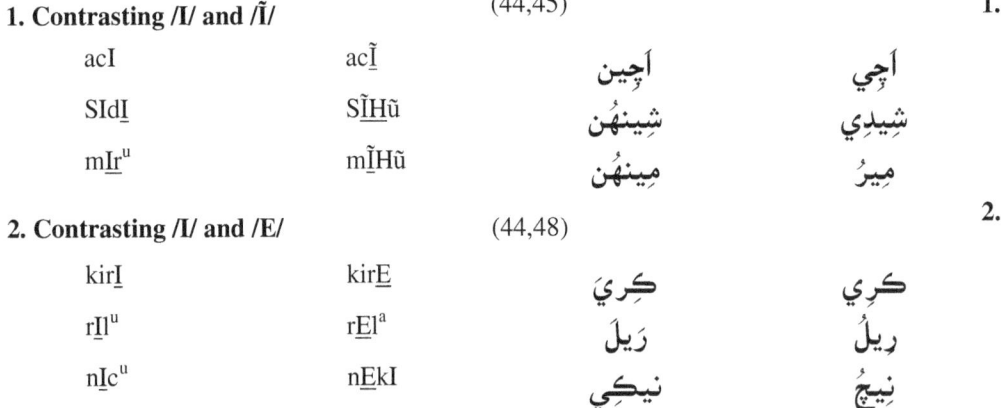

3. Contrasting /I/ and /i/ (44,46)

pItO	pitO	پِتو	پیِتو
dIn^u	din^u	دِنُ	دیِنُ
SIdI	bbiII	بِلِي	شِیدِي

4. Contrasting /i and /ĩ/ (46,47)

tan^i	taHĩ	تَنِهن	تَنِ
jAn^i	gÃĩ	گانءِ	جانِ
bhit^i	mãĩHĩ	مَینِهن	پِتِ

5. Contrasting /i/ and /u/ (46,60)

HitE	HutE	هُتي	هِتي
jAn^i	jaHAn^u	جَهانُ	جانِ
bhit^i	but^u	بُتُ	پِتِ

6. Contrasting /i/ and /a/ (46,52)

bhit^i	bhat^a	ڀَتَ	پِتِ
piT^i	paT^a	پَٽَ	پِٽِ
dil^i	maHal^a	مَحَل	دِلِ

7. Contrasting /E/ and /Ẽ/ (48,49)

tE	mẼ	مِ	تي
maHInE	dUHẼ mẼ	دُونهين مِ	مَهِینِي
rastE tE	kĨẼ mẼ	کِینئِین مِ	رَستي تي

8. Contrasting /E/ and /aĩ/ (48,51)

qEdI	qaĩcI	قَینچِي	قَیدِي
mEdO	maĩHĩ	مَینِهن	مَیدو
pEsO	ãI	ءَ	پَیسو

9. Contrasting /E/ and /A/ plus /i/ (48,56 plus 46)

pEsO	fAidO	فائِدو	پَيِسو
qEdI	qAidO	قاعِدو	قَيدِي
mEdO	mAit^u	مائِثُ	مَيدو

10. Contrasting /a/ and /ã/ (52,53)

badan^a tE	mũHã tE	مُنهن تي	بَدَن تي
kan^a	HOddÃHã	هوڏانهن	ڪَنَ
pan^a	ddÃHã	ڏانهن	پَنَ

11. Contrasting /ã/ and /ã õ/ (53,55)

mũHã tE	dhã õ dhã õ	ڏون ڏون	مُنهن تي
ddĨHã	Dhã õ g̃	ڍونگ	ڏينهن
ddÃHã	sã õ p^a	سَونپَ	ڏانهن

12. Contrasting /A/ and /Ã/ (56,57)

tAn^u	tÃ	ٹان	تانُ
chA?	chÃv^a	چائَوَ	چا
mAn^u	mÃ	مان	مانُ

13. Contrasting /A/ and /a/ (56,52)

vArI	varI	وَري	واري
HAl^u	Hal^u	هَلُ	حالُ
Acar^u	ac^u	اَچُ	آچر

14. Contrasting /O/ and /Õ/ (58,59)

sOn^u	dŨHÕ	ڏُونهون	سونُ
kInO	kĨÕ	ڪِينئون	ڪِينو
maHInO	sŨHÕ	سُونهون	مَهِينو

15. Contrasting /O/ and /U/ (58,62)

camcO	tambU	تنبو	چَمچو
panO	maR̃ HU	ماٹھُو	پَنو
zOr^u	sUr^u	سُورُ	زورُ

16. Contrasting /U/ and /Ũ/ (62,63)

raHAkU	vichŨ	وِچُون	رَهاکُو
tambU	marŨ	مَرُون	تَنبُو
khUh^u	dŨH Õ	دُونهون	کُوهُ

17. Contrasting /U/ and /u/ (62,60)

UcO	ucO	أچو	أوچو
UndAHI	umId^a	أمِيدَ	أونداهِي
raHAkU	mAlik^u	مالِکُ	رَهاکُو

18. Contrasting /O/ and /u/ (58,60)

OcitO	ucO	أچو	اوچتو
OtrO	utE	أتي	اوترو
rakhO	rakh^u	رَکُ	رَکو

19. Contrasting /u/ and /ũ/ (60,61)

muk^a	mũHũ	مُنهُن	مُکَ
mukO	mũHinjO	مُنهنجو	مُکو
uTh^u	mĩHũ	مِينهُن	أٹُ

20. Contrasting /u/ and /a/ (60,52)

kuTumb^u	kaTar^a	کَٹَرَ	کُٹنبُ
Hukum^u	Haq^a	حَقَ	حُکُمُ
umId^a	amIr^u	امِيرُ	أمِيدَ

3-B   Differential Drills – Consonants

1. Contrasting /p/ and /b/   (6,7)

ta<u>b</u>AH^u	ta<u>p</u>As^u	تَپاسُ	تَباهُ
<u>b</u>Ab^u	<u>p</u>Ap^a	پاپَ	بابُ
<u>b</u>alE	<u>p</u>alI	پلِي	بَلِي

2. Contrasting /p/ and /ph/   (6,9)

<u>p</u>Ap^a	<u>ph</u>AsI	قاسِي	پاپَ
kA<u>p</u>I	thA<u>ph</u>I	تاقِي	کاپِي
<u>p</u>Er^u	<u>ph</u>Er^u	قِيرُ	پيِيرُ

3. Contrasting /ph/ and /bh/   (9,10)

<u>ph</u>ikO	<u>bh</u>ik^a	پِکَ	قِکو
<u>ph</u>AsI	a<u>bh</u>IAsI	اَپِياسِي	قاسِي
thA<u>ph</u>O	<u>bh</u>A<u>bh</u>I	پاپِي	تاقُو

4. Contrasting /b/ and /bh/   (7,10)

<u>b</u>Ab^u	<u>bh</u>A^u	پاؤُ	بابُ
<u>b</u>alE	<u>bh</u>alI	پَلِي	بلِي
<u>b</u>Ahⁱ	<u>bh</u>Akur^u	پاکُرُ	باہِ

5. Contrasting /b/ and /bb/   (7,8)

<u>b</u>Ar^u	<u>bb</u>Ar^u	ٻارُ	بارُ
ta<u>b</u>AH^u	ka<u>bb</u>aT^u	کَٻَٹُ	تَباهُ
<u>b</u>Ab^u	<u>bb</u>Acⁱ	ٻاچ	بابُ

6. Contrasting /bh/ and /bb/   (10,8)

| <u>bh</u>alI | <u>bb</u>OlI | ٻولِي | پَلِي |
| a<u>bh</u>IAsI | ka<u>bb</u>aT^u | کَٻَٹُ | اَپِياسِي |

Lesson 3/ 21

7. Contrasting /t/ and /d/ (11,12)

tarsO	daru	دَرُ	تَرسو
tabilO	dAdilO	دادِلو	طِبلو
tinª	dinu	دِنُ	تِن

8. Contrasting /t/ and /th/ (11,18)

tAnu	thAnu	ثانُ	تانُ
tAlO	thulHO	ثُلهو	تالو
HitE	kithE	كِٿي	هِتي

9. Contrasting /d/ and /dh/ (12,15)

dAnu	dhIAnu	ڌيانُ	دانُ
dasu	dhartI	ڌَرتي	دَسُ
AdmI	khAdhO	كاڌو	آدمِي

10. Contrasting /th/ and /dh/ (18,15)

thAnu	dhAnu	ڌانُ	ثانُ
thIO	dhIAnu	ڌِيانُ	ٿِيو
patharu	padharO	پَڌرو	پَٿَرُ

11. Contrasting /d/ and /dd/ (7,10)

dAdilO	ddAddO	ڊاڊو	دادِلو
dasu	ddisu	ڊِسُ	دَسُ
irAdO	paRAddO	پَڙاڊو	اِرادو

12. Contrasting /T/ and /D/ (16, 17)

paTATO	DAHO	ڊاهو	پَٽاٽو
TAkª	DAkª	ڊاڪَ	ٽاڪَ
minTu	canDu	چَنڊُ	مِنٽُ

13. Contrasting /T/ and /Th/ (16,18)

Tap^u	Thap^u	ٹَپُ	ٿَپُ
vaT^i	vaTh^u	وَٹِ	وَٿُ
aTO	miThO	اَٹو	مِٿو

14. Contrasting /Th/ and /Dh/ (18,19)

Thagg^u	Dhigg^u	ٿَڳُ	ڈِڳُ
mATh^i	vADhO	ماٿِ	واڍو
kanThO	nanDhO	ڪَنٿو	نَنڍو

15. Contrasting /D/ and /Dh/ (17,19)

manDO	nanDhO	مَنڊو	نَنڍو
DAHO	vADhO	ڊاهو	واڍو
DaDO	DhaggO	ڊَڊو	ڍَڳو

16. Contrasting /D/ and /dd/ (17,13)

DOHI	ddOHI	ڊوهِي	ڏوهِي
DaHi	ddaHI	ڊَهِي	ڏَهِي
manDO	vaddO	مَنڊو	وَڏو

17. Contrasting /t/ and /T/ (11,16)

tan^u	Tin^i	تَنُ	ٽِنِ
HutE	pETI	هُتي	پيٽي
vAt^u	vAT^a	واتُ	واٽَ

18. Contrasting /d/ and /D/ (12,17)

mandO	manDO	مَندو	مَنڊو
dAdilO	DaDO	دادِلو	ڊَڊو
ddand^u	ddanD^u	ڏَندُ	ڏَنڊُ

Lesson 3/ 23

19. Contrasting /th/ and /Th/ (14,18)

sAth[u]	mATh[i]	ماتِ	ساتُ
pathar[u]	aThAsI	اَناسِي	پَٿَرُ
uth[u]	uTh[u]	اُٿُ	اُٿُ

20. Contrasting /dh/ and /Dh/ (15,19)

khAdhO	vADhO	واڍو	ڪاڌو
dhAggO	DhaggO	ڍڳو	ڌاڳو
andhO	nanDhO	نَنڍو	اَنڌو

21. Contrasting /k/ and /g/ (21,22)

kap[a]	gap[a]	گَپَ	ڪَپَ
nak[u]	nigAH[u]	نِگاهُ	نَڪُ
mOkal[a]	pAggal[i]	پاڳِلِ	موڪَلَ

22. Contrasting /kh/ and /gh/ (25,26)

khOlIO	ghOT[u]	گھوٽُ	ڪوليو
akh[i]	agh[u]	اَگھُ	اَکِ
pakhI	paghar[u]	پَگھَرُ	پَکِي

23. Contrasting /k/ and /kh/ (21,25)

kapE	khapE	کپِي	ڪپِي
pakI	pakhI	پَکِي	پَڪِي
likO	likhO	لِکو	لِڪو

24. Contrasting /g/ and /gh/ (22,26)

gAbO	ghATO	گھاتو	گابو
jung[i]	sagh[a]	سَگھَ	جَنگِ
pAggal[i]	paghAr[a]	پگھار	پاڳِلِ

25. Contrasting /K/ and /G/ (34,35)

KAs[u]	GAlib[u]	غالِبُ	خاصُ
iKtIArI	kAGazI	كاغذي	اِختياري
KAm[u]	laGAm[u]	لَغامُ	خامُ

26. Contrasting /g/ and G/ (22,35)

gAbO	GAlib[u]	غالِبُ	گابو
pAgal[i]	kAGaz[u]	كاغذُ	پاگلِ
nAng[u]	bAG[u]	باغُ	نانگُ

27. Contrasting /kh/ and /K/ (25,34)

khAdhO	KAsO	خاصو	کاڈو
pakhI	taKtI	تَختِي	پَکِي
pOkh[i]	puKtO	پُختو	پوکِ

28. Contrasting /gh/ and /G/ (26,35)

ghATO	GAlib[u]	غالِبُ	گھاٹو
paghAr[a]	GAr[a]	غارَ	پَگھارَ
ddAgh[u]	bAG[u]	باغُ	ڈاگھُ

29. Contrasting /c/ and /j/ (28,29)

cOr[u]	jOR[u]	جوڑُ	چورُ
acAnak[a]	ajarak[u]	أجَرَكُ	أچائكَ
lAlac[i]	suraj[u]	سُورَجُ	لالچِ

30. Contrasting /c/ and /ch/ (28,30)

cAr[i]	chA?	چا؟	چار
acO	achO	اچو	اچو
sac[u]	kach[u]	کچُ	سچُ

31. Contrasting /ch/ and /jh/ (30,31) **31.**

chOlIO	jhOliO	جهولِيو	چولِيو
achO	ajhO	اَجهو	اَچو
kuch^{u}	kujh^{u}	ڪُجهُ	ڪُڇُ

32. Contrasting /j/ and /jh/ (29,31) **32.**

jang^{i}	jhang^{u}	جَهنگُ	جَنگِ
ajarak^{u}	jhirk^{u}	جِهرڪُ	اَجَرَڪُ
sij^{u}	samjh^{u}	سَمجُهه	سِجُ

33. Contrasting /j/ and /jj/ (29,20) **33.**

jAn^{i}	jjAO	ڄائو	جانِ
Haj^{u}	ajj^{u}	اَڄُ	حَجُ
ajAIO	ajjOkO	اَڄوڪو	اَجايو

34. Contrasting /jh/ and /j/ plus /H/ (31,29+41) **34.**

jhERO	jaHiRO	جَهڙو	جهيڙو
jhang^{u}	jaHAz^{u}	جَهازُ	جَهنگُ
jhÃjh^{u}	jaHAn^{u}	جَهانُ	جَهانجهُ

35. Contrasting /f/ and /v/ (32,33) **35.**

faqIr^{u}	vakIl^{u}	وَڪِيلُ	فَقِيرُ
kAfir^{u}	kAvaR^{i}	ڪاوَڙِ	ڪافِرُ
dafa'O	davA	دَوا	دَفعو

36. Contrasting /g̃/ and /n/ plus /g/ (4, 2+22) **36.**

bhAg̃O	bhAngO	ڀانگو	ڀاڱو
cag̃O	ddingO	ڏِنگو	ڇَڱو
Ag̃ur^{i}	angUr^{u}	انگورُ	آڱرِ

37. Contrasting /r/ and /R/   (42,43)

cOrI	cORI	چوڙي	چوري
pArO	pARO	پاڙو	پارو
umir^i	amaR^i	اَمَڙِ	عُمِرِ

38. Contrasting /R/ and /R/ plus /H/   (43, 43+41)

piR^u	piRH^u	پِڙهُ	پڙُ
viR^u	viRH^u	وِڙهُ	وِڙُ
ghORO	ggORHO	ڳوڙھو	گھوڙو

39. Contrasting /R/ and /D/   (43,17)

chaRO	chiDO	چِڊو	چَڙو
tARO	manDO	مَنڊو	تاڙو
kUR^u	canD^u	چَنڊُ	ڪُڙ

40. Contrasting /R/ and /R̃/   (43,5)

vaR^u	vaR̃^{u}	وَڻُ	وَڙُ
tARO	tAR̃O	تاڻو	تاڙو
gOR^u	guR̃^{u}	ڳُڻُ	ڳوڙُ

41. Contrasting /n/ and /R̃/   (2,5)

pan^u	vaR̃^{u}	وَڻُ	پَنُ
pAn^u	pAR̃^{u}	پاڻُ	پانُ
kAnO	kAR̃O	ڪاڻو	ڪانو

42. Contrasting /jj/ and /dd/   (20,13)

ajj^u	chadd^i	چَڊِ	اَجُ
jjAO	ddAHO	ڊاھو	جائو
ajjOkO	gOddO	ڳوڊو	اِجوڪو

43. Contrasting /H/ and /K/ (41,34)

HutE	KudA	خُدا	هُتي
HAl^u	KAl^u	خالُ	حالُ
aHatIAj^u	aKtIArI	اختِیاری	اَحتِیاجُ

44. Contrasting /n/ and /Ñ/ (2,3)

panA	aÑA	اَجا	پَنا
un^a	uÑ^a	اُجَ	اَنَ
munO	maÑO	مَجو	مُنو

45. Contrasting /Ñ/ and /g̃/ (3,4)

vaÑaR̃^u	vAg̃aR̃^u	واڳُ	وَجَڱُ
suÑ^a	sig̃^u	سِڳُ	سُجَ
maÑO	ag̃aR̃^u	اڳُ	مَجو

LESSON FOUR

4-A   Pronunciation Drill[1]

This drill should be done only with the teacher. Never try to read the phonetic script, and pronounce the word by yourself. The teacher should pronounce each phrase several times while the student listens and tries to identify through hearing the sounds which one is being heard. If the student has difficulty hearing the difference in any particular contrasting pair of sounds, they may look at the phonetic script in order to check their hearing, and to know what they are listening for. Then they listen again to the teacher as s/he pronounces each pair several times. Only after listening should the student then attempt to mimic the teacher. The book should be closed at all times during this drill, except for checking when having some difficulty.

1.   Contrasting /r/ and /R/   (42, 43)   / ر ، /ڙ/

kArI tARI	(black bolt)	ڪاري تاڙي
mErA kapRa	(dirty clothes)	ميرا ڪپڙا
ghar[a] jI masivAr[a]	(house rent)	گهر جي مسواڙ
saRak[a] jE bharasÃ	(beside the road)	سڙڪ جي پرسان

2.   Contrasting /k/ and /K/   (21, 34)   / ڪ ، /خ/

KAs kam[u]	(special work)	خاص ڪم
saKt suk[a]	(severe drought)	سخت سڪ
kA bi Kabar[a]	(any news)	ڪا ب خبر
Kat[u] kitab[a] mẼ AHE	(the letter is in the book)	خط ڪتاب ۾ آهي

---

[1] In Lesson Three you practiced saying the Sindhi sounds using isolated words. Beginning with this lesson they will be practiced in phrases and sentences. Although the meanings are given in English, it is not important that the student learn them. They are given to demonstrate that the expressions are meaningful, and to assist the teacher.

4-B The cardinal numbers "one" to "five"

one:	Hik^u, or HikaRO	written in Sindhi as,	١	هِكُ يا هِكِڙو
two:	bba,	written in Sindhi as,	٢	بَ
three:	TE,	written in Sindhi as,	٣	ٽي
four:	cArⁱ,	written in Sindhi as,	٤	چار
five:	panj^a,	written in Sindhi as,	٥	پَنج

4-C The plural forms of masculine nouns

Hik^u darivAzO one door	هِكُ دروازو	Hik^u kamarO one room	هِكُ ڪَمَرو
bba darivAzA two doors	بَ دروازا	TE kamarA three rooms	ٽي ڪَمَرا
Hik^u ustad^u one teacher	هِكُ أُستادُ	hik^u qalam^u one pen	هِكُ قَلَمُ
cArⁱ ustAd^a four teachers	چار أُستادَ	panj^a qalam^a five pens	پَنج قَلَمَ
hik^u mA R̃ HU[2] one man	هِكُ ماڻهُو	hik^u tambU one tent	هِكُ تَنبُو
cArⁱ mA R̃ HU four men	چار ماڻهُو	bba tambU two tents	بَ تَنبُو

1. There are three main types of masculine nouns:

    (a) those which end in the sound /O/, as in darivAzO.
    (b) those which end in the sound /^u/, as in ustAd^u.
    (c) those which end in the sound /U/, as in tambU.

2. Regular plurals of masculine nouns are formed as follows:

    (a) those which end in /O/ are changed to /A/, as kamarO (room), kamarA (rooms).
    (b) those which end in /^u/ are changed to /^a/, as ustAd^u (teacher), ustAd^a (teachers).
    (c) those which end in /U/ do not change, as mA R̃ HU (man), mA R̃ HU (men).

---

[2] Sometimes the final /U/ is mA R̃ HU is nasalized because of the influence of /R̃/. Thus, it may be pronounced as mA R̃ HŨ.

4-D The masculine demonstrative pronouns: the third person present tense of the verb Hua$^R{}^u$ (to be).

Hi^u this	هِيءُ	HI these	هِي	HU that	هُو	HU those	هُو

also,

iHO this	اِهو	iHE these	اِهي	uHO that	أهُو	uHE those	أهي

Singular: AHE is	آهي	Plural: AHin are	آهن

HI^u ustAd^u AHE. This is a/the male teacher.	هِيءُ أستادُ آهي.
HI^u kitAB^u AHE. This is a book.	هِيءُ كتابُ آهي.
HI^u faraS^u AHE. This is the floor.	هِيءُ فَرشُ آهي.
HU darivAzO AHE. That is the door.	هُو دَروازو آهي.
HI SISO AHE. This is glass.	هِي شِيشو آهي.
HU SAgird^u AHE. That is a student.	هُو شاگِردُ آهي.
HU pardA AHin. Those are curtains.	هُو پَردا آهِن.
uHO kutO AHE. That is a dog.	أهو كُتو آهي.
HI gul^a AHin. These are flowers.	هِي گُلَ آهِن.
uHO mEvO AHE. That is fruit.	أهو ميوو آهي.
HI panA AHin. These are papers.	هِي پَنا آهِن.
uHO Kat^u AHE. That is a letter.	أهو خَطُ آهي.

iHE kitAb^a AHin. These are books.	اِهي ڪِتابَ آهِن.
HU qalam^u AHE. That is a pen.	هُو قَلَمُ آهي.
HU kabbaT^a AHin. Those are cupboards.	هُو ڪَٻَٽَ آهِن.

1. The two forms of the verb HuaR̃^u are introduced here for practice. They will be presented and explained in details in another lesson. AHE = is, singular; AHin = are, plural.

2. HU and HI are used in general statements of fact, iHO, uHO, iHE, and uHE are used somewhat more emphatically, to point out or indicate. Be alert as to the way in which Sindhi speakers distinguish these two types of demonstratives in actual use.

3. HI, iHO and iHE refer to something or someone <u>near</u> the speaker, while HU, uHO, and uHE refer to something or a person (or persons) <u>farther away</u>, or more <u>remote</u> from the speaker. They are all used both for people and things.

4. There are no indefinite or definite articles (a, an, the, as used in English) as such in Sindhi. This idea has to be supplied from the context. Sometimes indefiniteness can be shown by using the number "Hik^u," unstressed before a noun, as: HI^u Hik^u <u>kitAb^u</u> AHE (This is a <u>book</u>). if the stress is moved to the number, as: HI^u <u>Hik^u</u> kitAb^u AHE (This is <u>one</u> book), then the suggestion is rather that it is only one book, and not several.

5. Word order in Sindhi normally puts the subject first and the verb last in the sentence. Thus HU kitAb^u AHE, "That (a) book is" means, "That is (a) book",

4 -E   **The question words, chA (what?) and kEr^u (who?)**

HI^u chA AHE? What is this? HU kitAb^u AHE. That is a book.	هيءُ چا آهي؟ هُو ڪِتابُ آهي.
HI^u chA AHE? What is this? HU qalam^u AHE. That is a pen.	هيءُ چا آهي؟ هُو قَلَمُ آهي.
HI chA AHin? What are these? HU Kat^a AHin. Those are letters.	هِي چا آهِن؟ هُو خَطَ آهِن.
HI^u chA AHE? What is this? HU gul^u AHE. That is a flower.	هيءُ چا آهي؟ هُو گُلُ آهي.

HI chA AHin? What are these? HU gilAs^a AHin. Those are glasses.	هِي چا آهِن؟ هُو گِلاسَ آهِن.
HU kEr^u AHE? Who is that? HU ustAd^u AHE. He is a/the teacher.	هُو كيرُ آهي؟ هُو أستاذُ آهي.
HU kEr^a AHin? Who are they? HU SAgird^a AHin. They are students.	هُو كير آهِن؟ هُو شاگِردَ آهِن.
HU kEr^a AHin? Who are they? uHE mA R̃ HU AHin. They are men (people).	أهي كير آهِن؟ أهي ماݨُھو آهِن.

1. chA (referring to things) asks the question, "what?" while kEr^u asks the question, "Who?". Both can be singular or plural. chA does not change its form in the plural. Note, however, that the final short vowel ending /u/ in kEr^u changes to /a/ in the plural from, thus, kEr^a. As has already been noted, the short final vowel is very nearly voiceless, and dropped, or becomes a brief break between two consonant sounds. It is very important that the student observe and imitate the way Sindhi speakers pronounce these final short vowels.

2. Where no great importance is attached to the matter of nearness or remoteness, HI and HU may be used interchangeably. In other words, the answer to the question, HU chA AHE? could be HU kitAb^u AHE, or HI kitAb^u AHE. Both in this case would mean, "It's a book." However, when the speaker wishes to differentiate, that is, between something nearby or across the room, the difference is important.

3. When the question asked by chA or kEr^u is answered, the noun of the thing/person in question takes the place of chA or kEr^u, thus providing the answer. For example,

HI^u chA AHE?	هِيءُ چا آهي؟	HU kEr^u AHE?	هُو كيرُ آهي؟
HI^u kitAb^u AHe.	هِيءُ كِتابُ آهي.	HU ustAd^u AHE.	هُو استادُ آهي.

4. The Sindhi word order normally places the question word just before the verb.

5. Sindhi has absorbed many English words, and gilAs^u is one of them. The word SISO may also mean "a glass," but it has a wider meaning, as in English, which includes the material of glass.

4 -F   "Yes" and "no" questions with chA

Transliteration / Translation	Sindhi
chA HI kitAb^u AHE? Is this a book? HAO, HU kitAb^u AHE. Yes, that's a book.	چا هِي ڪِتابُ آهي؟ هائو، هُو ڪِتابُ آهي.
chA HI panA AHin? Are these papers? HAO HU panA AHin. Yes they are papers.	چا هِي پَنا آهِن؟ هائو هُو پَنا آهِن.
chA HU ustAd^a AHin? Are those teachers? na, HU ustAd^a na AHin. No, they're not teachers. uHE ustAd^a AHin. <u>Those</u> are teachers. HI SAgird^a AHin. These are students.	چا هُو أستادَ آهِن؟ نَ، هُو أستادَ نَ آهِن. اُهي استادَ آهِن. هِي شاگردَ آهِن.
chA HI^u kabbaT^u AHE? Is this a cupboard? na, HU kabbaT^u na AHE. No, that's not a cupboard. HU darivAzO AHE. That's a door. iHO kabbaT^u AHE. <u>This</u> is a cupboard.	چا هِيءُ ڪَبَٽُ آهي؟ نَ، هُو ڪَبَٽُ نَ آهي. هُو دَروازو آهي. اِهو ڪَبَٽُ آهي.
chA, HU pardO AHE? Is that a curtain? na, HU pardO na AHE, kapRA AHin. No, it isn't a curtain. They're clothes.	چا هُو پَردو آهي؟ نَ، هُو پَردو نَ آهي، ڪپڙا آهِن.
chA HI kAGaz AHE? Is this paper? na, kAGaz na AHE. uHO kapRO AHE. No, it isn't paper. It is cloth.	چا هِي ڪاغذ آهي؟ نَ ڪاغذ نَ آهي، اُهو ڪپڙو آهي.

1.   chA unstressed, at the beginning of a sentence is not translatable. It merely signals that a question is being asked. You will discover that it is sometimes placed at the end of the question. Thus, HI kitAb^u AHE chA? It may be omitted, and the question shown by the voice rising at the end of the sentence.

2. Except for the inclusion of chA at the beginning or the end of the question, the word order remains the same as for a statement. Only the tone of voice (intonation) is changed, rising at the end for a question, and remaining level or dropping slightly at the end of a statement.

3. HAO is the answer, "Yes," and na is the answer, "No." When translated as "not," na is placed immediately before the verb. HA also means "yes," and the two words are both used in Sindh. Use the word which is common in your area.

4. kapRO means "cloth," and its plural form, kapRA, means "clothes."

4-G   Vocabulary for Lesson Four

ustAdu teacher	أُستادُ	pardO curtain	پَردو
iHO this	اِهو	panja five	پَنجَ
uHO that	أهو	bba two	بَ
iHE these	اِهي	panO leaf, sheet of paper	پَنو
uHE those	أهي	cAri four	چار
tambU tent	ئَنبُو	chA what	چا
darivAzO door	دروازو	kamarO room	كَمَرو
SAgirdu student	شاگِردُ	kEru who	كيرُ
SISO glass	شيشو	gulu flower	گُلُ
na no, not	نَ	gilAsu glass	گلاسُ
faraSu floor	فرشُ	mAR̃HU man, people	ماٹھو
qalamu pen	قَلَمُ	mEvO fruit	ميوو
kAGazu paper	كاغَذُ	Hiku, HikaRO one	هِكُ, هكڑو
kabbaTu cupboard	كَبَٹُ	HU he, that, those	هُو
kitAbu book	كِتابُ	HIu He, this	هِيءُ
kapRA clothes	كَپڑا	HI these	هِي
kapRO cloth	كَپڑو	HAO, HA yes	هائو, ها

TE three	ٽي	Kat^u Letter	خط
kutO Dog	ڪُتو		

4-H Conversational Review

1. Pronounce each of the nouns given in this lesson's vocabulary with the number Hik^u and bba. For example,

    Hik^u ustAd^u   هِڪُ أستادُ   bba ustAd^a   بَ أستادَ

    Hik^u panO   هِڪُ پَنو   bba panA   بَ پَنا

2. Touching or pointing to the thing/ person if he/it is in the room, use the nouns in this vocabulary in the following pattern:

HU Kat^u AHE; HI^u qalam^u AHE.	هُو خطُ آهي؛ هِيُ قَلَمُ آهي.
HU mA R̃ HU AHE. HI pardA AHin.	هُو ماڻهو آهي. هي پَردا آهِن.

3. Touching or pointing to the various items in the room which are given in the vocabulary, ask and answer questions according to the following patterns:

Teacher: HI^u / HU chA AHE?	أستادُ: هِيُ/هُو چا آهي؟
Student: H^u gilAs^u AHE.	شاگردُ: هُو گلاسُ آهي.

4. Touching or pointing to the various items/ persons in the room which are given in the vocabulary and which are plural, ask and answer questions according to the following pattern:

Teacher: HI chA AHin?	أستادُ: هِي چا آهِن؟
Student: HU kitAb^a AHin.	شاگردُ: هو ڪتابَ آهِن.

5. Use as many items of this vocabulary as are available in the room in the following pattern, asking questions that will have to be answered, "Yes."

Teacher: chA, HI/ HU qalam^u AHE?	أستادُ: چا هي/ هُو قلمُ آهي؟
Student: HAO, HI/HU qalam^u AHE.	شاگردُ: هائو، هِي/ هُو قلمُ آهي.

6. Repeat exercise 5, using items in the plural when available. Thus,

Teacher: chA, HI/HU pardA AHin?	أستادُ: چا هِي/ هُو پردا آهِن؟
Student: HAO, HI/HU pardA AHin.	شاگردُ: هائو، هِي، هُو پردا آهِن.

7. Use as many vocabulary items of this lesson as are available in the room in the following pattern, asking questions so that the answer will have to be "no."

Teacher: chA, HI^u/HU darivAzO AHE?	أستادُ: چا هِيءُ/ هُو دروازو آهي؟
Student: na, darivAzO na AHE.	شاگردُ: نَہ دروازو نَہ آهي.

8. Repeat exercise 7, using items in the plural when available. Thus,

Teacher: chA HI panA AHin?	أستادُ: چا هِي پَنا آهِن؟
Student: na, HU/uHE panA na AHin.	شاگردُ: نَہ هُو/ أهي پَنا نَہ آهِن.

9. Go over the "yes" and "no" questions in 4-G again with your teacher. Repeat each one after him/her, taking special care to mimic not only his/her pronunciation but the rise and fall of his/her voice in each sentence also. Encourage your teacher to correct you when your pronunciation or voice intonation is not correct.

LESSON FIVE

5-A Pronunciation Drill

1. Contrasting /b/ and /bb/ (7, 8) ب ء ٻ

HU bAr^u AHE.	(That is a load.)	هُو بارُ آهي. هُو ٻارُ آهي.
HU bbAr^u AHE.	(That is a baby.)	
HI bUT^a AHin.	(These are shoes.)	هِي بُوٽ آهي. هِي ٻُوٽا آهِن.
HI bbUT^a AHin.	(These are bushes.)	
HI^u kabUtar^u AHE.	(This is a pigeon.)	هِيءُ ڪَبُوتَرُ آهي.
HU kabbirO AHE.	(It is spotted.)	هُو ڪَٻِرو آهي.

2. Contrasting /n/ and /R̃/ (2, 5) ن ء ڻ

nAnI pAR̃I khaR̃E thI.	(Grandmother is carrying water.)	ناني پاڻي کڻي ٿي.
pAn^u pAR̃a AR̃^u.	(Bring the pan-leaf yourself.)	پانُ پاڻ آڻُ.
kAR̃O mAR̃HU kAnO kapE thO.	(The one-eyed man is cutting cane.)	ڪاڻو ماڻهو ڪانو ڪَپي ٿو.

5-B The plural forms of feminine nouns

Hik^a kunjI one key	هِڪَ ڪُنجي	Hik^a kursI one chair	هِڪَ ڪُرسي
bba kunjIŨ two keys	ٻَ ڪُنجِيُون	TE kursIŨ three chairs	ٽي ڪُرسِيُون
Hik^a 'aorat^a one woman	هِڪَ عورت	Hik^a mEz^a one table	هِڪَ ميز
cArⁱ 'aoratŨ four women	چار عورتُون	panj^a mEzŨ five tables	پَنج ميزُون
hik^a davA one medicine	هِڪَ دوا	Hik^a KatA one mistake, fault	هِڪَ خطا
bba davAŨ two medicines	ٻَ دوائُون	bba KatAŨ two mistakes	ٻَ خطائُون

Hik^a pEnsilⁱ one pencil	هِڪَ پينسِلِ	Hik^a bhitⁱ one wall	هِڪَ ڀِتِ
TE pEnsilIŨ three pencils	ٽي پينسِليُون	cArⁱ bhitIŨ four walls	چار ڀِتيون

1. There are only two genders in Sindhi - masculine and feminine. There is no neuter gender. Gender in Sindhi is grammatical rather than natural; that is, it does not follow a practical pattern based on sex or the lack of it. In some instances the two may correspond, but in most cases one simply has to <u>learn</u> the gender of each noun. For example, there is nothing in experience that would tell us that to a Sindhi speaker qalam^u (pen) is masculine while pEnsilⁱ (pencil) is feminine.

2. There are four main types of feminine nouns:

    (a) those which end in /I/, as in kunjI.
    (b) those which end in /ᵃ/, as in 'aorat^a.
    (c) those which end in /A/, as in davA.
    (d) those which end in /ⁱ/, as in pEnsilⁱ.

3. Regular plurals of feminine nouns are formed as follows:

    (a) those which end in /I/ add /Ũ/, as kunjI (key), kunjIŨ (keys).
    (b) those which end in /ᵃ/ drop the /ᵃ/ and add /Ũ/, as 'aorat^a (woman), 'aoratŨ (women).
    (c) those which end in /A/ add /Ũ/, as davA (medicine), davAŨ (medicines).
    (d) those which end in /ⁱ/ lengthen the /ⁱ/ to /I/ and add /Ũ/, as pEnsilⁱ (pencil), pEnsilIŨ (pencils).

5 -C   The feminine demonstrative pronouns

HI^a this	هِيءَ	HI these	هِي	HU^a that	هوءَ	HU those	هُو

also,

iHA this	اِها	iHE these	اِهي	uHA that	أها	uHE those	أهي

HI^u kulf^u AHE. This is a lock.	هِيءُ ڪُلفُ آهي.
HI^a kunjI AHE. This is a key.	هِيءَ ڪنجِي آهي.
HI kunjIŨ AHin. These are keys.	هِي ڪنجيُون آهِن.
HI pEnsilIŨ AHin. These are pencils.	هِي پينسِليُون آهِن.

HU qalam^a AHin. Those are pens.	هُو قَلَمَ آهِن.
HU rabbaR^u AHE. That is an eraser.	هُو رَبِڙُ آهي.
HI^a mas^u AHE. This is ink.	هِيءَ مَسُ آهي.
HU^a chatⁱ AHE. That is the ceiling.	هُوءَ چَتِ آهي.
HU^a batI AHE. That's the light.	هُوءَ بَتي آهي.
bba kursIŨ AHin. (there) are two chairs.	بَ ڪُرسِيُون آهِن.
HI^a farAsI AHE. This is a rug (cotton carpet).	هِيءَ فِراسي آهي.
HU^a mEz^a AHE. That is a table.	هُوءَ ميزَ آهي.
HI cArⁱ bhitIŨ AHin. These are four walls.	هِي چار ڀِتِيون آهِن.
HU tasvIrŨ AHin. Those are pictures.	هُو تصويرُون آهِن.
HU jAnvar^a AHin. Those are animals.	هُو جانور آهِن.
HI^a bbilI AHE. This is a cat.	هِيءَ ٻِلي آهي.
chA, HU ghORO AHE? Is that a horse?	چا، هُو گهوڙو آهي؟
HU ghORO na AHE; ghORI AHE. That's not a (male) horse; (it's) a mare.	هو گهوڙو نَ آهي؛ گهوڙي آهي.
chA HU uTh^a AHin? Are those (male) camels?	چا هُو اُٺَ آهِن؟
HAO, HU uTh^a AHin. Yes, they are (male) camels.	هائو، هُو اُٺَ آهِن.
chA HU^a kukiRⁱ AHE? Is that a hen?	چا هُوءَ ڪُڪِڙِ آهي؟
na, kukiRⁱ na AHE; kukuR^u AHE. No, (it) is not a hen; (it) is a rooster.	نَ، ڪُڪِڙِ نَ آهي؛ ڪُڪُڙُ آهي.

uHA kukiRⁱ AHE. That is a hen.	أها كُكِڙِ آهي.
chA, HI pAR̃I AHE? Is this water?	ڇا، هِي پاڻي آهي؟
na, pAR̃I na AHE; davA AHE. No, (it) is not water; (it) is medicine.	نَ، پاڻي نَ آهي؛ دَوا آهي.
chA HU ustadIAR̃IŨ AHin? Are those (lady) teachers?	ڇا هُو استادياڻيُون آهِن؟
HAO, HU ustadIAR̃IŨ AHin. Yes, they are (lady) teachers.	هائو، هُو استادياڻيُون آهِن.
uHE kErᵃ AHin? Who are they?	أهي ڪير آهِن؟
HU chOkirIŨ AHin. They are girls.	هُو ڇوڪِريُون آهِن.
chOkirA ŋa AHin chA? Are (there) no boys?	ڇوڪرا نَ آهِن ڇا؟
HAO, Hikᵘ chOkirO AHE. Yes, (there) is one boy.	هائو، هِڪ ڇوڪرو آهي.
chA HI kitAbᵃ AHin? Are these books?	ڇا هِي ڪتاب آهِن؟
na, kApIŨ AHin. No, (they) are notebooks.	نَ، ڪاپيون آهِن.

1. Notice the similarities and difference between the feminine demonstrative pronouns and the masculine:

	Singular		Plural	
	Masc.	Fem.	Masc.	Fem.
Near	HIᵘ هِيُ	HIᵃ هِيءَ	HI هِي	HI هِي
Remote	HU هُو	HUᵃ هُوءَ	HU هُو	HU هُو

Near	iHO اِهو	iHA اِها	iHE اِهي	iHE اِهي
Remote	uHO أهو	uHA أها	uHE أهي	uHE أهي

2. They serve not only as demonstrative pronouns but personal pronouns as well. That is, the

singulars may be translated as "he/she/it" as well as "this/that," and the plurals may be translated as "they" as well as "these/ those."

3. The English word, "there," in such expressions as "there is one book," "there are four walls," is not really translatable. You will notice this in several examples in the above sentences.

4. Often the demonstrative or personal pronoun need not be repeated. For example, the answer to the question, "chA HU ghORO AHE?" (Is that a horse?) may be "HAO, ghORO AHE," leaving out the demonstrative, HU.

5. The word, mas^u (ink), ends in /^{u}/ and therefore is masculine in <u>form</u>. However, it is irregular since it is considered feminine. Similarly, pARĨ (water) appears in a feminine form, but is considered masculine. There are not many irregular nouns in Sindhi. However, the quality of the final short vowels which are the gender indicators are such that remembering the genders of those types of nouns may present a problem to the student. In the vocabulary lists at the end of each lesson the gender of each noun will be indicated as (m), masculine or (f), feminine.

6. Certain masculine nouns may change the masculine ending and thus become feminine. For example:

        chOkirO (boy) may become chOkirI (girl)

        uTh^u (camel) may become uTh^i (female camel)

        ustad^u (teacher) may become ustAdIARĨ (woman teacher)

5-D   Vocabulary for Lesson Five

uTh^u (m) camel	اُٽُ	batI (f) light, lamp	بَتي
bbilI (f) female cat	بِلي	bhit^i (f) wall	پِتِ
tasvIr^a (f) picture	تصويرَ	pARĨ (m) water	پاڻي
pEnsil^i (f) pencil	پينسلِ	jAnvar^u (m) animal	جانوَرُ
chat^i (f) roof, ceiling	چِتِ	chOkirO (m) boy	چوڪِرو
KatA (f) fault, mistake	خَطا	chOkirI (f) girl	چوڪِري
davA (f) medicine	دَوا	rabbaR^u (m) eraser	رَبَڙُ
'aorat^a (f) woman	عَورتَ	farAsI (f) rug, cotton carpet	فَراسي
kApI (f) notebook	ڪاپي	kursI (f) chair	ڪُرسي
kulf^u (m) lock	ڪُلفُ	kukuR^u (m) rooster	ڪُڪُڙُ

kunjI (f) key	ڪُنجي	ghOrO (m) horse	گھوڙو
mas^u (f) ink	مَسُ	mEz^a (f) table	ميزَ
zAl^a (f) wife	زالَ		

5-E Conversational Review

1. Pronounce each noun in this lesson's vocabulary list by prefixing the number Hik^u, then the numbers, bba, TE, cAr^j, and panj^a.

2. Touching or pointing to the thing/person if he/she/it is in the room, use nouns in the vocabulary of both lessons 4 and 5 with the appropriate demonstrative pronouns. For example,

HI^a mEz^a AHE.	هِيءَ ميزَ آهي.	HU^a chat^i AHE.	هُوءَ چت آهي.

3. Repeat exercise 2 using items/ persons in the plural where possible with the appropriate demonstrative pronouns. For example,

HI pEnsilI$\tilde{U}$ AHin.	هِي پينسليُون آهِن.	uHE bhitI$\tilde{U}$ AHin, etc.	اُهي ڀتيون آهِن.

4. Use as many items/ persons in both vocabularies as are available around you, asking questions so that the answer will have to be "yes". For example,

Teacher: chA HI^a tasvIr^a AHE?	أستاد: ڇا هِيءَ تصويرَ آهي؟
Student: HAO HU^a tasvIr^a AHE.	شاگرد: هائو هُوءَ تصويرَ آهي.

5. Repeat Exercise 4, using items/ persons in the plural when available.

6. Using nouns in both vocabularies, Lesson 4 and 5, ask questions so that the answers will have to be "no." For example,

Teacher: chA, HU^a chat^i AHE?	أستاد: ڇا هُوءَ چت آهي؟
Student: na, HU^a chat^i na AHE. HU^a bhit^i AHE.	شاگرد: هُوءَ چت نَہ آهي. هُوءَ ڀِت آهي.

In this exercise, use both singular and plural forms.

7. Go over section 5-C of this lesson again with your teacher. Repeat each sentence after him/her two or three times, taking care to mimic both his/her pronunciation of each word, and the rise and fall of his/her voice in the sentences. Encourage him/her to correct you when either your pronunciation or intonation is not correct.

LESSON SIX

6 - A   Pronunciation Drill

1. Contrasting /c/ and /ch/   (28, 30)   ج ءِ ڄ

cAr^i chOkarA	(four boys)	چار چوڪرا
coath Ẽ chanchar^a acO.	(Come the fourth Saturday.)	چوتين چنڃر اچو.
ucO achO AnO AR̃^{i}.	(Bring a fine white egg.)	اڃو اچو آنو آڙِ.
kacI chat^i	(poorly made roof)	ڪچي ڇت

2. Contrasting /T/ and /Th/   (16, 18)   ت ءِ ٿ

TE uTh^a Halan thA.	(Three camels are going)	ٽي اُٺ هلن ٿا.
HI miThA maTar^a AHin.	(Those are sweet peas.)	هي مِٺا مٽر آهِن.
HI suThI miTI AHE.	(This is good dirt)	هي سُٺي مٽي آهي.
puT^a jE puThIÃ	(behind the son)	پُٽ جي پٺيان

6 – B   The cardinal numbers "six" to "ten"

six	cha,	written as,	٦	ڇَھ
seven	sat^a,	written as,	٧	سَت
eight	aTh^a,	written as,	٨	اَٺ
nine	nava,	written as,	٩	نَوَ
ten	ddaHa,	written as,	١٠	ڏَھَ

6 – C Personal Pronouns as Subjects

Person	Singular			Plural		
1st	mÃ, AŨ	(I)	مان، آءُ	asĨ	(we)	اسين
2nd	tŨ	(you)	تُون	avHĨ, tavHĨ	(you)	اوهين، توهين
3rd masc:	HU	(he/it)	هُو	HU	(they)	هو
fem:	HUa	(she/it)	هُوءَ			

1. Except for the 3rd person singular, the forms are the same for both masculine and feminine.

2. For 1st person singular (I), mÃ is generally used in Upper Sindh and AŨ in lower Sindh.

3. The singular personal pronoun tŨ is allowed for use when addressing only one person who is a servant, a child, or someone well known to the individual. It is always with a singular verb.

While the use of "tŨ" does not necessarily imply a lack of respect, it is commonly used for a person one knows to be of lower social standing. The foreigner who has recently come into the culture may not be aware of social status in the way that Sindhis look at it. To use the singular "tŨ" for someone you have just met, and who may consider himself your equal or superior socially could be taken as an attitude of superiority. It may also indicate more intimacy than you intend to imply. Generally, if you are not very sure of the social situation, or not very well acquainted with the people, it is best to use the plural of respect, "tavHĨ".

Women and people with less education, villagers and children use the singular form commonly among themselves. In the cities and among educated people the plural form will often be used as a sign of respect. Don't be insulted if people use the singular form when addressing you, since there is not a strict rule for this in Sindhi. Simply be aware of the implications, and sensitive in each social situation. It is usually safer to show more respect and reserve than less when first meeting people.

The singular form "tŨ" is generally used in prayer when addressing God.

4. Whether "tavHĨ" is generally used in addressing more than one person, or as a plural of respect for one person, it is regarded as grammatically plural. Words modifying or qualifying it (e.g. adjectives) or controlled by it (e.g. verbs) will always be in the plural.

"avHĨ" is more commonly used in southern Sindh and regarded as proper Sindhi, but immigration of upper Sindhis to the south has meant both terms are used interchangeably. Listen to which is used most often in your area.

5. HU is the same for the 3rd person singular or plural. It is identical to the remote form of the demonstrative pronoun already introduced.

6 – D The present tense of the verb HuaR̃ᵘ (to be)

Person	Singular		Plural	
1st	(AŨ) AHIÃ (I am)	آءٌ آهيان	(asĨ) AHIŨ (We are)	(اسين) آهيون
2nd	(tŨ) AHĨ (You are)	تُون) آهين	(tavHĨ) AHIO (You are)	(توهين) آهيو
3rd	(HU) AHE (He/she/it is)	(هُو) آهي	(HU) AHin (They are)	(هُو) آهن

1. The infinitive form of the verb in Sindhi always ends in R̃ᵘ. This is the form of the verb found in dictionaries.

2. When R̃ᵘ is removed, the root of the verb is left. Thus the root of HuaR̃ᵘ is Hua-.

3. Actually the present tense of the verb HuaR̃ᵘ (to be) is irregular in that it does not retain the root form but replaces it with AH- as you will notice from the conjugation above of the present tense. In many other languages the present tense of the verb "to be" is irregular. For example in English, it is "am/are/is."

4. The present tense forms of the verb HuaR̃ᵘ given here also recur in tenses yet to be learned where they will function as auxiliary or helping verbs.

6 - E Statements, questions and negatives with the present tense of HuaR̃ᵘ.

AŨ ustAdᵘ AHIÃ. I am a / the teacher.	آءٌ استادُ آهيان.
AŨ DAkTar na AHIÃ. I am not a doctor.	آءٌ ڊاڪٽر نَ آهيان.
chA tŨ mAlHI AHĨ? Are you a /the gardener?	چا تون مالهي آهين؟
na sAI, aŨ mAlHI na AHIÃ. No Sir, I'm not a/the gardener.	نَ سائين، آءٌ مالهي نَ آهيان.
tŨ kErᵘ AHĨ? Who are you?	تُون ڪيرُ آهين؟
mÃ bOrcI AHIÃ. I'm the cook.	مان بورچي آهيان.
HU kErᵃ AHin? Who are they?	هُو ڪير آهن؟
HU bi naokarᵃ AHin. They are also servants.	هُو بہ نوڪَر آهن.
chA HU bi naokarᵘ AHE? Is he a servant too?	چا هُو بہ نوڪرُ آهي؟

na sAI, HU TapAlI AHE. No, sir, he's a/the postman	نَہ سائين، ھُو ٽپالي آهي.
chA tavHI SAgirdª AHIO? Are you students?	ڇا توهين شاگردَ آهيو؟
HAO sAI, asI SAgirdª AHIU. Yes, sir, we are students.	هائو سائين، اسين شاگردَ آهيون.
chA HU dhobbI AHin? Are they laundry men?	ڇا هُو ڌوٻي آهن؟
na sAI, HU dhobbI na AHin. No sir, they aren't laundry men.	نَہ سائين، هُو ڌوٻي نَہ آهن.
HU mazdUrª AHin. They are laborers.	هُو مزدورَ آهن.
chA avHI ustAdIARIU AHIO? Are you a/the lady teacher?	ڇا اوهين استادياڻيُون آهيو؟
na, AU DAkTarIARI AHIA. No, I'm a lady doctor.	نَہ، آءُ ڊاڪٽرياڻي آهيان.
chA, tavHI maolvI sAHibª AHIO? Are you a/the Muslim religious scholar	ڇا توهين مولوي صاحب آهيو؟
na, sAI, mA ustAdu AHIA. No, sir, I'm a teacher.	نَہ، سائين، مان استادُ آهيان.
HU mARHU kErª AHin? Who are those men?	هُو ماڻهو ڪير آهن؟
iHE pAdrI sAHibª AHin. They are Christian clergymen.	اِهي پادري صاحب آهن.

1. The nouns mAlHI (gardener), bOrcI (cook), TapAlI (postman), dhObI (laundry man), maolvI (Muslim religious), and pAdrI (Christian clergyman) end in /-I/, and therefore appear feminine. They are masculine however, and do not inflect (= change) for the simple plural. Thus Hikᵘ mAlHI (one gardener), bba mAlHI (two gardeners).

2. sAI is equivalent to the word, "Sir," and is used very commonly between men to address each other. While it is properly used to address a man older or of higher social status, it may be and is used by a man to address any man. Women speakers, however, should use the word cautiously because the Sindhi woman uses it to address only her husband and older male members of her household.

3. sAHibᵘ is equivalent to the word, "Sir," and is often added to the professional titles of men such as doctors, religious ministers, etc. When used in this way, it follows the professional title; thus, DAkTar sAHibᵘ.

4. mazUrᵘ is also pronounced as mazdUrᵘ. As always, use the pronunciation which is common in your area.

5. The adverb, bi, means "too, also" and is placed immediately after the word emphasized. For example,

   mÃ bi bOrcI AHIÃ, means "I, too, (as well as someone else mentioned) am a cook."

mÃ bOrcI bi AHIÃ, means "I'm a cook also" (as well as something else, for example, a gardener or laundry man).

6. The adverb, bi, can give the sense of "either" when negative. For example,

   asĨ mazdUrᵃ na AHIŨ, means "We aren't laborers."
   HU bi mazdUrᵃ na AHin, means "They aren't laborers either."

   You may hear this pronounced as "bᵘ," not as a rhyme to "na" or "ta."

6 - F   Introducing Adjectives

HU cagO bOrcI AHE. He is a good cook.	هُو چڱو بورچي آهي.
HU cagA SAgirdᵃ AHin. They are good students.	هُو چڱا شاگرد آهن.
Hi cagIŨ kApIŨ AHin. These are good notebooks.	هِي چڱيون ڪاپيون آهن.
HIᵘ vaddO kulfᵘ AHE. This is a big lock.	هيءُ وڏو ڪلف آهي.
iHE vaddA kamarA AHin. Those are big rooms.	اهي وڏا ڪمرا آهن.
HIᵃ vaddI tasvIrᵃ AHE. This is a big picture.	هِ وڏي تصوير آهي.
HIᵘ nanDhO darivAzO AHE. This is (it's) a small door.	هيءُ ننڊو دروازو آهي.
iHE nanDhA qalamᵃ AHin. Those are small pens.	اِهي ننڊا قَلَم آهن.
iHA nanDhI mEzᵃ AHE. That is a small table.	اِها ننڊي ميز آهي.
chA iHA nanDhI TOpI AHE? Is that a small cap?	ڇا اِها ننڊي ٽوپي آهي؟
HI panja SUHiRIŨ tasvIrŨ AHin. These (here) are five pretty pictures.	هِي پنج سُهڻيون تصويرون آهن.

HI cArⁱ mazbUt kulf^a AHin. These (here) are four strong locks.	هِي چار مضبوط كلف آهِن.
HI^a Hik^a pIlI pEnsilⁱ AHE. This/ it is a yellow pencil.	هِيءَ هِكَ پيلي پينسل آهي.
iHO nIrO kapRO AHE. That/it is blue cloth.	اِهو نيرو كپڙو آهي.
HI^u KAlI kamarO AHE. This is an empty room.	هِيءُ خالي كمرو آهي.
iHE KAlI pEtI Ũ AHin. These are empty boxes.	اِهي خالي پيتِيُون آهِن.

1. There are two kinds of adjectives in Sindhi:
    (a) Those ending in /O/ (masculine singular) which change as follows to agree with the noun modified or qualified:

        Masculine singular - /O/   Masculine plural   /A/

        Feminine singular - /I/   Feminine plural   /I Ũ/

    (b) Those ending in any other letter. These do not change but stay the same when modifying nouns of either gender, singular or plural. Two examples of this type of adjective are:
        mazbUt^u strong   KAlI empty

2. In the usual order of words the adjective comes just before the noun it qualifies, as in all the examples above.

6-G   Vocabulary for Lesson Six

aTh^a eight	اَٺَ	as Ĩ we	اَسِين
A Ũ, m Ã I	آءٌ، مان	avHĨ, tavHĨ you, plural	اُوهِين، توهِين
bOrcI (m) cook	بورچِي	t Ũ you, sing.	تُون
TapAlI (m) postman	ٽپالِي	TOpI (f) cap, hat	ٽوپِي
pAdrI (m) Christian clergyman	پادرِي	pIlO yellow	پِيلو
cagO good	چڱو	chA six	ڇَهَ

KAlI empty	خالي	suHiRO beautiful	سُهِڙو
dhObbI (m) Laundry man	ڏوبي	ddaHa ten	ڏَهَ
bi, bu also, too	بِہ, بُہ	pEtI (f) box	پيتي
DAkTaru (m) DAKTarIARI (f) Doctor, lady doctor	ڊاڪٽرُ ڊاڪٽرياڻي	sata seven	سَتَ
mAlHI, mAlI (m) gardener	مالھي، مالي	mazUru, mazdUru (m) laborer	مزورَ، مزدورَ
mazbUtu strong	مَضبوطُ	maolvI (m) Religious scholar	مَولوِي
nanDhO (m) small	نَنڍو	nava nine	نَوَ
naokaru (m) man servant	نَوڪَرُ	naokarIARI (f) woman servant	نَوڪَرياڻي
nIrO blue	نيرو	vaddO big, large, important	وَڏو
sAI~ Sir	سائين	sAHib Sir	صاحب

6 - H Conversational Review

1. Pronounce each noun given in the vocabularies of lessons 4 and 5 with an appropriate singular adjective chosen from the following:

       cagO, vaddO, nanDhO   چڱو وڏو نَنڍو

For example:

       cagO ustAdu, nanDhI batI, etc.   چڱو استادُ ننڍي بَتي

2. Repeat exercise 1, using an appropriate plural adjective chosen from the three adjectives given. For example:

       vaddA tambU; vaddIU~ KatAU~, etc. (Omit collective nouns like pARI)

       وڏا تنبو وڏيون خطائون

3. Repeat exercise 2, by prefixing the number chaHa, sat^a, ath^a, nava, ddaHa to each phrase. For example:

        chaHa vaddA darvAzA.   چَهَ وڏا دروازا

        sat^a nandHIŨ kunjIŨ, etc.   سَتَ نندِيون کنجيون

4. Pronounce each of the eleven nouns given in this lesson's vocabulary with the number cha, sat^a, ath^a, nava, or ddaHa and an appropriate plural adjective. For example:

        chaHa cagA borcI.   چَهَ چڱا بورچي

        sat^a nandHIŨ pEtIŨ, etc.   سَتَ نندِيون پيتيون

5. Answer the questions, HU kEr^u AHE/AHIN? with each of the professional titles given in this lesson's vocabulary. The teacher can ask the questions, and the student should reply with the full answer. For example:

    Teacher   HU kEr^u AHE?   اُستادُ: هُو ڪيرُ آهي؟

    Student: HU dhObbI AHE.   شاگردُ: هُو ڌوٻي آهي.

    Be sure to do them in the plural, too.

6. Carry on the following "conversation" with your teacher using all the professions given in the vocabulary of this lessons in this manner.

    Teacher: avHĨ kEr^a AHIO?   اُستادُ: اوهين ڪيرَ آهيو؟

    Student: AŨ DAkTar^u AHIÃ.   شاگردُ: آءُ ڊاڪٽر آهيان.

    (or AŨ DAkTar^u na AHIÃ) etc.   (يا آءُ ڊاڪٽر نَ آهيان)

7. Practice the conjugation of HuaR^u (to be) using at least six of the professions mentioned and using your hands to indicate the person. For example:

Pointing to yourself:	AŨ naokar^u AHIÃ	آءُ نوڪر آهيان.
Pointing to teacher	tŨ naokar^u AHĨ	تون نوڪرُ آهين.
Pointing to someone else	HŨ naokar^u AHE	هُو نوڪرُ آهي.
Pointing to both teacher and yourself	asĨ naokar^a AHIŨ	اسين نوڪر آهيون.
Pointing to teacher	tavHĨ naokar^a AHIO	توهين نوڪر آهيو.
Pointing to others	HŨ naokar^a AHin	هُو نوڪر آهن.

Repeat the exercise making the statements negative, and turning them into questions.

LESSON SEVEN

7-A Pronunciation Drill

1. Contrasting /dh/ and /Dh/

ڏ ء د

vADhE khE dhak^u laggO. (The carpenter got hurt.)	وادي کي ڏَڪُ لڳو.
nanDhI^a dhI^a khE Dhak^u AHE. (The small daughter has the cover.)	ننڍيءَ ڌيءَ کي ڏَڪُ آهي.
nanDhE dhObbI^a vADHE jA kapRA dhOtA. (The young washerman washed the carpenter's clothes.)	ننڍي ڌوٻيءَ وادي جا ڪپڙا ڌوتا.

2. Contrasting /t/ and /T/

ٽ ء ت

miTI hitE AHE. (The dust is here.)	مٽي هتي آهي.
TapAlI^a jA puT^a hutE tarsIA. (The postman's sons waited there.)	ٽپاليءَ جا پُٽَ هُتي ترسيا.
HaT^a tE TE mOtI AHin. (There are three pearls at the shop.)	هٽ تي ٽي موتي آهن.

7 – B   The Postposition jO (of) to make adjectives

HI^u TapAlI^a jO qalam^u AHE. This is the postman's pen.	هيءُ ٽپاليءَ جو قلم آهي.
HI^u nanDhE kamarE jO darivAzO AHE. This is the door of the small room.	هيءُ ننڍي ڪمري جو دروازو آهي.
HI^a darivAzE jI kunjI AHE. This is the key to (lit: of) the door.	هيءَ دروازي جي ڪنجي آهي.
HI^a DAktar^a sAHib^a jI pEnsilⁱ AHE. This is the doctor's pencil.	هيءَ ڊاڪٽر صاحب جي پينسل آهي.

chA HI^u DAkTarIA RI^a jO ghar^u AHE? Is this the lady-doctor's house?	چا هيءَ ڊاڪٽرياڻيءَ جو گهرُ آهي؟
HI^u naokar^a jO chOkarO AHE. This is the servant's boy.	هيءَ نوڪر جو چوڪرو آهي.
HU^a naokar^a jI chOkirI AHE. That is the servant's girl.	هُوءَ نوڪر جي چوڪري آهي.
HI^u ustAd^a jO bbAr^u AHE. This (he) is the teacher's child (little boy).	هيءَ استاد جو ٻارُ آهي.
HU ustAdIA RI^a jA bbAr^a AHin. They (those) are the lady-teacher's children.	هو استادياڻي جا ٻار آهن.
iHE ustAdan jŪ kursiŪ AHin. These are the teacher's chairs.	اِهي استادن جون ڪرسيون آهن.
HU naokaran jA chOkirA AHin. They (those) are the servant's boys.	هو نوڪرن جا چوڪرا آهن.
HU naokaran jŪ chOkirIŪ AHin. They (those) are the servant's girls.	هو نوڪرن جون چوڪريون آهن.
chA UHE SAgirdan jA kamarA AHin? Are those the student's rooms?	چا اُهي شاگردن جا ڪمرا آهن؟
HI vaddan darivAzan jŪ kunjIŪ na AHin. These aren't the keys to (lit: of) the big doors.	هي وڏن دروازن جون ڪنجيون نه آهن.
HI nanDhIun darIun jA pardA AHin. These are the curtains for (lit: of) the small windows.	هي ننڍين درين جا پردا آهن.
HI^u 'aoratun jO kamarO AHE. This is the women's room.	هيءَ عورتن جو ڪمرو آهي.
aI HI chOkirIun jA kamarA AHin. And these are the girls' rooms.	ءَ هي چوڪرين جا ڪمرا آهن.

1. jO is inflected in the same way as masculine singular nouns and adjectives ending in /O/ are inflected, to form the feminines and plurals in the nominative. That is, jO may take the following forms in the nominative position:

Singular		**Plural**	
masc.	fem.	masc.	fem.
jo جو	jI جي	jA جا	jŪ جون

2. When jO is added to a word it turns that word into an adjective, describing or showing special, often possessive, relationship with the following word or phrase. This is true of both persons and things.

3.   Its use is often equivalent to the English "of" although as the examples above show, "to," "for," and "____'s" are sometimes more idiomatic renderings than "of."

4.   Whereas in English "of" is a <u>pre</u>position, jO is a <u>post</u>position; that is, it comes <u>after</u> the word which it changes into an adjective. So TapAII^a jO qalam^u is literally "postman-of-pen" = pen of (the) postman = (the) postman's pen. Here it can be clearly seen that "postman," which is normally a noun, becomes "postman's," an adjective showing relationship of possession and given the information as to "whose" pen it is.

5.   The noun (or word) which jO turns into an adjective is changed, that is, inflected according to the following pattern:

For masculine words

   (a) Words ending in /O/ change to /E/. For example, kamarO (room) = kamarE jO (of the room). The plural /A/ is shortened to /a/ and /n/ is added. For example, kamarA (rooms) = kamaran jO (of the rooms).

   (b) Words ending in /^{u}/ change to /^{a}/. For example, kitAb^u (book) kitAb^a jO (of the book). To the plural /a/ ending /n/ is added. Thus, kitAb^a (books), kitAban jO (of the books).

   (c) Words ending in /U/ add /a/. For example, mARHU (man) mARHU^a jO (of the man). For the plural form /U/ is shortened to /u/ and /n/ is added. For example, mARHU (men), mARHun jO (of the men).

For feminine words

   (a) Words ending in /I/ add /^{a}/. For example, kursI (chair), kursI^a jO (of the chair). The plural ending /Ũ/ becomes /un/. For example, kursIŨ (chairs) kursIun jO (of the chairs).

   (b) Words ending in /^{a}/ remain unchanged. For example mEz^a (table) mEz^a jO (of the table.) The plural ending /Ũ/ becomes /un/. For example mEzŨ (tables), mEzun jO (of the tables).

   (c) Words ending in /A/ remain unchanged. For example, davA (medicine) davA jO (of the medicine). The plural addition /Ũ/ becomes /un/. For example, davAŨ (medicines), davAun jO (of the medicines).

   (d) Words ending in /^{i}/ remain unchanged. For example, bhit^i (wall), bhit^i jO (of the wall). The plural /IŨ/ ending becomes /Iun/. For example, bhitIŨ (walls), bhitIun jO (of the walls).

6.   The form a word takes because of the presence of jO or any other post position yet to be introduced will be called the oblique form. Thus, kutE is the oblique form of kutO; kutan is the oblique form of kutA, kursIun is the oblique form of kursIŨ, etc.

7. To summarize, the oblique forms of the various types of nouns are as follows:

Masculine		Nominative		Oblique	
(a)	those ending in /O/ sing.	kutO	کتو	kutE (jO)	کتي (جو)
	pl.	kutA	کتا	kutan (jO)	کتن (جو)
(b)	those ending in /O/ sing.	ghar^u	گهرُ	ghar^a (jO)	گهرَ (جو)
	pl.	ghar^a	گهرَ	gharan (jO)	گهرن (جو)
(c)	those ending in /U/ sing.	tambU	تنبو	tambU^a (jO)	تنبوءَ (جو)
	pl.	tambU	تنبو	tambun (jO)	تنبن (جو)

Feminine		Nominative		Oblique	
(a)	those ending in /I/ sing.	kursI	کرسي	kursI^a (jO)	کرسيءَ (جو)
	pl.	kursIŨ	کرسيون	kursIun (jO)	کرسين (جو)
(b)	those ending in /a/ sing.	mEz^a	ميز	mEz^a (jO)	ميز(جو)
	pl.	mEzŨ	ميزون	mEzun (jO)	ميزن (جو)
(c)	those ending in /A/ sing.	davA	دوا	davA (jO)	دوا (جو)
	pl.	davAŨ	دوائون	davaun (jO)	دوائن (جو)
(d)	those ending in /i/ sing.	bhit^i	ڀت	bhit^i (jO)	ڀت (جو)
	pl.	bhitIŨ	ڀتيون	bhitIun (jO)	ڀتين (جو)

8. Listen to your teacher pronounce the plural oblique forms with the post position jO Does s/he add a semi-vowel after the final /n/? If so it would be /^{i}/. That is, kutan^i jO, kursIun^i jO, etc.

9. Listen to your teacher pronounce the feminine plural oblique forms and notice where his/her accent (or stress) falls in the word. It is never on the final /Iun/ sound. For example, the accented syllable in such words as bhitIun jO, chOkirIun jO, kursIun jO is as underlined.

10. The postposition jO, since it acts like an adjective ending, must agree with the word or phrase it qualifies; that is, with what follows it. For example, naokar^a jA chOkirA (servant's boys), naokar^a jŨ chOkirIŨ (servant's girls). In both these phrases jO agrees with the noun that follows it in gender and number.

11. When adjectives or other qualifying words which are inflectable are used in a phrase before a form of /jO/ they are inflected according to the following pattern:

   (a) adjectives ending in the inflectable masculine form of /O/ change in the same way that nouns do (as described above). For example:

nanDhO kamarO	becomes	nanDhE kamarE jO	نندو کمرو ← نندي کمري جو
cagA chOkirA	"	cagan chOkiran jO	چڱا چوڪرا ← چڱن چوڪرن جو
nanDhI chOkirI	"	nanDhIa chOkirIa jO	نندي چوڪري ← نندية چوڪرية جو
nanDhIŨ chOkirIŨ	"	nanDhIun chOkirIun jO	نندیون چوڪریون ← نندین چوڪرین جو
vaddI mEza	"	vaddIa mEza jO	وڏي ميز ← وڏي ميز جو
vaddIŨ mEzŨ	"	vaddIun mEzun jO	وڏیون میزون ← وڏین میزن جو

   (b) adjectives ending in any other letter do not change. For example:

KAlI kamarO	remains	KAlI kamarE jO	خالي ڪمرو ← خالي ڪمري جو
KAlI pEtIŨ	"	KAlI pEtIun jO	خالي پیٹیون ← خالي پیٹین جو
mazbutu kulfu	"	mazbUtu kulfa jO	مضبوط ڪلف ← مضبوط ڪلف جو
mazbUtu kursIŨ	"	mazbUtu kursIun jO	مضبوط ڪرسیون ← مضبوط ڪرسین جو

7 - C   The Demonstrative Adjectives

HIa tasvIra nanDhI AHE This picture is small.	هيء تصوير نندي آهي.
HUa tasvIra suHiRI AHE. That picture is pretty.	هوء تصوير سهڻي آهي.
uHA tasvIra bi suHiRI AHE. That picture is pretty, too.	اها تصوير به سهڻي آهي.
HU mARHU kEru AHE? Who is that man?	هو ماٹھو ڪير آهي؟
HU DAkTaru sAHibu AHE. That's (He's) the doctor.	هو ڊاڪٹر صاحب آهي.
HUa 'aorata kEra AHE? Who is that woman?	هوء عورت ڪير آهي؟
HUa ustAdIARI AHE. She is a/the teacher.	هوء استادیاڻي آهي.

HI^a darI vaddI AHE. This window is large.	هي دري وڏي آهي.
uHE chOkirA miHinatI AHin. Those boys are hard-working.	اهي چوکرا محنتي آهن.
HU mARHU sust^u AHin. Those men are lazy.	هو ماڙهو سست آهن.
HI chOkirI U HOSIAr AHin. These girls are clever.	هي چوڪريون هوشيار آهن.
HU^a mEz^a DighI AHE. That table is long.	هوءَ ميز ڊگهي آهي.
HI^u kAGaz^u sanHO AHE. This paper is thin.	هيءُ ڪاغذ سنهو آهي.
HI^u kitAb^u dilcasp^u AHE. This book is interesting.	هيءُ ڪتاب دلچسپ آهي.
uHO bOrcI tamAm HOSIAr AHE. That cook is very clever.	اهو بورچي تمام هوشيار آهي.
HU chOkirA tamAm cagA AHin. Those boys are very good.	هو چوکرا تمام چڱا آهن.
HI kitAb^a dilcasp^u na AHin. These books aren't interesting.	هي ڪتاب دلچسپ نہ آهن.

1. The demonstrative words used above, previously learned as pronouns and twice so used above (with DAkTaru and ustAdIARI) – also function as adjectives. The same distinction of nearness and remoteness (e.g. HI and HU) and emphasis (e.g. iHO vs. uHO) are observed.

2. The ordinary adjectives in the examples given above follow the words that they describe just as predicate adjectives do in English. Note the difference this word order makes in the meaning.

HI^u pardO kArO AHE. This curtain is black.	هيءُ پردو ڪارو آهي.
HI^u kArO pardO AHE. This is a black curtain.	هيءُ ڪارو پردو آهي.
HI kapRA achA AHin. These clothes are white.	هي ڪپڙا اڇا آهن.
HI achA kapRA AHin. These are white clothes.	هي اڇا ڪپڙا آهن.
HU mARHU thulHO AHE. That man is fat.	هو ماڙهو ٿلهو آهي.

HU thulHO mARHU AHE. That/ he is a fat man.	هو ٿلهو ماٺهو آهي.
uHE tambU ggARHA AHin. Those tents are red.	اهي تنبو ڳاڙها آهن.
uHE ggARHA tambU AHin. Those are red tents.	اهي ڳاڙها تنبو آهن.

3. tamAm^u is an adverb which intensifies the meaning of the adjective. So, not just cagO (good) but tamAm cagO (very good).

4. You have been introduced to the suffix /IARI/ which is used to change a masculine title or occupation to the feminine form. Sometimes in place of this longer ending, the final short vowel may be changed. For example, ustAd^u becomes ustAdⁱ. Then the plural will be ustAdIU; rather than ustAdIARIU.

7-D The oblique forms of demonstratives and the question word, kEr^u and kaHiRO

HI^u kāHinjO kitab^u AHE? Whose book is this?	هيءُ ڪنهن جو ڪتاب آهي؟
HI^u ustAd^a jO kitab^u AHE. It's the teacher's book.	هيءُ اُستاد جو ڪتاب آهي.
kaHiRO kitAb^u cagO AHE? Which book is good?	ڪهڙو ڪتاب چڱو آهي؟
uHO vaddO kitAb^u cagO AHE. That big book is good.	اُهو وڏو ڪتاب چڱو آهي.
HI^a kaHiRE darivAzE jI kunjI AHE? Which door is this the key to?	هيءَ ڪهڙي دروازي جي ڪُنجي آهي؟
HI^a unHI^a nanDhE darivAzE jI kunjI AHE. It is the key to that small door.	هيءَ اُنهيءَ ننڍي دروازي جي ڪنجي آهي.
HIa kāHinjI batI AHE? Whose lamp is this?	هيءَ ڪنهن جي بتي آهي؟
iHA hin^a 'aorat^a jI batI AHE. That's this woman's lamp.	اها هن عورت جي بتي آهي.
Hun^a mARHU^a jO nAlO chA AHE? What is that man's name?	هن ماٺهوءَ جو نالو ڇا آهي؟

Hun^a jO nAlO mumtAz alI AHE. His name is Mumtaz Ali.	هن جو نالو ممتاز علي آهي.
HI kāHinjA panA AHin? Whose papers are these?	هي ڪنهن جا پنا آهن؟
HU Hin^a chOkiri^a jA panA AHin. Those are this girl's papers.	هُو هِنَ ڇوڪريءَ جا پنا آهن.
Hi kāHinjA kamarA AHin? Whose rooms are these?	هي ڪنهن جا ڪمرا آهن؟
HI hun^a ustAd^a jA kamarA AHin. These are that teacher's rooms.	هي هن استاد جا ڪمرا آهن.
Hi kaHiRIun chOkarIun jA kamarA Ahin? Which girls' rooms are these?	هي ڪهڙين ڇوڪرين جا ڪمرا آهن؟
HI ustAd^a jĒ chOkirIun jA kamarA AHin. These are the rooms of the teacher's girls.	هي استاد جي ڇوڪرين جا ڪمرا آهن.
Hinan 'aoratan jO kaHiRO kam AHE? What is the work of these women?	هنن عورتن جو ڪهڙو ڪم آهي؟
HU unHan chOkirIun jŨ ustAdIA R̃ IŨ AHin. They are those girl's teachers	هو انهن ڇوڪرين جون استادياٽيون آهن.
HI bbAr^a kāHinjA AHin? Whose children are these?	هي ٻار ڪنهن جا آهن؟
HU unHan naokaran jA bbAr^a AHin. They are those servant's children.	هو اُنهن نوڪرن جا ٻار آهن.
inHI^a mA R̃ Hu^a jO chOkirO tamAm^u HOSIAr AHE. That man's boy is very clever.	انهيءَ ماٺهوءَ جو ڇوڪرو تمام هوشيار آهي.
par^a unHI^a mA R̃ HU^a jO chOkirO sust^u AHE. But that man's boy is lazy.	پر انهيءَ ماٺهوءَ جو ڇوڪرو سست آهي.

1. kaHiRO, like kEr^u, is a question word, and it asks, "which?", "what?". Its /O/ ending must inflect to agree with the noun which follows it in gender and number.

2. The demonstratives and kEr^u can be turned into possessive adjectives by the addition of jO. However, when they are followed – either immediately (kāHinjO) or in a series (as, Hin^a kamarE jO) – by a form of jO, they change their form; that is, they are inflected. Thus, we cannot say HU jO, but Hunan jO, nor kEr^u jO, but kāHinjO. Note that when jO is added to kāHin it is attached, the two words becoming one word.

3. The inflected form of kEr^u is kāHin for the singular, and kin for the plural.

4. The position in the sentence of words like kaHiRO and kāHinjO may vary. For example, one may say:

HI^u kāHinjO kitAb^u AHE?   or,   HI^u kitAb^u kāHinjO AHE?

Hinan 'aoratun jO kam kaHiRO AHE?   or,   Hinan 'aoratun jO kaHiRO kam AHE?

5. The inflectional changes (to form the oblique) of this section are summarized in the following chart:

Nominative Form			Meaning	Oblique Form	
HI^u	(m)	هِيءُ	this/it/he	Hin^a	هِن
HI^a	(f)	هِيءَ	this/it/she	Hin^a	هِن
HU	(m)	هو	that/it/he	Hun^a	هُن
HU^a	(f)	هوءَ	that/it/she	Hun^a	هُن
iHO	(m)	اِهو	this/it/he	inHI^a	اِنهِيءَ
iHA	(f)	اها	this/it/she	inHI^a	اِنهِيءَ
uHO	(m)	أهو	that/it/he	unHI^a	أنهِيءَ
uHA	(f)	أها	that/it/she	unHI^a	أنهِيءَ
HI	(m and f)	هي	these/they	Hinan	هِنن
HU	(m and f)	هو	those/they	Hunan	هُنن
iHE	(m and f)	اِهي	these/they	inHan	اِنهن
uHE	(m and f)	أهي	those/they	unHan	أنهن

7 - E   The inflected personal pronouns

HI^u mūHīnjO kitAb^u AHE. This is my book.	هِيءُ منهنجو ڪتاب آهي.
HI^a mūHīnjI pEnsil^i AHE. This is my pencil.	هِيءَ منهنجي پينسل آهي.
HI mūHīnjA qalam^a AHin. These are my pens.	هي منهنجا قلم آهن.

chA HU tūHīnjO nAlO AHE? Is that your name?	چا هو تنهنجو نالو آهي؟
HI tūHīnjA panA AHin. These are your pages.	هي تنهنجا پنا آهن.
HIa tūHīnjI pEnsili na AHE. This isn't your pencil.	هيءَ تنهنجي پينسل نَ آهي.
chA HU Huna jŪ chOkirIŨ AHin? Are those/they his/her girls?	چا هو هُن جون چوڪريون آهن؟
HU Huna jO ustAdu AHE. He is his/her teacher.	هو هُن جو استاد آهي.
Huna jI tasvIra tamAmu suHiR̃I AHE. His/her picture is very pretty.	هن جي تصوير تمام سهڻي آهي.
Hu asÃjO mAlHI AHE. He is our gardener.	هو اسان جو مالهي آهي.
HI asÃja TE nanDhA bbAra AHin. These are our three young children.	هي اسان جا ٽي ننڍا ٻار آهن.
HI asÃjŨ kunjIŨ na AHin. These aren't our keys.	هي اسان جون ڪنجيون نَ آهن.
chA HIu tavHÃjO kam AHE? Is this your work?	چا هيءُ توهان جو ڪم آهي؟
HI avHÃjA vaddA achA pardA AHin. These are your large white curtains.	هي اوهان جا وڏا اڇا پردا آهن.
chA HUa tavHÃjI chOkirI AHE? Is she your girl?	چا هوءَ توهان جي چوڪري آهي؟
tavHÃ jE kitAba jO nAlO chA AHE? What is the name of your book?	توهان جي ڪتاب جو نالو چا آهي؟
chA HI bba HOSIAr chOkirA tavHÃ jA AHin? Are these two clever boys yours?	چا هي ٻَ هوشيار چوڪرا توهان جا آهن؟
tavHÃ jE kapRE jO rãgu kaHiRO AHE? Which is the color of your cloth?	توهان جي ڪپڙي جو رنگ ڪهڙو آهي؟
Hunan jE chOkirIa jO nAlO chA AHE? What is the name of their girl?	هُنن جي چوڪريءَ جو نالو چا آهي؟
HI bi hunan jŨ tasvIrŨ AHin. These are their pictures also.	هي ٻَ هُنن جون تصويرون آهن.

HI tavHĀ jE chOkirIun jA kapRA AHin. These are your girls' clothes.	هي توهان جي چوڪرين جا ڪپڙا آهن.
HI TOpIŨ mAlHIa jE chOkiran jŨ AHin. These caps belong to the gardeners' boys	هي ٽوپيون مالهي جي چوڪرن جون آهن.

1. The adjectival postposition jO may be added to the personal pronouns to make them possessives. When this happens changes take place in the pronouns, that is, they inflect. For example AŨ or mĀ becomes mũHĩnjO. The chart below details the changes.

Person	Singular		Plural	
1st	mũHĩnjO my, mine	منهنجو	asĀ jO our, ours	اسان جو
2nd	tũHĩnjO your, yours	تنهنجو	tavHĀ jO, AvHĀ jO your, yours	توهان جو، اوهان جو
3rd	Huna jO his, her, hers, its	هن جو	Hunan jO their, theirs	هنن جو

2. Often you will find jO attached to all six of the inflected pronouns in the Sindhi script. However, jO may remain detached from the 3rd singular and all plural forms as above. jO is <u>never</u> found detached from the 1st and 2nd singular forms.

3. The possessive adjectives may occur in both the subject and predicate positions. For example,

HIu mũHĩnjO nIrO qalamu AHE. This is my blue pen.	هيءُ منهنجو نيرو قلم آهي.
HIu nIrO qalamu mũHĩnjO AHE. This blue pen is mine.	هيءُ نيرو قلم منهنجو آهي.
HU HunajO kam AHE. That is his work.	هو هُن جو ڪم آهي.
HU kam HunajO AHE. That work is his.	هو ڪم هن جو آهي.

4. kaHiRO and chA can often be used interchangeably. For example,

Hina kapRE jO rāgu chA AHE? Hina kapRE jO rāgu kaHiRO AHE? What is the color of this cloth?	هن ڪپڙي جو رنگ چا آهي؟ هن ڪپڙي جو رنگ ڪهڙو آهي؟

5. When it inflects to form the oblique, jO acts differently from nouns and adjectives ending in /O/. The oblique form of jO is simply jE. This is true for both singular and plural in both their masculine and feminine forms. Thus,

naokarᵃ jE chOkirE jO......	نوکر جي چوکري جو ....
naokarᵃ jE chOkirIᵃ jO......	نوکر جي چوکريءَ جو ....
naokarᵃ jE chOkiran jO......	نوکر جي چوکرن جو ....
naokarᵃ jE chOkirIun jO......	نوکر جي چوکرين جو ....

You will notice however, that Sindhis will often inflect jO into the oblique as they do adjectives and nouns ending in /O/, especially when they use jO with the first and second personal pronouns, for example,

mūHĩnjIᵃ chOkirIᵃ jO......	منهنجي چوکري جو ....
mūHĩnjIun chOkirIun jO......	منهنجين چوکرين جو ....
tūHĩnjan chOkiran jO......	تنهنجن چوکرن جو ....
asÃ jan bbAran jO......	اسان جن بارن جو ....
tavHÃ jIᵃ chOkirIᵃ jO.......	توهان جيءَ چوکريءَ جو ....

In his grammar Dulamal Bulchand says, "Strictly speaking the first and second persons of the adjectives ending in jO, viz., mūHĩnjO, asÃjO, tūHĩnjO, and tavhÃjO have altogether four inflected forms like an ordinary adjective, but it is also a common custom among Sindhis to use only the masculine inflected form (jE) of the above four words before all inflected forms whether plural masculine nouns, feminine singular nouns or feminine plural nouns. The European student of Sindhi, however, is advised not to trouble himself about all the inflected forms of these four words, but to adhere to one form only, viz., the singular masculine (jE)..."[1]

Anandram T. Shahani says, "jE is the inflected from of jO, jA, jI, and jŨ. It is used for all oblique forms, i.e., if jO, jA, jI, or jŨ precedes a noun which is followed by a postposition (expressed or implied) it should be substituted by jE. ..."[2]

6. When a word is qualified by more than one adjective and these adjectives come before the noun they qualify or describe they usually occur in the following order:

(1) Possessive	(2) Number	(3) Intensity/size	(4) Quality	(5) Color	(6) Noun
asÃ jA	TE	nanDhA			bbArᵃ
tūHinjA		DighA		achA	pardA
	bba		HOsIAr		chOkirA
Hunan jA			KAlI		KamarA

---

[1] Bulchand, Dulamal, A Manual of Sindhi, 1901, p.73
[2] Shahani, Anandram T., The Sindhi Instructor, date unknown, p 23

7 - F Vocabulary for Lesson Six

achO white	اَچو	aĩ and	ءٍ
bbAr{u} (m) child	ٻارُ	kArO black	ڪارو
dilcasp{u} interesting, pleasing	دِلچَسپُ	darI (f) window	دَري
DighO long, tall	ڊِگهو	kam{u} (m) work	ڪَمُ
tamAm{u} very, quite	تَمامُ	kaHiRO which, what?	ڪِهِڙو
thulHO thick, fat	ٿُلهو	ggARHO red	ڳاڙهو
par{a} but	پَرَ	ghar{u} (m) house	گهرُ
rãg{u} (m) color	رَنگُ	miHinatI hard-working, industrious	مِحِنَتي
sust{u} lazy	سُستُ	nALO (m) name	نالو
sanHO thin	سَنهو	HOSIAr clever, intelligent	هوشيار

7 - G Conversational Review

1. Carry on the following dialogue, using each of these words:

batI, tasvIr{a}, pEnsil{i}, farAsI,

kApI, kunjI, mEz{a}, TOpI, chOkirI

بتي، تصوير، پينسِل، فراسي،

ڪاپي، ڪنجي، ميز، ٽوپي، چوڪِري

For example:

Teacher: HI{a}/ HU{a} kāHĩnjI batI AHE?	استاد: هي/ هُوَ ڪهِن جي بتي آهي؟
Student: HI{a}/HU{a} Hun{a} mAR̃HU{a} jI batI AHE.	شاگرد: هي/ هُوَ هن ماڻهُوءَ جي بتي آهي.

In your reply vary the answer to include other appropriate words in addition to mAR̃HU.

2. Carry on the following dialogue, using each of these words:

tambU, pardO, Kat^u, SISO, kitAb^u	تنبو، پردو، خط، شيشو، ڪتاب
kutO, kamarO, uTh^u, ghORO,	ڪتو، ڪمرو، اٺ، گھوڙو،
kukUR^u, kulf^u.	ڪُڪُرُ، ڪلف
Teacher: HI^u kāHīnjO tambU AHE?	استاد: هي ڪنهن جو تنبو آهي؟
Student: HU 'aorat^a jO tambU AHE.	شاگرد: هو عورت جو تنبو آهي.

3. Use the following words according to the pattern given:

batI, kunjI, chat^i, bhit^i,	بتي، ڪنجي، چٽ، ڀت،
faraS^u, darI, pardO, kulf^u	فرش، دري، پردو، ڪلف
Teacher: chA HI^a hin^a kamarE jI batI AHE?	استاد: ڇا هيءَ هن ڪمري جي بتي آهي؟
Student: na sAĪ, HI^a hin^a kamarE jI batI na AHE, par^a Hun^a kamarE jI (AHE.)	شاگرد: نَ سائين، هيءَ هِنَ ڪمري جي بتي نَ آهي، پر هُن ڪمري جي (آهي).

4. Repeat exercise 3, using the same pattern but nouns in the plural. Omit the words chat^i and faraS^u.

5. Use <u>inflected</u> plurals of the following nouns to answer the question.

HI^u kāHīnjO kam^u AHE?	هيءُ ڪنهن جو ڪم آهي؟
ustAd^u, DAkTar^u, SAgird^u, bOrcI,	استاد، ڊاڪٽر، شاگرد، بورچي
mAlHI, mazUr^u, chOkirO, mAR̃HU	مالهي، مزور، چوڪرو، ماڻهو
maolvI sAHib^u	مولوي صاحبُ
Teacher: HI^u kāHīnjO kam^u AHE?	استاد: هيءُ ڪنهن جو ڪم آهي؟
Student: HI^u ustAdan jO kam^u AHE.	شاگرد: استادن جو ڪم آهي.

6. Practice using from the following lists adjectives with the nouns given, according to the pattern shown:

Adjectives: cag̃O, vaddO, nanDhO

چڱو، وڏو، ننڊيو

mazbUt^u, miHinatI, suHiR̃O, sust^u, dilcasp^u, DighO

مضبوط، محنتي، سهڻو، سست، دلچسپ، ڊگهو

Nouns: darivAzO, bhit^i, chat^i, paR̃I, panO, kitAb^u, mAR̃HU, mazUr^u, chOkirO

دروازو، ڀت، ڇت، پاڻي، پنو، ڪتاب، ماڻهو، مزور، چوڪرو

chOkirI, mEz^a, tasvIr^a

چوڪري، ميز، تصوير

HI^u _____ darivAzO AHE.

هيءُ _____ دروازو آهي.

7. Repeat Exercise 6 with the adjectives in the predicate position. For example:

HI^u _____ darivAzO AHE.

هيءُ _____ دروازو آهي.

8. Repeat exercise 6 with nouns in the plural and adjective in the predicate position. (Omit nouns which are not normally used in the plural, such as pARĨ.) For example:

HI _____ darivAzA AHin.

هي _____ دروازا آهن.

9. Holding up or pointing to items around you which you have learned in the lessons thus far, the teacher should ask the following questions:

Teacher: chA HI^u kitAb^u tavHÃ jO AHE?	استاد: ڇا هيءُ ڪتاب توهان جو آهي؟
Student: na SAĨ, HU kitAb^u mūHinjO na AHE, (HU) tavÃ jO AHE.	شاگرد: نه سائين، هو ڪتاب منهنجو نه آهي، (هو) توهان جو آهي.

You can also make good use of picture books or magazines to practice words for which the items are not available. Answer according to real or imaginary owners of the items.

10. Repeat exercise 9, using the nouns in the plural. For example:

Teacher: HI tavHÃ jŨ kunjIŨ AHin chA?	استاد: هي توهان جون ڪنجيون آهن ڇا؟
Student: HU mūHĩnjŨ kunjIŨ AHin., etc	شاگرد: هو منهنجيون ڪنجيون آهن.

11. Using hand motions to signify the person, drill the declension of the possessive pronouns, using the following nouns:

pEnsilⁱ, qalam^u, kunjI, kitAb^u,

rabbaR^u, kApI, kursI

پينسل، قلم، ڪنجي، ڪتاب

ربڙ، ڪاپي، ڪرسي

For example:

HI^a muHĩnjI kunjI AHE   HI^a asÃ jI kunjI AHE.

HI^a tuHĩnjI kunjI AHE   HI^a tavHÃ jI kunjI AHE.

HI^a hunajI kunjI AHE   HI^a hunanjI AHE.

Repeat Exercise 11, using nouns in the plural. For example:

HI mūHinjŨ kunjIŨ AHin, etc.

LESSON EIGHT

8 – A   Pronunciation Drill

1.   Contrasting /d/ and /dh/   (12,15)   /ڏ/ /د/

dhI^a jI SAdI Huna Handh^a tE HUndI. (The daughter's wedding will be in that place).	ڏيءَ جي شادي هُنَ هنڌ تي هوندي.
AdmI Huna Handh^a mẼ khAdhO khAIndO. (The man will eat in that place.)	آدمي هُن هنڌ مِ کاڌو کائيندو.
dar^a tE dhIAn ddEO. (Pay attention to the door.)	در تي ڏيان ڏيو.

2.   Contrasting /R/ and /R̃/   (43,5)   /ڙ/ /ٽ/

bbOr^a mẼ zIAdaHa lUR̃^u AHE. (There's too much salt in the curry.)	ٻوڙ مِ زياده لوڻ آهي.
ghORO pAR̃^a nORI TORaR̃^a laggO. (The horse began to break the rope himself.)	گھوڙو پاڻ نوڙي توڙڻ لڳو.
mAR̃HU vaR̃^a jE HEThÃ bbOr^u khAiR̃^a laggO. (The man began to eat curry under the tree.)	ماڻھو وڻ جي ھيٺان ٻوڙ کائڻ لڳو.

8 - B   Location shown by the words kithE (where?) HutE (there) and HitE (here).

tavHÃ jO ggARHO qalam^u kithE AHE? Where is your red pen? HU HitE AHE. It's here.	توهان جو ڳاڙھو قلم ڪٿي آهي؟ هو هتي آهي.

mūHĩnjŪ kunjIŪ kithE AHin? Where are my keys? sAĨ, HU HitE AHin. Sir, they're here.	منهنجون ڪنجيون ڪٿي آهن؟ سائين هو هتي آهن.
mūHĩnjO risAlO kithE AHE? Where is my magazine? Kabar[a] na AHE, sAĨ. I don't know (lit: there's no information), sir.	منهنجو رسالو ڪٿي آهي؟ خبر نہ آهي، سائين.
chA tūHĩnjI aKbAr[a] HitE AHE? Is your newspaper here? na, HutE AHE. No, it's (over) there.	چا منهنجي اخبار ھِتي آھي؟ نہ، ھُتي آهي.
zanAnI ispatAl[a] kithE AHE? Where is the women's hospital? HU HutE AHE. It's there.	زنانو اسپتال ڪٿي آهي؟ هو هتي آهي.
bImAr[u] chOkirI kithE AHE? Where is the sick girl? HU[a] hutE AI IE. She is there.	بيمار چوڪري ڪٿي آهي؟ هو ھُتي آهي.
misTar ismith kithE AHE? Where is Mr. Smith? misTar ismith HutE AHE. Mister Smith is there.	مسٽر اسمٿ ڪٿي آهي؟ مسٽر اسمٿ ھُتي آهي.
iskUl[u] kithE AHE? Where is the school? HitE iskUl[u] kOnaHE. There's no school here.	اسڪول ڪٿي آهي؟ ھِتي اسڪول ڪون آهي.
chA HitE bAlTI AHE? Is there a bucket here? na, HitE bAlTI kAnaHE. No, there's no bucket here.	چا ھِتي بالٽي آهي؟ نہ ھِتي بالٽي ڪانہ آهي.
tavHÃ jI kApI AĨ kitAb[a] kithE AHin? Where are your notebook and books? mūHĩnjA kitAb[a] AĨ kApI hitE AHE. My books and notebook are here.	توهان جي ڪاپي ۽ ڪتابَ ڪٿي آهن؟ منهنجا ڪتاب ۽ ڪاپي هتي آهي.

1. kithE is the commonly used adverb for asking the location of something or someone --- Where? ---.

2. The two adverbs HitE (here) and HutE (there) often answer that question. You may also hear itE (here) and utE (There).

3. The "place" which answers the question "Where?" is mentioned in the place of kithE. As with chA, word order normally puts the question word just before the verb.

4. Although the subject may be repeated in the answer it is frequently replaced with HU/HI (he/she/it/they), or it may be omitted altogether. For example, chOkirA kithE AHin? HU HutE AHin, or HutE AHin.

5. The particle kO is sometimes attached to the negative word, na, and these two words attach to AHE to intensify the negative aspect in a sentence. Thus, kO na AHE, three separate words, become kOnaHE. kO inflects to become kA in the feminine form, as illustrated in the sentence above using bAlTI. kO is also used as a pronoun and adjective, and these uses will be explained later.

6. When Sindhis assimilate English words like "Smith" and "school" which begin with an /s/ followed immediately by a consonant, they often add /i/ at the beginning to facilitate pronunciation. The word hospital" is also treated similarly, in that the first two letters are dropped, and /i/ is added so that in Sindhi the word becomes ispatAl.

7. The last two sentences above illustrate certain details about agreement of words in Sindhi:

    (a) If two nouns are qualified by the same adjective, the adjective will agree with the noun nearest it. So tavHĀ jI kApI aĪ kitAb[a], and tavHĀ jA kitab[a] aĪ kApI.

    (b) If two or more nouns are the subject of the sentence, the verb will agree with the last one, that is, the one nearest to it, in gender and in number. Thus, in the second from the last sentence above the verb is AHin (where kitAb[a] is nearest to it) and in the last sentence the verb is AHE, agreeing with kApI.

8 – C   The postposition mẼ (in, at) and tE (on, at) to show location.

DAkTar sAHib[u] ispatAl[a] mẼ AHE. The doctor is in the hospital.	ڊاڪٽر صاحبُ اسپتال ۾ آهي.
tavHĀ jO chOkirO mardAR̃E kamarE mẼ AHE. Your boy is in the men's ward.	توهان جو چوڪرو مرداڻي ڪمري ۾ آهي.
TapAl Afis[a] mẼ ghaR̃A-I mAR̃HU AHin. There are many people in (at) the post office.	ٽپال آفيس ۾ گھڻا ئي ماڻھو آهن.
Hina ggOTh[a] mẼ ghaR̃A-I HaT[a] AHin. There are many shops in this village.	هن ڳوٺ ۾ گھڻا ئي هٽَ آهن.
chA Huna kabbaT[a] mẼ aTh[a] kApIŨ AHin? Are there eight notebooks in that cupboard?	ڇا هن ڪٻٽ ۾ اٺ ڪاپيون آهن؟

na sAĨ, Huna kabbaTᵃ mẼ ruggO TE AHin. No, sir, there are only three in that cupboard.	نَ سائين، هُنَ ڪَٻَٽَ مِ رڳو ٽي آهن.
mũHĩnjE khIsE mẼ Hikᵃ pEnsilⁱ AHE. There's a pencil in my pocket.	منهنجي کيسي مِ هِڪ پينسل آهي.
bEgam sidIqI gharᵃ mẼ na AHE. Begum Siddiqi is not at home.	بيگم صديقي گهرَ مِ نَ آهي.
kāHĩnjI kunjI farAsIᵃ tE AHE? Whose key is on the rug?	ڪنهن جِي ڪُنجِي فراسِيءَ تي آهي؟
avHĀ jI kunjI farAsIᵃ tE AHE. Your key is on the rug.	اوهان جِي ڪُنجِي فراسِيءَ تي آهي.
chA zanAnI ispatAlᵃ Hina rastE tE AHE? Is the women's hospital on this road?	ڇا زناني اِسپَتالَ هِن رستي تي آهي؟
chA ddaHᵃ kArIŨ kApIŨ mEzᵃ tE AHin? Are there ten black notebooks on the table?	ڇا ڏَهَ ڪاريُون ڪاپيُون ميزَ تي آهن؟
na, sAĨ ruggO panjᵃ mEzᵃ tE AHin. No, sir, there are only five on the table.	نَ سائين رڳو پنج ميزَ تي آهن.
Huna bhitⁱ tE ghaRIAl AHE. There is a clock on that wall.	هُنَ ڀِتِ تي گهڙيال آهي.
Hina gilAsᵃ mẼ kujh pARI AHE. There's some water in this glass.	هِنَ گلاسَ مِ ڪُجهہ پاڻي آهي.
misaz grIn gharᵃ mẼ na AHE. Mrs. Green isn't at home.	مِسز گِرين گهرَ مِ نَ آهي.
HUᵃ SaHarᵃ mẼ AHE. She's in town.	هُوءَ شَهرَ مِ آهي.
darivAzE tE kEru AHE? Who's at the door?	درۡوازي تي ڪيرُ آهي؟
aKbArᵃ faraSᵃ tE AHE. The newspaper is on the floor.	اخبارَ فرشَ تي آهي.
faraSᵃ tE aKbArᵃ AHE. There's a newspaper on the floor.	فرشَ تي اخبار آهي.

1. As postpositions, mẼ (in) and tE (on) <u>follow</u> the word which functions as its object. That object must be inflected into the oblique form. So,

   HI^u kamarO (nominative) becomes   <u>Hina</u> kamarE mẼ (oblique)

2. Note that while the basic meaning of mẼ is "in", and that of tE is "on", these postpositions sometimes carry the meaning of "at", as illustrated in the sentences above. There are still other meanings these postpositions can carry. For example, Hina ghar^a mẼ sat^a kamarA AHin means, "This house has seven rooms." Another way to express the same meaning is with the use of jO: Hina ghar^a jA sat^a kamarA AHin.

3. The last two examples above (with aKbar^a) show that definiteness or indefiniteness can often be conveyed by word order. In the first example the occurrence of aKbar^a at the beginning of the sentence suggests that we already know what is being talked about. Perhaps the statement is in answer to the question, "Where is the newspaper?" Hence in this statement the thing mentioned before, the aKbar^a, is definite or specific. On the other hand, when faraS^a tE (on the floor) comes first, and aKbar^a in a less conspicuous place, the idea of indefiniteness is conveyed. This is approximately equivalent to the indefinite phrase, "There is…" in English.

4. ruggO is an adverb and does not inflect. That is, the /O/ ending remains even though it precedes a noun with a feminine, or a plural ending. As an adverb it has no agreement with nouns near it in the sentence. For example,

   ruggO Hik^a kApI   only one notebook

   ruggO chOkirIŨ   only girls

5. Sometimes bEgam is placed before the name of a lady of high standing in the community. The masculine equivalent is bEg^u. These are the old Moghul titles meaning, "Lord", and "Lady".

6. Emphasis is added by the use of the particle "I" (see 8-D-3 below). Leaving out the particle in the examples above makes the sentence sound like a question.

8 – D   Some uses of the word kO

darivAzE tE kO chOkirO AHE. There is some boy at the door.	دروازي تي ڪو چوڪرو آهي.
ghar^a mẼ kO dAkTar^u AHE chA? Is there any doctor in the house?	گھر ۾ ڪو ڊاڪٽر آهي ڇا؟
na, ghar^a mẼ kOI DAkTar^u kOna AHE. No, there's no doctor (at all) in the house.	نَ گھر ۾ ڪوئي ڊاڪٽر ڪونَ آهي.
ghar^a mẼ kA DAkTarIAR̃I AHE chA? Is there some lady doctor in the house?	گھر ۾ ڪا ڊاڪٽرياڻي آهي ڇا؟
na, HitE kAI DakTarIAR̃I kAnaHE. No, there's no lady-doctor at all here.	نَ هِتي ڪائي ڊاڪٽرياڻي ڪانھي.
kamarE mẼ kE mAR̃HU AHin. There are some men in the room.	ڪمري ۾ ڪي ماڻھو آهن.

kamarE mẼ kE 'aoratŨ bi AHin. There are some women in the room, too.	کمري ۾ ڪي عورتون به آهن.
chA HI^u kāHĩjO qalam^u AHE? Is this anyone's pen?	ڇا هيءُ ڪنهن جو قَلَمُ آهي؟
kāHĩ chOkirE jA kitAb^a mEz^a tE AHin. Some boy's books are on the table.	ڪنهن ڇوڪري جا ڪتابَ ميز تي آهن.
kin chOkiran jA kitAb^a faraS^a tE AHin. Some boys' books are on the floor.	ڪِن ڇوڪرن جا ڪتابَ فرش تي آهن.
chA kamarE mẼ kO AHE? Is there anyone in the room?	ڇا ڪمري ۾ ڪو آهي؟
na, kamarE mẼ kOI kOnaHE. No, there's no one (at all) in the room.	نه ڪمري ۾ ڪوئي ڪونهي.
ghar^a mẼ kE mĀR̃HU AHin chA? Are there some (any) people in the house?	گهرَ ۾ ڪي ماڻهو آهن ڇا؟
na, ghar^a mẼ kE bi mĀR̃HU na AHin. No, there are no people at all in the house.	نه گهرَ ۾ ڪي به ماڻهو نه آهن.
HI^a kāHĩ bi chOkirE jI TOpI AHE. This is the cap of some boy or other.	هيءَ ڪنهن به ڇوڪري جي ٽوپي آهي.
iskUl^a mẼ kO bi ustAd^u kOnaHE. There's no teacher in the school at all.	اسڪول ۾ ڪو به استادُ ڪونهي.

1. The word kO, like the demonstratives, can be used as either a pronoun or an adjective, as illustrated in the above sentences. It is an indefinite word and gives the meaning, "some", "some one", "any", "anyone", etc.

2. kO inflects like iHO to form the nominative feminine (i.e., kA) and the plural (i.e., kE). But it inflects like kEr^u to form the oblique singular (i.e., kaHĩ) and plural (i.e., kin). To summarize,

	Nominative			Oblique	
Sing.	kO	(m)		kāHĩ	(m & f)
	kA	(f)			
Pl.	kE	(m & f)		kin	(m & f)

kaHin is the original form and may still be heard. kaHĩ is the usual present pronunciation.

3. kO is given emphasis by adding either "I" or "bi". The use of bi with kujh and kO is unique as a particle for emphasis, but the particle, "I" can follow virtually any word in order to give emphasis to that word.

8 – E   Some Postpositions with jE

Transliteration / English	Sindhi
pEnsilⁱ kursI^a jE HEThÃ AHE. The pencil is under the chair.	پينسل ڪرسيءَ جي هيٺان آهي.
kursI^a jE HEThÃ bbilI AHE. There's a cat under the chair.	ڪرسيءَ جي هيٺان ٻلي آهي.
Huna jI TOpI kithE AHE? Where is his hat?	هن جي ٽوپي ڪٿي آهي؟
Huna jI TOpI kabbaT^a jE puThIÃ AHE. His hat is behind the cupboard.	هُن جي ٽوپي ڪٻٽ جي پٺيان آهي.
Hunan pardan jE puThIÃ kujh^u bi na AHE. There's nothing behind those curtains.	هُن پردن جي پٺيان ڪجھ به نه آهي.
nanDhI^a pEtI^a jE andar ch^A AHE? What is in the small box?	ننڍيءَ پيتيءَ جي اندر ڇا آهي؟
nanDhI^a pEtI^a jE andar tavHÃ jŨ kunjIŨ AHin. Your keys are in the small box.	ننڍيءَ پيتيءَ جي اندر توهان جون ڪنجيون آهن.
chOkirO HaT^a jE bbAHirÃ na AHE. The boy isn't outside the shop.	ڇوڪرو هٽ جي ٻاهران نه آهي.
HU HaT^a jE andar AHE. He is inside the shop.	هو هٽ جي اندر آهي.
Huna jO HaT^u TapAl AfIs^i jE sAmHŨ AHE. His shop is opposite the Post office.	هن جو هٽ ٽپال آفيس جي سامهون آهي.
darivAzE jE sAmHŨ kursI AHE. There's a chair in front of the door.	دروازي جي سامهون ڪرسي آهي.
tasvIr^a darI^a jE vEjhO AHE. The picture is near the window.	تصوير دريءَ جي ويجهو آهي.
ispatAl^a mũHĩnjE ghar^a jE vEjhO AHE. The hospital is near my house.	اسپتال منهنجي گهر جي ويجهو آهي.
ustAd^a jO ghar iskUl^a jE bharsÃ AHE. The teacher's house is next to the school.	استاد جو گهر اسڪول جي ڀرسان آهي.
Huna jI kursI darivAzE jE bharsÃ AHE. His chair is next to the door.	هُن جي ڪرسي دروازي جي ڀرسان آهي.
batI mEz^a jE mathÃ AHE. The lamp is over (above) the table.	بتي ميز جي مٿان آهي.

chatⁱ mūHĩnjE mathÃ AHE. The ceiling is above me.	چت منھنجي مٿان آھي.
Hunan jE aggIÃ pardO AHE. There's a curtain in front of them.	ھُنن جي اڳيان پردو آھي.
kE bbAr^a 'aoratun jE aggIÃ AHin. Some children are in front of the women.	ڪي ٻار عورتن جي اڳيان آھن.

1. The above sentences illustrate the use of compound postpositions. These postpositions are preceded by jE, the masculine singular oblique form of jO. This in turn is preceded by a noun or pronoun also in the oblique form. Thus, pardan jE puThIÃ (behind the curtains).

2. aggIÃ and sAmHŨ have approximately the same meaning, "before", "in front of".

3. kujh^u means, "any", "something". kujhⁱ bi na means "nothing", "nothing at all". It can be used as an adjective: thus, kujh^u pAR̃I.

4. To summarize, these nine compound postpositions illustrated above are:

jE HEThÃ	under	جي ھيٺان
jE puThIÃ	behind	جي پٺيان
jE andarⁱ	inside	جي اندر
jE bbAHirÃ	outside	جي ٻاھران
jE sAmHŨ	before, in front of, opposite	جي سامھون
jE vEjhO	near	جي ويجھو
jE bharsÃ	beside, next to, near	جي ڀرسان
jE mathÃ	above, over	جي مٿان
jE aggIÃ	before, in front of	جي اڳيان

8 – F   Vocabulary for Lesson Eight

(jE) andar in, inside	(جي) اندر	ispatAl^a (f) hospital	اسپتال
aKbAr^a (f) newspaper	اخبار	iskUl^u (m) school	اسڪول
(jE) aggIÃ before, in front of	(جي) اڳيان	kO (m) any, some, someone, anyone	ڪو

Lesson 8/ 74

TapAl AfIsⁱ (f) Post office	ٽپال آفيس	khIsO (m) pocket	کيسو
bAzArⁱ (f) bazaar	بازار	ggOTh ᵘ (m) village	ڳوٺ
bAlTI (f) bucket	بالٽي	ghaRIalᵘ (m) clock	گھڙيال
bImArᵘ sick	بيمار	ghaR̃O much, many	گھڻو
bEgamⁱ Lady, Madame	بيگم	(jE) mathÃ above, over	(جي) مٿان
(jE) bharsÃ close to, beside next to	(جي) ڀرسان	(jE) bbAHirÃ outside	(جي) ٻاهران
(jE) puThIÃ behind, in back of	(جي) پٺيان	mẼ in, at	م
Kabarª (f) news	خبر	tE on, at	تي
risAlO (m) magazine	رسالو	HitE (itE) Here	هِتي (اِتي)
rastO (m) road	رستو	HutE (utE) There	هُتي (اُتي)
ruggO only	رڳو	HaTᵘ (m) Shop	هٽ
zanAnO female, ladies	زنانو	maradÃRO male, men's	مرداڻو
SaHarᵘ (m) city	شهر	(jE) HEThÃ under, below	(جي) هيٺان
kithE Where?	ڪٿي	(jE) sAmHŨ before, in front of, opposite	(جي) سامهون
kujhᵘ some, any	ڪجھ	(jE) vEjhO near	جي ويجھو
misTar Mr.	مِسٽر	misaz Mrs.	مِسَز

8 – G   Conversational Review

1. Use the following words for "things" and "places" in asking and answering questions about location, connecting them with mẼ and tE, as appropriate:

THINGS: aKbAr^a, risAlO, kunjI	اخبارَ، رسالو، کُنجي
Kat^u, qalam^u, pEnsilⁱ, kitAb^u	خطُ، قَلَمُ، پينسلِ، کتابُ
kApI, kulf^u, rabbaR^u, tasvIr^a	کاپي، کلفُ، ربڙُ، تصويرَ
kAGaz^u, panO, gilAs^u	کاغذُ، پنو، گلاسُ
PLACES: mEz^a, kursI, faraS^u	ميزَ، کرسي، فرشُ
kabbaT^u, kamarO, bhitⁱ	کَبَٽُ، کمرو، ڀتِ
pEtI, darivAzO, pardO	پيتي، دروازو، پردو

Dozens of sentences can be made on this model. No two sentences should be alike; variety will re-inforce the pattern. For example;

Teacher: tavHÃjO kitab^u kithE AHE?	استاد: توهان جو ڪتابُ ڪٿي آهي؟
Student: mũHĩnjO kitAb^u kabbaT^a mẼ AHE.	شاگرد: منهنجو ڪتاب ڪَبَٽَ ۾ آهي.
Teacher: asÃjI kunjI kithE AHE?	استاد: اسان جي ڪنجي ڪِٿي آهي؟
Student: asÃjI kunjI mEz^a tE AHE.	شاگرد: اسان جي ڪنجي ميز تي آهي.

Note: Wherever possible dramatize these situations by acting them out. Place books, letters, pens, etc. here and there and ask about them. Mix both plural and singular forms whenever possible.

2. Use the same pattern as exercise 1, and add the following adjectives where appropriate:

Adjectives:

vaddO, nanDhO, cağO, dilcasp^u,	وڏو، ننڍو، چڱو، دلچسپُ
suHiR̃O, kArO, achO, pIlO, nIrO	سهڻو، ڪارو، اڇو، پيلو، نيرو
ggARHO	ڳاڙهو

For example:

Teacher: avHÃjI suHiR̃I tasvIr^a kithE AHE?	استاد: اوهان جي سهڻي تصويرَ ڪِٿي آهي؟
Student: mũHinjI suHiR̃I tasvIr^a bhitⁱ tE AHE.	شاگرد: منهنجي سهڻي تصويرَ ڀتِ تي آهي.

3. Using the same objects mentioned in exercise I, ask and answer questions about location using the compound postpositions given in this lesson (see 8-E-4).

Teacher: mũHĩnjI pEnsilⁱ kithE AHE?	استاد: منهنجي پينسل ڪٿي آهي؟
Student: tavHÃjI pEnsilⁱ mEz^a jE HETHÃ AHE.	شاگرد: توهان جي پينسل ميز جي هيٺان آهي.

4. Repeating exercise 3, collect more than one object mentioned so that you can use numbers from two to ten. Place them in proximity to the various locations mentioned, and carry on dialogue like this:

Teacher: HunanjŨ panj^a kApIŨ kithE AHin?	استاد: هُنن جون پنج ڪاپيون ڪٿي آهن؟
Student: Hunan jŨ panj^a kApIŨ mEz^a jE HEThÃ AHin.	شاگرد: هُنن جون پنج ڪاپيون ميز جي هيٺان آهن.

5. Practice using the simple location words, HutE and HitE, using this pattern:

Teacher: tavHÃ jA kitAb^a kithE AHin?	استاد: توهان جا ڪتاب ڪٿي آهن؟
Student: mũHĩnjA kitAb^a HitE AHin.	شاگرد: منهنجا ڪتاب هتي آهن.
Teacher: tasvIrŨ kithE AHin?	استاد: تصويرون ڪٿي آهن؟
Student: tasvirŨ HutE AHin.	شاگرد: تصويرون هتي آهن.

6. Using the vocabulary you have learned in lessons thus far describe your house to your teacher. For example, begin by saying something like this:

mũHĩnjO ghar^u vaddE SaHar mẼ AHE.	منهنجو گهر وڏي شهر ۾ آهي.
HU DighE rastE ṭE AHE.	هو ڊگهي رستي تي آهي.
mũHĩnjO ghar^u nanDhO AHE; vaddO na AHE.	منهنجو گهر ننڍو آهي؛ وڏو نہ آهي.
Huna mẼ ruggO TE kamarA AHin.	هُن ۾ رِڳو تي ڪمرا آهن.

Etc.

Continue your description by telling how many rooms are big and how many are small. Include such things as the color of the house, its proximity to public buildings such as a school or post office, what things are in each room, etc.

7. Now describe and talk about the town you and your teacher are living in, using your limited vocabulary. Talk about the location of the school, post office, hospital, certain people's homes, etc. Talk about the color and size of those places, and their location in relation to each other.

REVIEW ONE

1. Practice the pronunciation drills again for Lessons Four to Eight.

2. All grammatical structures have been presented in "pattern sentences". The vocabulary has been presented in these patterns. The student should have "learned" these patterns and the vocabulary by the constant repetition of hearing and using them. In this review use the following vocabulary list to practice the patterns learned in Lessons Four to Eight, varying the choice of words, persons (I, you, he, etc.) and number (singular and plural) as much as possible to provide variety and repetition. (Conversational reviews at the end of each lesson give examples of the kind of practice that is called for.)

   The teacher or the student should point to or use real objects when these are available. Do not hesitate to walk around the room or place things here and there—in other words, "to act" – so as to produce real-life situations.

   Even though concentrating on structure, do not overlook poor pronunciation. Continue to remind the teacher to correct you in this area.

   Avoid translating into English. It is better from the beginning to develop the habit of <u>thinking in Sindhi</u> by keeping the simplest conversation or question/answer exchanges in the language you are learning.

3. Numbers in ( ) after the words given below refer to the lesson in which the word was first used and defined.

4. In actual practice the best plan may be to chose a particular structure that is to be practiced and write it down on a piece of paper that you can keep before you. As you go along, underline the words you want to substitute. For example, suppose you come to the structure given in 8-G-4, Hunan jŨ panj^a kApIŨ kithE AHin?

   (a) Begin your practice by underlining "Hunan jŨ". Substitute this with other <u>pronouns</u> and <u>people</u>.
   (b) Then underline "panja" and substitute other numbers up to ten. Also substitute <u>adjectives</u> (e.g. kArO, nanDhO, vaddO, etc.)
   (c) Underline "kapIŨ". Substitute this with other <u>things</u>.
   (d) Finally, underline "kithE". Here you can substitute with both <u>postpositions</u> and <u>places</u>. Also you can answer with "HAO" and "na" by changing the question to: Hunan jŨ panja kApIŨ kabbaT^a mẼ AHin chA?

When one pattern has been practiced sufficiently it should be replaced with another pattern. Ask your teacher to help you in this kind of practice by writing out a pattern in the Sindhi script which s/he can use to direct your drilling.

Review One

Questions		Postpositions		Persons (cont)		
chA (4)	چا	mẼ (8)	مٖ	mAlHI, mAlI (6)	m	مالهي, مالي
kEr^u (4)	ڪير	tE (8)	تي	mazUr^u (6)	m	مزور
kaHiRO (7)	ڪهڙو	jE HEThĀ (8)	جي هيٺان	mazdUr^u (6)	m	مزدور
kithE (8)	ڪٿي	jE puThIĀ (8)	جي پٺيان	maolvI (6)	m	مولوي
Answers		jE andar (8)	جي اندر	bbar^u (7)	m	ٻار
HAO, HA (4)	هائو, ها	jE bbAHirĀ (8)	جي ٻاهران	naokar^u (6)	m	نوڪر
na (4)	نہ	jE sAmHŨ (8)	جي سامهون	naokarIaR̃I (6)	f	نوڪرياڻي
Pronouns		jE vEjhO (8)	جي ويجهو	**Titles**		
HU/HU^a (4/5)	هُو/ هُوءَ	jE bharsĀ (8)	جي پرسان	sAĨ (6)	m	سائين
HI^u/HI^a (4/5)	هِيُ/هِيءَ	jE mathĀ (8)	جي مٿان	misTar (8)	m	مسٽر
iHO/iHA (4/5)	اِهو/ اِها	jE aggIĀ (8)	جي اڳيان	misaz (8)	f	مسز
uHO/uHA (4/5)	اُهو/اُها	**Persons**		sAHib^u (6)	m	صاحب
iHE (4/5)	اِهي	SAgird^u (4)	m شاگرد	bEgum (8)	f	بيگم
uHE (4/5)	اُهي	mAR̃HU (4)	m ماڻهو	**Places**		
AŨ/mĀ (6)	آءٌ / مان	ustAd^u (4)	m استاد	faraS^u (4)	m	فرش
tŨ (6)	تون	'aorat^a (5)	f عورت	tambU (4)	m	تنبو
asĨ (6)	اسين	zAl (5)	f زال	kabbaT^u (4)	m	ڪٻٽ
tavHĨ (6)	توهين	chOkirO (5)	m چوڪرو	kamarO (4)	m	ڪمرو
avHĨ (6)	اوهين	chOkirI (5)	f چوڪري	bhit^i (5)	f	ڀت
kO (8)	ڪو	bOrcI (6)	m بورچي	chat^i (5)	f	ڇت
Adverbs		TapAlI (6)	m ٽپالي	ghar^u (7)	m	گهر
bi, b^u (6)	بہ	pAdrI (6)	m پادري	ispatAl^a (8)	f	اسپتال
tamAm^u (7)	تمام	dhobI (6)	m ڌوٻي	bAzAr^i (8)	f	بازار
ruggO (8)	ڳرو	DakTar^u (6)	m ڊاڪٽر	TapAl Afis (8)	f	ٽپال آفيس

Places (cont'd)				Other Nouns (cont'd)				Other Nouns (cont'd)			
SaHar^u	(8)	m	شهر	batI	(5)	f	بتي	aKbAr^a	(8)	f	اخبار
rastO	(8)	m	رستو	bbilI	(5)	f	ٻلي	bAlTI	(8)	f	ٻالٽي
khIsO	(8)	m	کيسو	tasvIr^a	(5)	f	تصوير	Kabar^a	(8)	f	خبر
ggOTh^u	(8)	m	ڳوٺ	pARI	(5)	m	پاڙي	risalO	(8)	m	رسالو
HitE	(8)		هِتي	pEnsil^i	(5)	f	پينسل	khIsO	(8)	m	کيسو
HutE	(8)		هُتي	jAnvar^u	(5)	m	جانور	ghaRIAl^u	(8)	m	گهڙيال
Hat^u	(8)	m	هٽ	KatA	(5)	f	خطا	**Numbers**			
iskUl^u	(8)	m	اسکول	davA	(5)	f	دوا	Hik^u, HikaRO			هڪ/هڪڙو
Other Nouns				rabbaR^u	(5)	m	رٻڙ	bba	(4)		ٻه
pardO	(4)	m	پردو	farAsI	(5)	f	فراسي	TE	(4)		ٽي
panO	(4)	m	پنو	kApI	(5)	f	ڪاپي	cAr^i	(4)		چار
Kat^u	(4)	m	خط	kursI	(5)	f	ڪرسي	panj^a	(4)		پنج
darivAzO	(4)	m	دروازو	kulf^u	(5)	m	ڪلف	chaH^a	(6)		ڇھ
SISO	(4)	m	شيشو	kukuR^u	(5)	m	ڪڪڙ	sat^a	(6)		ست
qalam^u	(4)	m	قلم	kunjI	(5)	f	ڪنجي	aTh^a	(6)		اٺ
kAGaz^u	(4)	m	ڪاغذ	ghORO	(5)	m	گھوڙو	nava	(6)		نو
kitAb^u	(4)	m	ڪتاب	mas^u	(5)	f	مس	ddaHa	(6)		ڏھ
kutO	(4)	m	ڪتو	mEz^a	(5)	f	ميز	**Adjectives**			
kapRA	(4)	m	ڪپڙا	TOpI	(6)	f	ٽوپي	pILO	(6)		پيلو
kapRO	(4)	m	ڪپڙو	pEtI	(6)	f	پيٽي	cag̃O	(6)		چڱو
gul^u	(4)	m	گل	rãng^u	(7)	m	رنگ	KAlI	(6)		خالي
gilAs^u	(4)	m	گلاس	darI	(7)	f	دري	suHiR̃O	(6)		سھڻو
mEvO	(4)	m	ميوو	kam^u	(7)	m	ڪم	mazbUt^u	(6)		مضبوط
uTh^u	(5)	m	اٺ	nAlO	(7)	m	نالو	nanDhO	(6)		ننڍو

Adjectives (cont)						Conjunctions		
nIrO	(6)	نيرو	miHinatI	(7)	محنتي	aĩ	(7)	۽
vaddO	(6)	وڏو	HOSIAr	(7)	هوشيار	par^a	(7)	پر
achO	(7)	اچو	thulHO	(7)	ٿلهو			
dilcasp^u	(7)	دلچسپ	bImAr^u	(8)	بيمار			
DighO	(7)	ڊگهو	zanAnO	(8)	زنانو			
sust^u	(7)	سست	kujh^u	(8)	ڪجھ			
sanHO	(7)	سنهو	ghaR̃O	(8)	گهٽو			
kArO	(7)	ڪارو	maradAR̃O	(8)	مرداٽو			
ggARHO	(7)	ڳاڙهو						

LESSON NINE

9 – A Pronunciation Drill

1. Contrasting /D/ and /Dh/

ڊ ۽ ڍ

HI DhOr^u DighO AHE. (This animal is tall.)	هي ڍور ڊگهو آهي.
DhOlak aī Dhak^u kunD^a mẼ AHin. (The drum and the cover are in the corner.)	ڍولڪ ۽ ڍڪ ڪنڊ ۾ آهن.
DhanDh^a nanDhI par^a samunD^u nanDhO na AHE. (A pond is small, but a sea is not.)	ڍنڍ ننڍي پر سمنڊ ننڍو نہ آهي.

2. Contrasting /p/ and /b/   (11/16)

پ ۽ ب

puT^a bIAn kayO ta pI^u bImAr AHE. (The son explained that father is sick.)	پٽ بيان ڪيو تہ پيءُ بيمار آهي.
pI^u bAr^u jabal^a jE pAr^i khaR̃I vayO. (Father carried the load across the mountain.)	پيءُ بارُ جبل جي پار کڙي ويو.
bAH^i jE sababÃ kapaH^a baribAd thI vaI. (On account of the fire the cotton was destroyed.)	باھ جي سبباً ڪپھ برباد ٿي وئي.

9 - B   The cardinal numbers "eleven" to "sixteen"

eleven:	yAraHã	written in Sindhi as	۱۱	يارهن
twelve:	bbAraHã	" " " "	۱۲	ٻارهن
thirteen:	tEraHã	" " " "	۱۳	تيرهن
fourteen:	cOddaHã	" " " "	۱۴	چوڏهن
fifteen:	pandaraHã	" " " "	۱۵	پندرهن
sixteen:	sOraHã	" " " "	۱۶	سورهن

9 - C   Other uses of the question word, kaHiRO (Which?)

Sindhi (transliteration)	Sindhi (script)
Hunan jO gharu kaHiRE qisima jO AHE? What sort of a house do they have?	هنن جو گهر ڪهڙي قسم جو آهي؟
uHU kacO gharu AHE. It's a house of unbaked bricks.	اُهو ڪچو گهرُ آهي.
tavHÃ jO gharu kaHiRE qisima jO AHE? What sort of a house do you have?	توهان جو گهر ڪهڙي قسم جو آهي؟
mũHinjO gharu pakO AHE. My house is of baked brick.	منهنجو گهر پڪو آهي.
HI kaHiRE qisima jO rastO AHE? What kind of a road is this?	هي ڪهڙي قسم جو رستو آهي؟
HI rastO pakO AHE. It's a paved road.	هي رستو پڪو آهي.
tavHÃ jA pardA kaHiRE rāga jA AHin? What color are your curtains?	توهان جا پردا ڪهڙي رنگ جا آهن؟
iHE nIrE rāga jA AHin. They are blue. (lit; of blue color)	هو نيري رنگ جا آهن.
Hina 'aorata jO kaHiRO mizA ju AHE? What's the disposition of this woman?	هن عورت جو ڪهڙو مزاج آهي؟
HUa KuS mizAja 'aorat AHE. She has a happy disposition.	هوءَ خوش مزاج عورت آهي.
HI kaHiRE qisima jA kitAb AHin? What kind of books are these?	هي ڪهڙي قسم جا ڪتاب آهن؟
uHE sindhI kitAb AHin. They are Sindhi books.	اهي سنڌي ڪتاب آهن.
Huna jO bhAu KaHiRE qisima jO mARHU AHE? What sort of man is her brother?	هن جو ڀاءُ ڪهڙي قسم جو ماڻهو آهي؟
HU tamAm suThO mARHU AHE. He's a very fine man.	هو تمام سٺو ماڻهو آهي.

1. In the above sentences kaHiRO is followed by a noun in order to express such questions as, "What kind of?", "What color?", "What disposition?", etc.

2. Notice that one may vary the order of the words in such a sentence. For example, one may say, HI kaHiRE qisima jO gharu AHE or, HI gharu kaHiRE qisima jO AHE. However, the particle, jO, when it follows nouns like qisimu, rāgu, mizAju must agree with the noun it is referring to. For example, HI 'aoratŨ kaHiRE mizAja jŨ AHin? Although mizAja jŨ is placed <u>after</u> the noun it

refers to, it <u>must</u> agree with that noun, 'aoratŨ, just as if it preceded it (i.e., HI kaHiRE qisim^a jŨ 'aoratŨ AHin?).

3. kacO and pakO are two very common and useful adjectives which convey a wide range of meaning. Some of these meanings are listed in the vocabulary section.

4. suThO is an adjective with approximately the same meaning as cag̃O. However, they are not entirely interchangeable. The student will learn from usage that in certain sentences suThO may be preferred and in others cag̃O will be used.

9 - D   Greetings and courtesies

asalAm 'alEkum, sAĨ. Hello, sir! (also good-bye)	السلام عليكم، سائين.
va'alEkum asalAm. Hello. (also good-bye)	وعليكم السلام.
avHÃ jO kaHiRO HAl^u AHE? How are you?	اوهان جو کهڙو حال آهي؟
or, avHĨ KuS AHIO na? How are you?	يا اوهين خوش آهيو نه؟
maHarbAnI, mÃ KuS AHIÃ. Thank you, I'm fine.	مهرباني مان خوش آهيان.
tavHÃ jA bbAr^a bbacA kIã AHin? How is your family?	توهان جا ٻار ٻچا ڪيئن آهن؟
KudA jO Sukur AHE, bbAr^a bbacA bi cag̃ A bhalA AHin. Thank God, the family is well, too.	خدا جو شڪر آهي، ٻار ٻچا به چڱا ڀلا آهن.
sabh^u KairIat AHE. Everything (all) is alright.	سڀ خيريت آهي.
tavHÃ jI maHarbAnI. Thank you.	توهان جي مهرباني.
tavHÃ jI vaddI maHarbAnI. Thank you very much.	توهان جي وڏي مهرباني.
KudA Hafiz. Good-bye.	خدا حافظ.

1. The above are some of the basic patterns of greeting people. You will observe variations of these.

2. asalAm 'alEkum and va'alEkum salAm are Arabic constructions used throughout the Muslim world.

3. Both bbAr^u and bbacO mean child, infant. Used together – bbAr^a bbacA—means children, and by extension, family.

4. kIã is a question word meaning "How?" It can be used in other contexts. For example,

tavHÃ jA SAgird^a kIã AHin? How are your students?	توهان جا شاگرد ڪيئن آهن؟
HU tamAm HOSIAr AHin. They're very clever.	هو تمام هوشيار آهن.
iHO risAlO kIã AHE? How's that magazine?	اهو رسالو ڪيئن آهي؟
iHO dilcasp AHE. It's interesting.	اهو دلچسپ آهي.

5. ca͠gO bhalO is another term (like bbAr^a bbacA) which uses two words meaning the same. Both words mean fine, well, etc.

6. KairIat also means fine, well. Often Kair which means the same will be used.

7. KudA jO Sukur means thanks to God, and tavHÃ jI maHarbAnI is used to say thank you to a person. It means literally, your kindness. When speaking directly to someone, the pronoun tavHÃ jI may be omitted.

9 - E The question word kEtrO, how many?, and gha͠RO, how much?

mEz^a tE kEtrIŨ akbArŨ AHin? How many newspapers are on the table?	ميز تي ڪيتريون اخبارون آهن؟
kabbaT^a m͠E kEtrA kitAb^a AHin? How many books are there in the cupboard?	ڪٻٽ ۾ ڪيترا ڪتاب آهن؟
HikaRO bi na. HU bilkul KAlI AHE. Not even one. It's completely empty.	هڪڙو به نه. هو بلڪل خالي آهي.
tavHÃ jA ketrA chOkarA aĨ chOkarIŨ AHin? How many boys and girls have you?	توهان جا ڪيترا چوڪرا ۽ چوڪريون آهن؟
tavHÃ jE darjE m͠E kEtrA SAgird^a AHin? How many students are there in your class?	توهان جي درجي ۾ ڪيترا شاگرد آهن؟
kam^u gha͠RO AHE? How much work is there?	ڪم گهڻو آهي؟
bAlTI^a m͠E pA͠RI gha͠RO AHE? How much water is in the bucket?	بالٽيءَ ۾ پاڻي گهڻو آهي؟

kujh bi kOnaHE. HU bilkul KAlI AHE. None at all. It's completely empty.	كجھ بہ ڪونھي. ھو بلڪل خالي آھي.
tavHÃ kEtrA bhAurᵃ AHIO? How many brothers are you? (= How many brothers do you have?)	توھين ڪيترا ڀائر آھيو؟
asĨ bba bhAurᵃ AHIŨ. We are two brothers. (=I have two brothers.)	اسين ٻہ ڀائر آھيون.
tavHÃ jŨ kEtrIŨ bhEnarŨ AHin? How many sisters do you have?	توھان جون ڪيتريون ڀينرون آھن؟
mũHinjI ruggO HikaRI bhER̃ᵘ AHE. I have only one sister.	منھنجي رڳو ھڪڙي ڀيڻ آھي.
tavHĨ kEtrIŨ bhEnarŨ aĨ bhAurᵃ AHIO? How many brothers and sisters are you?	توھين ڪيتريون ڀينرون ۽ ڀائر آھيو؟
asĨ TE bhEnarŨ aĨ bba bhAurᵃ AHIŨ. We are three sisters and two brothers.	اسين ٽي ڀينرون ۽ ٻہ ڀائر آھيون.
tavHÃ jŨ kEtrIŨ dhIarŨ AHin? How many daughters have you?	توھان جون ڪيتريون ڌيئرون آھن؟
mũHinjI faqat HikaRI dhIᵃ AHE. I have only one daughter.	منھنجي فقط ھڪڙي ڌيءَ آھي.
gharᵃ mẼ ghaR̃A-I mAR̃HU AHin. There are many people in the house.	گھر ۾ گھڻا ئي ماڻھو آھن.
Hina darjE mẼ ghaR̃A chOkirA na AHin. There aren't many boys in this class.	ھن درجي ۾ گھڻا ڇوڪرا نہ آھن.
kEtrA AHin? ruggO yAraHÃ. How many are there? Only eleven.	ڪيترا آھن؟ رڳو يارھن.
gilAsᵃ mẼ khIrᵘ ghaR̃O AHE? How much milk is in the glass?	گلاس ۾ کير گھڻو آھي؟
thOrO khIrᵘ AHE. ghaR̃O na AHE. There's a little milk. It's not much.	ٿورو کير آھي. گھڻو نہ آھي.
thElHIᵃ mẼ ghaR̃I khanDᵘ AHE? How much sugar in the bag?	ٿيلھي ۾ گھڻي کنڊ آھي؟

1. Generally kEtrO means "How many?" and ghaR̃O means "How much?" However, you will hear people use kEtrO and ghaR̃O for both.

2. Remember that ghaR̃O also means "much" or lots" in contrast to thOrO meaning "little".

3. kujh means "some", and kujh bi na means "none at all". This is another example of the use of the emphatic particle, bi.

4. When asking the number of brothers you have, the question is put, "How many brothers are you?", and the answer is in the form, "we are ____ brothers". The speaker, a man or a boy, includes himself as one of the brothers. The same goes, of course, for the number of sisters if the speaker is one of the sisters being inquired about.

5. faqat^i means "only, merely". It has approximately the same meaning as ruggO.

9 - F The use of the postpositions vaT^i and khE with the verb HuaR̃^{u}?

ma^u vaT^i bba rupIA AHIn. Mother has two rupees.	ماءُ وٽ ٻہ رپيا آهن.
Huna vaT^i mūHinjO kitAb^u AHE. She has my book.	هن وٽ منهنجو ڪتاب آهي.
mŨ khE mathE mẼ sUr^u AHE. I have a headache.	مون کي مٿي ۾ سور آهي.
mŨ khE dhI^a kAnaHE. I don't have a daughter.	مون کي ڌيءَ ڪانهي.
asÃ khE bba puT^a AHin. We have two sons.	اسان کي ٻہ پُٽ آهن.
chA tO vaT^i mūHinjI kApI AHE? Do you have my notebook?	ڇا تو وٽ منهنجي ڪاپي آهي؟
na, HU ustAd^a vaT^i AHE. No, the teacher has it.	نہ هو استاد وٽ آهي.
zamIndAr^a khE ghaR̃I zamIn AHE. The landlord has a lot of land.	زميندار کي گھڻي زمين آهي.
mūHinjE pI^u khE vaddO ghar^u AHE. My father has a large house.	منهنجي پيءُ کي وڏو گھر آهي.
Hina kamarE khE cAr^a darivAzA AHin. This room has four doors.	هِن ڪمري کي چار دروازا آهن.
Hunan khE umId^a kAnaHE. They have no hope.	هُنن کي اميد ڪانهي.
Huna chOkirE khE faqat^i HikaRO Hath^u AHE. That boy has only one hand.	هن ڇوڪري کي فقط هڪڙو هٿ آهي.
mU khE afsOs AHE. I'm sorry.	مون کي افسوس آهي.

1. The English verb, "to have", has no simple equivalent in Sindhi. The idea is expressed by the postposition vaT^i or khE after the noun or pronoun (inflected into the oblique form) which denotes the owner. This phrase is followed by the appropriate form of the verb HuaR̃^{u}, "to be", which agrees with the object possessed in both gender and number. (It has already been noted that in the simple present tense the masculine and feminine forms are the same.) When you say, mŨ vaT^i HikaRO kitAb^u AHE (I have one book) you are saying literally "To me one book is". When you say, mŨ vaT^i chaH^a kitAb^a AHin (I have six books) you are saying literally, "To me six books are". The basic meaning of both vat^i and khE is "to".

2. Ownership or possession of articles which are movable or separate from the possessor is expressed by the postposition vaT^i. For example,

mŨ vaT^i bba rupIA AHin. I have two rupees.	مون وٽ ٻہ رپيا آهن.
Huna vaT^i mūHinjO kitAb^u AHE. He/she has my book.	هن وٽ منهنجو ڪتاب آهي.

3. The postposition khE is used following the possessor:

    a) When speaking about kinship and relatives. For example,

Huna khE bba puT^a AHin. He has two sons.	هن کي ٻہ پٽ آهن.
mŨ khE dhI^a na AHE. I have no daughter.	مون کي ڌيءَ نہ آهي.

    b) In referring to land and property. For example,

tavHÃ khE ghaR̃I zamIn^a AHE? How much land have you?	توهان کي گهٽي زمين آهي؟
mŨ khE bba ghar^a AHin. I own two houses.	مون کي ٻہ گهر آهن.

    c) In referring to parts of the body or conditions that cannot be separated from the possessor. For example,

Huna khE ruggO HikaRO Hath^u AHE. He has only one hand.	هن کي رڳو هڪڙو هٿ آهي.
Hina ghar^a khE panj^a darivAzA AHin. This house has five doors.	هن گهر کي پنج دروازا آهن.
mŨ khE tap^u AHE. I have a fever.	مون کي تپ آهي.

d) When the object is an abstract noun. For example,

Huna khE vaqt^u na AHE. He has no time.	هن کي وقت نہ آهي.

4. The personal pronouns before vaTⁱ and khE are inflected into an oblique form which is different from that used with jO only in the first and second persons singular. Thus,

HI mūHinjO kitAb^u AHE. This is my book.	هي منهنجو ڪتاب آهي.
mŨ khE kitAb^u AHE. I have a book.	مون کي ڪتاب آهي.
HI tūHinjO kitAb^u AHE. It's your book.	هي تنهنجو ڪتاب آهي.
tO vaTⁱ kitAb^u AHE. You have a book.	تو وٽ ڪتاب آهي.

Thus, the oblique forms of personal pronouns with postpositions such as vaTⁱ and khE are:

mŨ khE AHE (I have)	مون کي آهي	asÃ khE (we have)	اسان کي
tO khE AHE (you have)	تو کي آهي	tavHÃ khE (you have)	توهان کي
Huna khE AHE (he/she has)	هن کي آهي	Hunan khE (they have)	هنن کي

5. The nouns of kinship listed below are irregular in the way they form the nominative plural and oblique forms.

	Nom. Sg.		**Obl. Sg.**		**N. Pl.**		**Obl. Pl.**	
father	pI^u	پيءُ	pI^u	پيءُ	pIur^a	پيئر	pIuranⁱ	پيئرن
mother	ma^u	ماءُ	ma^u	ماءُ	mAir^a, maŨ	مائر، مائون	mAunⁱ	مائن
brother	bhA^u	ڀاءُ	bhA^u	ڀاءُ	bhAuranⁱ	ڀائرن	bhAuranⁱ	ڀائرن
sister	bhER̃^a	ڀيڻ	bhER̃^a	ڀيڻ	bhEnarŨ	ڀينرون	bhEnarunⁱ	ڀينرن
daughter	dhI^a	ڌيءَ	dhI^a	ڌيءَ	dhIarŨ, dhIŨ ڌيئرون، ڌيئون		dhIarunⁱ	ڌيئرن
son	puT^u	پُٽ	puT^a	پُٽ	puT^a	پُٽ	puTanⁱ	پُٽن

9-G Vocabulary for Lesson Nine

asalAm 'alEkum Greetings, good-bye	السلام عليكم	va'alEkum asalAm Return greetings, or "good-bye"	وعليكم السلام
afsOs (m) sorrow, grief regret, Woe! Alas!	افسوس	umId^a (f) hope	اميد
bilkul very, quite alongther	بلكل	bbAra bbacA (m. pl) children, family	بار بچا
bbacO (m) child	بچو	bbAraHã twelve	بارهن
bhA^u (m) brother	ڀاءُ	bhER̃^{a} (f) sister	ڀيڻ
tap^u fever	تپ	tEraHã thirteen	تيرهن
thOrO little, few, small amount	تورو	thElHI (f) bag	ٹيلهي
pakO strong, well=built of stone, baked brick, cooked, fast (color), ripe	پكو	pandaraHã fifteen	پندرهن
pI^u (m) father	پيءُ	cag̃O bhalO fine, well	چڱو ڀلو
cOddaHã fourteen	چوڏهن	HAl^u condition	حال
KudA God	خدا	KuS^i happy, pleased	خوش
Kair^u, KairIat fine, well	خير خيريت	darjO (m) class, grade, standard	درجو
dhI^a (f) daughter	ڌيءَ	rupIO, rupayA rupee, rupees	رپيو، رپيا
zamIn^a (f) land	زمين	zamIndAr^u (m) landlord	زميندار
sabh^u all, the whole entire	سڀ	suThO good, fine, nice	سٹو

sUr^u (m) pain	سورُ	sOraHã sixteen	سورهن
Sukur^u (m) thanks	شڪر	faqatⁱ only, merely	فقط
qisim^u (m) kind	قسم	kacO weak, not well-built of unbaked brick, raw, unripe, not fast (color)	ڪچو
kEtrO How many?	ڪيترو	kĨa How?	ڪيئن
khanD^u (f) sugar	کنڊ	khE to	ڪي
khIr^u (m) milk	کير	mA^u (f) mother	ماءُ
mathO (m) head	مٿو	muRas^u (m) husband	مڙس
mizAj^u (m) disposition	مزاج	maHarbAnI (f) thanks, kindness, favor	مهرباني
vaTⁱ to	وٽ	vaqt^u (m) time	وقت
Hath^u (m) hand	هٿ	yAraHã eleven	يارهن
ghaR̃O how much?	گھڻو		

9 - H   Conversational Review

1. Ask questions using kaHirE qisim^a jO and kaHiRE rãg^a jO using various objects around you. You can extend this exercise by using magazine pictures or children's picture books. For example,

Teacher: HI kaHiRE rãg^a jI pEnsilⁱ AHE?	استاد: هي ڪهڙي رنگ جي پينسل آهي؟
Student: HU pIlE rãg^a jI pEnsilⁱ AHE.	شاگرد: هو پيلي رنگ جي پينسل آهي.

    Get from your teacher the words used for other colors besides those learned thus far in these lessons.

2. Repeat exercise 1, with the student asking the questions and the teacher answering.

3. Use the words given in the vocabulary to inquire about the condition of various relatives. (In the inquiry either kIã or kaHiRO HAI[u] may be used. Both should be practiced.) For example,

Teacher: tavHÃ jO bbacO kIã AHE?	استاد: توهان جو ٻچو ڪيئن آهي؟
Student: mūHinjO bbacO cag̃O bhalO AHE, maHarbAnI.	شاگرد: منهنجو ٻچو چڱو ڀلو آهي، مهرباني.

During this exercise, the student should learn from the teacher the relatives one does <u>not</u> ask about, as man inquiring about the health of female relatives, and a woman asking about male relatives.

Reverse the exercise with the student asking the questions.

4. Have your teacher ask kEtrO (How many?) or ghaR̃O (How much?) of the following you have.

puT[a], naokar[a], bbAur[a], bhEnarŨ   پٽ، نوڪر، ڀائر، ڀيڻرون

kutA, naokar[a], kitAb[a], kamarA   ڪتا، نوڪر، ڪتاب، ڪمرا

kunjIŨ, pAR̃I, khanD[u], kApIŨ   ڪنجيون، پاٽي، ڪنڊ، ڪاپيون

risAlA, Kat[a], ghORA, zamIn[a]   رسالا، خط، گهوڙا، زمين

pEnsilIŨ, bbAr[a], ghar[a], khIr[u]   پينسلون، ٻار، گهر، کير

Give true answers, using numbers up to sixteen or negative answers with na AHE. For example,

Teacher: tavHĨ kEtrA bhAur[a] AHIO?	استاد: توهين ڪيترا ڀائر آهيو؟
Student: asĨ TE bhAur[a] AHIŨ.	شاگرد: اسين ٽي ڀائر آهيون.
Teacher: tavHÃ vaT[i] kEtrIŨ kunjIŨ AHin?	استاد: توهان وٽ ڪيتريون ڪنجيون آهن؟
Student: mŨ vaT[i] ruggO HikaRI kunjI AHE.	شاگرد: مون وٽ رڳو هڪڙي ڪنجي آهي.
Teacher: tavHÃ khE gha R̃I zamIn[a] AHE?	استاد: توهان ڪي گهڻي زمين آهي؟
Student: mŨ khE zamIn[a] kAnaHE.	شاگرد: مون ڪي زمين ڪانهي.

5. Repeat exercise 4. with the student asking the questions and the teacher answering.

9 - I   Introduction to the Sindhi Writing System (Part I)

The Sindhi writing system, like the Persian, is based on that of Arabic. It makes use of the Persian innovations, and thus is called a Persian Arabic Script. Sindhi also adds its own modifications in order to symbolize the many sounds not found in Arabic or Persian. For example, in the Sindhi alphabet, the original Arabic /t/, written ت, is extended to include /th/, /T/ and /Th/, written as ٿ, ٽ, and ٺ, respectively, -- all sounds not found in Arabic. You will notice that this was done by taking the basic shape of the letter ت and adding or rearranging dots. In this way Sindhi has extended the 28 Arabic characters to 51[*] so that the sounds unique to Sindhi may be symbolized.

These 51 letters, written from right to left, are divisible into sixteen basic "shape groups." Various letters may have the same basic shape, but are differentiated from each other within the group by the use of dots above, within or below the basic shape of the letter. Thus, /H/, /J/, /c/, /ch/, /Ñ/, /jj/, and /K/ share the same basic shape. They are respectively:

ح   ج   چ   ڇ   ڃ   جھ   خ

The basic shape of a letter may vary according to its position in the word, and also according to its connecting or not connecting to adjacent letters. A connector letter may have as many as four different forms:

(1)   C-   Initial: Used at the beginning of a word or after a non-connector.

(2)   -C-   Medial: used between two connectors and joined to both.

(3)   -C   Final: used after a connector at the end of a word.

(4)   C   Independent: unconnected on either side.

A non-connector may have only two forms:

(1)   N   **Initial independent:** used at the beginning of a word, after another non-connector at the end of a word, or between two non-connectors within a word

(2)   -N   **Medial-Final:** used after a connector either within or at the end of a word.

The 51 letters of the Sindhi alphabet do not included any symbols for the short vowels, which are represented by diacritical marks above or below the letter representing the consonant sound. In common usage, these diacritical marks are not printed or written at all unless needed to clarify some possible ambiguity.

Because of the rich heredity of Sindhi in its Sanskrit origins, and the later additions of many Arabic and Persian words, the alphabet contains some sounds which are represented by more than one letter. The letter used is determined by the origin of the words. This makes spelling more difficult although on the whole Sindhi is very phonetic in its spelling. The following are the sounds which may be represented by more than one letter:

/t/   ت , the common letter, and   ط , in words of Arabic origin.

/s/   س , common, and   ص، ث , in words of Arabic origin.

---

[*] This number excludes /hamzo/ which is not really a letter of the Sindhi alphabet, but a special symbol used to separate two vowel sounds that come together within a word. (See Lesson 11, The Sindhi Writing System Part III.)

/z/ ذ and ز, common; ظ and ض, in words of Arabic origin.

/H/ ھ, common; ح, found in words of Arabic origin.

English words which have been taken into Sindhi will always be spelled with the more common symbol.

Three other letters are found only in words of Arabic origin. These are:

/q/ ق /'/ ع and /G/ غ.

In the remainder of this section five letter groups will be introduced. The other letter groups, diacritical marks, and numerals will be introduced in lessons 10 and 11.

Letter Group 1

This group contains only ا /A/. It is a non-connector. When found at the beginning of word, the diacritic "madd" will be written over ا. For example, آنا. It is not usually found over ا in the medial or final position.

An important function of ا is as a "carrier" of other vowels when a word begins with a vowel. The diacritical marks representing the short vowels must always be carried by ا when at the beginning of a word. In other positions in the word they are carried by the relevant consonant symbol. The short vowels are represented as follows:

/a/ ◌َ as in اَچو achO = زَبَر zabar

/ı/ ◌ِ as in اِھو iHO = زِیرَ zEr

/u/ ◌ُ as in اُھو uHO = پِیشُ pES

When found in the middle of a word, the vowel sign or diacritic will be written either directly above or below the consonant, or above or below the previous consonant.

For example, Hath[a] bhit[i] uTh[u]

هَٺَ پِتِ اُٺُ

Letter Group 2

This group contains ب/b/, ٻ/bb/, ڀ/bh/, ت /t/, ٿ/th/, ٽ /T/, ٺ /Th/, ث /s/, پ /p/, and partially ن /n/, ڙ /R̃/ and ي /y/.

Letters of this shape group are connectors and have the following basic forms:

	Initial	Midial	Final	Independent
	بـ	ـبـ	ـب	ب

Letters of this group are thus:

	/b/	/bb/	/bh/	/t/	/th/	/T/	/Th/	/s/	/p/
Initial	بـ	بـ	ڀـ	تـ	تــ	ٿـ	ٿـ	ثـ	پـ
Medial	ـبـ	ـبـ	ـڀـ	ـتـ	ـتــ	ـٿـ	ـٿـ	ـثـ	ـپـ
Final	ـب	ـب	ـڀ	ـت	ـت	ـٿ	ـٿ	ـث	ـپ
Independent	ب	ب	ڀ	ت	ت	ٿ	ٿ	ث	پ

The letter ث is an "uncommon Arabic consonant," that is, it is not frequently used in Sindhi.

The letters ن /n/ and ڻ /R̃/ differ somewhat from those above:

Illustrations:

Initial	نـ	ڻـ	pAR̃I	پاڻي	nanDhO	نئنڊو
Midial	ـنـ	ـڻـ	HaR̃O	هڻو	panO	پَنو
Final	ـن	ـڻ	bhER̃u	ڀيڻُ	panu	پَنُ
Independent	ن	ڻ	paR̃a	پاڻ	jAni	جانِ

Notice that the final and independent forms of ن and ڻ are more rounded than the others in group 2. Also, they drop below the main lines of writing, while those presented above are even or level with the main line of writing.

The letter ي also has special forms:

Illustrations:

Initial	يـ	yAdi	ياد
Midial	ـيـ	pETI	پيٽي
Final	ـي	TE	ٽي
Independent	ي	ddE	ڏي

Initial ي stands only for the consonant sound /y/. /I/, /E/, or /ai/ is symbolized by ي plus ا.

For example, aiT^u   ayaT^a   eddo   ImAn^u

ايٽ   آيَتَ   ايڏو   اِيمانُ

Note that the only difference between /I/ and /E/ sound as symbolized is the inclusion of the diacritic "zer", ي , thus ي . However it is almost never written, so it is imperative that the student learn the correct pronunciation of the word. When reading new words that have not been learned orally, the help of a Sindhi will be very important.

Medial ـيـ may represent either the consonant sound /y/ or anyone of the vowels /I/, /E/, or /ai/, as illustrated above.

Letter Group 4

This group contains د /d/, ڌ /dh/, ڊ /D/, ڍ /Dh/, ڏ /dd/ and ذ /z/. Letters of this group are non-connectors and have the following basic form:

Initial- Independent   د

Medial-final   ـد

Letters of this group are thus:

	/d/	/dh/	/D/	/Dh/	/dd/	/z/
Initial	د	ڌ	ڊ	ڍ	ڏ	ذ
Medial-final	ـد	ـڌ	ـڊ	ـڍ	ـڏ	ـذ

Examples   dar^u   nanDhO

دَرُ   نڊيو

The letter ذ is an "uncommon Arabic consonant." Thus it is not found frequently in Sindhi.

Letter Group 5

This group contains ر /r/, ڙ /R/ and ز /z/. Letters of this group have the following basic form:

Initial- Independent   ر

Medial-final   ـر

---

* Refer to Letter Group 8, Lesson 11 for explanation of how to write the small ط as a diacritic in ڙ /r/.

Letters of this group are thus:

	/r/	/R/	/z/	Illustrations:		
Initial- independent	ر	ڙ	ز	rAt^i	tAr^u	رات تارُ راتِ
Medial- final	‍ـر	‍ـڙ	‍ـز	mEz^a	kapRA	ميز کپڙا

This letter ز is the most common representative of /z/ in Sindhi. Notice the difference in the shape of the ر group and that of the د group. Students sometimes confuse the two in their writing. The د is written with a relatively closed angle. Also, the ر drops down below the line of writing and the د does not.

Letter Group 15

This group contains only و /v/. It is a non-connector and has the following forms:

Illustrations			
Initial-independent	و	vaddO	وڈو
Initial-independent	‍ـو	uHO	أهو

When و is found at the beginning of a word, it stands for the consonant sound /v/. When it is used to represent an initial vowel sound, /O/, /U/, or/ aO/ it is found with ا . For example,

vaTh^i وَٺِ   aOggar   أوگر   OcitO   اوچتو   UcO   اوچو

In the medial and final position, و may represent either the consonant sounds or any of the vowel sound. The only difference in representation between /o/ and /U/ and the diphthong /aO/ is the presence or absence of the diacritical marks. Since they are not normally written, the student must learn the correct pronunciation of the words.

Letter Group 16

The only member of this group is ھ /H/, a connector. The basic forms of the consonant are:

Initial	Medial	Final	Independent
ھ	‍ـھـ	‍ـہ	ہ

Examples:

Hath^u	t ã Hin	vIHa	paRH^u
هَٿُ	تَنهن	ويھ	پَڙهُ

This letter also functions as the symbol for aspiration in جھ /jh/, and گھ /gh/, as will be noted in the sections on Groups 3 and 12.

Reading Exercises

1. Letters of all groups +/alif/, ا :

	نا	با	ڈا	تا	دا	ٹا	ذا	وا
نا	تا	ٹا	ڈا	ڑا	پا	با	دا	را
	دا	ها	را	یا	ٹا	زا	یا	وا	دا

2. Letters of all groups +/yE/, ي :

ژي	وي	شي	ڈي	تي	دي	ري	پي
ني	ذي	پي	ري	ٹي	ڍي	ٹي	ٹي
ڈي	زي	بي	ٹي	ڈي	ڀي	بي	ڊي

3. Letters of all group +/vAu/, و :

وو	ذو	تو	ژو	یو	ثو	دو	رو
نَو	رو	تو	ڎو	ڈو	ڌو	ڀو	ہو
تو	پُو	تو	ڀُو	بُو	زو	وُو	دو

4. Mixed sequences of the above:

ني	ژي	وا	ڈي	تو	دا	ري	پَي
تو	ني	پُو	رُو	تَو	دا	تَو	تا
رو	بي	نو	ڊو	یا	نَو	ڍي	ٹي

5. Sequences of two consonants:

یا	وَتِ	وَنُّ	پِٹُ	پَر	پُٹُ	پَنُ	دَپ
	هتي	یِتِ	تَپُ	هُنَ	دَر	دَبَ	ڈَدِ
ڎه	نَوَ	وَنُّ	دوا	بتي		دَري	هَٹُ

6. Initial short vowels:

	اهو	اُهو	اُهي	اُها	اِهو	اَٹ	اُٹ
	اُر	اَتو	اَبو	اَبا	اِهي	اَدي	اَڈ

7. Initial long vowels and diphthongs:

آب   آيَتَ   اِيران   آبادُ   ايڊو

اَويرُ   اوترو   آيا

8. Medial long vowels and diphthongs:

روز   پيدا   پيرُ   رات   دُور

ٻارُ   تارُ   راتِ   زور   بابا

9. Final long vowels and diphthongs:

پاٽي   وڏو   ڏاڏو   نيرو   پورو

اِهي   دَوا   هَوا   ٽوپي   پيتي   دري

10. Final nasalized vowels:

اَنون   هِتان   پيتيون   بتيون   دريون

LESSON TEN

10-A Pronunciation Drill

1. Contrasting /th/ and /Th/   (14-18)   /ٿ/ /ٽ/ /ث/

The camel's head is fat.	اٺ جو مٿو ٿلهو آهي۔
The hand got better.	هٿ نيڪ ٿي ويو۔
The elephant was seen in the village.	هاٿي ڳوٺ ۾ ڏٺو ويو۔

2. Contrasting /ph/ and /bh/   (9/10)   /ڀ/ /ڦ/ /ڀ/

Brother's wife turned and went away.	ڀاڄائي ڦري وئي۔
The vegetables are tasteless.	ڀاڄيون ڦڪيون آهن۔
Brother's firecracker fell near the gate.	ڀاءُ جو ڦٽاڪو ڦاٽڪ جي ڀرسان ڪري پيو۔

10-B The formation of the simple imperative

darivAzO khOlⁱ. Open the door.	دروازو کول۔
maHarbAnI karE darivAzO khOllO. Please open the door.	مهرباني ڪري دروازو کوليو۔
ghar^a m Ẽ ac^u. Come into the house.	گهر ۾ اچ۔
ghar^a m Ẽ acO. Please come into the house.	گهر ۾ اچو۔
HEddÃHã ac^u. Come here.	هيڏانهن اچ۔
maHarbAnI karE HOddÃHã na vaÑO. Please don't go there.	مهرباني ڪري هوڏانهن نہ وڃو۔

Huna iskU^a ddÃHā na vaÑO. Don't go to that school.	هن اسڪول ڏانهن نـ وجو.
vaddan chOkiran jE iskU^a ddÃHa vaÑO. Go to the big boy's school.	وڏن چوڪرن جي اسڪول ڏانهن وجو.
HI SaI ddisO. See this thing.	هي شيءِ ڏسو.
Huna ddÃHā na ddis^u. Don't look toward that/ him/her.	هن ڏانهن نـ ڏس.
HitE tars^u. Wait here.	هتي ترس.
maHarbAnI karE tarsO. Please wait.	مهرباني ڪري ترسو.
HutE raH^u. Remain there.	هتي رَهُ.
HutE raHO. Please remain there.	هتي رهو.
Kat^u ajj^u mOkil^i. Send the letter today.	خط اڄ موڪلِ.
maHarbAnI karE kat^u ajj^u mOkilIO. Please send the letter today.	مهرباني ڪري خط اڄ موڪليو.
HAR̃E na ggAlHA^i. Don't speak now.	هاڻي نـ ڳالهاءِ.
chOkarIŨ, bhit^i tE na caRHO. Girls, don't climb on the wall.	چوڪريون ڀت تي نـ چڙهو.
Huna sAf farAsI^a tE na HalO. Don't walk on the clean carpet.	هن صاف فراشي تي نـ هلو.
maHarbAnI karE HI ggAlH^i samjhAyO. Please explain this matter.	مهرباني ڪري هي ڳالھ سمجهايو.
HAR̃E HI ggAlh^i samjhO. Now understand this thing.	هاڻي هي ڳالھ سمجهو.

1. Look at the verbs in the examples above. In their infinitive forms they are:

khOlaR̃ᵘ	کولڻ	to open	ggAlHAiR̃ᵘ	ڳالهائڻ	to speak
acaR̃ᵘ	اچڻ	to come	caRHaR̃ᵘ	چڙهڻ	to climb
vaÑaR̃ᵘ	وڃڻ	to go	HalaR̃ᵘ	هلڻ	to walk
tarsaR̃ᵘ	ترسڻ	to wait	ddisaR̃ᵘ	ڏسڻ	to see
raHaR̃ᵘ	رهڻ	to remain	samjhAiR̃ᵘ	سمجهائڻ	to explain
mOkilaR̃ᵘ	موڪلڻ	to send	samjhaR̃ᵘ	سمجهڻ	to understand

In Lesson 6-D-1,2 we stated that the infinitive form of the verb ends in –R̃ᵘ, and that when this is removed, the root of the verb remains. However, it is not precisely true that by dropping the –R̃ᵘ ending one can see the verb root. In the infinitives given above you will notice that most infinitives have the "a" sound immediately before –R̃ᵘ. (There are two exceptions above, ggalHAiR̃ᵘ and samjhAiR̃ᵘ. For further comment see 10-B-1-d). This "a" sound does not belong in the verb root; it is there for the sake of euphony. When –R̃ᵘ is removed, the correct final short vowel of the root appears in the Sindhi speaker's pronunciation. It is essential to know precisely what that final short vowel is because it affects the verb's inflections into various forms to show tense number, gender, aspect, and mood. The root of the Sindhi verb must end in either /u/ or /i/. The student's problem is to determine which is the correct ending. Here are some guidelines:

(a) The root of an <u>intransitive</u> verb[1] <u>always</u> ends in /u/. For example, the root of acaR̃ᵘ is acᵘ; The root of vaÑaR̃ᵘ is vaÑᵘ.

(b) The root of a <u>transitive</u> verb[2] <u>generally</u>, but not always, ends in /i/. For example, the root of mOkilaR̃ᵘ is mOkilⁱ; the root of khOlaR̃ᵘ ends in /i/. But the transitive verb ddisaR̃ᵘ (to see) is an exception; its root ends in /u/, as do the roots of intransitive verbs.

(c) The root of a transitive verb which has /r/ or /R/ as its final consonant nearly always ends in /i/. For example, the root of sEkhAraR̃ᵘ (to teach) is sEkhArⁱ: the root of jORaR̃ᵘ (to make) is jORⁱ.

(d) The root of a transitive verb which has –Ai- before the final –Rᵘ of the infinitive, with few exceptions ends in /i/. For example, the root of ggAlHAiR̃ᵘ is ggAlHAⁱ; the root of samjhAiR̃ᵘ is samjhAⁱ.

2. The <u>singular</u> imperative is generally the same as the root of the verb. For example, tarsᵘ (Wait!), acᵘ (Come!), mOkilⁱ (Send!).

3. The plural imperative is formed by:

(a) changing the final /u/ of the root to /O/. For example, acᵘ becomes acO; vaÑᵘ becomes vaÑO.

---

[1] Intransitive verbs are those which do not require an object to complete their meaning. Thus, acaR̃ᵘ and vaÑaR̃ᵘ are examples of intransitive verbs. We cannot "come" or "go" something or somebody.

[2] Transitive verbs are those which assume an object, either expressed or understood. Thus, verbs like khOlaR̃ᵘ and mOkilaR̃ᵘ are transitive because it is possible to "open" or "send" something or somebody.

(b) changing the final /i/ of the root to /I/ and adding /O/. For example, khol[i] becomes khOlIO; mOkil[i] becomes mOkilIO. If the verb root ends in –Ai (as in ggAlHA[i] and samjhA[i]) this course transcribes the plural imperative ending as –AyO instead of –AIO. For example, ggAlHAyO (speak), samjhAyO (explain).

4. The imperative form of the verb is used to give commands or orders. The singular (or familiar) form is used when speaking to one person. The pronoun tŨ is understood but is not usually expressed. The proper usage of tŨ is explained in Lesson 6-C-3. The <u>plural</u> (or polite) form is used when speaking to more than one person, or as a plural of respect. The pronoun tavHĨ is understood, but not usually expressed. Its proper usage is explained in Lesson 6-0-4.

5. maHarbAnI karE is a combination of the noun maHarbAnI meaning "kindness" (and "thanks" in the previous lesson) and a form of the verb karaR̃[u] (to do). This form, karE, will be learned in a later lesson. Put together the expression means simply, "Please". When it is omitted, and only the polite form (plural) of the verb is used, the "please" is implied.

6. ddÃHā is a postposition meaning "to/toward". It is used with verbs of motion. In Upper Sindh you will hear ddE instead of ddÃHā.

7. HEddÃHā and HOddÃHā are place words meaning "here" and "there". They are used with verbs of motion, while the two similar words, HitE and HutE are static, and do not suggest motion. HEddE and HOddE are variations heard in Upper Sindh.

8. SaI and ggAlH[i] may both be rendered in English by "thing," but there is a difference:

(a) SaI always refers to things you can see and touch. HI[a] kaHiRI SaI AHE? (What is this?), for example.

(b) ggAlH[i] refers to word, utterance, event, idea. It is intangible. For example, HI[a] vaddI ggAlH[i] AHE. (This is an important matter.)

10-C The postposition khE as a sign of the object

mŨ khE ddisO. See me!	مون کي ڏسو.
maHarbAnI karE Huna khE kitAb[u] ddEO. Please give him the book.	مهرباني ڪري هن کي ڪتاب ڏيو.
asÃ khE hitE na chadd[i]. Don't leave us here.	اسان کي هتي نہ ڇڏ.
Hunan[i] khE bi iHA ggAlH[i] bbudhAyO. Tell them this thing also.	هنن کي بہ اها ڳالھ ٻڌايو.
HI Kat[u] ustAd[a] khE mOkilIO. Send this letter to the teacher.	هي خط استاد کي موڪليو.
maHarbAnI karE HI ggAlH[i] chOkirIun[a] khE bbudhAyO. Please tell this (thing) to the girls.	مهرباني ڪري هي ڳالھ ڇوڪرين کي ٻڌايو.
mũHĩnjI bbudh[u]. Listen to me.	منهنجي ٻڌ.

maHarbAnI karE varI caO. Please say it again.	مهرباني ڪري وري چئو.
darIŨ khOliO. Open the windows.	دريون کوليو.
darivAzA na, darIunᵃ khE khOliO. Not the doors, open the <u>windows</u>.	دروازا نـ، درين کي کوليو.
maHarbAnI karE mŨsÃ ggAlHAyO. Please speak/talk with me.	مهرباني ڪري مون سان ڳالهايو.

1.   The object of a sentence may – but need not always – be indicated by the postposition khE. This is true of both <u>direct</u> and <u>indirect</u> objects. When used in this way khE is not always translatable, although "to" is understood with indirect objects. Some guidelines for the use of khE are:

       (a)   When the direct or indirect object of the verb is a pronoun, as a rule the pronoun is followed by khE. This is illustrated in the examples above.

       (b)   When the object of the verb is to be emphasized, it is generally followed by khE. In the next to the last example above, the speaker wants to emphasize that he wants the <u>windows</u>, not the doors, opened. Thus he emphasizes the object with khE.

       (c)   When the clause contains both a direct and an indirect object, usually the indirect object is followed by khE. The direct object remains in the uninflected nominative form.

2.   To say, "Listen to me," Sindhis do not use khE, but the possessive. Thus, mũHinjI (ggAlH[i]) bbudh[u]. That is, one does not listen to the person, but to his word – ggAlHi. Most often ggAlH[i] will be omitted although understood, and one will say simply mũHinjI bbudh[u].

3.   In Sindhi one does not talk <u>to</u> someone, but <u>with</u> him. Thus, mŨ sÃ ggAlHAyO (talk with me). SÃ is a postposition meaning "with".

4.   Notice these additional verbs introduced in this section;

ddIaR̃[u]	ڏيڻ	to give	ddEkhAraR̃[u]	ڏيکارڻ	to show
chaddaR̃[u]	ڇڏڻ	to leave	bbudhaR̃[u]	ٻڌڻ	to listen
bbudhAiR̃[u]	ٻڌائڻ	to tell	cavaR̃[u]	چوڻ	to say

       ddIaR[u] is an irregular verb. The singular imperative form is ddE and the plural imperative form is ddEO. bbudhaR̃[u] is irregular in that its root ends in /u/; thus, it inflects as do intransitive verbs. The imperative singular is bbudh[u] and the plural is bbhudhO. cavaR̃[u] is irregular in that the /v/ is sometimes dropped in the inflections. For example, the singular imperative is ca[u] and the plural is caO.

10-D The formation of the present tense

			اچ	اچُ
Infinitive: acaR̃ᵘ	root: acᵘ			
mÃ acÃ thO/thI I come	asĨ acŨ thA/thIŨ We come		مان اچان ٿو /ٿي	اسين اچون ٿا /ٿيون
tŨ acĨ thO/thI You come (sing.)	tavHĨ acO thA/thIŨ You come (pl.)		تون اچين ٿو /ٿي	توهين اچو ٿا /ٿيون
HU acE thO/thI He comes	HU acan thA/thIŨ They come		هو اچي ٿو /ٿي	اُهي اچن ٿا /ٿيون
Infinitive: khOlaR̃ᵘ	Root: khOlⁱ		کول	کولُ
mÃ khOlIÃ thO/thI I open	asĨ khOlIŨ thA/thIŨ We open		مان کوليان ٿو /ٿي	اسين کوليون ٿا /ٿيون
tŨ khOlĨ thO/thI You open	tavHĨ khOlIO thA/thIŨ You open		تون کولين ٿو /ٿي	توهين کوليو ٿا /ٿيون
HU khOlE thO/thI He opens	HU khOlin thA/thIŨ They open		هو کولي ٿو /ٿي	هو کولن ٿا /ٿيون

1. The present tense describes action or state/ condition which is not completed, but is still going on, taking place or in progress at the time of the statement. It is also used to indicate something about to happen, that is the immediate future, and is used for general statements of fact.

2. The present tense inflections attach to the root of the verb. These inflections indicate the person and number but not gender. (The present tense indicator, thO, shows the gender. See below.) Notice that the inflections in the second and third persons singular are the same with verbs whose roots end in /u/ or /i/. There is a slight difference, however, in the other personal inflections between those whose roots end in /u/ and those which end in /i/. Note the difference:

root: acᵘ – drop /u/ and add: root: khOlⁱ – drop /i/ and add:

- -Ã   (mÃ acÃ thO)   - IÃ   (mÃ khOlIÃ thO)
- -Ĩ   (tŨ acĨ thO)   - Ĩ   (tŨ khOlĨ thO)
- -E   (HU acE thO)   - E   (HU khOlE thO)
- -Ũ   (asĨ acŨ thA)   - IŨ   (asĨ khOlIŨ thA)
- -O   (tavHĨ acO thA)   - IO   (tavHĨ khOlIO thA)
- -an   (HU acan thA)   - in   (HU khOlin thA)

3. The particle thO indicates the present tense, and like jO, it is inflectable according to gender and number. Thus when the subject is masculine thO is used with the singular and thA with the plural. When the subject is feminine, thI is used with the singular and thIŨ with the plural. For example:

chOkarO acE thO. The boy comes.	چوکرو اچي ٿو.
chOkarA acan thA. The boys come.	چوکرا اچن ٿا.
chOkarI acE thI. The girl comes.	چوکري اچي ٿي.
chOkarIŨ acan thIŨ. The girls come.	چوکريون اچن ٿيون.

10-E   Statements, questions and negatives in the present tense

kEr^u acE thO? Who is coming?	ڪير اچي ٿو؟
mũHinjO pI^u acE thO. My father is coming.	منھنجو پيءُ اچي ٿو.
mũHinjI mA^u bi acE thI. My mother is coming, too.	منھنجي ماءُ بہ اچي ٿي.
tŨ kEddÃHā vaÑĪ thO? Where are you going?	تون ڪيڏانھن وڃين ٿو؟
AŨ bAzAr^i ddÃHā vaÑÃ thO. I am going to the bazaar.	آءٌ بازار ڏانھن وڃان ٿو.
tŨ chA thO karĪ? What are you doing?	تون ڇا ٿو ڪرين؟
mÃ HI lifAfO khOllÃ thO. I'm opening this envelope.	مان هي لفافو کوليان ٿو.
HU chA thA kan? What are they doing?	ھو ڇا ٿا ڪن؟
HU kitAb^a kabbaT^a mẼ rakhan thA. They are putting books into the cupboard.	ھو ڪتاب ڪٻٽ ۾ رکن ٿا.
mEz^a tE avHĨ chA thA rakhO? What are you putting on the table?	ميز تي اوھين ڇا ٿا رکو؟
mEz^a tE aŨ kujh bi na thO rakhÃ. I'm not putting anything on the table.	ميز تي آءٌ ڪجھ بہ نہ ٿو رکان.
mEza tE AŨ mAnI rakhÃ thO. I'm putting food (lit: bread) on the table.	ميز تي آءٌ ماني رکان ٿو.

avHĨ Huna lifAfE mẼ chA thA mOkillO? What are you sending in that envelope?	اوهين هن لفافي مِ چا ٿا موڪليو؟
AŨ mAlHIa jE pIu khE kujh pEsa mOkillĨA thO. I'm sending some money to the gardener's father.	آءُ مالهي جي پيءُ ڪي ڪجھ پئسا موڪليان ٿو.
tavHÃ jA mAu pIu kithÃ thA acan? Where are your parents coming from?	توهان جا ماءُ پيءُ ڪٿان ٿا اچن؟
HU karAcIa khÃ acan thA. They are coming from Karachi.	هو ڪراچيءَ ڪان اچن ٿا.
tŨ chA thO paRHĨ? What are you reading?	تون چا ٿو پڙهين؟
mÃ sindhI aKbAra paRHÃ thO. I'm reading a Sindhi newspaper.	مان سنڌي اخبار پڙهان ٿو.
mÃ ãgrEzI aKbAra na thO paRHÃ. I'm not reading an English newspaper.	مان انگريزي اخبار نَ ٿو پڙهان.
'aoratŨ chA thIŨ kan? What are the women doing?	عورتون چا ٿيون ڪن؟
HU qurAn SarIf paRHan thIŨ. They are reading the Holy Koran.	هو قرآن شريف پڙهن ٿيون.
tavHĨ chA thA karIO? What are you doing?	توهين چا ٿا ڪريو؟
asĨ sabh kitAba Hina pEtIa mÃ kadhŨ thA. We are taking all the books out of this box.	اسين سڀ ڪتاب هن پيتي مان ڪڍون ٿا.
asĨ subh SAIŨ thElHIa mÃ kaDhŨ thA. We are taking all the things out of the bag.	اسين سڀ شيون ٿيلهي مان ڪڍون ٿا.
chOkarA iskUla vaÑan thA. Boys go to school.	چوڪرا اسڪول وڃن ٿا.
suThA chOkarA ustAda jI bbudhan thA. Good boys listen to the teacher.	سٺا چوڪرا استاد جي ٻڌن ٿا.

1. Note the position of the inflectable particle thO (present tense indicator) in relation to its verb:

(a) In general statements thO follows the verb. For example, HU ghar^a ddÃHā vaÑE thO.

(b) When the negative particle na is used, then thO precedes the verb. For example, mÃ ghar^a na thO vaÑA. (Note that although ddÃHā is understood after ghar^a, it does not have to be expressed.)

(c) With other question words thO is often placed before the verb. For example, HU chA thO karE?

(d) With other question words thO is often placed before the verb. For example, HU kEddÃHā thO vaNe? However, this is not a rule, and it may be placed after the verb as in general statements. For example, HU kithÃ acan thA?

2. Notice the additional verbs in the examples:

| karaR̃^{u} | کرڻ | to do | paRHaR̃^{u} | پڙهڻ | to read |
| rakhaR̃^{u} | رکڻ | to place, put | kaDhaR̃^{u} | ڪڍڻ | to take out |

All these verbs are transitive, but only one has a root ending in /i/, karaR̃^{u}. The rest have roots ending in /u/ and must inflect as do the intransitive verbs whose roots end in /u/. For example, mÃ paRHÃ thO (I am reading); asĨ paRHŨ thA (we reading), etc.

3. karaR̃^{u} is very common verb and its inflections are often irregular. For example, in the third person plural, one does not say, Hu karan thA, but HU kan thA, dropping the /r/ out of the root. You will also notice that Sindhi speakers drop the /r/ sometimes in other personal inflections. One may say either mÃ karIÃ thO or mÃ kayÃ thO; one may say either saĨ karIŨ thA or asĨ kayŨ thA.

4. ma^u pI^u is the term generally used for parents.

5. khÃ is a postposition meaning "from". mÃ also means "from" but it has the more precise meaning of "out of". To take any thing from a box, pocket, room, house implies that you are taking it from within an enclosed area. In such cases you should use mÃ rather than khÃ.

6. kEddÃHā asks "to/ toward where?" when used with a verb of motion. In Upper Sindh you will hear kAddE.

7. kithÃ asks "from where?" when used with verbs of motion.

8. sabh means "all." sabh kujh means "everything" and sabh kO means "everyone". The oblique form of <u>sabh</u> is <u>sabhanI</u>. For example, sabhanI mÃR̃Hun jA bbAr (all the people's children)

10-F   The reflexive pronouns

mÃ pAR̃ª vaÑÃ thO. I'm going myself.	مان پاڻ وڃان ٿو.
Katᵘ pAR̃ª likhO. Write the letter yourself.	خط پاڻ لکو.
asĨ pAR̃ª kam karIŨ thA. We are doing the work ourselves.	اسين پاڻ ڪم ڪريون ٿا.
'aoratŨ paR̃ª ustAdª sÃ ggAlHAin thIŨ. The women themselves are talking to the teacher.	عورتون پاڻ استاد سان ڳالهائين ٿيون.
mAᵘ paR̃ª kapRA dhOE thI. Mother washes the clothes herself.	ماءُ پاڻ ڪپڙا ڌوئي ٿي.
chOkarA paR̃ª mẼ ggAlHAin thA. The boys are talking among themselves.	ڇوڪرا پاڻ ۾ ڳالهائين ٿا.
HŨ paR̃EHI kam karE thO. He is doing the work by himself.	هو پاڻيهي ڪم ڪري ٿو.
pAR̃EHI thÃvª dhO. Wash the dishes yourself.	پاڻيهي ٿانئَو ڌوءُ.
HŨª paR̃EHI acE thI. She is coming on her own (voluntarily).	هوءَ پاڻيهي اچي ٿي.
mÃ pāHinjO kitAbᵘ paRHÃ thO. I'm reading my own book.	مان پنهنجو ڪتاب پڙهان ٿو.
mŨ khE pāHinjI pEnsilⁱ ddE. Give me your (own) pencil.	مون کي پنهنجي پينسل ڏي.
asĨ pāHinjE gharª (ddÃHã) vaÑŨ thA. We are going (to our own) home.	اسين پنهنجي گهر (ڏانهن) وڃون ٿا.
pāHinjO kam karⁱ. Do your own work. Mind your own business.	پنهنجو ڪم ڪر.
maᵘ pIᵘ pāHinjan bbAran sÃ Halan thA. Parents are going with their (own) children.	ماءُ پيءُ پنهنجن ٻارن سان هلن ٿا.
pāHinjA hathª mEzª tE rakhO. Put your hands on the table.	پنهنجا هٿ ميز تي رکو.

asĨ pāHinjan bhAuran sÃ ggAlHAyŨ thA. We are talking to our (own) brothers.	اسين پنهنجن ڀائرن سان ڳالهايون ٿا.
HI ggAlHⁱ pāHinjlᵃ mAᵘ khE bbudhAⁱ. Tell this to your mother.	هي ڳالھ پنهنجي ماءُ کي ٻڌاءِ.
chOkarE khE sandus kitAbᵘ ddE. Give the boy his (own) book.	چوڪري کي سندس ڪتاب ڏي.
chOkaran khE sandan kApIŨ ddEO. Give the boys their (own) notebooks.	چوڪرن کي سندن ڪاپيون ڏيو.
HU AĨ sandus puTᵘ kam thA kan. He and his (own) son are working.	هو ۽ سندس پٽ ڪم ٿا ڪن.
mÃ chOkarE khE sandus TOpI ddIÃ thO. I'm giving the boys his (own) cap.	مان چوڪري کي سندس ٽوپي ڏيان ٿو.

1. The reflexive pronoun pÃR̃ᵃ (self), refers back to the subject of the clause as illustrated in examples above. In its nominative form pAR̃ᵃ does not change for the masc. or fem. plural or for the fem. sing. For example, naokarᵘ pAR̃ᵃ (the servant himself), naokarᵃ pAR̃ᵃ (the servants themselves), 'aoratᵃ pAR̃ᵃ (the woman herself), 'aoratŨ pAR̃ᵃ (the women themselves).

2. With all postpositions except jO, pAR̃ᵃ remains pAR̃ᵃ. For example, HU pAR̃ᵃ mẼ ggAlHAIn thA. (They are talking among themselves).

3. The adverbial form illustrated in several sentences above with the form pAR̃EHI, has the meaning "by_____ self", "voluntarily".

4. When used with jO, pAR̃ᵃ inflects to pāHin+jO. In a Sindhi clause when a possessive pronoun refers back to the verb's subject (of that same clause) then the reflexive pronoun pāHinjO must always be used. One must be sure that the possessive pronoun and the subject are exactly the same. For example, in the sentence, mÃ AĨ mũHinjO bhAᵘ Katᵘ paRHŨ thA, (I and my brother are reading a letter), one cannot use pāHinjO bhAᵘ. The reason is that in this case it would only partially reflect the subject. However, if the letter belongs to both mÃ and bhAᵘ mutually, pāHinjO could be used with Katᵘ (letter). Thus, mÃ AĨ mũHinjO bhAᵘ pāHinjO Katᵘ paRHU thA. (I and my brother are reading our (own) letter). "Our" in this case exactly reflects the subject.

5. Sometimes pāHinjO is repeated in order to denote a distributive sense. For example,

HU pāHinjA pāHinjA kitAbᵃ paRHan thA. They are each reading their own books (or their respective book).	هو پنهنجا پنهنجا ڪتاب پڙهن ٿا.
asĨ pāHinjE pāHinjE gharᵃ (ddÃHā) HalŨ thA. We are going each to his own home (or, our respective homes.)	اسين پنهنجي پنهنجي گهر (ڏانهن) هلون ٿا.

6. In the last four sentences above the pronoun, sandus^u, is introduced. In English ambiguity can arise when one say, "Give the boy his book." Do we mean the boy's book, or someone else's book? If we mean the boy's book, then the Sindhi would say, chOkarE khE sandus kitAb^u ddE. When the Sindhi says chOkarE khE pāHinjO kitAb^u ddE, he would mean, "Give the boy your (own) book". The subject of the verb in this command is "you". Actually the rule governing the use of sandus^u is not so clear-cut and precise. Sindhi speakers will use it in all cases where a 3rd person possessive pronoun (e.g. "his", "her", "their") refers back to a nearby noun; but that noun does not necessarily have to be in the same sentence.

7. sandus^u is from the old Sindhi postposition, sandO which, like jO, expresses possession. It is often used in poetry. For example, rAjAan^i sandO rAjA (king of kings), DAkTaran^i sandO DAkTar^u (Doctor of doctors). But more often it occurs in constructions like those in examples above. The most common forms are:

(a) sandus^u: used with masculine singular nouns, both in the nominative and oblique, meaning "his/hers/its". For example, sandus^u puT^u (his/her son) sandus^u kitAb^a mẼ, (in his/her book).

(b) sandus^u: used with feminine singular nouns, both in the nominative and the oblique, meaning "his/her/its". For example, sandus^u dhI^u (his/her daughter), sandus^u pEtI^a mẼ (in his/her box).

(c) sandan^u: used with masculine plural nouns, both in the nominative and oblique, meaning "their". For example, sandan^u bhAur^a (their brothers) sandan^u bhAuran^i sÃ (with their brothers).

(d) sandan^u: used with feminine plural nouns, both in the nominative and oblique, meaning "their". For example, sandan^u dhIurŨ (their daughters), sandan^u dhIuran^i sÃ (with their daughters).

8. In Lesson 7-8-5 you learned that Sindhi grammars instruct us to inflect the postposition jO as jE in all oblique forms. However, you will hear Sindhi speakers inflecting the plural oblique form of paHinjO as paHinjan. For example, paHinjan bhAuran^i sÃ.

10- G   Vocabulary for Lesson Ten

ajj^u today	اج	ddÃHā toward	ڏانهن
acaR̃^{u} (acu)[1] to come	اچڻ (اچُ)	ddisaR̃^{u} (ddis^u) to see	ڏسڻ (ڏسُ)
thÃv^u (m) dish, vessel	ٿانوُ	ddIaR̃^{u} (ddE^u) to give	ڏيڻ (ڏي)
bbudhaR̃^{u} (bbudh^u) to listen, hear	ٻڌڻ (ٻڌُ)	rakhaR̃^{u} (rakh^u) to place, put, keep	رکڻ (رکُ)

---

[1] After each infinitive in the vocabulary the verb root will be given in parentheses.

bbudhAiR̃u (bbudhAi) to tell	بڌائڻ (بڌاءِ)	raHaR̃u (raHu) to remain, reside	رھڻ (رھُ)
tarsaR̃u (tarsu) to wait	ترسڻ (ترسُ)	sÃ with	سان
pAR̃a self	پاڻ	samjhaR̃u (samjhu) to understand	سمجھڻ (سمجھُ)
paRHaru (paRHu) to read, study	پڙھڻ (پڙھُ)	samjhAiR̃u (samjhAi) to explain	سمجھائڻ (سمجھاءِ)
pEsa (m.pl.) money	پيسا	sandusu his, hers	سندس
caRHaR̃u (caRHu) to climb	چڙھڻ (چڙھُ)	SaI (f) Thing	شيءَ
cavaR̃u (cau) to say	چوڻ (چئُ)	sAf clean	صاف
chaddaR̃u (chaddi) to leave	ڇڏڻ (ڇڏِ)	qurAn SarIf (m) Holy Koran	قرآن شريف
dhOaR̃u (dhOi) to wash	ڌوئڻ (ڌوءِ)	kithÃ from where?	ڪٿان
kaDhaR̃u (kadhu) to take out	ڪڍڻ (ڪڍُ)	mOkilaR̃u (mOkili) to send	موڪلڻ (موڪلِ)
karaR̃u (kari) to do	ڪرڻ (ڪرِ)	vaThaR̃u (vaThu) to take	وٺڻ (وٺُ)
kEddÃHã where to?	ڪيڏانھن	vaÑaR̃u (vaÑu) to go	وڃڻ (وڃُ)
khOlaR̃u (khOli) to open	کولڻ (کولِ)	varI again	وري
ggAlHi (f) matter	ڳالھ	HAR̃E Now	ھاڻي
ggAlHAiR̃u (ggAlHAi) to speak, talk	ڳالھائڻ (ڳالھاءِ)	HalaR̃u (Halu) To go walk	ھلڻ (ھل)
lifAfO (m) envelope	لفافو	HOddÃHã Toward there	ھوڏانھن

Lesson Ten/ 111

likhaR̃u (likhu) to write	لکڻ (لکُ)	HEddÃHā Toward here	هيڏانهن
mAnI (f) bread, food general	ماني	mÃ from out of	مان
khÃ from	کان	mAu pIu parents	ماءُ پِيءُ
kithÃ from where	کتان	vijhaR̃u to put in, insert	وجهڻ

10-H Conversational Review

1. The teacher should give commands using the verbs listed below and the student should silently carry out the commands to show that he understands what the teacher is saying:

khOlaR̃u, ggAlHAiR̃u, karaR̃u likhaR̃u   کولڻ، ڳالهائڻ، کرڻ، لکڻ

acaR̃u halaR̃u rakhaR̃u paRHaR̃u   اچڻ، هلڻ، رکڻ، پڙهڻ

vaÑaR̃u ddIaR̃u tarsaR̃u   وڃڻ، ڏيڻ، ترسڻ

mOkilaR̃u cavaR̃u kaDhaR̃u vaThaR̃u   موڪلڻ، چوڻ، ڪڍڻ، وٽڻ

For example:

Teacher: darivAzO khOllO. Student: (goes and opens the door)	استاد: دروازو کوليو.
Teacher: HEddÃHā acO. Student: (walks toward the teacher)	استاد: هيڏانهن اچو.

2. Repeat Exercise 1 by switching roles. The student gives the commands and the teacher carries them out.

3. Repeat Exercise 1, and while carrying out the command say what you are doing, using the present tense. For example,

Teacher: darivAzO khOllO.	استاد: دروازو کوليو.
Student: (opening the door) mÃ darivAzO khOllÃ thO/thI.	شاگرد: مان دروازو کوليان ٿو/ ٿي.

4. Using the nouns and pronouns listed below as subjects of the verb, karaR̃u, the teacher should ask, for example, mAR̃HU chA thO karE? avHĨ chA thA karIO? Etc.

The student should give imaginary answers, or true ones, as the case may be, using all the verbs given in this lesson's vocabulary.

maR̃HU (sing. & pl.), SAgird^u, avHĨ   ماٺهو، شاگرد، اوهين

bbacO, bOrcI, bbAr^a bbacA, avHÃ jO bhA^u   بچو، بورچي، ٻار ٻچا، اوهان جو ڀاءُ

TapAlI, avHÃ jI mA^u, HU (sing. & pl)   ٽپالي، اوهان جي ماءُ، هو

HU^a, uHE 'aoratŨ, maolvI sAHib^u   هوءَ، اهي عورتون، مولوي صاحب

avHÃ jA mA^u pI^u, mAlHI^a jI dhI^u   اوهان جا ماءُ پيءُ، مالهي جي ڌيءُ

5. Place on the table these three objects: book, pencil (or pen) and notebook. Mark each object as belonging to "teacher", "student" and "boy". Now the teacher should request:

mŨ khE mũHinjO (or, pãHinjO, or chOkirE jO/jI) _____ ddEO.   مون کي منهنجو (يا پنهنجو، يا چوڪري جو/ جي) .... ڏيو.

The student answers by silently carrying out the command.

6. Repeat Exercise 5, by requesting as follows:

ddisaR̃^u, bbudhaR̃^u, likhaR̃^u   ڏسڻ، ٻڌڻ، لکڻ

mOkilaR̃^u, dhOaR̃^u, ddIaR̃^u   موڪلڻ، ڌوئڻ، ڏيڻ

khOlaR̃^u, paRHaR̃^u, KaDhaR̃^u   کولڻ، پڙھڻ، ڪڍڻ

For example:

Teacher: tavHĨ chA thA ddisO?	استاد: توهين ڇا ٿا ڏسو؟
Student: mÃ kutO (kutE khE) ddisÃ thO/thI.	شاگرد: مان ڪتو (ڪتي کي) ڏسان ٿو/ٿي.
Teacher: tavHĨ kãHinjO kutO ddisO tha? etc.	استاد: توهين ڪنهن جو ڪتو ڏسو ٿا؟ وغيره

8. Put the following nouns and verbs together with kithE, kithÃ, and kEddÃHã. The teacher may ask the question first, and the student may answer using HitE, HutE, HEddÃHã. Then change roles with the student asking and the teacher answering.

dhobi	ڌوٻي	acaR̃u	اچَڻُ	kithE?	ڪٿي؟
HunajI dhiu	هن جي ڌيءُ	vaÑaR̃u	وَڃَڻُ	kithÃ?	ڪٿان؟
SaI	شيءِ	AHE, AHin	آهي، آهن	kEddÃHā?	ڪيڏانهن؟
kitAbu	ڪتابُ	tarsaR̃u	تَرسَڻُ	HitE	هِتي
lifAfO	لفافو	chaddaR̃u	چَڏَڻُ	HutE	هُتي
mAu pIu	ماءُ پيءُ	raHaR̃u	رَهَڻُ	HEddÃHā	هيڏانهن
SAgirdu	شاگرد	rakhaR̃u	رَکَڻُ	HOddÃHā	هوڏانهن
chOkirA	چوڪرا	HalaR̃u	هَلَڻُ		
chOkirIŨ	چوڪريون	vaThaR̃u	وَٺَڻُ		

10-I Introduction to the Sindhi Writing System- Part II

Six letter groups will be introduced in this lesson.

Letter Group 3

This group includes ج /j/, ڄ /jj/, جھ /jh/, ڃ /Ñ/, چ /c/, ڇ /ch/, ح /H/, خ /K/. Letters of this shape group are connectors and have the following basic forms:

Initial   Medial   Final   Independent

Letters of this group are thus:

	/j/	/jj/	/jh/	/Ñ/	/c/	/ch/	/H/	/K/	Illustrations:
Initial:	جـ	ڄـ	جھـ	ڃـ	چـ	ڇـ	حـ	خـ	chA چا
Medial:	ـجـ	ـڄـ	ـجھـ	ـڃـ	ـچـ	ـڇـ	ـحـ	ـخـ	bacO بچو
Final:	ـج	ـڄ	ـجھ	ـڃ	ـچ	ـڇ	ـح	ـخ	sacu سَچُ
Independent:	ج	ڄ	جھ	ڃ	چ	ڇ	ح	خ	ajju اَجُ

The letter ح /H/ occurs only in words of Arabic origin.

Letter Group 6

This group includes س /s/ and ش /S/. Letters of this group are connectors and have the following basic forms.

Initial   Medial   Final   Independent

Letters of this group are thus;

			Illustrations:
Initial:	ســ	شــ	sAlu سال
Medial:	ـســ	ـشــ	SISO شیشو
Final:	ـس	ـش	basu بَس
Independent:	س	ش	tarsu ترسُ

The letter س is the most common representative of /s/.

Letter Group 11

This group contains only ک /k/. It is a connector and has the following forms:

Initial   Medial   Final   Independent

Illustrations: kutO   kukuRu   naku   dhaku
                 کتو   کُکُرُ   نک   ڈک

Letter Group 12

This group includes ک /kh/ گ /g/ ڳ /gg/ گھ /gh/ ݢ /g̃/. Letters in this group are connectors and have the following basic forms:

Initial   Medial   Final   Independent

	/kh/	/g/	/gg/	/gh/	/g/	Illustrations:	
Initial:	کــ	گــ	ڳــ	گھــ	ݢــ	ggOThu	ڳوٹُ
Medial:	ـکــ	ـگــ	ـڳــ	ـگھــ	ـݢــ	cag̃O	چݢو
Final:	ـک	ـگ	ـڳ	ـگھ	ـݢ	rãgu	رنگ
Independent:	ک	گ	ڳ	گھ	ݢ	rakhu	رکُ

Before "alif," /A/ and /l/, special initial and medial forms are found: ڪ and ڪــ. For example: کل khal^u, کاٹ khaTⁱ, پگّل bhaggal^u etc. Notice the extra stroke that distinguishes the voiced velar stops from the voiceless ک.

Letter Group 13

The only member of this group is ل /l/. It is a connector and has the following basic forms:

Initial	Medial	Final	Independent
ل	ـلـ	ـل	ل

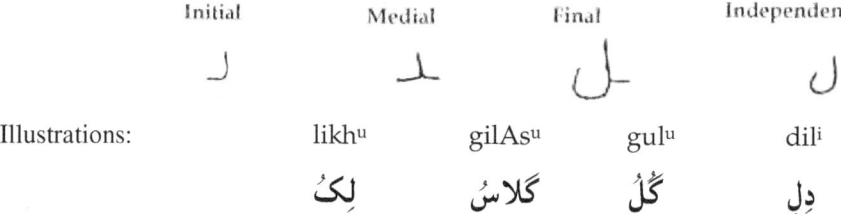

Illustrations: likh^u   gilAs^u   gul^u   dilⁱ

لِکُ   گلاسُ   گُلُ   دِلِ

Letter Group 14

The only member of this group is م /m/. It is a connector and has the following basic forms:

Initial	Medial	Final	Independent

Illustrations:

مَسُ   آسمانُ   کَمرُ   تمامُ

Exercises:

Reading Drills:

1. Letters of all new groups +/alif/:

جا   ݄جا   سا   شا   جھا   کا   ݨجا   کا

چا   گا   ݨچا   ݨگا   حا   خا   گھا   ما   لا

2. Letters of all new groups +/yE/:

چی   لی   جی   گی   می   سی   ڇی   ݨگی   شی

حی   جھی   ݨجی   خی   ݨچی   ڇی   گھی   کی   ݨجی

3. Letters of all new groups +/vAv/:

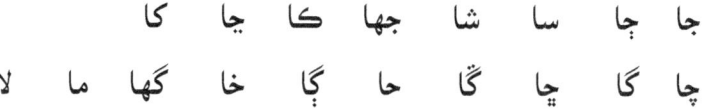

کو   کو   سو   گھو   ݨگو   لو   شو   خو   چو

چو   ݨچو   گو   ݨجو   جو   جھو   ݨگو   مو

4. Medial letters of all new groups:

تمامُ   کمرو   رستو   کیسو   شیشو

کُرسي   چگّو   پیلو   بِیمارُ   سستُ

اچو   خالي

5. Final letters of all new groups:

گُلُ   رنگُ   کَرُ   مَسُ   گِلاسُ   پنجَ

هِکُ   اِسکُولُ   نپال   رَکُ   کولِ   اَچُ

وَجُ   ڈِسُ   هَلُ   سَمجُهه   ترسُ

LESSON ELEVEN

11-A   **Pronunciation Drill**

1. Contrasting /p/ and /ph/   (6, 9)   /ڦ/   ء   /پ/

پيءُ ڦري پٽ جو ڦاڪو پڪڙيو.
ٿپالي ڦاٽڪ جي ڦنيان ڦري ويو.
پٽ پڇيو تہ چانھ ڇو ڦڪي آھي.

2. Contrasting /A/ and /a/   (52, 56)   /آ/   ء   /ا/

ماڻھو وري واري ڪٽي آيو.
مزور جا بار وري ھلن ٿا.
ڪمري ۾ سامان آھي ڇا؟ سامان ڪونھي.

11-B   **The cardinal numbers seventeen to twenty**

seventeen:	sataraHã,	written as,	۱۷	سترهن
eighteen:	araRahã,	written as,	۱۸	ارڙهن
nineteen:	uR̃avIHa,	written as,	۱۹	اڻويھ
twenty:	vIHa,	written as,	۲۰	ويھ

11-C   The oblique form of cardinal numbers

mA^u pāHinjan bbin bbAran sÃ gadd^u HalE thI. The mother is walking with (lit., together with) her two children.	ماءُ پنهنجن ٻن ٻارن سان گڏ هلي ٿي.
HI ruggO HikaRE mA R̃HU^a jO kam AHE. This is just one man's work.	هي رڳو هڪڙي ماڻهوءَ جو ڪم آهي.
ca-in kamaran m Ẽ sAmAn^a kOnaHE. There is no furniture in four rooms.	چئن ڪمرن ۾ سامان ڪونهي.
Hinan Tin pEtIunⁱ m Ẽ kujh bi kOnaHE. There is nothing in these three boxes.	هنن ٽن پيتين ۾ ڪجھ بہ ڪونهي.
Hunan ddaHan bbAran sÃ gadd^u vaÑO. Go with those ten children.	هنن ڏهن ٻارن سان گڏ وڃو.
Hinan aThan chOkarIun jA mA^u pI^u HitE na AHin. The parents of these eight girls aren't here.	هنن اٺن چوڪرين جا ماءُ پيءُ هِتي نہ آهن.
mAlHIun jE tEraHan chOkiran vaTⁱ mAnI kAnaHE. The thirteen boys belonging to the gardeners have no food.	مالهين جي تيرهن چوڪرن وٽ ماني ڪانهي.
Hunan vIHan SAgirdan jE puThIÃ Hik^a vaddI bhitⁱ AHE. There's a high wall behind those twenty students.	هنن ويهن شاگردن جي پٺيان هڪ وڏي ڀت آهي.

1.   Numbers from 2 to 48 inflect before plural nouns in the oblique and, with the exception of numbers 2, 3, and 4, the inflected ending is –an.

2.   The inflected forms of 2, 3, and 4, are irregular. Note:

bbin chOkiran khE To two boys	ٻن چوڪرن ڪي
Tin kursIun tE On three chairs	ٽن ڪرسين تي
ca-in kamaran mE In four rooms	چئن ڪمرن ۾

11-D   The comparison and superlative of adjectives

Sindhi (transliteration)	Sindhi (script)
HI^u kulf^u maHÃgO AHE. This lock is expensive.	هيءُ ڪلف مهانگو آهي.
HI^u kulf^u Huna (kulf^a) khÃ maHÃgO AHE. This lock is more expensive than that (one).	هيءُ ڪلف هُن (ڪلفَ) کان مهانگو آهي.
HI^u sabhanI khÃ maHÃgO kulf^u AHE. This lock is the most expensive of all.	هيءُ سيني کان مهانگو ڪلف آهي.
HI^u sabha khÃ maHÃgO AHE. This is the most expensive of all.	هيءُ سڀ کان مهانگو آهي.
HI^a tasvIr^a Hunan (tasvIrun) khÃ suHiRĨI AHE. This picture is prettier than those (pictures).	هي تصوير هنن (تصويرن) کان سُهڻي آهي.
par^a HI^a sabh^a khÃ suHiRĨI AHE. But this is the prettiest of all.	پر هيءَ سَڀَ کان سُهڻي آهي.
kaHiRO mEvO sastO AHE? Which fruit is the cheapest? (Which fruit is cheap?)	ڪهڙو ميوو سستو آهي؟
nArãgIŨ sUfan khÃ sastIŨ AHin. The oranges are cheaper than the apples.	نارنگيون صوفن کان سستيون آهن.
par^a amb^a sabh^a khÃ sastA AHin. But mangoes are the cheapest of all.	پر انب سڀ کان سستا آهن.
kaHiRI bhAjjI sastI AHE? Which vegetable is the cheapest?	ڪهڙي ڀاڄي سستي آهي؟
ajj^u kalH^a paTATA aĨ gaJarŨ bbaI sastIŨ AHin. Nowadays potatoes and carrots are both cheap.	اڄڪلھ پٽاٽا ۽ گجرون ٻئي سستيون آهن.
par^a basar^a Hunan khÃ bi sastA AHin. But onions are even cheaper than they.	پر بصر هنن کان بہ سستا آهن.
HI kAGaz^u maHÃgO AHE. par^a bbIE qism jO (kaGaz^u) vadhIk maHÃgO AHE. This paper is expensive, but the other kind (of paper) is more expensive.	هي ڪاغذ مهانگو آهي، پر ٻئي قسم جو (ڪاغذ) وڌيڪ مهانگو آهي.

bOrcI, HI nArãgIŨ kacIŨ AHin. Hinan khÃ pakIŨ bAzAr mẼ na AHin? Cook, these oranges are unripe. Aren't there any riper ones in the bazaar?	بورچي، هي نارنگيون ڪچيون آهن. هنن کان پڪيون بازار ۾ نه آهن؟
mÃ Hunan khE vApas karIÃ thO. I'm returning them.	مان هنن کي واپس ڪريان ٿو.
Hunan khÃ pakIŨ aĨ miThIŨ KarId karIÃ thO. I'm buying riper and sweeter ones.	هنن کان پڪيون ۽ مٺيون خريد ڪريان ٿو.

1. When making comparisons in Sindhi, the postposition khÃ (from) is often used in the sense of "than" or "in comparison with". It follows the mention of the person or thing being compared.

2. In the case of the superlative, the word sabh^u (all) is used before khÃ or, if the noun being compared is mentioned, before it and khÃ.

3. Used as an adjective the word sabh^u inflects to become sabhanI. For example,

    sabh^u chOkirA   all the boys

    sabhanI chOkiran khE   to all the boys

Used as a pronoun, it inflects to become sabh^a. For example,

    sabh^u vaddA AHin.   All are big.

    HI^u sabh^a khÃ vaddO AHe.   This is the biggest of all.

However, the fine line of distinction between the use of sabh^u as an adjective or as a pronoun is in the mind of the speaker. Therefore, he may say either sabh^a khÃ or sabhani khÃ. The latter is required, though, when the person or thing being compared is mentioned. For example, one cannot say, sabh^a kitAban khÃ but sabhanI kitAban khÃ. Of course, this is true not only with the use of khÃ but with the use of all postpositions with sabh^u.

4. The word order in these statements may vary, depending on style and emphasis. For example,

HI^a (chOkirI) sabh khÃ vaddI (chOkirI) AHE. This (girl) is the biggest/ oldest (girl).	هيءَ (چوڪري) سڀ کان وڏي (چوڪري) آهي.
HI^a sabhanI (chOkirIun) khÃ vaddI (chOkirI) AHE. This is the biggest/oldest girl of all.	هيءَ سڀني (چوڪرين) کان وڏي (چوڪري) آهي.
HI^a (chOkirI) sabhanI (chOkirIun) khÃ vaddI AHE. This (girl) is the biggest/oldest of all (the girls).	هيءَ (چوڪري) سڀني (چوڪرين) کان وڏي آهي.

sabhanI chOkirIun khĀ hIᵃ vaddI AHE. Of all the girls, this (one) is the biggest/oldest.	سڀني چوڪرين کان هيءَ وڏي آهي.
sabhᵃ khĀ HIᵃ vaddI (chOkirI) AHE. This is the biggest/oldest (girl) of all.	سڀ کان هيءَ وڏي (چوڪري) آهي.

As shown by the words in ( ), it is often possible to omit the noun entirely, if the situation is clear. Notice those places where either sabhᵘ or sabhanI may be used, and those when one must use sabhanI.

5. Sometimes a situation may be so clear that it is possible to dispense with both khĀ and sabhᵘ, and to simply use the adjective alone to give the idea of comparison. The two examples above with mEvO (fruit) and bhAjjI (vegetable) illustrate this as do the following two examples:

kaHIRO chOkirO nanDhO AHE? Which boy is young (er)?	ڪهڙو چوڪرو ننڍو آهي؟
HIᵘ nanDhO AHE. This one is young (er).	هيءُ ننڍو آهي.

If many things are being compared – as with mEvO and bhajjI, above, - then one can express the superlative idea in the same way. For example,

kaHiRA sUfa miThA AHin? Which apples are (the) sweet (est)?	ڪهڙا صوف مٺا آهن؟
HI miThA AHin. These are (the) sweet (est).	هي مٺا آهن.

6. In the last two examples above there are two compound verbs – vApas karaR̃ᵘ and KarIdᵃ karaR̃ᵘ. Sindhi has many compound verbs which in English should be expressed by a single word. These are generally expressed by a noun, adjective, or adverb plus any of a certain number of common verbs. vApas means "back", "again", and with the verb karaR̃ᵘ means "to return, refund". KarId means "purchasing", "buying", and with karaR̃ᵘ means "to do purchasing", to buy". In section 11-E more compound verbs are introduced.

7. ajjᵘ kAlHᵘ means nowadays ("today-yesterday"). kAlHᵘ by itself will be introduced again in 13-F, and is also commonly pronounced kalHᵘ.

11-E   Compound verbs

chA naokarᵘ gudAmᵘ sAf karE thO? Is the servant cleaning the storeroom?	ڇا نوڪر گدام صاف ڪري ٿو؟
na, HU ArAm karE thO. No, he's resting.	نه، هو آرام ڪري ٿو.
chA, bOrci cĀHi tayAr karE thO? Is the cook preparing tea?	ڇا بورچي چانهه تيار ڪري ٿو؟
na, HU nimAzᵃ paRHE thO. No, he's praying.	نه، هو نماز پڙهي ٿو.

chA sabh^u naokar^a nimAz^a paRHan thA? Are all the servants praying?	ڇا سڀ نوڪر نماز پڙهن ٿا؟
mAlHI bAG^a mẼ kam karE thO. The gardener is working in the garden.	مالهي باغ ۾ ڪم ڪري ٿو.
maHarbAnI karE, asÃkhE madad ddEO. Please help us.	مهرباني ڪري، اسان ڪي مدد ڏيو.
asĨ sabh^u darIŨ aĨ darivAzA band karIŨ thA. We are closing all the doors and windows.	اسين سڀ دريون ۽ دروازا بند ڪريون ٿا.
HU DAkTar sAHib^a jE ghar^a khE rãg^u kan thA. They are painting the Doctor's house.	هو ڊاڪٽر صاحب جي گهر ڪي رنگ ڪن ٿا.
chOkirIŨ mũHinjE kamarE mẼ rAndⁱ kan thIŨ. The girls are playing in my room.	ڇوڪريون منهنجي ڪمري ۾ راند ڪن ٿيون.
chA tavHÃ jO vaddO bhA^u HaR̃E kam karE thO? Is your oldest brother working now?	ڇا توهان جو وڏو ڀاءُ هاڻي ڪم ڪري ٿو؟
na, HU HAR̃E kam na thO karE. No, he isn't working now.	نه، هو هاڻي ڪم نه ٿو ڪري.
HU rOzO rakhE thO. He is fasting.	هو روزو رکي ٿو.
sabh^u mÃR̃HU rOzO rakhan thA. All the people are fasting.	سڀ ماڻهو روزو رکن ٿا.

1. Each of the above sentences contains an example of a compound verb. They are as follows:

sAf (clean) +	karaR̃^u (to do, make)	=	to clean
ArAm^u (rest) +	" "	=	to rest
tayAr (ready) +	" "	=	to prepare
nimAz (prayer) +	paRHaR̃^u (to read)	=	to pray
madadⁱ (help) +	ddIaR̃^u (to give)	=	to help
band^u (close) +	karaR̃^u (to do make)	=	to close
rãg^u (color) +	" "	=	to paint, color
rAndⁱ (play) +	" "	=	to play
rOzO (fast) +	rakhaR̃^u (keep)	=	to (keep) fast

2. When a compound verb is put in the negative, the negative comes between the noun, adjective or adverb and the verb: IN other words, just before the verbal element of the compound. For example,

    darivAzO band na karⁱ   Don't close the door.

11-F The formation of the subjunctive tense

mÃ vaÑÃ I may go	asĪ vaÑU we may go	اسين وجون	مان وجان
tŪ vaÑĪ you may go	tavHĪ vaÑO you may go	توهين وجو	تون وجين
HU vaÑE He may go	HU vaÑan They may go	هو وجن	هو وجي
mÃ mOkilIÃ I may send	asĪ mOkilIŨ We may send	اسين موڪليون	مان موڪليان
tŪ mOkilĪ you may send	tavHĪ mOkilIO You may send	توهين موڪليو	تون موڪلين
HU mOkilE He may send	HU mOkilIan They may send	هو موڪلين	هو موڪلي

1. The subjunctive mood denotes an action or state as conceived but not yet as a fact. It can express a great variety of meanings – a wish, an inquiry. An exhortation, or a hypothetical, conditional or prospective event. Only some of these various uses are illustrated under 11-G.

2. As may be seen from the two examples given above, the subjunctive is formed exactly like the present tense <u>minus</u> the present tense indicator, the inflectable thO.

11-G Some uses of the subjunctive

jEkaddaHĪ DAkTar acE ta mŨ khE bbudhAyO. If the doctor should come (then) tell me.	جيڪڏهن ڊاڪٽر اچي تہ مون کي ٻڌايو.
jEkaddaHĪ mEvO KarAb HujE ta na khAᵘ. If the fruit is bad don't eat it.	جيڪڏهن ميوو خراب هجي تہ نہ کائو.
jekaddaHĪ pEsa mOkilIO ta mŨ khE bbudhAyO. If you should send money (then) tell me.	جيڪڏهن پيسا موڪليو تہ مون کي ٻڌايو.
SAyad mĪHũ pavE. Perhaps it may rain (rain may fall).	شايد مينهن پوي.
mumkin AHE ta HavA tEz laggE. It's possible that the wind may blow hard.	ممڪن آهي تہ هوا تيز لڳي.

Sayad asĨ ajj^u sakhar na vanŨ. Perhaps we won't go to Sukkur today.	شايد اسين اڄ سکر نہ وڃون.
mumkin AHE ta asÃjO pI^u ajj^u kam na karE. It's possible that our father may not work today.	ممکن آهي تہ اسان جو پيءُ اڄ کم نہ ڪري.
zarUrI AHE ta asĨ sindhI ggAlHAyŨ We must speak Sindhi (Lit.: It's necessary that….).	ضروري آهي تہ اسين سنڌي ڳالهايون.
zarUrI AHE ta subhA R̃E mÃ naokaran khE paghAr^a ddIÃ. Tomorrow I have to pay the servants. (Lit.: it is necessary that….).	ضروري آهي تہ سڀاڻي مان نوڪرن کي پگهار ڏيان.
zarUrI na AHE ta asĨ Huna zamindAr lAi kam karIŨ. We don't have to work for that landlord.	ضروري نہ آهي تہ اسين هن زميندار لاءِ کم ڪريون.
munAsib^u na AHE ta HU zAlŨ ddisan. It isn't proper that they see the women.	مناسب نہ آهي تہ هو زالون ڏسن.
chA mÃ cÃHĨ yA kAfI tayAr karIÃ? Should I prepare tea or coffee?	چا مان چانھہ يا ڪافي تيار ڪريان.
asĨ hunan sÃ HalŨ chA? Should we go with them?	اسين هنن سان هلون چا؟
asĨ kaHiRO sabaq^u paRHŨ? Which lesson should we read?	اسين ڪهڙو سبق پڙهون؟
chA AŨ tavHÃ khE madad ddIÃ? May I help you?	چا آءُ توهان کي مدد ڏيان؟
mÃ chA karIÃ? What may I do?	مان چا ڪريان؟
ijAzat AHE (ta mÃ va Ñ̃Ã)? Is there permission (that I go)?	اجازت آهي (تہ مان وڃان)؟
asĨ cAHIŨ thA ta tŨ subhA R̃E acĨ. We want you (lit.: that you might) to come tomorrow.	اسين چاهيون ٿا تہ تون سڀاڻي اچين.
mÃ na thO cAHIÃ ta tavHÃ khE taklIf ddIÃ. I don't want to bother you.	مان نہ ٿو چاهيان تہ توهان کي تڪليف ڏيان.
KudA karE ta HU salAmatI^a sÃ paHucan. May God grant that they arrive safely.	خدا ڪري تہ هو سلامتيءَ سان پهچن.

Sal KudA tavHÃ khE salAmat rakhE. May the Lord keep you safe.	شال خدا توهان کي سلامت رکي.

1. jEkaddaHĩ (if) is commonly used with the subjunctive although it may be used with other verb forms also. It normally introduces the first clause while ta (then), which can be omitted, introduces the second.

2. HujaR̃ᵘ (to be) is another form of HuaR̃ᵘ (to be), and the personal inflections of the subjunctive are attached to its root, Huj ͧ.

3. SAyad (perhaps, maybe) and the clause, mumkin AHE ta (It is possible that...) are interchangeable when followed by a subordinate clause using the subjunctive. Notice here that ta means "that". In other examples it has the meaning, "then". Even when not translated or expressed in English, it may not normally be omitted in Sindhi.

4. "To rain" is mĩHũ pavaR̃ᵘ, a compound verb which combines the noun mĩHũ (rain) with the verb pavaR̃ᵘ (to fall). This verb also has other meanings and uses which will be encountered later.

5. To ask permission to leave one says, ijAzat AHE? In such a context as leaving, ta mã vaÑã is understood. That is, "Is there permission that I may leave?" Theoretically any verb might be understood after it, asking permission to do this or that depending on the circumstances. It is used commonly as a formula to ask permission to leave after a visit, interview or meeting with someone. When used as a statement, ijAzat AHE, it means that the speaker is giving permission to the listener to leave, or asking him to leave.

6. The last two illustrations contain the phrase, KudA karE ta. To most Sindhi speakers, religion is a part of life, and they have no hesitancy in using the name of God, and attributing many commonplace occurrences in life to God's activity and will. Thus, while an English speaker is more likely to say, "I hope...", a Sindhi speaker will often put this as "God grant that..." (lit.; God do this or that...).

7. tEz is an adjective with various meanings. In the above context it means, "swift", but it carries the meanings also of "sharp", "pointed", "pungent", "hot", "fiery", "active", "smart".

8. laggaR̃ᵘ is a verb with many meanings. In the above context it means, "to blow". Some other meanings are, "to be applied to", "to be fixed", "to strike" and "to stick or adhere to".

11-H   Vocabulary for Lesson Eleven

ijAzatᵃ (f) permission	إِجازَتَ	ArAmᵘ karaR̃ᵘ to rest	آرامُ کَرَڻُ
ajjᵘ kAlHᵘ nowadays	أجُ کالهـ	araRahã eighteen	أَرَڙَهَن
ãmbᵘ (m) mango	أنبُ	KarIdᵃ karaR̃ᵘ to buy	خَرِيدَ کَرڻُ
uR̃avIHa nineteen	أُٺوِيهَ	rãgᵘ karaR̃ᵘ to paint, color	رَنگُ کَرَڻُ

basar^u (m) onion	بَصَرُ	rAndⁱ karaR̃u to play	رانڌِ کرڻ
band karaR̃u to close	بَندُ کَرَڻُ	rOzO rakhaR̃u to fast	روزو رَکڻُ
bhAjjI (f) vegetable	ڀاڄِي	zAl^a (f) woman, wife	زالَ
bbaI both	بَئِي	sabaq^u (m) lesson	سَبَقُ
ta that, then	تَ	subhAR̃E tomorrow	سُڀاڻي
taklIf^a trouble, difficulty, hardship	تَڪلِيفَ	sataraHã seventeen	سَتَرَهَن
tayAr karaR̃u to prepare, make ready	تيارُ کَرَڻُ	sastO cheap	سَستو
tEz, tikhO swift, sharp, hot	تيز، تِکو	salAmatI (f) safety	سَلامَتِي
paTATO (m) potato	پَٽاٽو	SAyadⁱ perhaps	شايَدِ
paghAr^a (f) pay, salary	پَگھارَ	sAf karaR̃u to clean	صاف کرڻ
paHucaR̃u (paHuc^u-) to arrive	پَهِچَڻُ (پَهَچُ)	zarUrI necessary	ضَرُورِي
jEkaddaHĩ if	جيڪَڏَهِن	pavaR̃u (pau-) to fall	پَوَڻُ
cAHaR̃u to want, wish	چاهَڻُ	sUf^u (m) apple	صُوفُ
cÃHi (f) tea	چانهِ	kam^u karaR̃u to work	ڪَمُ کَرَڻُ
KarAb bad	خَرابُ	gudAm^u (m) storeroom	گُدامُ
gadd^u together	گڏُ	maHÃgO expensive	مَهانگو
gajar^a (m) carrot	گَجَرَ	mĩHũ (m) rain	مِينهُن

laggaR̃u to blow, strike, adhere to	لَڳُڻ	vApas karaR̃u to return	واپَس ڪَرَڻُ
lAi for, on behalf of	لاءِ	vadhIkᵘ more	وَڌِيڪَ
nArāgI (f) orange	نَارَنگِي	vIHa twenty	وِيھَ
nimAz paRHaR̃u to pray	نِمَازَ پَڙَهَڻُ	HujaR̃u (Hujᵘ) to be	هُجَڻُ (هُجُ)
madadᵃ ddIaR̃u to help	مَدَدَ ڏِيَڻُ	HavA (f) air	هَوَا
mu'Af karaR̃u to forgive	مُعاف ڪَرَڻُ	yA or	يا
mumkin possible	مُمڪِن	miThO sweet	مِٺو
thudhO cold	ٿَڌو		

11-I Conversational Review

1.   Form complete sentences using each of the following phrases. The numbers in brackets are to be put into the oblique form.

Hinan (2) kursIun jE puThIÃ...............	هِنن ڪرسين جي پُٺيان
Hunan (4) chOkiran sÃ....	هُنن چوڪرن سان...............
(6) mÃR̃Hun jO kam	ماٺهن جو ڪم
(8) kamaran mẼ	ڪمرن ۾
(1) SISE mẼ	شيشي ۾
Hunan (9) mÃR̃Hun khE	هُنن ماٺهن ڪي
(3) mazUran khE	مزورن ڪي

Go through the exercise again changing the numbers to any of the other numbers you have learned thus far.

2. Notice the people and objects around you – chairs, tables, lamps, pictures, boys, girls, men, women, pencils, papers, magazines, etc. and talk about the comparative sizes of each. For example,

HI^a kursI hunan kursI^a khÃ vaddI AHE.	هي ڪرسي هن ڪرسيءَ کان وڏي آهي.
HI^a kursI sabhanI kursIan khÃ vaddI AHE.	هي ڪرسي سيني ڪرسين کان وڏي آهي.

3. Ask your teacher to act out each of the following actions and ask you, "mÃ chA thO karIÃ?" you should answer in the present tense.

Aram kara R̃^u, nimAz paRHa R̃^u	آرام ڪرڻ، نماز پڙھڻ
kam kara R̃^u, rãgu kara R̃^u, rAnd^i kara R̃^u,	ڪم ڪرڻ، رنگ ڪرڻ، راند ڪرڻ
rOzO rakha R̃^u, KarId^a kara R̃^u, vApas kara R̃^u	روزو رکڻ، خريد ڪرڻ، واپس ڪرڻ

For example,

Teacher: (lying down) mÃ chA thO karIÃ?	استاد: مان ڇا ٿو ڪريان؟
Student: tavHĨ ArAm karIO thA.	شاگرد: توهان آرام ڪريو ٿا.
Then, (lying down), mÃ bi ArAm karIÃ thO.	مان به آرام ڪريان ٿو.
HAR̃E asĨ bbaI ArAm karIŨ thA.	هاڻي اسين به آرام ڪريون ٿا.

4. Complete the following, using the subjunctive form of a verb in the first phrases and the imperative form in the second:

jEkaddaHĩ asĨ .... ta   جيڪڏهن اسين .... ته

.... tŨ .... تون .... ته

.... tavHĩ .... توهين .... ته

.... zAlŨ .... زالون .... ته

.... HI sabaq^u .... هي سبق .... ته

.... pÃR̃I .... پاڻي .... ته

.... chOkirA .... تہ چوکرا ....

.... iHA chOkirI .... تہ چوکري اها ....

.... mAlHI .... تہ مالهي ....

.... bOrcI .... تہ بورچي ....

5. Make at least five different statements beginning with each of these phrases:

mumkin AHE ta......, mumkin na AHE ta.....   ممكن آهي تہ......، ممكن نہ آهي تہ......

zarUrI AHE ta......, zarUrI na AHE ta.....   ضروري آهي تہ......، ضروري نہ آهي تہ...

SAyad ...., munAsib AHE ta......   شايد ....   مناسب آهي تہ..........

munAsib na AHE ta............   مناسب نہ آهي تہ ....

6. Ask your teacher for permission to do the following activities:

paRHaR̃^{u}, cĀHī tayAr karaR̃^{u},   پڙهڻ، چانھ ٽيار ڪرڻ

kat^u likhaR̃^{u}, darvAzO khOlaR̃^{u} خط لکڻ، دروازو کولڻ

darI band karaR̃^{u}, mAnI khAiR̃^{u} دري بند ڪرڻ، ماني کائڻ

kitAb^a mEz^a tE rakhaR̃^{u}, HalaR̃^{u} ڪتاب ميز تي رکڻ، هلڻ

You have by now acquired a vocabulary adequate for simple conversations both with your teacher and with other Sindhis. Plan to spend the first five to ten minutes of each hour with your teacher in conversation practice. You should also take advantage of every opportunity to talk with other Sindhis, using the vocabulary, and verb tenses you have been learning. Constant and regular usage will re-enforce the patterns of Sindhi that you are learning. If you have a problem getting a conversation started, prepare questions on different subjects as starters. It should be a habit by now to use proper greetings and leave-takings with your teacher and all other Sindhis. These are not optional in the Sindhi culture, but a necessary part of proper behavior.

11-J Introduction to the Sindhi Writing System- Part III

This final lesson in the writing system will include: (1) the four remaining letter groups, (2) the /hamzO/ as a special symbol used to mark the occurrence of two vowels without an intervening consonant, (3) various other diacritics that Sindhi employs, especially in words borrowed from Arabic and Persian, and (4) numerals.

Letter Group 7

This group includes ص /s/ and ض /z/. Letters of this group are connectors and have the following basis forms:

Initial	Medial	Final	Independent

Letters of this group are thus:

	/s/	/z/		
Initial:	ص	ض	sUf^u	صُوفُ
Medial:	ص	ض	mazbUt^u	مَضْبُوطُ
Final:	ص	ض	marIz^u	مَرِيضُ
Independent:	ص	ض	KAs^u	خاصُ

These letters are found only in loan words of Arabic origin.

Letter Group 8

This group includes ط /t/ and ظ /z/. They are connectors and have the following basic forms:

Initial	Medial	Final	Independent

Letters of this group are thus:

	/t/	/z/	Illustrations	
Initial			tOtO	طوطو
	ط	ظ		
Medial			nazarⁱ	نَظَرِ
	ط	ظ		
Final			Kat^u	خَطُ
	ط	ظ		
Independent			mazbUt^u	مَضْبُوطُ
	ط	ظ		

Letter Group 9

This group contains ع /'/ and غ /G/. Letters of this shape group are connectors and have the following basic forms:

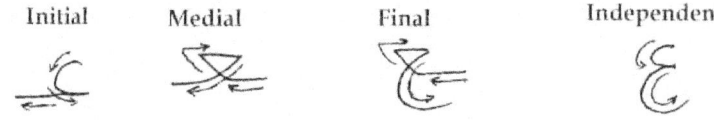

Letters of this group are thus:

	/'/	/G/	Illustrations:	
Initial:	عـ	غـ	'aorat[a]	عَوَرَتَ
Medial:	ـعـ	ـغـ	t'Allm[a]	تَعْلِيمَ
Final:	ـع	ـغ	jamau[a]	جَمَعَ
Independent:	ع	غ	bAg[u]	باغُ

As noted in Lesson one ع has no easily assignable phonemic value in Sindhi. It occurs only in very literary pronunciations of Arabic loan words. Sindhi speakers usually omit the pronunciation entirely. Various functions of this letter are:

(1) Initially, ع is like initial ا; that is, it has no effect on the following vowel and serves only as the "carrier" of the initial vowel.

For example,	'aorat[a]	umir[i]	Am[u]
	عورت	عِمِرِ	عامُ

(2) between vowels ع functions as a marker to separate two vowels which come together in a word.

For example,	jamA'it[a]	mu'Af[u]
	جَمَاعَتَ	مُعافُ

(3) after a consonant ع has no discernible phonemic representation when ordinarily pronounced.

For example,	mAna	inAm[u]
	مَنْعَ	اِنعامُ

(4) after a short vowel and before a consonant ع has the effect of lengthening the vowel. Listen to the sound of the vowel just before ع as your teacher pronounces:

For example,	ta'Allm[a]	mOjizO
	تَعلِيمَ	مِعجِزو

(5) At the end of a word following a consonant, ع is pronounced /A/.

For example,   jamA   daf'a

                    جَمَعَ   دَفَعَ

Letter Group 10

This group contains ڦ /ph/ ف /f/ and ق /q/. Letters of this shape are connectors and have the following basic forms:

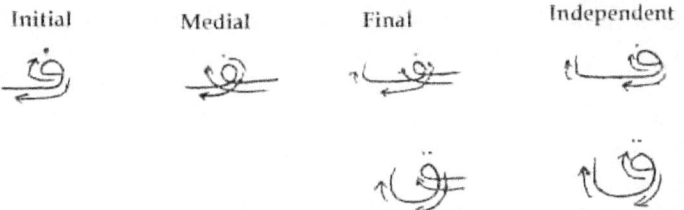

Letters of this group are thus:

	/ph/	/f/	/q/		Illustrations:
Initial:	ڦــ	فــ	قــ	phikO	ڦکو
Medial:	ـڦـ	ـفـ	ـقـ	lafazu	لَفظُ
Final:	ـڦ	ـف	ـق	kulfu	قلف
Independent:	ڦ	ف	ق	mUAfu	معاف

Medial ـفـ may sometimes be confused with medial ـغـ. The loop of the former should be rounded, however, while the latter is written with sharp corners and a flattened top.

For example: lifAfO   pEGAmu

                    لِفافو   پیغامُ

Final and independent forms of ڦ and ف differ from those of ق.

The final stroke of ڦ and ف should be longer and flatter, where as that of ق should be more round. However, initial and medial forms of these letters differ only in the number of dots.

/hamzO/

When within a word any syllable ends with a vowel (long or short) and the following syllable begins with one, the two vowels are separated by /hamzO/ ء. It serves the same purpose that a hyphen does in English, that is to separate two syllables.

In the initial and medial forms /hamzO/ must be written over a "carrier" which is the same basic shape as letter group 2. For example:

Initially: mAiTu   مائِثُ   AŨ   آئون

Medially: naŨ   نئون   SaI   شَيءِ

At the end of word, however, when it occurs with a final short vowel after a long vowel, it is written without the usual carrier.

Examples: jAi   bhAu   poi
                 جاءِ   ياءُ   پوءِ

Traditionally, /hamzO/ is counted as a letter of the Sindhi alphabet. It comes between هـ and ي.

/tanvin/ ً

There are two uses of this symbol in Sindhi.

(1) It occurs in loan words from Arabic as a double /zabar/ ً over alif/, thus, اً. In such words /alif/ becomes a "carrier" for /zabar/; that is, the /alif/ is not pronounced as /A/ but as /a/, and the doubling of the /zabar/ indicates that the word's final sound is the consonant /n/. Examples are:

            itafAqan   اتفاقاً   maslan   مثلاً   fOran   فَوْراً

(2) But a more common use of /tanvin/ in Sindhi is to indicate a shortened form (in writing, not in pronunciation) of some words ending in nasalized ‍ين /Ĩ/ and وُن /Ũ/.

For example: چيائين /cayA-Ĩ/ is written چياءً. آئون /AŨ/ is written آءً.

In these examples you will notice that the /zEr/ and the /pES/ are doubled and this indicates that in pronunciation, the final vowel is lengthened and nasalized.

/taSdId/ ّ

Occasionally you may see ّ /taSdId/ written over a consonant. Its purpose is to double or strengthen the consonant. However, in ordinary spoken Sindhi this is not noticeable.

Examples: قُوَّتَ   quvvata   أنَّ   unna   مُقَدَّسُ   muqaddasu

/jazm/ ْ

In Sindhi a consonant is usually followed by a vowel. In some Arabic loan words, however, two consonants may appear within a word without a vowel between them. For example, خشك /KuSk/. In this word the /S/ and the /k/ have no vowel between them as Sindhi words usually do. To indicate this /jazam/ may be written over the first consonant, thus

Other examples: maqdUru   maqsadu   Hikmata
                     مَقْدُورُ   مَقْصَدُ   حِكْمَتَ

Special /alif/

Final /A/ in certain Arabic loan words is written ىٰ, that is, a small /alif/ written on /yE/. It is relatively rare, but does occur in some common biblical words, such as,

مُوسىٰ /mUsA/ (Moses) and عِيسىٰ /'IsA/ (Jesus).

Numerals

The basic numerals in Sindhi are as follows:

English	Sindhi	
1	١	Hik^u
2	٢	bba
3	٣	TE
4	٤	cAr^i
5	٥	panj^a
6	٦	chaHa
7	٧	sat^a
8	٨	aTh^a
9	٩	nav^a
10	١٠	ddaHa

Sindhi numbers, unlike Sindhi words, are written from left to right as in English. Thus, 23 is written ٢٣ and 498 is written ٤٩٨.

Reading Drills

1. Letters of all new groups + /alif/:

صا ضا طا ظا غا قا فا قا

2. Letters of all new groups + /yE/:

صِي ضِي طِي ظِي غِي قِي فِي قِي

3. Letters of all new groups + /vAv/:

صُو ضُو طُو ظُو غُو قُو فُو قُو

4. Medial letters of all groups:

بَصَرُ لَغُزُ خَطا تَصْوِيرَ مَضْبُوطٌ طاقَتَ

نَظَرَ دُعا فَقِيرُ هَفْتو قاعِدو

5. Final letters of all groups:

حَوْضُ صُوفُ كُلَفُ حَقُ خَطُ

نَبضَ داغُ باغُ مَضْبُوطٌ لائِقُ

6. Mixed combinations of the new groups:

هِيءُ صُوفُ كاءُ ۔ هِيءُ صوفُ آهي.

طوطي تي ظلم نه كَرِ ۔ هُو طوطو آهي.

تَفاوَتُ فائدو ۔ هُو مائِثُ آهي.

هائو مَرضِي

LESSON TWELVE

12-A   Pronunciation Drill

1. Contrasting /O/ and /ao/   (58 / 50)   /اَو/ /او/

چوٽين چوڪري ڪي مَوَقعو مليو.
هن موسم ۾ موڪل ملڻ جو مَوَقعو نہ ملندو.
نَوَجوان چوڪرو اَوَزار، زور سان هَٽي تو.

2. Contrasting /b/ and /bh/   (7/10)   /ڀ/ /ب/

ياءُ هڪ ڀيرو پِٽَ تي ڀِيٽو.
ڀاڀي بہ بيمار آهي.
ٻاھر ايرندي ۾ ياءُ جو باغ برباد ڪيو.

12-B   Cardinal numbers by "ten"

10	١٠	ddaHa	ڏھ
20	٢٠	vIHa	ويھ
30	٣٠	TIHa	ٽيھ
40	٤٠	cAlIHa	چاليھ
50	٥٠	panjAHu	پنجاھ
60	٦٠	saThⁱ	سٺ
70	٧٠	satarⁱ	ستر
80	٨٠	asI	اسي
90	٩٠	navE	نوي
1,00	١٠٠	(Hik^u) saO	(ھڪ) سو
1,000	١,٠٠٠	(Hik^u) HazArⁱ	(ھڪ) ھزار

| 1,00,000 | ۱،۰۰،۰۰۰ | (Hik^u) lakh^u | (هڪ) لکُ |
| 100,00,000 | ۱۰۰،۰۰،۰۰۰ | (Hik^u) kirOr^u | (هڪ) ڪروڙ |

1. Note the different position of the commas in dividing up Sindhi numbers so that they can be clearly seen to be multiples or 100.

	Sindhi no.	Sindhi name	English name	English no.
100 x 10 =	1,000	(Hik^u) HazAr^u	one thousand	1,000
100 x 1,000=	1,00,000	(Hik^u) lakh^u	100 thousand	100,000
100 x 1,00,000=	100,00,000	(Hik^u) kirOR^u	10 million	10,000,000

2. If saO (hundred) and HazAr^u (thousand) are used alone they would mean "one hundred" and "one thousand" respectively. But it is common to use the number with them for emphasis or to avoid ambiguity.

12-C The formation of the present habitual tense

tarsaR̃^{u} root: tars(u)-plus -andO with the present tense of HuaR̃^{u} (to be)

mÃ tarsandO AHIÃ I wait	asĨ tarsandA AHIŨ We wait	اسين ترسندا آهيون	مان ترسندو آهيان
tŨ tarsandO AHĨ You wait	avHĨ tarsandA AHIO you wait	اوهين ترسندا آهيو	تون ترسندو آهين
HU tarsandO AHE He waits	HU tarsandA AHin They wait	هو ترسندا آهن.	هو ترسندو آهي

khOlaR̃^{u} root: khOl (i) – plus – IndO with the present tense of HuaR̃^{u} (to be)

mÃ khOlIndO AHIÃ I open	asĨ khOlIndA AHIŨ We open	اسين کوليندا آهيون	مان کوليندو آهيان
tŨ khOlIndO AHĨ You open	avHĨ khOlIndA AHIO You open	اوهين کوليندا آهيو	تون کوليندو آهين
HU khOlIndO AHE He opens	HU khOlIndA AHin They open	هو کوليندا آهن	هو کوليندو آهي

1. The present habitual tense is used to state action that <u>regularly</u> or <u>habitually</u> happens. It may be sometimes used for stating a general truth or an established fact, but more commonly the simple present tense is used in such cases.

2. This tense makes use of these two grammatical constructions:

(a) the imperfect participle which is formed by adding –andO to the root of verbs which end in /u/ and –IndO to the root of verbs which end in /i/. The imperfect participle indicates an action or state /condition not completed, finished (or "perfected") at the time described – although this aspect in some verb formations seems to be almost lost. The imperfect participle will appear in several other verb forms as well. It is inflectable according to the number and gender of the subject. For example, HUᵃ tarsandI AHE (she waits). HU (fem) tarsandIŨ AHin (they are waiting).

    (b)   The present tense forms of HUaR̃ᵘ appeared in Lesson 6-D. Here these forms of HuaR̃ᵘ are used as auxiliary or "helping" verbs. The same personal pronouns are used with this expanded verb form.

3.   A few of the common verbs have irregular imperfect participles:

Infinitive	Imperfect Participle		
vaÑaR̃ᵘ	vEndO	ویندو	وڃڻ
acaR̃ᵘ	IndO	ایندو	اچڻ
HuaR̃ᵘ	HUndO	ھوندو	ھئڻ
karaR̃ᵘ	kandO	ڪندو	ڪرڻ

12-D Statements, questions, and negatives in the present habitual tense

mūHinjO bhAu Har rOzᵘ HitE tarsandO AHE. My brother waits here every day.	منھنجو ڀاءُ ھر روز ھتي ترسندو آھي.
garamIᵃ jE maosam mẼ AŨ subuHᵃ jO darIŨ band kandO AHIÃ. In the hot season I close the windows in the morning.	گرميءَ جي موسم ۾ آءٌ صبح جو دريون بند ڪندو آھيان.
Sam jO darIŨ khOlIndO AHIÃ. In the evening I open the windows.	شام جو دريون کوليندو آھيان.
sIArE mẼ asĨ mAnI manjhandⁱ jO khAIndA AHIŨ aĩ cÃvarⁱ rAtⁱ jO. In the winter we eat bread at noon and rice at night.	سياري ۾ اسين ماني منجھند جو کائيندا آھيون ۽ چانور رات جو.
chA tŨ Hina gharᵃ mẼ raHandO AHĨ? Do you live in this house?	ڇا تون ھن گھر ۾ رھندو آھين؟
HU Har rOzᵘ aThᵃ kalAkᵃ kam kandA AHin. They work eight hours every day.	ھو ھر روز اٺ ڪلاڪ ڪم ڪندا آھن.
chA bOrcI Har rOzᵘ bAzAr vEndO AHE? Does the cook go to the bazaar every day?	ڇا بورچي ھر روز بازار ويندو آھي؟

Hina kilAsᵃ mẼ kEtrA SAgirdᵃ paRHandA AHin? How many students study in this class?	هن ڪلاس ۾ ڪيترا شاگرد پڙهندا آهن؟
Hina kilAsᵃ mẼ cAlIHᵃ SAgirdᵃ paRHandA AHin. Forty students study in this class.	هن ڪلاس ۾ چاليہ شاگرد پڙهندا آهن.
Hina kamarE mẼ kEru sumHandO AHE? Who sleeps in this room?	هن ڪمري ۾ ڪير سمهندو آهي؟
Hunan jŨ chOkarIŨ Hina kamarE mẼ sumHandIŨ AHin. Their girls sleep in this room.	هنن جون چوڪريون هن ڪمري ۾ سمهنديون آهن.
chA TapAlI HitE IndO AHE? Does the postman come here?	چا ٽپالي هتي ايندو آهي؟
HAO sAĨ. HU ddiHARI HitE IndO AHE. Yes, sir, he comes here.	هائو سائين، هو ڏهاڙي هتي ايندو آهي.
HU ddiHARI HikaRO sabaqu paRHandA AHin. They do (read) one lesson every day.	هو ڏهاڙي هڪڙو سبق پڙهندا آهن.
chA tavHĨ ddiHARI kOT paHarIndA AHIO? Do you wear a coat every day?	چا توهين ڏهاڙي ڪوٽ پهريندا آهيو؟
HAO sAĨ, mÃ ddiHArI kOT paHarIndO AHIÃ, parᵃ TOpI na paHarIndO AHIÃ. Yes, sir, I wear a coat every day, but I don't wear a hat.	هائو سائين مان ڏهاڙي ڪوٽ پهريندو آهيان پر ٽوپي نہ پهريندو آهيان.
chA sindhᵃ mẼ sArIun jI pOkhᵃ cag̃I thIndI AHE? Is there good cultivation of rice in Sindh?	چا سنڌ ۾ سارين جي پوک چڱي ٿيندي آهي؟
HAO, tamAm cag̃I thIndI AHE. Yes, it's very good.	هائو تمام چڱي ٿيندي آهي.
tavHĨ pāHinjA kapRA dhOIndA AHIO? Do you wash your own clothes?	توهين پنهنجا ڪپڙا ڌوئيندا آهيو؟

na, AŨ pāHinjA kapRA na dhOIndO AHIA. dhObI (Hunan khE) dhOIndO AHE. No, I don't wash my own clothes. The washerman washes them.	نہ، آءٌ پنهنجا ڪپڙا نہ ڌوئيندو آهيان. ڌوٻي (هنن کي) ڌوئيندو آهي.
aī HU pāHinjE Hat^a mẼ kapRan jI istrI kandO AHE. And he irons the clothes in his shop.	۽ هو پنهنجي هٽ ۾ ڪپڙن جي استري ڪندو آهي.
naokar jI zAl^a bbAr^a lAi ddĨHã mẼ TE dafA khIr^u garam kandI AHE. The servant's wife heats the milk for the baby three times a day.	نوڪر جي زال ٻار لاءِ ڏينهن ۾ ٽي دفعا کير گرم ڪندي آهي.
asĨ Har maHInE pāHinjI^a mA^u khE Kat^u likhandA AHIŨ. We write our mother a letter every month.	اسين هر مهيني پنهنجي ماءُ کي خط لکندا آهيون.
zamIndAr Har sAl^a naĩ gAddI KarId kandO AHE. The landlord buys a new car every year.	زميندار هر سال نئين گاڏي خريد ڪندو آهي.

1.   In each of the above examples the verb tense suggests that which happens regularly or habitually.

2.   To express "day" ddĨHũ is used. rOz^u also means "day", but it is usually used with a suffix or another word. For example, Har rOz^u means "daily", "every day". Thus there are three words which can convey the idea of "daily":   Har rOz^u, rOzAnO, and ddiHarI.

3.   garamI is a noun meaning "heat", "warmth". The adjective is garam. Both are common words, and it is very important to use them correctly since these words can also have a sexual connotation that should be avoided in speech. Animals may be garam (in heat), and people may be garam (angry, passionate), or have garamI (sexual passion; used also for venereal disease). In the summer months when you want to express the idea of feeling hot, you should say, mŨ khE garamI laggE thI. Literally this means, "To me heat is attached."

4.   subuH^u (morning), manjhand^i (noon), Sam (evening) and ddĨHũ (day) are like adverbs when used with jO and in such constructions mean "at", "by", or "in". For example, ddĨHã jO means "by day", "in the daytime". manjhand^i jO means "at noontime", and SAm jO "in the evening", etc.

5.   Note the difference between the two words given for "rice". sArI means "a grain of rice in the husk". It is also used to refer to fields of growing rice. cÃvar^u is white rice after it has been husked in the mill. Thus one eats cÃvar^a and grows sArIŨ. Both words are generally used in the plural.

6.   Notice that one usually says Har HaftE or Har maHinE. That is, HaftO (week) and maHinO (month) are used in the oblique because a postposition is understood.

7.   istrI means "a flat iron" (used for pressing clothes). With kara$\tilde{R}^u$ it forms a compound verb

meaning "to iron". However, if you state what is being ironed, you must use jI after the object. Thus, "to iron clothes" kapRan jI istrI karaR̃ᵘ. This is true of many compound verbs formed by combining a noun and a verb. Some may require khE after the object. For example, HU naokarᵃ khE Hukum kandO AHE. (He orders the servant.) Still others require no postposition to learn how each compound is used when it has an object. (2009 Note: this rule does not seem to be emphasized as it once was. Listen to what your teacher say and copy him/her. If in doubt, use the "jI".)

8. gAddI means "carriage", "vehicle", rEl gAddI means "train".

9. naÕ means "new" and is inflected in this way:

Singular

Nominative		Oblique	
Masculine	Feminine	Masculine	Feminine
naÕ kitAbᵘ	naĨ istrI	naẼ kitAbᵃ mẼ	naĨ istrIᵃ khE

Plural

| navÃ kitAbᵃ | nayŨ istrIŨ | navan kitAban mẼ | nayun istrIun khE |

10. garamIᵃ jI maosamᵃ means "hot season (weather)". The word for summer is unHArO. "Winter" is sIArO. One can also say thadhIᵃ jI maosamᵃ, meaning literally, "cold season". thadhI is a noun which means "cold", and thadhO is the adjective.

11. dafaO means "a time", "a turn". Notice how your informant pronounces it. This word and bhErO are synonymous. bhErO is the more common of the two.

12-E   The use of the vocative

aI chOkirI! HEddE acᵘ. O girl! Come here.	اي چوڪري! هيڏي اچ.
aI saHRIŨ! asĨ pardE mẼ raHŨ (woman speaker) O friends! Let's remain in purdah (veiled)	اي ساهڙيون! اسين پردي ۾ رهون.
aI chOkirIŨ! pāHinjE gharᵃ vaÑO. Girls, go home!	اي چوڪريون! پنهنجي گهر وڃو.
aRE bbacA! band karⁱ! Stop it, child.	اڙي ٻچا! بند ڪر!
mazUrᵃ! bAlTI HitE rakhᵘ. Laborer, put the bucket here.	مزور! بالٽي هتي رک.
E KudA, asÃ jI du'A bbudhᵘ. O God, hear our prayer.	اي خدا! اسان جي دعا ٻڌ.
E chOkirA tŨ chA thO karĨ? Boy, what are you doing?	اي چوڪرا تون ڇا ٿو ڪرين؟

chOkiraO! pāHinjO kam karIO. Boys! Mind your own business. (Lit. : do your own work).	چوڪرو! پنهنجا ڪم ڪريو.
E bhAurO, mūHinjI bbudhO. O brothers, listen to me.	اي ڀائرو، منهنجي ٻُڌو.
aRE bbArO! KabardAr thIO. Children! Be careful!	اڙي ٻارو! خبردار ٿيو.
E dOstO, asĪ KudA khE maÑŨ. (man speaker) O friends, Let us obey God.	اي دوستو، اسين خدا ڪي مڃون.
E bbacO, pāHinjan rAndIkan sÃ rAndⁱ karIO. O children, play with your own toys.	اي ٻچو، پنهنجن رانديڪن سان راند ڪريو.

1. Often in English we prefix "O" before the person (s) we are addressing. In Sindhi E (aI- feminine) is the normal equivalent of "O". aRE (aRI- feminine) may be used when calling those who are subordinate in age and status. The student should use the latter with care since they may imply an attitude of superiority or intimacy not intended.

2. When speak directly to someone, Sindhi has a special, or vocative, form for the person(s) being addressed.

   (a) The vocative of all feminine (singular and plural) is the same as their nominative, as illustrated in the first three examples.

   (b) The vocative of masculine nouns in the singular is the same as their nominative plural. This is illustrated in the next four examples above. KudA being irregular remains the same.

   (c) The vocative of masculine nouns in the plural is formed by adding –O to the nominative plural, as aI bhAurO (O brothers!) and aI dOstO (O friends). When the nominative plural ends in –A it is shortened to –a before the vocative ending. Thus, aI chOkaraO (O boys!).

3. One must be careful in Sindhi to use the word "friend" in the proper context. It is not culturally proper to use <u>any</u> word that suggests a friend of the opposite sex since one does not ordinarily mention such a "friend". To avoid the suggestion of improper intimacy the word dOstᵘ is used <u>by men of men friends</u>, while the word saHErI is used <u>by women of women friends.</u>

4. The word band means "closed". However, when used with karaR̃ᵘ in a compound verb, it may mean, "to stop doing something". See sentence four above.

12-F The word khapE (need, want) in impersonal constructions

tavHÃ khE chA khapE? What do you want?	توهان ڪي چا ڪپي؟
mŨ khE ggARHO qalamᵘ khapE. I want a red pen.	مون ڪي ڳاڙهو قلم ڪپي.

Huna chOkirI^a khE chA khapE? What does that girl need?	هن چوڪريءَ کي ڇا کپي؟
Huna khE Hik^a pEnsil^i khapE. She needs a pencil.	هن کي هڪ پينسل کپي.
SAgirdan khE chA khapE? What do the students need?	شاگردن کي ڇا کپي؟
mūHinjO KayAl AHE ta Hunan khE navÃ kitab^a khapan. I think (my idea is) that they need new books.	منھنجو خيال آھي تہ ھنن کي نوان ڪتاب کپن.
mAlHI^a khE kEtrA rupIA khapan? How many rupees does the gardener need?	ماليءَ کي ڪيترا رپيا کپن؟
Huna khE vIH^a rUpIA khapan. He needs twenty rupees.	هن کي ويھ رپيا کپن.
HI^a vAc^a purARĨ AHE aĨ cag̃I^a taraH^a na thI HalE. mŨ khE naĨ vAc khapE. This watch is old and doesn't run properly. I need a new watch.	ھي واچ پراڻي آھي ۽ چڱيءَ طرح نہ ٿي ھلي، مون کي نئين واچ کپي.
chA tavHÃ khE palang^u khapE? Do you need a bed?	ڇا توھان کي پلنگ کپي؟
Huna kamarE mẼ fAltU palang^u AHE. There's an extra bed in that room.	ھن ڪمري ۾ فالتو پلنگ آھي.
chA kãHin bbIE khE aKbAr khapE? Does anyone else need a newspaper?	ڇا ڪنھن ٻئي کي اخبار کپي؟
jI HA, mŨ khE aKbAr khapE. Yes, sir/ madam, I need a newspaper.	جي ھا، مون کي اخبار کپي.
chA tO khE vadhIk kAGaz khapE? Do you want more paper?	ڇا توکي وڌيڪ ڪاغذ کپي؟
na sAĨ, mŨ vat^i kAfI AHE. vadhIk na khapE. No sir, I have enough. I don't need (any) more.	نہ سائين، مون وٽ ڪافي آھي. وڌيڪ نہ کپي.

1. Although in English when we say, "I need....", the thing needed is the object of the

sentence, in Sindhi the same idea is commonly expressed impersonally as follows:

(a) the thing needed becomes the subject.

(b) the impersonal khapE (for either gender) is the verb. This is pluralized to khapan when the subject is plural.

(c) the person who needs (that is, the subject in English) becomes the indirect object, followed by khE.

So, in the example above, we have, literally, "To you what is wanted/needed?" "To me a red pen is wanted/needed."

2. taraH^a means "manner", "way" cag̃I^a taraH^a means "in a good way", "right", "well". A postposition is understood; therefore, the phrase is in the oblique.

3. Notice that the verb HalaR̃^{u} is used to mean "to run", "to function", as it relates to a watch.

4. jI HA is equivalent to HAO sAĨ. jI can mean both "sir" or "madam". It is simply a title of respect. HA is another form of HAO.

5. bbIO means "other", "else". For example, chA kāHin bbIE khE aKbAr khapE? (does anyone else need a newspaper?) mŨ khE bbIO kitAb^u khapE. (I need another book.)

6. kAFI means "enough". In some contexts it means "plenty". For example, mŨ khE kAfI AHE can mean, "I have enough." Or "I have plenty."

7. There is another word which may also be used to mean "need", "want". It is ghurjE. (plural: ghurjan). Like khapE, it is used in the same type of impersonal construction. You will hear both these forms used frequently. ghurjE will be treated more completely in a later lesson.

12-G   The use of ordinal numbers

HI^u asÃ jO paHarIÕ kitAb^u AHE. This is our first book.	هي اسان جو پهريون ڪتاب آهي.
Hunan jO bbIO puT^u iskUl na vEndO AHE. Their second son doesn't go to school.	هنن جو ٻيو پٽ اسڪول نه ويندو آهي.
HAR̃E TIÕ chOkirO vaÑE. Now the third boy may go.	هاڻي ٽيون چوڪرو وڃي.
HAR̃E TIẼ chOkirE jO bhErO (vArO) AHE. Now it's the third boy's turn.	هاڻي ٽئين چوڪري جو ڀيرو (وارو) آهي.
HIa ajj^u jI cOthĨ ciThI AHE. This is the fourth letter today.	هي اڄ جي چوٿين چٺي آهي.
panjÕ chOkirO kithE raHandO AHE? Where does the fifth boy live?	پنجون چوڪرو ڪٿي رهندو آهي؟
chA tavHÃjI chOkirI chaHẼ kilAs^a mẼ paRhandI AHE?	چا توهان جي چوڪري ڇهين ڪلاس ۾ پڙهندي آهي؟

Does your girl study in the sixth class?	پڙهندي آهي؟
HI^a ggAlHⁱ satẼ sabaq^a mẼ AHE. This thing is in the seventh lesson.	هي ڳالھ ستين سبق ۾ آهي.
aThÕ bAb^u paRHO. Read the eighth chapter.	اٺون باب پڙهو.
kEtrA chOkirA aThẼ kilAs^a mẼ paRHandA AHin? How many boys are studying in the eighth class?	ڪيترا ڇوڪرا اٺين ڪلاس ۾ پڙهندا آهن؟
HI^u nAÕ sabaq^u na AHE. asĨ ddaHÕ sabaq^u paRHandA AHIŨ. This isn't the ninth lesson. We are studying the tenth lesson.	هي نائون سبق نہ آهي. اسين ڏهون سبق پڙهندا آهيون.
naokar^u kāHin bbIE kamarE khE sAf karE thO. The servant is cleaning some other room.	نوڪر ڪنهن ٻئي ڪمري ڪي صاف ڪري ٿو.
mũHinjO KayAl AHE ta HU bbIan khE bi pEsa ddIndA AHin. I think that they give money to others also.	منهنجو خيال آهي تہ هو ٻين ڪي بہ پيسا ڏيندا آهن.
chA kO bi bbIO mAR̃HU AHE? Is there someone else?	چا ڪو بہ ٻيو ماڻهو آهي؟
na sAĨ, bbIO kO bi na AHE. No sir, no one else.	نہ سائين، ٻيو ڪو بہ نہ آهي.

1. The ordinals are formed by adding –Õ to the cardinal number. However, the first four and the ninth are irregular. Notice:

Cardinal	**Ordinal**		**Cardinal**	**Ordinal**	
Hik^u	paHarIÕ	پهريون	chaHa	chaHÕ	ڇهون
bba	bbIO	ٻيو	sat^a	satÕ	ستون
TE	TIÕ	ٽيون	aTh^a	aThÕ	اٺون
cArⁱ	cOthÕ	چوٿون	nava	nAÕ	نائون
panj^a	panjÕ	پنجون	ddaHa	ddaHÕ	ڏهون

2. Ending in -Õ, ordinals must inflect to –Ĩ to form the feminine. For example,

    bbAraHÕ kitAb^u bbAraHĨ pEnsil^i
    the twelfth book   the twelth pencil

    pandaraHÕ kitab^u pandaraHĨ pensil^i
    the fifteenth book   the fifteenth pencil

    TIÕ kitAb^u TĨ pEncil^i
    The third book   the third pencil

They must also inflect to form the oblique. Remember that ordinals are numerical adjectives and inflect like other adjectives ending in -Õ.

    bbAraHẼ kitAb^a mẼ   bbAraHI^a chOkirI^a khE
    in the 12th book   to the 12th girl

3. Notice that three words may be used for "time", "turn". bhErO, vArO, and dafaO all mean the same in this context.

4. Both kat^u and ciThI can be used to mean "letter". However, ciThI is generally used to mean a short note, usually sent by hand, not in the mail.

5. The word bbIO is used to mean either "second", as an ordinal number, or to mean, "other", "else". The context tells which is the meaning intended. Notice that this is the only ordinal number that is not nasalized.

12-H Vocabulary for Lesson Twelve

istrI karaR̃^{u} to iron	اِستري کرڻُ	dafaO (m) time, turn	دَفَعو
asI eighty	اَسي	dost^u (m) friend	دوستُ
UnHArO (m) summer	اُونھارو	ddĨHũ (m) day	ڏِينھُن
bhErO (m) time, turn	ڀيرو	ddiHARI daily	ڏِهاڙي
bbIO other, second	ٻيو	rAt^i (f) night	راتِ

thIaR̃u (thIu-) to be, to become	ٽِيڻ (ٿِيُ)	rAndikO (m) toy	رانڊيڪو
TIHa thirty	ٽِيهَ	rOzu (m) day	روزُ
TIÕ third	ٽِيون	rOzAnO daily	روزانو
parAR̃O old	پراڙو	sArI (f) rice (in husk)	ساري
panjaHu fifty	پَنجاهُ	satari seventy	سَتَرِ
pOkha (f) cultivation	پوکَ	saThi sixty	سَٺِ
paHaraR̃u (paHaru-) to wear	پَهَرَڻُ	saO (m) hundred	سَو
paHarIÕ first	پَهَرِيون	sAHERI (f) friend	ساهيڙي
cÃvara (m.pl) rice (husked)	چانورَ	sumHaR̃u to sleep	سمهڻ
cAlIHa forty	چاليهَ	sIArO (m) winter	سِيارو
ciThI (f) letter, note	چِٺي	SAma (f) evening	شام
caOthÕ fourth	چَوٿون	subuHu (m) morning	صُبُحُ
KabardAr careful	خَبَردار	kapaHa (f) cotton	ڪَپَهَ
kirOru 10 million	ڪِروڙُ	maHInO (m) month	مَهِينو
khAiR̃u to eat	کائڻ	naram soft	نَرَم
gAddI (f) carriage, car, vehicle	گاڏِي	navE ninety	نَوِي
gAhu grass	گاهُ	naÕ new	نَئون
garam	گَرَم	vArO (m)	وارو

warm, hot		turn, time	
garam karaR̃ᵘ to heat	گَرَمُ ڪَرَڻُ	HaftO (m) week	هَفتو
garamI (f) heat	گَرَمِي	HazArᵘ (m) thousand	هَزارُ
lakhᵘ (m) 100,000	لَکُ	Harⁱ every	هَرِ
manjhandⁱ (f) noon	مَنجَهندِ	taraHa (f) manner, way	طَرَحَ
maosamᵃ (f) season, weather	مَوسَمَ		

12-I Conversational Review

1. Use the following phrases to answer the question given below:

Huna jO chOkirO, Hunan jI chOkirI   هن جو چوڪرو، هنن جي چوڪري

tavHã jO mAlHI, asÃ jO TapAlI,   توهان جو مالهي، اسان جو ٽپالي

cOddaHã SAgirdᵃ, dhObI, ustAdᵃ,   چوڏهن شاگرد، ڌوٻي، استاد

mũHinjO bhAᵘ, tũHinjI bhER̃ᵘ,   منهنجو ڀاءُ، تنهنجي ڀيڻ

bOrcIᵃ jA bbArᵃ, DAkTar sAHib,   بورچي جا ٻار، ڊاڪٽر صاحب

uHE TE mAR̃HU, DAkTarIAR̃I,   اهي تي ماڻهو، ڊاڪٽرياڻي

Teacher: Har rOz bAzAr ddÃHÃ kErᵘ vEndO AHE?	استاد: هر روز بازار ڏانهن ڪير ويندو آهي؟
Student: Har rOz _____	شاگرد: هر روز ....

2. Use the cardinal number up to 100, by tens, to answer the question below:

Teacher: TavHĨ ddiHARI kEtrIŨ ciThIŨ likhandA AHIO?	استاد: توهين ڏهاڙي ڪيتريون چنيون لکندا آهيو؟
Student: ddiHARI AŨ _____ ciThIŨ	شاگرد: ڏهاڙي آءُ .... چنيون لکندو

likhandO AHIÃ.	آهيان.

Go through the exercise a second time using "kitAb^a paRHAR̃^{u}".

3. Carry on a conversation with your teacher, talking about the things you generally do every day, using the verbs learned thus far. Include questions as to what he does, and comments on things that someone else does everyday. (For example, your spouse, child, servant, friend.) If appropriate, include the time of day such as, subuH^a jO, manjhand^i jO, SAm jO, rAt^i jO.

4. Converse with your teacher about the season of the year. Is it hot, cold, rainy? Do you go to Quetta or Murree? Do you wear a coat? What do you eat in this season?

5. Practice using the vocative form to tell the following people to "Come here", or "Go there", using the appropriate form for each.

mAlHI, bOrcI, DAkTar, sAĨ, chOkirO,	مالهي، بورچي، ڊاکتر، سائين، چوکرو
chOkirA, chOkirI, bbacA, mAR̃HU (pl)	چوکرا، چوڪري، ٻچو، ماڇهو،
naokar^u, bhaur^a, dOst^a.	نوڪرُ، ڀائرَ، دوستَ

6. Place some common objects on the table. For example, rupees, books, pencils, sheets of paper, etc. Tell your teacher that you want a particular item or items. For example,

Student: mŨ khE pEnsilIŨ khapan.	شاگرد: مون کي پينسلون کپن.
Teacher: tavHÃ khE kEtrIŨ pEnsilIŨ khapan?	استاد: توهان کي ڪيتريون پينسلون کپن؟
Student: mŨ khE TE khapan.	شاگرد: مون کي ٽي کپن.

7. Line up the objects on the table so there will be a first, second, third, etc. Then carry on the exercise in this way:

Student: mŨ khE Hik^u kitAb^u khapE.	شاگرد: مون کي هڪ ڪتاب کپي.
Teacher: tavHÃ khE kaHiRO kitAb^u khapE?	استاد: توهان کي ڪهڙو ڪتاب کپي؟

Student: mŨ khE caOthÕ kitAb^u khapE.	شاگرد: مون کي چوٽون کتابُ کپي.

8. Change each of the following verbs which are now in the present tense, to the present habitual tense, keeping the person, number, and gender the same. The teacher should call out the forms below, and the student reply with the new forms. For example,

Teacher: AŨ acÃ thO/thI.	استاد: آءٌ اچان ٿو/ ٿي.
Student: AŨ IndO/ I AHIÃ.	شاگرد: آءٌ ايندو/ ي آهيان.
chA tŨ ArAm karI thO?	چا تون آرام کرين ٿو؟
HU vaÑE thO.	ھو وڃي ٿو.
asĨ kam karIŨ thA.	اسين کم کريون ٿا.
tavHĨ chA thA karIO?	توهين چا ٿا کريو؟
HU^a Kat^a likhE thI.	ھوءَ خط لکي ٿي.
asĨ paRHŨ thIŨ.	اسين پڙھون ٿيون.
mÃ Huna khE ddisÃ thI/ thO.	مان ھن کي ڏسان ٿي / ٿو.
chA tŨ pEsA ddiĨ thO?	چا تون پيسا ڏين ٿو؟
HU sumHE thO.	ھو سمھي ٿو.
chA tŨ mEvO khAĨ thO?	چا تون ميوو کائين ٿو؟
asĨ Huna jI bbudhŨ thA.	اسين ھن جي ٻڌون ٿا.
chA naokar^u kam karE thO?	چا نوکر کم کري ٿو؟

LESSON THIRTEEN

13-A   Pronunciation Drill

1. Contrasting /U/ and /u/   (62/60)   / اُوْ /   / ءُ /

کُئو ءِ کلف کُوھ مِ کري پيا.
اونھاري مِ استاد مري شھر وڃي تو.
تنبوءَ مِ کلف ءِ کئو آھن.

2. Contrasting /g/ and /gh/   (22/26)   / گھ /   / گ /

گھوڙي تي گورو ويٺو آھي.
پاڳل کي پگھار نہ ڏيو.
گھٽا گھوڙا گاھ پيا کائين.

13-B   Cardinal numbers by "five"

5 ۵	panj[a]	پنج
15 ۱۵	pandaraHã	پندرھن
25 ۲۵	panjavIH[a]	پنجويھ
35 ۳۵	panjaTIH[a]	پنجتيھ
45 ۴۵	panjEtAlIH[a]	پنجيتاليھ
55 ۵۵	panjavanjAH[u]	پنجونجاھ
65 ۶۵	panjaHaTh[i]	پنجھٺ
75 ۷۵	panjaHatar[i]	پنجھتر
85 ۸۵	panjAsI	پنجاسي
95 ۹۵	panjAnavE	پنجانوي
105 ۱۰۵	Hik saO panj[a]	ھڪ سو پنج

1. It will be noticed that, beginning with 25, there is a consistent pattern when counting by "fives". 25 is panj^a (5) plus vIH^a (2), and 35 is panj^a (5) plus TIH^a (30, and so on. Notice however, that slight changes take place in certain combinations with panj^a. panjaHaTh^i, not panjasaTh^i. panjaHatar^i, <u>not</u> panjasatar^i. Notice that in 85, the short /a/ of /asI / is lengthened to become panjAsI.

2. While in English, one would say, "one hundred and five", in Sindhi, "and" is not used in such combinations. Thus in Sindhi you would say simply, Hik sao panja (one hundred five).

13-C Asking the cost of something

Hina jI qImat chA AHE? What's the price of this?	هن جي قيمت ڇا آهي؟
Hina kursI^a jI qImat chA AHE? How much (what's the price of) is this chair?	هن ڪرسيءَ جي قيمت ڇا آهي؟
Hina jI qImat vIH^a rupayA AHE. It's price is Rs. 20.	هن جي قيمت ويھ رپيا آهي.
HI^a kursI ddADhI maHÃgI AHE. This chair is very expensive.	هيءَ ڪرسي ڏاڍي مهانگي آهي.
ajj^u khanD^a jO agh^u chA AHE? What's the rate of sugar today?	اڄ کنڊ جو اگھ ڇا آهي؟
sAĨ, ajj^u kalh^a tamAm qImtI AHE; bba saO rupaE maR̃^{u}. Sir, it's very expensive nowadays Rs. 200 per maund.	سائين، اڄ ڪلھ تمام قيمتي آهي، ٻہ سو رپئي مڻ.
kAThI^a jO agh^u chA AHE? What's the rate of wood?	ڪاٺيءَ جو اگھ ڇا آهي؟
covIHẼ rupaẼ maR̃^{u}. Rs. 24 per maund.	چوويھين رپئي مڻ.
HI sastI na AHE! This isn't cheap!	هي سستي نہ آهي!
basar^a ghaR̃E kilO AHin? How much are onions per kilogram?	بصر گھٽي ڪلو آهن؟
bbI rupaẼ kilO AHin. Rs. 2 per kilo.	ٻي رپئي ڪلو آهن.
paTATA panj^a kilA ghaR̃E AHin? How much are five kilograms of potatoes?	پٽاٽا پنج ڪِلا گھٽي آهن؟

TI rupaẼ kilO AHin. ajj^u sastA AHin. Rs. 3 per kilo. Today they're cheap.	ٽي رپئي ڪلو آهن. اڄ سستا آهن.
sUf^a ghaR̃E kilO AHin? How much are apples per kilo?	صوف گهٽي ڪلو آهن؟
chaHẼ rupaẼ kilO AHin. Rs. 6 per kilo.	ڇھين رپئي ڪلو آهن.
ajj^u maTar^a ghaR̃E pAu AHin? How much are peas per quarter kilo today?	اڄ مٽر گهٽي پاءُ آهن؟
caẼ AnE pAu, yAnE panjavIHẼ pAsE AHin. Four annas per pao, that is 25 pAsa.	چئين آني پاءُ، يعني پنجويھين پيسي آهن.
HI^u kapRO ghaR̃E vAl^u AHE? How much is this cloth per yard?	هي ڪپڙو گهٽي وال آهي؟
ajj^u kalH^a vAl^u na thO HalE. asĨ mITar istimAl kandA AHIŨ. Nowadays the yard doesn't "go". We use the meter.	اڄ ڪلھ وال نہ ٿو هلي. اسين ميٽر استعمال ڪندا آهيون.
mITar jI qImat chA AHE? What's the price per meter?	ميٽر جي قيمت ڇا آهي؟
coddaHẼ rupaẼ mITar AHE. Rs. 14 per meter.	چوڏھين رپئي ميٽر آهي.

1. As the examples above show, there are a number of ways to ask the price of something in Sindhi. Above only three of the more common ways are illustrated. You will become familiar with others as you shop in the bazaar. The three forms illustrated above are:

   (a) with the use of qImat. This is used when referring to the price of something which is a separate or single entity, such as a chair, table, rug, book, etc. Thus,

   Hina kitAb^a jI qImat chA AHE?   What is the price of this book?

   Hina jI qImat bba rupayA AHE.   It's price is Rs. 2.

   (b) with the use of agh^u. In contrast to qImat, you are not asking the price, but the <u>rate</u> of something when you use agh^u. This word is used for items sold by the <u>unit</u>, rather than as separate items. This may be by quantity, weight or whatever. Thus,

   khanD^a jO agh^u chA AHE?   What's the rate of sugar?

   kAThI^a jO agh^u chA AHE?   What's the rate of wood?

   (c) with the use of ghaR̃E. When mentioning the unit (such as pao, kilo, maund) in your question, ghaR̃O is used <u>in the oblique</u> because some postposition is understood, probably mẼ or tE. For example,

   basar^a ghaR̃E kilO AHin?   How much are onions per kilo?

kAThI ghaR̃E maR̃ᵘ AHE?	How much is wood per maund?

2. In answering a question such as sUfᵃ ghaR̃E kilO AHin? (How much are apples per kilo?), you simply replace the ghaR̃E with the price per kilogram. Like ghaR̃E, the price quotation must be in the oblique since a postposition is understood after it. Thus,

caẼ rupaẼ kilO.	Rs. 4 per kilogram.

3. When stating the price per unit, the numbers from 2 to 48 take on a special oblique form. The special oblique forms of the ordinal numbers two, three, and four are irregular, as in the following illustrations:

bbI rupaẼ pAu	at Rs. 2 a pao
TI rupaẼ kilO	at Rs. 3 a kilogram
caẼ rupaẼ maR̃ᵘ	at Rs. 4 a maund.

The special oblique form of ordinal numbers from 5 to 48 attaches -Ẽ to the number. For example,

panjẼ rupaẼ pAu	at Rs. 5 per pao
aThẼ rupaẼ kilO	at Rs. 8 per kilogram
TIHẼ rupaẼ maR̃ᵘ	at Rs. 30 per maund

4. In this lesson another monetary unit is introduced – the paiso. Nowadays Pakistan has 100 paisas to the rupee, having done away with the old system of sixteen annas (AnA) to the rupee and four paisa (pAsa) to the anna. However, many people still use the anna equivalent for 25 paisa (cAr AnA), 50 paisa, (aTh AnA), and 75 paisa (bbArhᵃ AnA).

Pakistan is also converting to the metric system of weights and measures. Thus, units of measurement and weight are changing. vAIᵘ (yard) is being replaced by mITarᵘ (meter), sErᵘ (2.075 lbs) by kilo (kilogram = 2.2 lbs). pAu (pao), formerly used to mean one-quarter of a seer, is now used for one-quarter of a kilo. maR̃ᵘ which used to be 40 seer is now 40 kilograms.

In liquid measure, liters have replaced gallons in buying petrol, but for other liquids such as milk, the sErᵘ (32 oz. liquid) is still commonly used in many places.

5. The monetary units pAsẼ and rupaẼ are in the singular, <u>not plural</u>, oblique form in such constructions having to do with unit price quotations. And normally the final –E of the oblique singular is nasalized in agreement with the preceding numerical form. Thus,

aThẼ rupaẼ kilO	at Rs. 8 per kilogram

6. For price quotations per unit above the number 48 the regular cardinal form of the number is used with the oblique <u>unnasalized</u> form of the monetary unit. Thus,

panjAHᵃ rupaE kilO	at Rs. 50 per kilogram
bba saO rupaE maR̃ᵘ	at Rs. 200 a maund

7. Notice that the unit of measure is in the nominative, and is usually in the singular because normally the rate for <u>one</u> (kilo, maund, etc.) is asked for. Thus, TI rupaẼ kilO (at 3 rupees a kilogram).

However, in the example panjᵃ kilA paTATA ghaR̃E AHin (How much are 5 kilos of potatoes?), the nominative plural must be used. In this case we are not asking the rate per kilogram, but the price for 5 kilograms.

8. Both maHÃgO and qImtI mean "expensive", "dear", "costly". However, maHÃgO is inflectable according to gender and number and qImtI is not. sastO is an inflectable adjective meaning "cheap".

9. ddADhO, like tamAm, may be used to mean "very", but unlike tamAm it is inflectable according to gender and number.

10. ajj^u kAlH^a (literally, "today yesterday") has the meaning of "nowadays". kAlH^a means "yesterday" when used alone.

11. In this lesson you have used these units of weight:

> pAu – pao = 1/4 kilogram,   .54 lbs, or 8 oz. liquid measure
>
> kilO – kilogram = 2.2 lbs.
>
> sEr^u – formerly, 2.957 lbs dry measure; 32 oz. or 1 qt. liquid measure
>
> maR̃^{u} - maund = 40 kilograms.

13-D   Fractions

Sindhi (transliteration)	Sindhi (script)
adh^u sEr^u khIr^u qAfI na AHE. One pint of milk isn't enough.	اڌ سير کير ڪافي نہ آهي.
mŨ khE ddEDh^u sEru ddE. Give me 1 ½ quarts.	مون کي ڏيڍ سير ڏي.
mŨ khE adh^u mAnI ddEO. Give me half a loaf.	مون کي اڌ ماني ڏيو.
aTkal ddEdh^u kalAk^u mŨ lAi tarsO. Wait for me about 1 ½ hours.	اتڪل ڏيڍ ڪلاڪ مون لاءِ ترسو.
aDhAI kilA vaddO gOSt^u vaTh^u. Get 2 ½ kilos of beef.	اڍائي ڪِلا وڏو گوشت وٺ.
aDhAI kilA nanDhO gOSt^u bi AR̃i. Bring 2 ½ kilos of mutton also.	اڍائي ڪِلا ننڍو گوشت بہ آڻ.
na, nanDhO gOSt^u qImtI AHE. ruggO pOR̃^{a} bba kilA AR̃i. No, mutton is expensive. Bring only 1 ¾ kilo.	نہ، ننڍو گوشت قيمتي آهي. رڳو پوڻا بہ ڪِلا آڻ.
aDhAI mITar mūHinjE kam lAi qAfI na AHin. 2 ½ meters isn't enough for my use.	اڍائي ميٽر منهنجي ڪم لاءِ ڪافي نہ آهن.
mŨ khE sADhA TE mITar ddEO. Give me three and a half meters.	مون کي ساڍا ٽي ميٽر ڏيو.
ghaR̃E mITar AHE? What's the price per meter?	گھٽي ميٽر آهي؟

bEgam, sADhE bbAraHẼ rupaẼ AHE. Madam, it's 12.50 a meter.	بيگم، ساڍي ٻارهين رپئي آهي.
maHarbAnI karE sADhE yAraHẼ rupaẼ mITar ddEO. Please give it for 11.50 a meter.	مهرباني ڪري ساڍي يارهين رپئي ميٽر ڏيو.
pORẼ bbAraHẼ rupaẼ vaThO. Take it for 11.75.	پوٽي ٻارهين رپئي وٺو.
ruggO thorO ghaT AHE. That's only a little less.	رڳو ٿورو گهٽ آهي.
tavHĨ ruggO munE rupaẼ jI ra'Ayat karIO thA. You are only giving 75 pAsa concession (discount).	توهين رڳو مني رپئي جي رعايت ڪريو ٿا.
bEgam, munE rupaẼ jI ri'Ayat cagĨI AHE. Madam, .75 concession is good.	بيگم، مني رپئي جي رعايت چڱي آهي.
bbiyan HaTan mẼ mITar jI qImat savA tEraHã rupayA AHE. In other shops its price is 13.25 a meter.	ٻين هٽن ۾ ميٽر جي قيمت سوا تيرهن رپيا آهي.
savA pAu gIHᵘ ddEO. Give me 1 ¼ pao of cooking oil.	سوا پاءُ گيهه ڏيو.
tavHĨ zIAdaHᵃ ddEO thA. You're giving me too much.	توهين زياده ڏيو ٿا.
savA pAu qAfI AHE. na vadhIkᵘ, na ghaTⁱ. 1 ¼ pao is enough. Not more, not less.	سوا پاءُ ڪافي آهي. نه وڌيڪ، نه گهٽ.
pUrO savA Hik pAu. Exactly 1 ¼ pao.	پورو سوا هڪ پاءُ.
mazUr, HI sADhA panjᵃ maR̃ᵃ kAThI na AHE. Laborer, this isn't 5 ½ maunds of wood.	مزور، هي ساڍا پنج مڻ ڪاٺي نه آهي.
ddisᵘ, ruggO pORA panjᵃ maR̃ᵃ AHin. Look, it's only 4 and ¾ of a maund.	ڏس، رڳو پوٽا پنج مڻ آهي.
kujh vadhIK ddE. Give me some more.	ڪجهه وڌيڪ ڏي.
HAR̃E tŨ savA chaHᵃ maR̃ᵃ ddĨ thO. Now you are giving 6 ¼ maunds.	هاڻي تون سوا ڇهه مڻ ڏئين ٿو.

HI zIAdaH^a AHE. pUrO munO maR̃^u zIAdaH^a. that's too much. It's exactly ¾ of a maund too much.	هي زياده آهي، پورو مڻو مَٽُ زياده.
Hin^a kilAs^a mẼ savA saO SAgird^a AHin. There are 125 students in this class.	هن ڪلاس ۾ سوا سو شاگرد آهن.
bbIE kilAs^a mẼ ddEDh^u saO AHin. In the other class there are 150.	ٻئي ڪلاس ۾ ڏيڍ سو آهن.
mŨ khE Hik^u kilO khanD^u ddEO. Give me a kilo of sugar.	مون کي هڪ ڪلو کنڊ ڏيو.
sAĨ mŨ khE afsOs AHE. ruggO munO kilO bAqI AHE. Sir, I'm sorry. There's only ¾ of a kilo left.	سائين مون کي افسوس آهي. رڳو مڻو ڪلو باقي آهي.
cag̃O, munE kilE jI qImat chA AHE? All right, how much is ¾ of a kilo?	چڱو مڻي ڪلي جي قيمت ڇا آهي؟
pOR̃A panj^a rupayA, saĨ. Rs. 4.75, sir.	پوڻا پنج رپيا، سائين.

1. To express "half of (a whole)", use adh^u. It is not used before numbers, but just before nouns that express a whole. Thus, adh^u kalAk^u (½ hour), adh^u kilO (½ a kilogram), adh^u vAl^u (½ yard).

2. ddEDh^u is used to express "one and a half". For example, ddEDh^u kilO, (1½ kilos), ddEDh^u kalAk^u, (1½ hours), ddEDh^u mITar^u (yards). Note, that while in English we treat these fractions of one as plural, they are treated as singular in Sindhi.

3. aDhAI is used to express "two and a half". For example, aDhAI kalAk^a (2 ½ hours), aDhAI sEr^a (2 ½ quarts).

4. sADhA is used with numbers above two to express "… and a half". For example,

    sADhA cArⁱ kalAk^a   four and a half hours

    sADhA panj^a kilA   five and a half kilos

    sADhA chaH^a vAl^a   six and a half yards

When used with numbers qualifying nouns is the oblique it is inflected to become sADhE. For example,

    sADhE satẼ rupaẼ   at Rs. 7.50

5. To express a quarter of anything use pAu. Like adh^u it is not used with numbers but with nouns, pAu vAl^u (¼ yard), sEru jO pAu (¼ of a quarter). But pAu is often used alone, with the unit understood, as, Hik^u pAu ddEO. (Give one pao).

6. To express "three quarters" (of a whole) use munO. This is inflectable adjective used to qualify nouns. for example,

> munO kilO   three-fourths of a kilo.
>
> munE kilAka mẼ   in three quarters of an hour.

7. To express "… and a quarter", use savA which means "a quarter more". Like sADhA it is generally used with numbers. For example, savA bbAraHā sE^{ra} (12 ¼ quarts). But unlike sADhA it is not inflectable. Thus, savA caẼ rupaẼ (at Rs. 4.25). It may sometimes be used without a number, if one is implied or understood. Thus savA kilo (1 ¼ kilo).

8. To express "… and three quarters", use pOR̃A which means "a quarter LESS". It is used with numbers, but you must remember that it is a quarter less than the number used. For example, pOR̃A nao (eight and three quarters), pOR̃A cAri mITar^a (three and three quarters of a yard). Like sADhA it is inflectable when used with numbers qualifying nouns in the oblique. Thus, khanD^u pOR̃E chaHẼ rUpaẼ kilo AHE. (Sugar is Rs. 5.75 a kilo).

9. The English word "of" used before the noun which indicates what is being measured is omitted in Sindhi. Thus, Hik^u gilAs pAR̃I (one glass of water), pOR̃A TE kilA khanD^u (two and three-fourths kilos of sugar).

10. qAfI means "enough", and it can have the meaning of "plenty". For example, Huna khE sandas khIsE mẼ qAfI pEsa AHin. (He has plenty of money in his pocket.)

11. Other adverbs introduced in these examples are:

> zIAdaH^a too much, very much
>
> aTkal   about, almost, approximately
>
> bAqI   remaining, left

12. Notice the expression vaddO gOSt^u meaning "beef". This includes both cow and buffalo meat. nanDhO gOSt^u can mean either lamb or mutton.

13. pUrO means "whole", "complete". It also carries the meaning of "finished" or "fulfilled".

14. "To give a concession (or discount)" or simply "to reduce the price" is ri'Ayat karaR̃^{u}. Because ri'Ayat is a noun (feminine) it is necessary to use jI after the item to be reduced. For example, to say, "Please reduce the price", you would say in Sindhi, qImat jI ri'Ayat karIO.

15. bbIO meaning "another", "other" is inflectable as follows:

bbIO	بيو	masc. sing	بيئي	bbIE	masc. sing. oblique
bbI	بي	fem. sing	بيءَ	bbI^a	fem. sing. oblique
bbIA	بيا	masc. pl.	بين	bbiyan	masc. pl. oblique
bbIŨ	بيون	fem. pl.	بين	bbiyun	fem. pl. oblique

13-E The past tense of the verb HuaR̃ᵘ (to be)

The past tense of HuaR̃ᵘ has separate masculine and feminine forms:

	Masculine	Feminine	Feminine	Masculine
Sing:	mÃ HOs I was	mÃ HuIas	مان هُيَس	مان هوس
	tŨ HuI you were	tŨ HuIa	تون هُئِين	تون هُئِين
	HU HO, HuIO he was	HUa HuI she was	هُوَء هئي	هُو هو، هيو
Pl:	asĨ HuAsĨ or, HuAsŨ we were	asĨ HuIŨsĨ	اسين هيونسين	اسين هئاسين
	tavHĨ HuA you were	tavHĨ HuIŨ	توهين هُيُون	توهين هئا
	HU HuA they were	HU HuIŨ	هو هُيُون	هو هُئا

13-F Statements, questions and negatives with the past tense of HuaR̃ᵘ

kAlHa tavHĨ kithE HuA? Where were you yesterday?	كالهہ توهين ڪٿي هئا؟
AŨ gharᵃ mẼ HOs. I was at home.	آءٌ گهر ۾ هوس.
tavHÃ jA chOkarA kithE HuA? Where were your boys?	توهان جا چوکرا ڪٿي هئا؟
uHE iskUlᵃ mẼ HuA. They were in school.	اهي اسکول ۾ هئا.
sabh chOkirIŨ iskUlᵃ mẼ HuIŨ. All the girls were in school.	سڀ چوڪريون اسڪول ۾ هيون.
guzrEl sAlᵃ jO fasalᵘ cag̃O HO. Last year's crop was good.	گذريل سال جو فصل چڱو هو.
guzrEl maHInE jI garamI vadhIk HuI. It was hotter last month.	گذريل مهيني جي گرمي وڌيڪ هئي.

sArIun jI pOkh[i] guzrEl sAl Hina bbanI[a] mẼ HuI. Last year there was rice cultivation in this field.	سارين جي پوک گذريل سال هن بني ءِ مِ هئي.
Hik[u] lakh mAR̃HU masjid mẼ HuA. There were 100,000 people in the mosque.	هڪ لک ماڻهو مسجد مِ هئا.
chA avHĨ maojUd HuA? Were you present?	چا اوهين موجود هئا؟
na, mÃ maojUd na HOs. kAlH[a] mÃ bImAr HOs. No, I wasn't present. I was sick yesterday.	نہ، مان موجود نہ هوس. ڪالھ مان بيمار هوس.
chA HŨ avhÃ jŨ saHErIŨ HuIŨ? Were they your friends?	چا هو اوهان جون ساهيڙيون هيون؟
ruggO Hik[a] mũHinjI saHERI HuI. Only one was my friend.	رڳو هڪ منهنجي ساهيڙي هئي.
asĨ 'aoratŨ ghar[a] mẼ HuIŨsĨ. We women were in the house.	اسين عورتون گهر مِ هيونسين.
asĨ marad ghar[a] khÃ bbAHir HuAsĨ. We men were outside the house.	اسين مرد گهر کان ٻاهر هئاسين.
chA tŨ bbI[a] chokirI[a] sÃ HuI[a]? Were you with the other girl?	چا تون ٻيءَ چوڪريءَ سان هئين؟
na, AŨ akEll HuIas. No, I was alone.	نہ آءٌ اڪيلي هيس.

1. For the third person, singular, masculine form, HO, you will hear HuIO in Upper Sindh.

2. guzrEl means, "last", "past". Actually, it is one of the past participial forms of the verb, guzraR̃[u], meaning "to pass time", "to pass away".

3. maojUd means "present". Another common word meaning "present" is HAzur[u].

13-G Vocabulary for Lesson 13

aTkal about, approximately	اٽڪل	zIAdaH[a] too much, very much	زياده
adh[u] half	اڌ	sADhA … and a half	سَاڍا
aDhAI two and a half	اڍائي	savA …. and a quarter	سَوا

istimAlu karaR̃u to use	اِستعمالُ	sEr^u 2.057 lbs. dry or 1 qt. liquid measure	سيرُ
akElO alone	اكيلو	fasal^u crop	فصلُ
agh^u (m) rate	اگهُ	qImat^a (f) price	قيمَتَ
AR̃aR̃^u (AR̃i-) to bring	آڻُ (آڻِ)	qImatI expensive, costly	قيمَتي
bAqI remaining, left	باقي	kAThI (f) wood	كاٹي
tAĨ till, until up to	تائين	kAfI enough, plenty	كافي
pAu (m) a quarter of anything	پاءُ	kalAk^u (m) hour	كَلاكُ
panjAsI eighty-five	پَنجاسِي	kilO kilogram, 2.2 lbs	كِلو
panjAnavE ninety-five	پَنجائوي	kalH^a, kAlH^a yesterday	كلھ، كالھ
panjEtAlIHa forty-five	پَنجيتاليهَ	guzrEl last, past	گُذريل
panjaTIH^a thirty-five	پَنجَتيهَ	gIH^u (m) butter-oil, vegetable oil	گِيهُ
panjavanjAH^u fifty-five	پنجوَنجاهُ	ghaTⁱ less	گهَٹِ
panjavIH^a twenty-five	پَنجوِيهَ	maTara (m. pl.) peas	مَٹَرَ
panjaHatarⁱ seventy-five	پَنجَهَتَرِ	masjid (f) mosque	مسجدِ
panjaHaThⁱ sixty-five	پَنجَهَٹِ	munO three-quarters of a whole	مُنو
pUrO while, complete	پُورو	maR̃^u (m) maund, 40 kilograms	مَڻُ
pOR̃A a quarter less than	پوڻا	mITar^u (m) meter = 39 in.	ميٹرُ

ddADhO very	ڈاڍو	vAl[u] (m) yard=36 in.	وَالُ
ddEDh[u] one and a half	ڈيڍُ	yAnE that is	يعني

13-H   Conversational review

1. Discuss the prices of things in the room, or of things in magazine pictures. The teacher can act as a shopkeeper, and set the prices. The student acting as the customer, can decide whether it is too expensive, and if he wants one cheaper. These should be items for which qImat[a] would be used. For example,

Student: Hina vAc[a] jI qImat chA AHE?	شاگرد: هن واچ جي قيمت ڇا آهي؟
Teacher: Hina jI qImat _____ rupayA AHE.	استاد: هن جي قيمت .... رپيا آهي.
Student: iHA ddADhI maHÃgI AHE.	شاگرد: اها ڈاڍي مهانگي آهي.
Teacher: mŨ vaT Hina khÃ sastI na AHE. para avHÃ lAi ruggO _____ rupayA AHE. etc .	استاد: مون وٽ هن کان سستي نه آهي. پر اوهان لاءِ رڳو .... رپيا آهي.

The student should vary his answers to provide a variety of responses. In acting out a shopkeeper situation, remember to open with correct greetings, and close with proper leave-takings.

2. Discuss the cost of things which are sold at a certain agh[u] and decide how much you want to buy. Let the teacher act as the shopkeeper.

Items: kAThI, basar[a], paTATA sUf[u], maTar[a], gajar[a], nArãgI, cÃvar[a], khanD[u], AnA

ڪاٺي، بَصَرَ، پٽاٽا
صوف، مٽر، گجر، نارنگي
چانور، کنڊ، آنا

Adjectives: cağO, vaddO, nanDhO, suThO, sAf, pakO, kacO, thOrO

چڱو، وڏو، ننڍو
سٺو، صاف، پڪو، ڪچو، ٿورو

Adverbs: zIAdaHa, aTkal, vadhIk[a], ghaT[u], faqat[i], ruggO

زياده، اٽڪل، وڌيڪ
گھٽ، فقط، رڳو

For example,

Student: sAĨ, ajjᵘ _____ jO aghᵘ chA AHE?	شاگرد: سائين. اج .... جو اگھ چا آهي؟
Teacher: sAĨ, HI _____ rupaẼ kilO /pAu/ maR̃ᵘ/ Dazan AHE/AHin.	استاد: سائين، هي .... رپئي کلو/ پاءُ/ مڻ/ ڏزن آهي/ آهن.
Student: cag̃O, para mŨ khE suThA khapan. _____ kilO/ etc ddEO.	شاگرد: چڱو، پر مون کي سٺا کپن. .... کلو (وغيره) ڏيو
Teacher: vaThO, sAĨ. vadhIk chA khapE? etc., etc.	استاد: وٺو سائين، وڌيڪ چا کپي؟

3. With the teacher acting as a cloth shopkeeper, practice asking the price and buying cloth.

4. Practice using fractions in the above exercises, and also in the following way. Place bills and change on the table, and converse along this line:

Teacher: mŨ khE adhᵘ rupayO ddEO.	استاد: مون کي اڌ رپيو ڏيو.
Student: HAO sAĨ. adhᵘ rupayO vaThO.	شاگرد: هائو سائين. اڌ رپيو وٺو.
Teacher: mŨ khE pOR̃E TE rupayA ddEO. etc.	استاد: مون کي پوٽا ٽي رپيا ڏيو.

6. Change the tense of the verb HuaR̃ᵘ below to the past tense, keeping the person, number and gender the same. The teacher should read the sentences, and the student reply with the past tense form. For example,

Teacher: mÃ gharᵃ mẼ AHIÃ.	استاد: مان گھر ۾ آهيان.
Student: mÃ gharᵃ mẼ HOs/ HuIas.	شاگرد: مان گھر ۾ هوس/ هيس.
tavHĨ kithE AHIO?	توهين ڪٿي آهيو؟
'aoratŨ kithE AHin?	عورتون ڪٿي آهن؟
TE qalamᵃ mEzᵃ tE AHin.	ٽي قلم ميز تي آهن.
cAr pEnsillŨ bi mEzᵃ tE AHin.	چار پينسليون بہ ميز تي آهن.
E chokarO! tavHĨ pardE jE puthIÃ chO AHIO?	اي چوڪرو! توهين پردي جي پٺيان آهيو؟

E chokarIŨ! tavHĨ pardE jE puthIÃ chO AHIO?	اي چوڪريون! توهين پردي جي پنيان چو آهيو؟
asĨ pāHinjE kamarE mẼ AHIŨ.	اسين پنهنجي ڪمري ۾ آهيون.
mÃ bImAr na AHIÃ.	مان بيمار نہ آهيان.
tasvIrŨ suHiR̃IŨ AHin.	تصويرون سهٽيون آهن.
mAnI garam na AHE.	ماني گرم نہ آهي.
tavHÃjO puT^u kithE AHE?	توهان جو پٽ ڪٿي آهي؟
tavHÃjI dhI^u bImAr AHE chA?	توهان جي ڌيءُ بيمار آهي ڇا؟

LESSON FOURTEEN

14-A   Pronunciation Drill

1. Contrasting /I/ and /Ĩ/   (44/45)   /ي / ين/

سائين چوڪري مينهن ۾ اچي ٿي.
اسين جلدي وينداسين. ڏينهن - ڏيندو
مائيءَ اجا تائين ماني نہ کاڌي. مينهن - ميهار

2. Contrasting /t/ and /d/   (11/12)   / ت / د /

اميد اهي تہ جلدي خط ايندو.
ديانتدار استاد دولتپُر ويندو.
طوطو ۽ ڪتو دوست آهن. دولت، تولو.

14-B   Cardinal numbers by "one"

11	۱۱	yAraH^a	يارهن
21	۲۱	EkavIH^a, EkIH^a	ايڪويھ، ايڪيھ
31	۳۱	EkaTIH^a	ايڪتيھ
41	۴۱	EkEtAlIH^a	ايڪيتاليھ
51	۵۱	EkavanjAH^u	ايڪونجاھ
61	۶۱	EkaHaTh^i	ايڪهٺ
71	۷۱	EkaHatar^i	ايڪهتر
81	۸۱	EkAsI	ايڪاسي
91	۹۱	EkAnavE	ايڪانوي
101	۱۰۰	saO Hik^u	سو هڪ

14-C The Formation of the Simple Future Tense

tarsaR̃ᵘ   (tarsᵘ-)   Imperfect participle: tarsand- plus personal endings

MASCULINE		مذكر	
Singular	Plural	جمع	واحد
mÃ tarsandus I shall wait	asĨ tarsandAsĨ (or, tarsandAsŨ) we shall wait	اسين ترسنداسين	مان ترسندس
tŨ tarsandẼ you will wait	tavHĨ tarsandA You will wait	توهين ترسندا	تون ترسندين
HU tarsandO He will wait	HU tarsandA They will wait	هو ترسندا	هو ترسندو
FEMININE		مؤنث	
Singular	Plural	جمع	واحد
mÃ tarsandIas I shall wait	asĨ tarsandIŨsĨ we shall wait	اسين ترسنديونسين	مان ترسنديس
tŨ tarsandĨᵃ You will wait	tavHĨ tarsandIŨ You will wait	توهين ترسنديون.	تون ترسندينءَ
HUᵃ tarsandI She will wait	HU tarsandIŨ They will wait	هو ترسنديون	هو ترسندي

1. The simple future tense is formed by adding personal endings to the imperfect participle of the verb. These personal endings are very similar to the past tense endings introduced in Lesson 13-E with the verb HuaR̃ᵘ.

2. The tense is used in the same way that it is used in English- to describe events or conditions which have not yet taken place, but which are going to occur.

14-D Statements, Questions and Negatives in the Simple Future Tense

darvAzO kErᵘ khOlIndO? Who will open the door?	دروازو كير كوليندو؟
mÃ khOlIndus. I'll open it.	مان كوليندس.

mÃ thadhO pARĩ pIandus. I shall drink cold water.	مان ٺڌو پاڻي پيئندس.
HU mŨ khE kujh pEsa ddIndO. He will give me some money.	هو مون کي ڪجھ پيسا ڏيندو.
asĨ TE lifAfA vaThandAsĨ. We will take three envelopes.	اسين ٽي لفافا وٺنداسين.
HU kaddaHĩ IndA? When will they come?	هو ڪڏهن ايندا؟
AŨ Huna khE ddisandus/ ddisandIas. I will see him.	آءٌ هن کي ڏسندس/ ڏسنديس.
tavHĨ kaddaHĩ ARIndA? When will you bring (it)?	توهين ڪڏهن آڻيندا؟
tŨ HARE chA kạndẼ? What will you do now?	تون هاڻي ڇا ڪندين؟
HU kaddaHĩ vIndO? When will he go?	هو ڪڏهن ويندو؟
tavHĨ kEddÃHĩ HalandA? Where will you go?	توهين ڪيڏانهن هلندا؟
HU jaldI IndO. He will come quickly.	هو جلدي ايندو.
chA cÃHi pIandA? Will you drink tea?	ڇا ڇانھ پيئندا؟
asĨ bbIE ddĨHᵃ HOddÃHā vIndAsĨ. We'll go there the day after tomorrow.	اسين ٻئي ڏينهن هوڏانهن وينداسين.
tavHĨ Katᵘ kaddaHĩ likhandA? When will you write the letter?	توهين خط ڪڏهن لکندا؟
asĨ ajjᵘ sAnjhĩᵃ jI mAnI bbAHir khAIndAsI. We will eat dinner out tonight.	اسين اڄ سانجهيءَ جي ماني ٻاهر کائينداسين.
tavHĨ Huna khE kEtrA pEsa ddIndA? How much money will you give him?	توهين هن کي ڪيترا پيسا ڏيندا؟
HU HitE kaddaHĩ pOHucandO? When will he arrive here?	هو هتي ڪڏهن پهچندو؟
chokirIŨ kithE vEHandIŨ? Where will the girls sit?	ڇوڪريون ڪٿي ويهنديون؟

'auratŨ HitE bIHandIŨ. The women will stand here.	عورتون هتي بيهنديون.
AŨ pāHinjI gAddI vikaR̃andus. I shall sell my car.	آءٌ پنھنجي گاڏي وڪڻندس.
jAnvar^u pEtI^a mÃ nikarandO. The animal will come out of the box.	جانور پيتيءَ مان نڪرندو.
pakhI vaR̃an^a mẼ uddAmandA. The birds will fly into the trees.	پکي وڻن ۾ اڏامندا.
HU bAHⁱ na visAIndA. They won't put out the fire.	ھو باھ نہ وسائيندا.
Hina Halat mẼ HI jAnvar^u zarUr marandO. In this condition the animal will surely die.	ھن حالت ۾ ھي جانور ضرور مرندو.

1. kaddaHĩ asks the question, "when"?

2. jaldI means, "soon", "quickly".

3. sAnjhI, like SAm, means, "evening".

4. IndaR^a means, "coming", thus "next". It is similar to the English gerund, or the "-ing" form of the verb when it is used as an adverb or adjective. In Sindhi it is formed by adding –aR to the imperfect –aR^a participle.

5. Notice these verbs introduced above for the first time:

vEHaR̃^u	(vEH^u-)	to sit	ويھڻُ	(ويھُ)
bIHaR̃^u	(bIH^u-)	to stand	بيھڻُ	(بيھُ)
vikaR̃aR̃^u	(vikaR̃^u-)	to sell	وڪڻڻُ	(وڪڻُ)
nikaraR̃^u	(nikar^u-)	to come out	نڪرڻُ	(نڪرُ)
uddAmaR̃^u	(uddAm^u-)	to fly	اڏامڻُ	(اڏامُ)
visAiR̃^u	(visAi-)	to put out, extinguish	وسائڻُ	(وساءِ)
maraR̃^u	(mar^u-)	to die	مرڻُ	(مرُ)

14 -E   The Formation of the past Habitual Tense

kholaR̃ᵘ   (kholⁱ-)   Imperfect participle: khOlindO/I/A/IŨ plus the past tense of HuaR̃ᵘ (to be)

MASCULINE		مذكر	
Singular	Plural	جمع	واحد
mÃ khOlindO HOs I used to open	asĨ khOlindA HuAsĨ We used to open	اسين کوليندا هئاسين	مان کوليندو هوس
tŨ khOlindO HuĨ You used to open	tavHĨ khOlindA HuA You used to open	توهين کوليندا هئا	تون کوليندو هئين
HU khOlindO HO He used to open	HU khOlindA HuA They used to open	هو کوليندا هئا	هو کوليندو هو
FEMININE		مؤنث	
mÃ khOlindI HuIas I used to open	asĨ khOlindIŨ HuIŨsĨ We used to open	اسين کوليندیون هيوسين	مان کوليندي هيس
tŨ khOlindI HuĨᵃ You used to open	tavHĨ khOlindIŨ HuIŨ You used to open	توهين کوليندیون هيون	تون کوليندي هئينءَ
HUᵃ khOlindI HuI She used to open	HU khOlindIŨ HuIŨ They used to open	هو کوليندیون هيون	هوءَ کوليندي هئي

1. This tense states what was usually, generally or regularly true- hence, "used to".

2. This tense is formed similarly to the present habitual tense. The only difference is that, whereas in the present habitual tense the auxiliary verb HuaRᵘ, is used in the <u>present</u> tense, in the past habitual tense, the auxiliary verb is used in the past tense. (See 13-E for the <u>past</u> tense of HuaR̃ᵘ.)

14 -F   Statements, Questions, and Negatives in the Past Habitual Tense.

Hunan jO bhAᵘ asÃ khE likhandO HO. Their brother used to write to us.	هنن جو ڀاءُ اسان کي لکندو هو.
tavHĨ kaHiRIᵃ taraHᵃ ggOThᵃ ddAHᵃ vEndA HuA? How did you used to go to the village?	توهين ڪهڙيءَ طرح ڳوٺ ڏانهن ويندا هئا؟

chA Hunan ddĩHan mẼ tavHĩ ghaR̃O karE safar kandA HuA? Did you used to travel a lot in those days?	چا هنن ڏينهن ۾ توهين گهڻو ڪري سفر ڪندا هئا؟
HAO, AŨ ghaR̃O karE safar kandO HOs. Yes, I traveled a lot.	هائو، آءُ گهڻو ڪري سفر ڪندو هوس.
TE suHiR̃IŨ tasvIrŨ Huna bhit^i tE HUndIŨ HuIŨ. There used to be three pretty pictures on that wall.	ٽي سهڻيون تصويرون هن ڀت تي هونديون هيون.
chA tavHÃ jA mAiT^a Hina rastE tE raHandA HuA? Did your relatives used to live on this road?	چا توهان جا مائٽ هن رستي تي رهندا هئا؟
lArI Huna ggOTh^i ddÃh^a na vEndI HuI. The bus didn't used to go to that village.	لاري هن ڳوٺ ڏانهن نه ويندي هئي؟
guzrEl sAl^a asĩ ghar^a jI masvAR^a ddIndA HuAsĩ. Last year we were paying house rent.	گذريل سال اسين گهر جي مسواڙ ڏيندا هئاسين.
asĩ panjAH^a rupayA maHInE (mẼ) ddIndA HuAsĩ. We used to pay (give) Rs. 50 per month.	اسين پنجاهه رپيا مهيني (۾) ڏيندا هئاسين.
lArI^a mẼ acaR̃a vaÑaR̃a jO bhARO chA thIndO IIO? How much did the round-trip bus fare used to cost?	لاري ۾ اچٽ وڃٽ جو ڀاڙو چا ٿيندو هو؟
Hunan jO iskUl cag̃Ia taraH^a HalandO HO. Their school used to run well.	هنن جو اسڪول چڱي طرح هلندو هو.
borcI kaHiRE HaT^a tã gOSt vaThandO HO? Which shop did the cook used to get meat from?	بورچي ڪهڙي هٽءَ تان گوشت وٺندو هو؟
HU Hitã vaddO gOSt vaThandO HO, aĩ nanDhO gOSt kãHin KAs jAi tã. He used to get beef from here, and mutton from some special place.	هو هتان وڏو گوشت وٺندو هو، ۽ ننڍو گوشت ڪنهن خاص جاءِ تان.
chA tŨ manjhand jO sumHandO HuĩĨ? Did you used to sleep at noon?	چا تون منجهند جو سمهندو هئين؟

HutE tavHĨ ghaR̃I paghAr^a kamAIndA HuA? How much pay did you used to earn there?	ھُتي توھين گھٹي پگھار ڪمائيندا ھئا؟
mÃ pOR̃^a bba saO rupayA kamAIndo HOs. I used to earn Rs. 175.	مان پوٽا ٻہ سو رپيا ڪمائيندو ھوس.
tavHÃ jE ghar^a mẼ kEr^u thÃv^a dhOIndO HO? Who used to wash dishes in your house?	توھان جي گھر ۾ ڪير ٿانو ڌوئيندو ھو؟
tũHinjO kam SOlO HUndO HO yA muSkil? Did your work used to be easy or hard?	تنھنجو ڪم سولو ھوندو ھو يا مشڪل؟

1. kaHiRI^a taraH^a means, "in which way, manner".

2. Note the correct pronunciation of ddĨH^a (day) in the plural oblique. The final "n" sound is pronounced: thus, Hunan ddĨHan mE.

3. safar^u karaR̃u is a compound verb. safar^u means "journey", and combined with karaR̃u means "to travel".

4. HUndO is the imperfect participle of HujaR̃^u which, like HuaR̃^u, means "to be". You have been introduced to three verbs all of which may be used to mean "to be".

   thIaR̃^u   HuaR̃^u   HujaR̃^u

Begin now to develop an awareness of how Sindhi use these three verbs.

5. acaR̃^a vaÑaR̃^a jO bhARO uses two infinitives as nouns: "the fare of 'coming'—lit., to come—and 'going' –lit., to go". When thus joined, they do not take any equivalent conjunction to "and". This has the meaning of "round trip" or "return trip", that is, both ways.

6. Notice how HalaR̃^u is used with iskUl^u in the sense of "to operate", "to function".

7. kamAiR̃^u (kamAi-) means "to earn". paghAr^a is a feminine noun meaning "pay", "salary". You will find that Pakistanis are quite free in asking such questions. Don't be offended at this, but do learn how to give an indirect answer.

8. sOlO and muSkil are adjectives meaning "easy" and "difficult", respectively.

14 –G   Other Forms of the Imperative

subhAR̃E varI acijO. Come again tomorrow.	سڀاڻي وري اچجو.
Huna khE mũHinjA salAm ddijO. Give him my compliments.	ھن کي منھنجا سلام ڏجو.
mũ khE mu'Af kajO. Please forgive me/ excuse me.	مون کي معاف ڪجو.
mũ khE uHO kitAb^u ddijO. Please let me have that book.	مون کي اھو ڪتاب ڏجو.

chA tavHĨ darvAzO khOlIndA? Will you please open the door?	چا توهين دروازو کوليندا؟
HAR̃E HI kam kandA. Please do this work now.	هاٹي هي ڪم ڪندا.
pOi acijO. Come later.	پوءِ اچجو.
pOi Huna khE kitAb^u ddij^i. Give him the book later.	پوءِ هن کي کتاب ڏج.
HI kam subhAR̃E kaj^i. Do this work tomorrow.	هي ڪم سڀاڻي ڪج.

1. The simple imperative was introduced in Lesson 10-B. the above questions illustrate "future imperatives". When the command given is to be carried out some time later, the next day, or at an indefinite time further in the future, the future imperative form is used.

2. Occasionally, when one wants to be so polite and respectful that he should rather not use any form of the imperative, he may simply use the future plural. This is illustrated in examples above:

> chA tavHĨ darvAzO khOlIndA?
>
> HAR̃E HI kam kandA.

Notice, however, that although the request is in the future tense, it is really something requested for the present moment. It is simply an extremely polite way to give a command.

3. The usual "future imperative", however, is formed by adding –ji for the singular, and –jO for the plural to the root of the verb. For example,

> subhAR̃E acij^i Come tomorrow
>
> subhAR̃E acijO   Please come tomorrow.

Sometimes you will hear –jÃi instead of simply –ji for the singular form ending. For example,

> pOi acijÃi   Come afterwards.

4. The future imperative of some verbs is irregular. For example,

> karaR̃^{u} (to do) is kaj^i; ddIaR̃^{u} (to give) is ddij^i.

5. As mentioned in explanation 2, above, in some instances the future imperative, instead of denoting future time, is also used to show a high degree of honor, respect, and politeness to the one addressed. This situation is illustrated in the following examples:

> mŨ khE mu'Af kajO.   Please excuse/forgive me.
>
> mŨ khE uHO kitAb^u ddijO.   Please give me that book.

14- H   Vocabulary for Lesson 14

uddAmaR̃u to fly	اُڏامڻ	pakhI (m) bird	پکي
EkAsI eighty-one	ايڪاسي	paghAra pay	پَگھار
EkAnavE ninety-one	ايڪانوي	jaldI quickly	جَلدِي
EkEtAlIHa forty-one	ايڪيتاليھَ	jAi (f) place	جاءِ
EkaTIHa thirty-one	ايڪَتِيھَ	HAlata (f) condition, state	حالَت
EkavanjAhu fifty-one	ايڪَونجاھُ	KAs special, unique	خاصُ
EkaHatari seventy-one	ايڪَھَتَرِ	sAnjhI (f) evening	سانجھي
EkavIHa twenty-one	ايڪَوِيھَ	kaddaHī when	ڪَڏھِن
EkaHathi sixty-one	ايڪَھَٺِ	kamAiR̃u (kamAi-) to earn	ڪَمائڻ (ڪماءِ)
IndaRa next, coming	اِينڊَڙَ	maraR̃u (maru-) to die	مَرڻ (مَرُ)
bIHaR̃u (bIHu-) to stand	بِيھَڻ (بيھُ)	masvARa (f) rent	مَسواڙ
bAHi (f) fire	باھِ	muSkil difficult, hard	مُشڪِل
bhARO (m) fare	ڀاڙو	safaru karaR̃u to travel	سَفَرُ ڪَرَڻُ
sOlO easy	سولو	zarUr surely, certainly	ضَرُورُ
lArI (f) bus	لاري	vEHaR̃u (vEHu) to sit	ويھَڻ (ويھُ)
nikaraR̃u (nikaru-) to come out, exit	نِڪرڻ (نِڪرُ)	yArAHā eleven	يارهن
visAiR̃u (visAi) to extinguish	وسائڻ (وساءِ)	vaR̃u (m) tree	وڻ

vikaR̃aR̃ᵘ (vikAR̃ᵘ-) to sell	وڪڻ (وڪڻ)	pIaR̃ᵘ (pIᵘ) to drink	پيئڻ

14 - I Conversational Review

1. Work on the following conversational topics with your teacher and with other Sindhi friends, using the verb tenses learned thus far in the course.

   a. Personal habits and customs: practice the use of the habitual tenses, and make special use of this exercise to learn all you can about Sindhis and the way they do things. It would be best for women students to do this with a woman teacher or friend.

   b. Village and city life in Pakistan.

   c. The customs and life-style of your home country.

2. Change the verbs given below from the simple present tense to the future tense, keeping the person, number and gender the same. For example,

Teacher: HU karE thO.	استاد: هو ڪري ٿو.
Student: HU kandO etc.	شاگرد: هو ڪندو وغيره.
mÃ HitE rakhÃ thO.	مان هتي رڪان ٿو.
HU kam karE thO.	هو ڪم ڪري ٿو.
asĨ kam karIŨ thA.	اسين ڪم ڪريون ٿا.
HU Huna khE kitAbᵃ ddian thA.	هو هن کي ڪتاب ڏين ٿا.
AŨ acÃ thO/thI.	آءٌ اچان ٿو/ ٿي.
pakhI uddAmE thO.	پکي اڏامي ٿو.
'auratŨ bbAran khE khIrᵘ ddIan thIŨ.	عورتون ٻارن کي کير ڏين ٿيون.
mÃ Katᵘ likhÃ thI/ thO.	مان خط لکان ٿي/ ٿو.
HUᵃ kujh cÃHⁱ AR̃E thI.	هوءَ ڪجھ چانھ آڻي ٿي.
tavHĨ Huna sÃ ggAlHAyO thA.	توهين هن سان ڳالهايو ٿا.
lArI HitE na thI HalE.	لاري هتي نہ ٿي هلي.

3. Ask and answer the following questions with such time words/ phrases as ajj^u, subhA R̃E, manjhand jO, SAm jO, rAt^i jO, subuH^a jO, subhA R̃E subuH^a jO, ajj^u rat^i jO, IndaR^a maHInE mE, bbIE ddĨHā. For example,

	Teacher: lArI kaddaHī HalandI?	استاد: لاري ڪڏهن هلندي؟
	Student: lArI subuH^a jO HalandI.	شاگرد: لاري صبح جو هلندي.
(a)	tŨ kaddaHī HalandẼ?	تون ڪڏهن هلندين؟
(b)	bbAr^a kaddaHī ArAm kandA?	ٻار ڪڏهن آرام ڪندا؟
(c)	dhobi HI kam kaddaHī kandO?	ڌوٻي هي ڪم ڪڏهن ڪندو؟
(d)	asĨ kaddaHī bbIO sabaq paRHandAsĨ?	اسين ڪڏهن ٻيو سبق پڙهندا سين؟
(e)	naokar^u kamrE khE kaddaHī sAf kandO?	نوڪر ڪمري کي ڪڏهن صاف ڪندو؟
(f)	Huna jI bbacI kaddaHī IndI?	هن جي ٻچي ڪڏهن ايندي؟
(g)	DAkTAr sAHib kaddaHī paHucandO?	ڊاڪٽر صاحب ڪڏهن پهچندو؟
(h) 'auratŨ cÃH^i kaddaHī pIandIŨ?	عورتون چانهه ڪڏهن؟ پيئنديون؟

4. Fill in the blanks below using a form, first of the present habitual tense, then of the past habitual tense of the infinitive given in parentheses.

(a)	Huna jI zAl^a bAG^a mẼ kam (karaR̃^{u}).	هن جي زال باغ ۾ ڪم (ڪرڻ).
(b)	chOkirO Huna naokirI^a mẼ ghaR̃O karE safar (karaR̃^{u}).	ڇوڪرو هن نوڪريءَ ۾ گهڻو ڪري سفر (ڪرڻ).
(c)	mũHinjO mURs^u ghaR̃O karE safar (karaR̃^{u}).	منهنجو مڙس گهڻو ڪري سفر (ڪرڻ).
(d)	'auratŨ HitE (vEHaR̃^{u}) aĨ mAR̃HU HutE (vEHaR̃^{u}).	عورتون هتي (ويهڻ) ۽ ماڻهو هتي (ويهڻ).

Lesson 14/ 176

(e)	tavHĨ bbAran^a khE KaHiRE qisim^a jO khIr^u (ddIa R̃^u)?	توهين ٻارن کي ڪهڙي قسم جو کير (ڏيڻ)؟
(f)	mÃ Har haftE pāHinjE mA^u pI^u khE Kat^u (likha R̃^u).	مان هر هفتي پنهنجي ماءُ پيءُ کي خط (لکڻ).

5. Expand each sentence into a story or dialogue with your teacher. Change it to a question, respond to his answer, expand it. Use your imagination and a good variety of the vocabulary at your command.

6. Practice using the different forms of the imperative in your daily activities.

LESSON FIFTEEN

15-A   **Pronunciation Drill**

1. Contrasting /O/ and /U/   (58/62)   و ء وُ

وڏو ماٺھو گھوڙو وني ويو.
اھو ماٺھو تنبوُ جو رھاڪوُ ھو.
اوچتو اُوچتو تنبوُ ڪري پيو.

2. Contrasting /D/ and /dd/   (17,13)   ڊ ء ڏ

گڏھ گاڏيءَ جي پنيان ڊوڙي ويو.
ڊگھي ڊڪڻ ڊوھ ڪري ڏنڊ ڏنو.
وڏو ڊيڍر ڊجي ڪڏ مِ ڊوڙيو.

15-B   **The Cardinal Numbers by "twos"**

12	١٢	bbAraH[a]	ٻارھن
22	٢٢	bbAvIH[a]	ٻاويھ
32	٣٢	bbaTIH[a]	ٻتيھ
42	٤٢	bbAEtAlIH[a]	ٻائيتاليھ
52	٥٢	bbAvanjAH[u]	ٻاونجاھ
62	٦٢	bbAHaTh[i]	ٻاھٺ
72	٧٢	bbAHatar[i]	ٻاھتر
82	٨٢	bbIAsI	ٻياسي
92	٩٢	bbIAnavE	ٻيانوي
102	١٠٢	saO bba	سؤ ٻہ

15 -C The days of the week

Transliteration / English	Sindhi
ajj^u mOkal^a AHE—as$\tilde{I}$ jum'E jE ddĪhā kam na kandA AHIŨ. Today is a holiday – we don't work on Friday.	اڄ موڪل آهي – اسين جمعي جي ڏينهن ڪم نَ ڪَندا آهيون.
as$\tilde{A}$ jA mAiT^a sUmar^a jE ddĪhā IndA. Our relatives will come on Monday.	اسان جا مائٽ سومر جي ڏينهن ايندا.
mũHinjA mA^u pI^u ghaR̃O karE ag̃ArE tE IndA AHin. My parents often come on Tuesday.	منهنجا ماءُ پيءُ گهڻو ڪري اڱاري تي ايندا آهن.
mũHinjO KayAl AHE ta as$\tilde{I}$ araba jE ddĪhā aThÕ sabaq^u pUrO kandAsĪ. I think that we'll finish the eighth lesson on Wednesday.	منهنجو خيال آهي تَ اسين اربع جي ڏينهن اٺون سَبقُ پُورو ڪنداسين.
as$\tilde{I}$ KamIs^a jE ddĪhā nAÕ sabaq^u SarU' kandAsĪ. We'll begin the ninth lesson on Thursday.	اسين خميس جي ڏينهن نائون سبق شروع ڪندا سين.
'ISAI mAR̃HU Acar^a jE ddĪhā 'ibAdat^a kandA AHin. Christians worship on Sunday.	عيسائي ماڻهو آچر جي ڏينهن عبادت ڪندا آهن.
as$\tilde{I}$ chanchar^a jE ddĪhā iskUl na vInda AHIŨ. We don't go to school on Saturday.	اسين ڇنڇر جي ڏينهن اسڪول نَ ويندا آهيون.

1. The days of the week are:

Sindhi (Latin)		English	Sindhi
Acar^u		Sunday	آچرُ
sUmar^u		Monday	سومرُ
ag̃ArO		Tuesday	اڱارو
araba'^{a}	(f)	Wednesday	اربع
KamIs^a	(f)	Thursday	خميس
jum'O		Friday	جمعو
chanchar^u		Saturday	ڇنڇر

2. Notice the gender of the days. They inflect according to the usual rules of inflection for masculine and feminine nouns.

3. In the illustration above all the days of the week are in the oblique. Of course, this is because a postposition is understood, the postposition, tE. One may either use the name of the day alone or add jE ddĪhā.

4. Pakistan uses both the Muslim and English calendars. Sindhis commonly use the English names for the twelve months. Note, however, the slight variations in Sindhi-izing the

pronunciations. For example, fEbarvarI, (February). You will notice that on many calendars printed in Pakistan, the week begins with Friday, the official weekly holiday.

5. Hindu Sindhis use a different set of names for the days of the week. They are:

AratvAr^u	Sunday	آرتوار
sUmar^u	Monday	سومرُ
mangal^u	Tuesday	منگلُ
bbudhar^u	Wednesday	ٻُڌرُ
vispatⁱ	Thursday	وسپت
SukarvAr^u	Friday	شڪروار
chanchar^u	Saturday	چنڇر

6. KayAl means "thought", "idea", "opinion". To say "I think", one usually says "My thought is …" (mũHinjO KayAl AHE ta…)

7. There are three compound verbs in the examples above, each using karaR̃^u:

    pUrO karaR̃^u   to complete, finish
    SarU' karaR̃^u   to begin, commence
    'ibAdat^a karaR̃^u   to worship

15 -D The positions (jE) pArⁱ (across), (jE) rUbarU (face to face, in front of, before), (jE) cOdhArI (around), (jE) vicamẼ (between) and khÃ aggE (before)

asĨ vaHa jE pAr HalandAsĨ. We'll go across the channel.	اسين واھ جي پار هلنداسين.
bbERI HAR̃E darIAHa jE pAr vaÑE thI. The boat is crossing the river now.	ٻيڙي هاڻي درياھ جي پار وڃي ٿي.
HU tavHÃ jE rUbarU bIThO AHE. He's standing in front of you.	هو توهان جي روبرو بيٺو آهي.
Huna khE mũHinjE rubarU vaThI acO. Bring him to me. (lit: in front of me)	هن کي منهنجي روبرو وٺي اچو.
sabh chOkirIŨ pãHinjE ustAd^a jE cOdhArI vEthIŨ HuIŨ. All the girls were seated around their teacher.	سڀ چوڪريون پنهنجي اُستاد جي چوڌاري ويٺيون هيون.

Huna jE ghar^a jE cOdhArI Hik^a UcI bhit^i AHE. There's a high wall around his house.	هن جي گهَرَ جي چوڌاري هڪ اوچي ڀِتِ آهي.
Hinan bbin kitAban jE vicamẼ kaHiRO tafAvat^u AHE? What is the difference between these two books?	هنن ٻِن ڪِتابَن جي وچ ۾ ڪهڙو تفاوتُ آهي؟
HU pãHinjE pI^u aĨ vaddE bhA^u jE vica mẼ bIThO AHE. He is standing between his father and (his) elder brother.	هو پنهنجي پيءُ ۽ وڏي ڀاءُ جي وچ ۾ بيٺو آهي.
HU Tin ddIhan kHÃ pOi mOkal^a tE vEndO. He'll go on leave after three days.	هو ٽن ڏينهن کان پوءِ موڪل تي ويندو.
mÃ bbin Haftan khÃ pOi Indus. I'll come after two weeks.	مان ٻِن هفتن کان پوءِ ايندس.
mÃ SAdI^a jE vaqt^a khÃ aggE zarUr Indus. I'll surely come before the time of the wedding.	مان شاديءَ جي وقت کان اڳي ضرور ايندس.

1. The postposition vicamẼ, is a combination of two words, vic^u, meaning middle, centre, and mẼ, the common postposition meaning "in". Thus, vicamẼ means, quite literally, "in between", "in the midst of". It is generally used with jE.

2. khÃ pOi and khÃ aggE are generally used in the context of time.

3. bIThO and vEThO are past particles of the verbs, bIHaR̃^{u} (to stand) and vEHAR̃^{u} (to sit), respectively. They are frequently used as adjectives. For examples,

    chOkirO bIThO AHE.   The boy is standing.
    chOkirA bIThA AHin.   The boys are standing.
    chOkirI vEThI AHE.   The girl is seated.
    chOkirIU vEThIŨ AHin.   The girls are seated.

15-E   Infinitives as Nouns

HAR̃E sumHaR̃^{a} jO vaqt AHE. Now it's time to sleep.	هاڻي سمهڻ جو وقت آهي.
Huna jO ggAiR̃^{u} tamAm mIThO AHE. Her singing is very sweet.	هن جو ڳائڻ تمام مٺو آهي.
dU'A ghuraR̃^{u}, sumHaR̃^{u} khÃ vadhIk suThI AHE. Prayer is better than sleep.	دعا گهرڻ، سمهڻ کان وڌيڪ سٺي آهي.

tavhÃ jO HitE acaR̃ ᵘ cag̃O na AHE. Your coming here is not good.	توهان جو هتي اچڻ چڱو نـ آهي.
sumHaR̃ ª jE kamrE jO farSᵘ sAf na AHE. The bedroom floor isn't clean.	سمهڻ جي ڪمري جو فرش صاف نـ آهي.
khAiR̃ ª jO kamrO mErO piR̃ ᵘ AHE. The dining room is also dirty.	کائڻ جو ڪمرو ميرو پڻ آهي.
mÃ tavHÃ jO samjhAiR̃ ᵘ na thO samjhÃ. I don't understand your explanation.	مان توهان جو سمجهائڻ نـ ٿو سمجهان.
padrI sAHib jO ggAlHAiR̃ ᵘ takiRO AHE. The Pastor's speaking is fast.	پادري صاحب جو ڳالهائڻ تڪڙو آهي.
AHistE AHistE ggAlHAyO. sindhI samjHa R̃ ª mE aŨ takiRO (takiRI) na AHIÃ. Speak slowly. I am not quick in understanding Sindhi.	آهستي آهستي ڳالهايو. سنڌي سمجهڻ ۾ آءٌ تڪڙو (تڪڙي) نـ آهيان.

1. The above illustrations are only a few of the many ways in which the Sindhi infinitive may be put to use as a noun. The infinitive of a verb is in reality a verbal noun, that is, a noun with a verbal idea. As such it inflects according to the rules for masculine nouns. That is, the masculine singular –u ending becomes –a when inflected.

2. In Sentence 3 above, the adjective suThI is in agreement with dU'A, a feminine noun. It is possible to consider it in agreement with the infinitive, a masculine noun, and thus it would be suThO. In practice you will hear both usages.

3. Note the adjective above: takiRO (fast, quick), and sAf (clean) and mErO (dirty). takiRO may also be used as an adverb. AHistO is an adjective meaning slow. AHistE AHistE becomes an adverb meaning "slowly".

15-F   The use of the infinitive with vArO to indicate the doer of an action

ajjᵘ jO ggAlHAiR̃ ª vArO kErᵘ HO? Who was the speaker today?	اڄ جو ڳالهائڻ وارو ڪيرُ هو؟
ajjª jO ggAlHAiR̃ ª vArO kO mizmAn HO. Today's speaker was some guest.	اڄ جو ڳالهائڻ وارو ڪو مزمان هو.
mũHinjO samjHAiR̃ ª vArO na AHE. I don't have anyone to explain it to me. (lit: explainer)	منهنجو سمجهائڻ وارو نـ آهي.
Hina Kataª jO likhaR̃ ª vArO kEr AHE? Who is the writer of this letter?	هن خط جو لکڻ وارو ڪير آهي؟

Hu^a bAIbal muqqadas jI paRha R̃ ª vArI AHE. She is the Bible read<u>er</u>.	هُوءَ بائيبل مقدس جي پڙھڻ واري آهي.
subhA R̃E mÃ paRha R̃ ª vArO/vArI thIndus/thIndius. Tomorrow I'll be the reader.	سڀاڻي مان پڙھڻ وارو / واري ٿيندس / ٿينديس.

1. vArO may be added to the infinitive of any verb to show the doer or performer of an action, in the same way that –er does to English verbs. The infinitive is inflected before vArO, thus ggAlHai R̃ ª vArO.

2. bAIbal muqqadas means, "Holy Bible", muqqadas being the Persian adjective "holy".

3. It may function as noun (e.g. bbudha R̃ ª vArO KudA – a hearing God).

4. "mizmAn" means guest. You will also hear "maHmAn" meaning the same thing. Use the word you hear in your area.

15-G The use of the Infinitive with vArO to indicate imminent action

mÃ ispitAl vaÑaR̃ ª vArO AHIÃ. I'm about to go to the hospital.	مان اسپتال وڃڻ وارو آهيان.
Huna jO pI^u mara R̃ ª vArO AHE. His father is about to die.	هن جو پيءُ مَرڻ وارو آهي.
pAdrI sAHib ggAlHAi R̃ ª vArO AHE. The Padre Sahib is just going to speak.	پادري صاحب ڳالهائڻ وارو آهي.
HaR̃E asĨ SarU' kara R̃ ª vArA AHIŨ. Now we're ready to start.	هاڻي اسين شروع ڪرڻ وارا آهيون.
nars bImAran khE davA ddI R̃ ª vArI AHE. The nurse is just about to give the medicine to the patients.	نرس بيمارن کي دوا ڏيڻ واري آهي.
mÃ tavHÃ jO fOTO kaDha R̃ ª vArO AHIÃ. I'm ready to take your picture.	مان توهان جو فوٽو ڪڍڻ وارو آهيان.

1. The use of vArO in this context means that the action is about to take place. Notice the various ways it can be translated into English.

2. Another way to express imminent action is with use of the postposition tE (on) instead of vArO. This is illustrated in the next section.

3. Notice that bImAr^u, learned earlier as an adjective "sick", may be used as a noun meaning "patient". Some other adjective may also be used in this way. For example, GarIb (poor) is used as a noun meaning "poor ones", "poor people".

15-H   The use of tE (on) to indicate imminent action

chA tŨ vaÑaR̃ª tE AHĨ? Are you about to go?	چا تون وڃڻ تي آهين؟
mÃ Hunan khE dA'vat ddIaR̃ª tE HOs. I was just about to invite them.	مان هنن کي دعوت ڏيڻ تي هوس.
mAlHI navÃ gUlª pOkhaR̃ª tE AHE. The gardener is about to plant new flowers.	مالهي نوان گل پوکڻ تي آهي.
chA tavHĨ fOTO kaDhaR̃^u tE AHIO? Are you about to take the picture now?	چا توهين فوٽو ڪڍڻ تي آهيو؟
bOrcI cÃH ĩ tayAr karaR̃ª tE AHE. The cook is about to make tea.	بورچي چانھ تيار ڪرڻ تي آهي.
Hunan jA mAiTª kAlH^u acaR̃ª tE HuA. Their relatives were about to come yesterday.	هنن جا مائٽ ڪالھ اچڻ تي هئا.

1. This idiom is equivalent to the vArO form used immediately above. However, this form is less ambiguous than the vArO form, and may imply a greater degree of intensity.

2. Note the two compound verbs introduced in the above two selections: fOTO kaDhaR̃^u, literally, "to take out a photo", hence "to photograph" and dA'vat^a ddIaR̃^u, literally, "to give an invitation", hence, "to invite".

15-I   Using the infinitive plus ghuraR̃ª to express necessity and compulsion

tavHÃ khE kujh khAiR̃^u ghurjE. You ought eat something.	توهان کي ڪجھ کائڻ گهرجي.
bbAran^a khE HAR̃E sumhaR̃ ghurjE. The children ought to go to sleep.	ٻارن کي هاڻي سمهڻ گهرجي.
mŨ khE bba kitAb paRHaR̃ª ghurjan. I need to read two books.	مون کي ٻہ ڪتاب پڙهڻ گهرجن.
Hina chokirE khE TE kApIŨ KarId^a karaR̃ª ghurjan. This boy needs to buy three notebooks.	هن ڇوڪري کي ٽي ڪاپيون خريد ڪرڻ گهرجن.

jAi tamAm parE AHE, tavHÃ khE TAngE tE vaÑaR̃ᵘ ghurjE. The place is quite far. You ought to go by tonga.	جاءِ تمام پري آهي. توهان کي ٽانگي تي وڃڻ گھرجي.
asÃ khE EtrI dEr HutE raHaR̃ᵘ na ghurbO HO. We ought not to have stayed there so late/long.	اسان کي ايتري دير هتي رهڻ نه گھربو هو.
mÜ khE subhAR̃E uHO kitAb vaThaR̃ᵘ ghurjE. I will need to bring that book tomorrow.	مون کي سڀاڻي اهو ڪتابُ وٺڻ گھرجي.
mÜHinjIᵃ bhER̃ᵃ khE agArE tE HI cAr kursIÜ ghurjan/ghurbIÜ. My sister will need these four chairs on Tuesday.	منهنجيءَ ڀيڻ کي اڱاري تي هي چار ڪرسيون گھرجن/ گھربيون.

1. Obligation or necessity is expressed in Sindhi by using the infinitive of a verb with various forms of ghurjE. The subject is inflected and followed by khE. In the present tense, the verb agrees with any stated object in number only.

      mÜ khE HikaRO kitAb paRHaR̃ᵘ ghurjE.   I need to read one book.

      mÜ khE bba kitAb paRHaR̃ᵃ ghurjan.   I need to read two books.

There is no change in form when the objective is feminine noun, as,

      Huna khE kursI KarIdᵃ karaR̃ᵃ ghurjE.   He needs to buy a chair.

2. The use and meaning of ghurjE is quite similar to khapE (Lesson 12-F). It was briefly referred to in 12-F-7.

3. The past idea, "ought to have" is expressed by ghurbO HO. This is inflected to agree with any stated object in gender and number.

4. The future tense is expressed by ghurbO, inflected to agree with the object when stated, in gender and number. This is illustrated in the last sentence above. ghurjE or ghurbO may be used without the infinitive to mean "are required", "are needed", or "will be required", "will be needed".

For example,

      subHAR̃E mÜ khE kitAb ghurjE.

      Tomorrow I will need that book. (Tomorrow that book will be required by me.)

      subHAR̃E asÃ khE vadhIk kursIÜ ghurbIÜ/ghurjan.

      Tomorrow we will need more chairs. (More chairs will be required by us.)

When the context indicates a future time, ghurjE is often used instead of ghurbO.

5. The subject may sometimes be omitted giving a strictly impersonal idea, as,

    kujh khAiR̃ᵘ ghurjE.   Something ought to be eaten.

    thIarR̃ᵘ na ghurjE.   It ought not to be.

15-J Using the "long" form of the infinitive plus HuaR̃ᵘ to show necessity, compulsion, obligation

mŨ khE pāHinjE pIᵘ khE Katᵘ likhaR̃O AHE. I have to write a letter to my father.	مون کي پنھنجي پيءُ کي خط لکڻو آهي.
mŨ khE pāHinjE pIᵘ khE Katᵘ likhaR̃O HO. I had to write a letter to my father.	مون کي پنھنجي پيءُ کي خط لکڻو ھو.
mŨ khE pāHinjE pIᵘ khE Katᵘ likhaR̃O pavandO. I shall have to write a letter to my father.	مون کي پنھنجي پيءُ کي خط لکڻو پوندو.
Huna khE ciThI likhaR̃I HUI. He had to write a note.	ھن کي چني لکڻي ھئي.
mŨ khE vaÑaR̃O AHE. I have to go.	مون کي وڃڻو آهي.
tO khE kaddaHẼ vaÑaR̃O AHE? When do you have to go?	توکي ڪڏھن وڃڻو آهي؟
tO khE kEddÃHā vaÑaR̃O AHE? Where do you have to go?	توکي ڪيڏانھن وڃڻو آهي؟
mŨ khE kEtrA-I kam karaR̃A AHin. I have to do many things.	مون کي ڪيترائي ڪم ڪرڻا آهن.
insAnᵃ khE Hina jaHanᵃ mẼ chA karaR̃O AHE? What has man to do in this world?	انسان کي ھن جھان ۾ ڇا ڪرڻو آهي؟
Huna khE faqat khAiR̃O , pIa R̃O aĨ sumHaR̃O AHE, chA? Has he only to eat, drink and sleep?	ھُن کي فقط کائڻو، پيئڻو ۽ سُمھڻو آهي ڇا؟
na, Huna khE Hina khÃ cag̃A kam karaR̃A AHin. No, he has something better to do.	نہ، ھُن کي ھن کي چڱا ڪم ڪرڻا آهن.

tO khE subHAR̃E subUHᵃ jO savEr uthaR̃O pavandO. You'll have to get up early tomorrow morning.	توکي سڀاڻي صبح جو سوير اٿڻو پوندو.
Hunan khE subHAR̃E TE ciThiŨ likhaR̃I Ũ pavandIŨ. They'll have to write three notes tomorrow.	هُنن کي سڀاڻي ٽي چٺيون لکڻيون پونديون.
tO khE ajjᵘ imtiHAn ddIaR̃O AHE chA? Do you have to take an examination today?	توکي اڄ امتحان ڏيڻو آهي ڇا؟
ajjᵘ na, paraᵃ subHAR̃E mŨ khE TE imtiHAn ddIAR̃A pavandA. Not today but tomorrow I'll have to "take" three exams.	اڄ نه، پَر سڀاڻي مون کي ٽي امتحان ڏيڻا پوندا.

1. This construction shows necessity, compulsion and / or obligation. The helping verb is in the appropriate tense HuaR̃ᵘ or pavaR̃ᵘ in the present and past tenses, but only pavaR̃ᵘ is used in the future tense.

2. When the verb pavaR̃ᵘ is used in this way to express compulsion, it implies a much stronger degree of necessity or obligation. Since the verb literally means "to fall", its use in this way suggests an element of external compulsion, something outside the speaker's control. It is that which "falls" to one to do, usually with no choice in the matter. The compulsion is much stronger than when HuaR̃ᵘ is used.

3. The verb pavaR̃ᵘ, both here and in its other idiomatic uses, implies suddenness, unexpectedness, or unavoidability, as for example,

    mŨ khE Kabar paI ta …   I found out, (suddenly and unexpectedly)

    mŨ khE Kabar HuI ta…   I found out… (came to know, perhaps by my own effort or inquiry.)

4. Since the pattern of this construction is quite different from the way we express the same thought in English, it may be helpful for the student to notice the say it is formed in Sindhi.

    mŨ khE vaÑaR̃O AHE = To me to go is = I have to go.

    tO khE ciThI likhaR̃I AHE = To you a note to write is = You have to write a note.

    Huna khE TE rUpayA ddIaR̃A HuA = To him three rupees to give were = He had to give three rupees.

    asÃ khE subHAR̃E vaÑaR̃O pavandO = to us tomorrow to go will fall / happen = We will have to go tomorrow.

    tavHÃ khE HI kitAbᵃ paRHaR̃A pavandA = to you these books to read will fall.= You will have to read these books.

As with khapE and ghurjE, this is an impersonal construction. That is the subject (in English) is followed by khE, and what is the object in the English sentence becomes the logical subject in the Sindhi sentences. Thus the infinitive, in its lengthened form with /O/, and the verb inflect to agree with that logical subject. This agreement is in gender and number.

5. Note the way imtiHAn (test, examination) is used in Sindhi. The student "gives" the exam, i.e., imtiHAn ddIaR̃ᵘ, while the teacher or examiner "takes" the exam, imtiHan vaThaR̃ᵘ. For example,

Hi vIHᵃ SAgird imtiHAn ddIndA. These 20 students will "give" the exam.	هي وِيھ شاگرد امتحان ڏيندا۔
uHO ustAd imtiHAn vaThandO. That teacher will "take" the exam.	اهو استادُ امتحان وٽندو۔

6. kEtrA-I when used in the context illustrated above, means "many".

15-K Vocabulary for Lesson 15

uthaR̃ᵘ (uthᵘ -) To rise, get up	اُٿڻ (اُٿُ)	bbAvIHᵃ twenty-two	ٻاويھ
Acarᵘ (m) Sunday	آچر	bbaTIHᵃ thirty-two	ٻَٽيھ
araba'ᵃ (f) Wednessday	اربع	bbaHatari seventy-two	ٻاهتر
ag̃ArO (m) Tuesday	اڱارو	bbaHaTHi sixty-two	ٻاهٺ
imtiHAnᵘ (m) test, examination	امتحانُ	bbIAsI eighty-two	ٻِياسي
imtiHAn vaThaR̃ᵘ to "give" an exam	امتحان وٽڻ	bbIAnavE ninety-two	ٻِيانوي
UcO High	اُوچو	bbERI (f) boat	ٻيڙي
AHistE AHistE slowly	آهستي آهستي	tafAvatᵘ (m) difference	تفاوت
bIThO standing	بيٺو	takaRO fast, quick	تڪڙو
bbAEtAlIHᵃ forty-two	ٻائيتاليھ	TAngO (m) horse-drawn buggy	ٽانگو
bbAvajAHᵘ fifty-two	ٻاونجاھُ	jE pAri across	جي پار

jum'O (m) Friday	جمعو	SarU' karaR̃ to begin, start	شروع کرڻ
jaHAnu (m) world	جهان	ibAdata (f) worship	عبادت
(jE) cOdhArI around	(جي) چوڌاري	ibAdata karaR̃u to worship	عبادت کرڻ
chancharu Saturday	ڇنڇر	fOTO photograph	فوٽو
KamIsa (f) Thursday	خميس	fOTO kaddaR̃ to take a photo	فوٽو کڍڻ
KayAl (m) though, idea, opinion	خيال	khÃ aggE before	کان اڳي
dariyAHu, darIyAu (m) river	درياهُ، درياءُ	khÃ poi after	کان پوءِ
du'A (f) prayer, blessing	دعا	mazmAn (m) guest	مزمان
du'A ghuraR̃u to pray, (lit: to ask for blessing)	دعا گهرڻ	maHmAn (m) guest	مهمان
dEri (f) delay, lateness	دير	mOkila holiday, leave	موڪل
(jE) rUbarU before, in front of, face to face	(جي) روبرو	narsa (f) nurse	نرسَ
sUmaru (m) Monday	سومر	vArO doer, person	وارو
savEra early	سوير	vAHu (m) canal	واهُ
SAdI (f) wedding	شادي	vETHO seated	ويٺو
SarU' beginning	شروع		

15-L Conversional Review

1. Ask and answer the question below, listening the teacher ask the question while the student answers. Repeat the drill with the student doing the asking. Remember this in not a reading lesson. The student should have his book closed, using the pattern and freely substituting vocabulary he knows.

Teacher: kAlHa tavHÃ khE kāHin khE likhaR̃O HO?

استاد: ڪالھ توهان کي ڪنهن کي لکڻو هو؟

Student: mŨ khE pāHinjE pI˞ khE likhaR̃O HO.

شاگرد: مون کي پنهنجي پيءُ کي لکڻو هو.

(a)	ajj^u rAt^a jO tavHÃ khE chA karaR̃O AHE?	اڄ رات جو توهان کي ڇا ڪرڻو آهي؟
(b)	kalH^a tavHA khE kEddÃHā vaÑaR̃O HO?	ڪالھ توهان کي ڪيڏانهن وڃڻو هو؟
(c)	Acar^u jE ddĨhā tavHÃ khE chA karaR̃O pavandO?	آچر جي ڏينهن توهان کي ڇا ڪرڻو پوندو؟
(d)	IndaR HaftE tavHÃ khE kaHiRO sabaq^u parHaR̃O pavandO?	ايندڙ هفتي توهان کي ڪهڙو سبق پڙهڻو پوندو؟
(e)	bOrcI khE bazAr khÃ chA KarId karaR̃O AHE?	بورچيءَ کي بازار کان ڇا خريد ڪرڻو آهي؟
(f)	tavHÃ jE mA^u pI^u khE kithÃ acaR̃O pavandO?	توهان جي ماءُ پيءُ کي ڪٿان اچڻو پوندو؟
(g)	mŨ khE ghaR̃A kilA/pAO/maR̃ vaThaR̃^a ghurjE?	مون کي گهڻا ڪلا/پاء / مڻ وٺڻ گهرجن؟
(h)	tavHÃ khE kEtrA dafA Hina sabaq khE paRHaR̃^u ghurjE?	توهان کي ڪيترا دفعا هن سبق کي پڙهڻ گهرجي؟
(i)	tavHÃ khE kaHiRI SaI bAzAr mÃ vaThaR̃^u ghurjE?	توهان کي ڪهڙي شيءِ بازار مان وٺڻ گهرجي؟
(j)	garamI^a jE maosam^a mẼ asÃ khE chA khAiR̃^u ghurjE?	گرميءَ جي موسم ۾ اسان کي ڇا کائڻ گهرجي؟

2. (a) Practice using the days of the weak to tell your teacher which days to come or not to come:

Acar^a tE na acO, para sUmar^a tE acO. etc.,	آچر تي نہ اچو، پر سومر تي اچو.

(b) Using a calendar, the teacher can point to the days of the week in mixed order, and say a sentence in the following pattern, leaving out the day of the next week. The student should repeat the sentence filling in the blank.

T.	mÃ _____ sakhar na vIndus.	مان ـــــــــ سكر نہ ويندس
S.	mÃ (jUm'E jE ddĪHā) sakhar na vIndus.	مان (جمعي جي ڏينهن) سكر نہ ويندس.
T.	tavHI kaddahĪ sakhar vInda? Etc.	توهين ڪڏهن سکر ويندا؟

3. Substitute the following phrases in the model shown:

ciThi likaR̃ᵃ vArO – khAdhO tayAr	چٺي لکڻ وارو – ڪاڏو تيار
karaR̃ᵃ vArO – kapRA dhOaR̃ᵃ vArO	ڪرڻ وارو – ڪپڙا ڌوئڻ وارو
vaÑaR̃ᵃ vArO - acaR̃ᵃ vArO - rāgᵘ	وڃڻ وارو – اچڻ وارو – رنگ
karaR̃ᵃ vArO - madadⁱ ddIaR̃ᵃ vArO	ڪرڻ وارو – مدد ڏيڻ وارو
imtiHAn ddIaR̃ᵃ vArO – imtiHAn vaThaR̃ᵃ vArO - uthaR̃ᵃ vArO - paRHaR̃ᵃ vArO	امتحان ڏيڻ وارو – امتحان وٺڻ وارو – اٿڻ وارو – پڙهڻ وارو
T. ciThI likhaR̃ᵃ vArO kErᵘ AHE/HO?	چٺي لکڻ وارو ڪير آهي / هو؟
S. ciThI likha R̃ᵃ vArO mūHinjO dOst AHE/HO.	چٺي لکڻ وارو منهنجو دوست آهي / هو.

(b) Vary the answers using the following pattern:

ciThI likhaR̃ᵃ vArI mūHinjI bheR̃ᵘ HUI.	چٺي لکڻ واري منهنجي ڀيڻ هئي.

4. Answer the following questions. The teacher should vary the questions by changing the question word.

Question words: chA, kaddaHĪ, kEddAHā   ڪيڏانهن   ڪڏهن   ڇا

Q.	tavHI kEddÃHā vaÑaR̃ᵃ tE AHIO/HuA?	توهين ڪيڏانهن وڃڻ تي آهيو / هئا؟
Q.	zAlᵃ chA karaR̃ᵃ tE HUI/AHE?	زال ڇا ڪرڻ تي هئي / آهي؟
Q.	chOkirO kEddÃHā vaÑaR̃ᵃ tE HO?	ڇوڪرو ڪيڏانهن وڃڻ تي هو؟

Substitute vArO for tE in the above drill. Substitute freely from the vocabulary you have learned.

5. Complete the following sentences using as many different endings as your vocabulary and imagination allow.

mAnI khAiR̃ª khÃ pOⁱ	ماني کائٽ کان پوءِ ....
bAzAr vaÑaR̃ª khÃ aggE......	بازار وڃڻ کان اڳي. ....
sindhI paRHaR̃ª khÃ aggE......	سنڌي پڙھڻ کان اڳي ....
gharª acaR̃ª khÃ pOⁱ......	گھر اچڻ کان پوءِ ....

6. Use the following postpositions, nouns and verbs to make a variety of statements and questions according to the pattern.

zAlŨ dariyAHª jE pAr na IndIŨ.	زالون درياءَ جي پار نَہ ايندِيون.
<u>People</u>: HU, chOkirI, zAlŨ, mÃ	ھُو چوڪِري زالون مان
asĨ, tavHĨ, tŨ, mAR̃HŨ, chOkirA	اسين توهين تون ماٿھو چوڪرا
<u>Places</u>: iskUl, rastO, gharᵘ,	اسڪول رستو گھر
ispitAl, dariyAHᵘ kamarO.	اسپتال درياءُ ڪمرو
<u>Postpositions</u>: jE parⁱ, jE rUbarU,	جي پار جي روبرو
jE cOdhArI, jE vicamE	جي چوڌاري جي وچ ۾
<u>Verbs</u>: acaR̃ᵘ, vaÑaR̃ᵘ, bIhaR̃ᵘ, vEHaR̃ᵘ	اچڻ وڃڻ بيھڻ ويھڻ

7. As you converse with your teacher and with other friends, make a point of using the days of the week; find opportunities to tell someone what you are about to do, what you have or had to do, and on which day you did or will do it. The patterns of Sindhi have to be etched into your brain by your conscious use of each new pattern until it becomes automatic, and until you have mastered it.

LESSON SIXTEEN

16-A   Pronunciation Drill

1. Contrasting /A/ and /Ã/   (56/57)   /ا/ ء /ان/

اسان آسان ڪتاب پڙھيو.
اسان ڪلام مان ايمان بابت سکيو.
توھان سامان چانو مان ڪڍيو چا؟

2. Contrasting /g/ and /gg/   (23/24)   /ڳ/ ء /گ/

گوشت ڳري ويو.
گانءِ ڳوٽريءَ ڪي ڪائٽ لڳي.
ڪاريگر گاڏيءَ ھر گانو ڳائٽ لڳو.

16-B   The Use of the Conjunctive Participle

andar acI vEHO. Come in and sit down.	اندر اچي ويھو.
maHarbanI karE vEHI mũ SÃ cÃHĩ pIO. Please take a seat and have some tea with me.	مھرباني ڪري ويھي مون سان چانھ پيو.
HI Kat^u TapAl mẼ vijhI tavHĩ jaldI mOTI IndA chA? After posting this letter, will you come back quickly?	ھي خط تپال ۾ وجھي توھين جلدي موٽي ايندا چا؟

puTa, AlA kapRA pAE bImAr na thIndẼ chA? Son, won't you get sick from wearing wet clothes?	پٽ، آلا ڪپڙا پائي بيمار نہ ٿيندين چا؟
HU nEran karE iskUla vIndA AHin. After taking breakfast, they go to school.	هو نيرن ڪري اسڪول ويندا آهن.
chOkirO farAsIa tE vEHI pāHinjA kitAba paRHandO AHE. Sitting on the carpet the boy uses to read his books.	چوڪرو فراسيءَ تي ويهي پنهنجا ڪتاب پڙهندو آهي.
asĪ HoddE vaÑI chOkirani sÃ milandAsĪ. We'll go there and meet the boys.	اسين هوڏي وڃي ڇوڪرن سان ملنداسين.
mÃ kapRA dhOI ArAm kandus/kandius. After washing the clothes, I'll rest.	مان ڪپڙا ڌوئي آرام ڪندس / ڪنديس.
HunajE ghara vaÑI huna khE Kabar bbudhAIO. Go to his house and tell him the news.	هن جي گھر وڃي هن کي خبر ٻڌايو.
asĪ bAG mẼ vEHI siju laHaR̃u ddisandAsĪ. We'll sit in the garden and see the sun set.	اسين باغ ۾ ويهي سج لهڻ ڏسنداسين.
savEr uthI sij ubharR̃u bi ddisandAsĪ. We'll get up early and see the sun rise, too.	سوير اٿي سج اڀرڻ بہ ڏسنداسين.
usa mẼ vEHI asÃ khE garamI laggandI. We'll get hot from sitting in the sun.	اُس ۾ ويهي اسان کي گرمي لڳندي.
mAlHI, aggu mẼ HI kam KarE bazaar vaÑu. Gardener! First do this work and then go to the bazaar.	مالهي! اڳ ۾ هي ڪم ڪري بازار وڃ.
asĪ nEran karE AfIs gaddajI vEndA HuAsĪ. We used to eat breakfast and then go to the office together.	اسين نيرن ڪري آفيس گڏجي ويندا هئاسين.
tavHĪ ddaHẼ bajE jI gAddIa tE HalI vaqta tE paHucahandA. Going by ten o'clock train, you'll arrive on time.	توهين ڏهين بجي جي گاڏيءَ تي هلي وقت تي پهچندا.
mÃ ddisI acÃ (thO/thI). I'll go and see (lit: Having seen, I'll come)	مان ڏسي اچان (ٿو/ ٿي).
tavHÃ sÃ milI mŨ khE ddADhI KuSI thI AHE. I'm very happy to meet you.	توهان سان ملي مُون کي ڏاڍي خوشي ٿي آهي.

tO khE ddisI mÃ HamESa KuS AHIÃ (mŨ khE KusI thIndI AHE.) I'm always happy to see you.	توکي ڏِسي مان هميشہ خوش آهيان (مون کي خوشي ٿيندي آهي.)
E chOkiraO, HalIA vaÑO! Go away boys!	اي چوڪرؤ، هليا وَجو!

1. The conjunctive participle is formed by dropping the final short vowel of the root, and adding /I/ to roots ending in /u/:

    Thus, vaÑ^u becomes vaÑI.

    Verbs with roots ending in /i/ and /E/ to form the conjunctive participle. Thus, kar^i becomes karE.

2. In English we say "Come and sit down", or "Go and tell him", using two imperatives with the conjunction "and ." In Sindhi this idea is expressed by omitting the conjunction and using a conjunctive participle to express the first verbal idea. See sentence 1-3, 9 and 13 above.

3. This participle is also used to express ideas which may be said in various ways in English. Sentence five above could be said as follows:

    Having eaten breakfast, they go to school.

    After eating breakfast, they go to school.

    Before going to school, they eat breakfast.

    They eat breakfast and then go to school.

No matter how we say it in English, it is clear that the eating preceded the going to school. In Sindhi, the verbal idea expressed by the conjunctive participle always precedes the other action.

4. Besides its normal function of joining two verbal ideas without using "aĨ" (and), this participle is used in a variety of idiomatic ways in both colloquial and literary Sindhi. Watch for them as you listen to Sindhis talking and as you read. The last four examples above are illustrations of such idiomatic usage.

5. There are few irregular conjunctive participles not formed according to the above principles:

    cavaR̃^{u} (to say) becomes caI.

    ddiaR̃^{u} (to give) becomes ddEI.

    pIaR̃^{u} (to drink) becomes PI.

    paHaR̃^{u} (to wear) becomes PaE.

6. Sometimes an /O/ is added to the conjunctive participle. The effect of this is to add a continuous idea. Its usage in compound verbs will be discussed in a later lesson. HalIO is the only continuous conjunctive participle used very commonly. It is also the only one that is declined:

    HalIO vaÑ^u!   Go away! (singular)

    HalIA vaÑO!   Go away (plural)

7. milaR̃ᵘ means "to meet" someone. Notice that in Sindhi we meet "with" a person. The postposition sÃ is used, as in sentence 7 above. Other idiomatic use of milaR̃ᵘ will be introduced later.

8. sijᵘ (the sun) and usᵃ (sunshine) must be distinguished in Sindhi. As shown in example above, we do not sit in the sun, but in the sunshine, i.e. usᵃ mẼ.

9. aggu mẼ means "before, first" and is used in an adverbial sense. Its usage must be distinguished from that of khÃ AggE which is used with nouns or pronouns as a postposition, and also means "before" in relation to time.

16-C The Formation of the Present Continuous Tense

The use of raHIO plus the conjunctive participle.

Masculine		مذكر	
Singular	Plural	جمع	واحد
mÃ karE raHIO AHIÃ I am doing (in the act of, now)	asĨ karE raHIA AHIŨ We are doing	آسين كري رهيا آهيون.	مان كري رهيو آهيان.
tŨ karE raHIO AHĨ Your are doing	tavHĨ karE raHIA AHIO You are doing	توهين كري رهيا آهيو.	تون كري رهيو آهين.
HU karE raHIO AHE He is doing	UHE karE raHIA AHin They are doing	اهي كري رهيا آهن.	هُو كري رهيو آهي.

Feminine		مؤنث	
mÃ karE raHI AHIÃ I am doing	asĨ karE raHIŨ AHIŨ We are doing	آسين كري رهيون آهيون.	مان كري رهي آهيان.
tŨ karE raHI AHĨ Your are doing	tavHĨ karE raHIŨ AHIO You are doing	توهين كري رهيون آهيو.	تُون كري رهي آهين.
HU karE raHI AHE She is doing	UHE karE raHIŨ AHin They are doing	اهي كري رهيون آهن.	هُو كري رهي آهي.

1. This form of the present continuous tense uses the conjunctive participle of the main verb + aHIO with the present tense of the verb "to be", HuaR̃ᵘ. It describes action which is taking place at the time of speaking, continuously in the present.

The use of payO with the present tense

Masculine		مذكر	
Singular	Plural	جمع	واحد
AŨ acÃ thO payO. I am coming. (in the act or process)	asĪ acŨ thA payA. We are coming.	آسين اچون ٿا پيا.	آءٌ اچان ٿو پيو.
tŨ acĪ thO payO. You are coming.	avHĨ acO thA payA. You are coming.	اوهين اچو ٿا پيا.	تون اچين ٿو پيو.
HU acE thO payO. He is coming.	UHE acan thA payA. They are coming.	اُهي اچن ٿا پيا.	هو اچي ٿو پيو.

Feminine		مؤنث	
AŨ acÃ thI paI. I am coming.	asĪ acŨ thIŨ payŨ. We are coming.	آسين اچون ٿيون پيون.	آءٌ اچان ٿي پئي.
tŨ acĪ thI paI. You are coming.	avHĨ acO thIŨ payU. You are coming.	اوهين اچو ٿيون پيون.	تون اچين ٿي پئي.
HUª acE thI paI. He is coming.	UHE acan thIŨ payŨ. They are coming.	اُهي اچن ٿيون پيون.	هُو اَچي ٿي پئي.

2. A continuous sense is given to the ordinary present tense by adding to the verb the continuous particle payO. This agrees with the subject in gender and number. It may precede or follow the main verb. The present tense indicator thO may be omitted when payO is used, thus,

      HU payO acE   He is coming

      HU acE payO   He is coming

The Use of VEThO and bIThO to Express Continuous Action

Masculine		مذكر	
Singular	Plural	جمع	واحد
mÃ vEThO / bIThO paRHÃ. I am reading.	asĪ vEThA / bIThA paRHŨ. We are reading.	اسين وينا / بيتا پڙهون.	مان وينو / بيتو پڙهان.
tŨ vEThO / bIThO paRH Ĩ. You are reading.	tavHĨ vEThA / bIThA paRHO. You are reading.	توهين وينا / بيتا پڙهو.	تون وينو / بيتو پڙهين.
HU vEThO / bIThO paRHE. He is reading.	UHE vEThA / bIThA paRHan. They are reading.	اُهي وينا / بيتا پڙهن.	هو وينو / بيتو پڙهي.

	Feminine	مؤنث	
mÃ vEThI / bIThI paRHÃ. I am reading.	asĨ vEThIŨ / bIThIŨ paRHŨ. We are reading.	آسين ويٺيون / بيٺيون پڙهون.	مان ويٺي / بيٺي پڙهان.
tŨ vEThI / bIThI paRHĨ. You are coming.	tavHĨ vEThIŨ / bIThIŨ paRHO. You are reading.	توهين ويٺيون / بيٺيون پڙهو.	تُون ويٺي / بيٺي پڙهين.
HUa veThI / bIThI paRHE. She is reading.	UHE vEThIŨ / bIThIŨ paRHan. They are reading.	اُهي ويٺيون / بيٺيون پڙهن.	هُوءَ ويٺي / بيٺي پڙهي.

3. If the action is done while sitting or standing, and the speaker wishes to call attention to that fact, vEThO or bIThO may be used to express continuous action. It indicates that the action is being done while the subject is sitting or standing. In this case, the appropriate form of vEThO or bIThO is added to the present tense in place of the participle, thO. These will agree with the subject in gender and number, and always <u>precede</u> the main verb.

4. All the above forms convey the idea of an action taking place continuously in the present. They are frequently used in colloquial spoken Sindhi, and each form has its own distinction as to usage and the shade of meaning expressed. Some are more frequently used in one area or with a certain verb. Observe carefully how they are used in your own are and which particular form of the continuous each verb takes more commonly.

5. The present continuous tense must be carefully distinguished from both the present tense and the present habitual tense as to the different meaning expressed by each.

16 -D Statements, Questions, and negatives in the present Continuous Tense.

mÃ sindhI sikhI raHIO AHIÃ / raHI AHIÃ. I am learning Sindhi.	مان سنڌي سکي رهيو آهيان / رهي آهيان.
zAlŨ cAH ĩ tayAr karE raHIŨ AHin. The women are making tea.	زالون چانھ تيار ڪري رهيون آهن.
chOkirA chA karE raHIA AHin? What are the boys doing?	چوڪرا ڇا ڪري رهيا آهن؟
HU gAHa tE khEddI raHIA AHin. They are playing on the grass.	هو گاھ تي کيڏي رهيا آهن.
avHĨ chA paRHI raHIA AHIO? What are you reading?	اوهين ڇا پڙهي رهيا آهيو؟
mÃ risAlO paRHI raHIO AHIÃ. I'm reading a magazine.	مان رسالو پڙهي رهيو آهيان.
kEr acE thO payO? Who is coming?	ڪير اچي ٿو پيو؟

mūHinjO bhAᵘ acE thO payO. My brother is coming.	منهنجو ڀاءُ اچي ٿو پيو.
HunajI gharavArI aĨ bbArᵃ bi acan thA payA. His wife and children are coming, too.	هن جي گهر واري ۽ ٻار ٻہ اچن ٿا پيا.
zAIŨ vaÑan thIŨ payŨ. The women are going.	زالُون وَڃَن ٿِيُون پيون.
mARHU kam kan payA. The men are working.	ماڻهو ڪم ڪن پيا.
tŨ chA (thO) payO karĨ? What are you doing?	تون ڇا (ٿو) پيو ڪرين؟
mÃ kitAbᵘ vEThO paRHÃ / vEThI paRHÃ. I'm (sitting) reading a book.	مان ڪتاب ويٺو پڙهان/ ويٺي پڙهان.
darzI, tavHĨ HAR̃E mūHinjI qamIsᵃ sibI raHIA AHIO chA? Tailor! Are you sewing my shirt now?	درزي! توهين هاڻي منهنجي قميص سبي رهيا آهيو ڇا؟
mOcI jutIŨ vEThA ThAHan. The shoemakers are making shoes.	موچي جُتيون ويٺا ٺاهن.
chOkirI āmbᵘ bIThI khAE. The girl is eating a mango.	چوڪري أنب ويٺي کائي.
DAkTar sAHib HAR̃E kāHin khE ddisI raHIO AHE chA? Is the doctor seeing anyone right now?	ڊاڪٽر صاحب هاڻي ڪنهن کي ڏسي رهيو آهي ڇا؟
na, HU kāHin khE ddisI na raHIO AHE. HU khAdhO khAI raHIO AHE. No, he isn't seeing anyone. He is eating his meal.	نہ، هو ڪنهن کي ڏسي نہ رهيو آهي. هو کاڌو کائي رهيو آهي.
uHO chOkirO HaTᵃ tÃ chA vaThI raHIO AHE? What is that boy getting from the shop?	اهو ڇوڪرو هٽ تان ڇا وٺي رهيو آهي؟
mūHinjO KayAl AHE ta HU naÕ qalam KarId karE raHIO AHE. I think he is buying a new pen.	منهنجو خيال آهي تہ هو نئون قلم خريد ڪري رهيو آهي.

1. Notice that in sentence 9 above, Huna jI possesses both gharavArI and bbArᵃ. It is in the feminine form in agreement with gharavArI which is closest to it. The <u>verb</u> is in the plural masculine form to agree with the plural masculine form to agree with the plural nature of the subject, that is, wife <u>and</u> children.

The order could be changed as follows:

        HunajA bbArᵃ aĨ gharavArI acan thA payA.

        His children and wife are coming too.

16 -E   The use of saghaR̃ᵘ (to be able)

uHO mAR̃HU halI na thO saghE. That man can't walk.	اُهو ماٹھو هلي نہ ٿو سگھي.
andhO mAR̃HU ddisI na thO saghE. A blind man is not able to see.	انڌو ماٹھو ڏسي نہ ٿو سگھي.
tavHĨ jumE' jE ddĨHã acI saghandA? Will you be able to come on Friday?	توهين جمعي جي ڏينهن اچي سگھندا؟
na, mÃ acI kO na saghhandus. No, I can't.	نہ، مان اچي ڪونہ سگھندس.
chOkirI paRHI saghE thI, parᵃ HinajI mAᵘ paRHI na thI saghE. The girl can read, but her mother can't read.	چوڪري پڙهي سگھي ٿي، پر هن جي ماءُ پڙهي نہ ٿي سگھي.
HitÃ tavHĨ HunanjO gharᵃ ddisI saghO thA. You can see their house from here.	هتان توهين هن جو گھر ڏسي سگھو ٿا.
subhAR̃E mistrI kam karE saghE thO. Tommorow the artisian will be able to work.	سڀاڻي مستري ڪم ڪري سگھي ٿو.
IndaR sAl HI bba chOkirIŨ imtiHAn ddEI na saghandIŨ. Next year these two girls won't be able to give the examination.	اِيندڙ سال هي ٻہ چوڪريون امتحان ڏئي نہ سگھنديُون.

1. saghaR̃ᵘ means "to be able to" do something. In English this idea is conveyed by "can" or "could", as well as "to be able to". In Sindhi it is always used with another verb which is in the form of the conjunctive participle, and does not change. The other verb may be left out and simply understood in English, as in sentence four above, but it may not be omitted in Sindhi. It must be expressed.

2. saghaR̃ᵘ is often used in the present tense in English even when a future time is meant. This is also true in Sindhi if a near future is intended, as in sentence seven above. However generally in Sindhi the future tense is used if a future time is meant.

3. saghaR̃ᵘ is an intransitive verb, and agrees with the subject in gender, number and person as do other intransitive verbs.

16-F   Vocabulary

AlO wet	آلو	gharavArI (f) wife, woman of the house	گهرواري
agg^u mE first, before	اڳ مِ	qamIs^a (f) shirt, dress	قميص
andhO blind	اندو	sibaR̃^{u} (sibu-) to sew	سبڻُ (سبُ)
andar inside, in	اندر	sij^u (m) sun	سج
ubharaR̃^{u} (ubhari-) to rise (as the sun)	اُڀرڻُ (اُڀر)	laHaR̃^{u} (laHu-) to set (as the sun)	لهڻُ (لهُ)
us^a (f) sunshine	اُس	maHarbAni karE please	مهرباني كري
TapAl^a (f) mail	ٽپال	milaR̃^{u} (milu) to meet	ملڻُ (مل)
TapAl vijhaR̃^{u} to post, mail	ٽپال وجهڻ	mOTi acaR̃^{u} to come back	موٽي اچڻ
ThAHaR̃^{u} (ThAHu) to make	ٺاهڻُ (ٺاهُ)	mOcI (m) Shoemaker	موچي
jutI (f) shoe	جُتي	mistrI (m) artisan, skilled workman	مستري
khAdhO (m) food	کاڌو	nEran^a (f) breakfast	نيرنَ
khAiR̃^{u} (khAu-) to eat	کائڻُ (کاءُ)	uthaR̃^{u} (uthu-) to get up	اُٺڻُ (اُٺُ)
khEddaR̃^{u} (khEdd^u) to play	کيڏڻُ (کيڏُ)	savEr^a early	سويرَ
darzI (m) tailor	درزي		

16-G   Conversational Review

1. Change the infinitive in each phrase to conjunctive participle. For example

(a)	kam (karaR̃u) acO: kam karE acO.	کم (کرڻُ) اچو: کم ڪري اچو
(b)	mŨHinjI qamIs (sibaR̃u) mŨ khE ddEO.	منهنجي قميص (سبڻُ) مون کي ڏيو.
(c)	khaTᵃ tE (vEHaR̃u) ArAm karIO.	ڪٽ تي (ويھڻُ) آرام ڪريو.
(d)	khAdhO (khAiR̃u) mOTI acO.	کاڏو (کائڻُ) موٽي اچو.
(e)	mistri mŨHinjI kursI (ThaHaR̃u) mŨ khE ddIndO.	مستري منهنجي ڪرسي (ٺاهڻُ) مون کي ڏيندو.

Go through the exercise changing the verb, changing the subject, and where possible changing the tense of the second verb.
For example, a) above could be as follows:

kam karE vaÑO, HU kam karE vEndO, mÃ kam karE acI saghundus, etc

2. Use the following verbs to pantomime actions. The first time ask your teacher to do the action, stating what he is doing. The student may then answer, stating what the teacher is doing. Use the appropriate form of the Present Continuous tense.
For Example:

Teacher: mÃ khAdO khAE raHIO AHIA.	استاد: مان ڪاڏو ڪائي رھيو آھيان.
Student: tavHĨ khADO khAE raHIA AHIO.	شاگرد: توهين ڪاڏو ڪائي رھيا آھيو.

randⁱ khEddaR̃u, qamIsᵃ sibaR̃u   راند ڪيڏڻُ،   قميص سبڻُ

kapRan jI istrI karaR̃u, paR̃I pIaR̃u   ڪپڙن جي استري ڪرڻ، پاڻي پيئڻُ

dOstᵃ sÃ milaR̃u, khAdhO khAiR̃u   دوست سان ملڻُ،   ڪاڏو ڪائڻُ

Switch roles, so that the student does the action, stating what he is doing. The teacher should then reply stating what the student is doing.

3. Bring a magazine or children's picture book to class with pictures of children, men and women doing various activities. Use the verbs in this lesson and previous lessons to talk about what the people in the pictures are doing, using the present continuous tense.

In your conversations with neighbors and friends make a point of bringing this tense into your discussions. Be sure to distinguish between the usage of this tense (what is being done right now) and the present habitual (those actions that are done regularly or habitually).

Note: If your teacher says that a certain verb is not used in one form of the Present Continuous, make a note of this. These usages vary according to local dialectical variations. You will have to learn this by careful listening.

4. Use the following phrases in the model below:

ciThI likhaR̃u, pāHinjI tasvIra mOkilaR̃u   چٹي لکڻ،   پنهنجي تصوير موڪلڻ

kapRA dhOaR̃u, bAGa mẼ vEHaR̃u   ڪپڙا ڌوئڻ،   باغ ۾ ويهڻ

madad ddIaR̃u, tayAr karaR̃u   مدد ڏيڻ،   تيار ڪرڻ

imtiHAn vaThaR̃u, mŨHinjE ghar vaÑaR̃u   امتحان وٺڻ   منهنجي گهر وڃڻ

mŨ khE bbudhAiR̃u, dEra sÃ tarasaR̃u   مون کي ٻڌائڻ   دير سان ترسڻ

T: avHĨ _____ saghO thA?	اوهين ( ) سگھو ٿا؟
S: HAO mÃ _____ saghÃ thO/thI. (or, na, mÃ _____ na thO/thI saghÃ.	هائو، مان ( ) سگھان ٿو/ ٿي. يا نہ، مان ( ) نہ ٿو/ ٿي سگھان.
chA avHĨ bi _____ saghO thA?	ڇا اوهين بہ ( ) سگھو ٿا؟
T: chA uHO maR̃HU _____ sagHE thO?	ڇا هو ماڻهو _____ سگھي ٿو؟

REVIEW TWO

1. **Review the Pronunciations Drills**, especially for any sounds that you are still having trouble with. Ask your teacher to pick out those words which you are mispronouncing, and to give you extra drill on those. Never assume that because you "can't make that sound", or "that sound is difficult" that you should not continuously <u>try</u> to do it. It is much easier to learn new sounds early in the course of learning and the language than to unlearn bad habits later.

2. Use the vocabulary on the following pages to practice the structures you have learned in lessons nine to sixteen. Go back over the "Conversational Review" sections using the patterns there for further practice.

    Remember that you now have the vocabulary and structures from four to eight in addition to that on this review list. So you have much more freedom within the scope of these lessons to develop and expand a pattern.

For example, one type of practice could be as follows:

    Teacher: mÃ jumE jE ddĨHã Indus.

    Student: jumE' jE ddĨHã na acijO, par[a] chanchar[a] tE acijO.

It can be seen that in this sentence there are three areas that land themselves to substitution.

Subjects: mÃ, mÃ aĨ pāHunjI gharvArI, DAkTar sAHib, asājA mAiT[a], hunajŨ bba bhEnarŨ, cAr SAgird[a], tavHÃ jA bbArabbacA, etc,

Time Phrases: jumE' jE ddĨhã, ag̃ArE tE, subuH[u], SAm, manjhand[i], kAlH[a], gUzrEI HaftE, IndaR maHinE, etc, etc,

Verbs: Indus (acaR̃[u]), Look through the list of verbs in the word list on the pages following, and use as many as you can, changing tenses according to the time phrase, person and number according to the subject.

Take another pattern, such as, in lesson 16-B:

    HU nEran karE iskUl[a] vIndA AHin.

Here you can see that the areas of substitution are the subject, the first verbal clause, in the form of the conjunctive participle, and the principal verb with iskUl[a]. With only this one pattern, there are a large number of variations and combinations, using only the vocabulary included in these lessons thus far.

4. In short, using the vocabulary and patterns learned so far, hundred of sentences, and hours of practice can be developed. By taking only one pattern from each structure, and putting it on a card, try to make up as many variations as you can. Explain to the teacher what you want to do, and he will be able to help you to review in this way. However, remember this is a review. You should not be trying to learn anything new, but rather to firmly fix these structures and patterns in your memory so that they become automatic.

5. In the list following the numbers in parenthesis after the vocabulary words indicate the lesson in which the words was first given and defined.

6. Finally, remember that the explanations in each lesson are for you to read, and to help you to understand. You should not be spending time on these in English in your class time. **At this point all your class time with your teacher should be in Sindhi.**

Questions		Postpositions (Cont'd)		Numbers (cont)	
kEtrO (9)	کيترو	(jE) rUbarU (15)	(جي) روبرو	cAllH^a (12)	چاليھ
ghaR̃O? (9)	گھڙو	(jE) vicam̃E (15)	(جي) وچ م	panjAH^u (12)	پنجاھ
kĨa (9)	کيئن	khÃ aggE (15)	کان اڳي	saTh^i (12)	ست
kithÃ? (10)	کٽان	khÃ pOi (15)	کان پوءِ	satar^i (12)	ستر
kEddÃha? (10)	کيڏانھن	**Greetings & Courtesies**		asI (12)	اسي
kaddaHĨ (14)	کڏھن	asalAm 'alEkum (9)	السلام عليکم	navE (12)	نوي
Conjunctions		va 'alEkum asalAm (9)	وعليکم السلام	saO (12)	سو
jEkaddaHĨ ta (11)	جيکڏھن ت	maHarbAnI (9)	مھرباني	HazAr^u (12)	ھزار
yA (11)	يا	maHarbAnI karE (16)	مھرباني ڪري	lakh^u (12)	لک
Postpositions		**Numbers**		kirOR^u (12)	ڪروڙ
khE (9)	کي	yAraHã (9)	يارھن	panjavIH^a (13)	پنجويھ
vaT^i (9)	وٽ	bbAraHã (9)	بارھن	panjaTIH^a (13)	پنجٽيھ
ddÃH^a (10)	ڏانھن	tEraHã (9)	تيرھن	panjEtAlIH^a (13)	پنجيتاليھ
sÃ (10)	سان	cOddaHã (9)	چوڏھن	panjavanjAH^u (13)	پنجونجاھ
mÃ (10)	مان	pandaraHã (9)	پندرھن	panjaHaTh^i (13)	پنجھٺ
khÃ (10)	کان	sOraHã (9)	سورھن	panjaHatar^i (13)	پنجھتر
gadd^u (11)	گڏ	sataraHã (11)	سترھن	panjAsI (13)	پنجاسي
lAi (11)	لاءِ	araRaHã (11)	ارڙھن	panjAnavE (13)	پنجانوي
tAĨ (13)	تائين	uR̃avIHa (11)	اٽويھ	EkavIHa, EkIha (14)	ايڪويھ ايڪيھ
(jE) pAr^i (15)	جي پار	vIHa (11)	ويھ	EkaTIHa (14)	ايڪٽيھ
(jE) cOdhArI (15)	جي چوڌاري	TIHa (12)	ٽيھ	EkEtAlIHa (14)	ايڪيتاليھ

Numbers (cont)		Frequency/ Time Words		Other Adverbs	
EkavanjAH^u 14	ایکونجاہ	ajj^u (10)	اڄ	bilkul (9)	بلکل
EkaHaTh^i (14)	ایکہٹھ	HA$\tilde{R}$E (10)	ہاڙي	faqat^i (9)	فقط
EkaHatar^i (14)	ایکہتر	varI (10)	وري	HOdd$\tilde{A}$Hā (10)	ہوڏانہن
EkAsI (14)	ایکاسي	bbaI (11)	ٻئي	HEdd$\tilde{A}$Hā (10)	ہيڏانہن
EkAnavE (14)	ایکانوي	subhA$\tilde{R}$E (11)	سياڙي	SAyad^i (11)	شاید
bbAvIHa (15)	ٻاویہہ	ajj^u kAlH^a (11)	اڄکلھ	KabardAr (12)	خبردار
bbaTIHa (15)	ٻتیہہ	vadhIk^a (11)	وڌیک	aTkal (13)	اٽکل
bbaEtAlIHa (15)	ٻائیتالیہہ	ddiHARI (12)	ڏہاڙي	ddADhO (13)	ڏاڍو
bbavanjAH^u (15)	ٻاونجاہُ	rOzAnO (12)	روزانو	yAnE (13)	یعني
bbaHaTh^i (15)	ٻاہٹ	Har^i (12)	ہرِ	zarUr (14)	ضرور
bbaHatari (15)	ٻاہتر	aTkal (13)	اٽکل	agg^u m$\tilde{E}$ (16)	اڳ مَ
bbIAsI (15)	ٻیاسي	bAqI (13)	باقي	andar (16)	اندر
bbIAnavE (15)	ٻیانوي	zIAdaH^a (13)	زیادہ	savEr^a (16)	سویر
Fractions		kAfI (13)	کافي	Pronouns	
adh^u	اڌُ	ghaT^i (13)	گھٽِ	pA$\tilde{R}$^{a} (10)	پاڙ
aDhAI	اڍائي	kalH^a (13)	کلھ، کالھ	sandas^u (10)	سندس
pA^u (13)	پاءُ	jaldI (14)	جلدي	Numerical Adjectives	
pO$\tilde{R}$A (13)	پوڙا	AHistE (15)	آہستي	bbIO (12)	ٻیو
ddEDh^u (13)	ڊیڍُ	takiRO (15)	تکڙو	TIÕ	ٹیون
sADha (13)	ساڍا	savEr^a (15)	سویر	paHarIÕ	پہریون
savA (13)	سوا			cOthÕ	چوٹون
munO (13)	مُنو				

Adjectives			Adjectives (cont)			Nouns – Persons	
thOrO	(9)	تورو	akElO	(13)	اڪيلو	bbArabbacA (m.pl.) (9)	ٻار ٻچا
pakO	(9)	پڪو	pUrO	(13)	پورو	bbacO (m) (9)	ٻچو
ca$\tilde{g}$O bhalO	(9)	چڱو ڀلو	qImtI	(13)	قيمتي	bhA^u (m) (9)	ڀاءُ
KuS^i	(9)	خوش	guzrEl^u	(13)	گذريل	bhE$\tilde{R}^u$ (f) (9)	ڀيڻ
KEr	(9)	خير	IndaR^a	(14)	اينڊڙ	pI^u (m) (9)	پيءُ
sabh^u	(9)	سڀ	KAs	(14)	خاصُ	KudA (m) (9)	خدا
suThO	(9)	سٺو	sOlO	(14)	سولو	dhI^a (f) (9)	ڌيءَ
kacO	(9)	ڪچو	muSkIl	(14)	مشڪل	zamIndAr^u (m) (9)	زميندار
sAf^u	(10)	صاف	UcO	(15)	اوچو	mA^u (f) (9)	ماءُ
tEz^u	(11)	تيز	bIThO	(15)	بيٺو	mURas^u (m) (9)	مڙس
tikhO	(11)	تکو	vEThO	(15)	ويٺو	mA^u pI^u (m.Pl) (10)	ماءُ پيءُ
thadhO	(11)	ٿڌو	AlO	(16)	آلو	dOst^u (m) (12)	دوست
KarAb^u	(11)	خرابُ	andhO	(16)	انڌو	sAHERI (f) (12)	ساهيڙي
sastO	(11)	سستو	**Days of week**			naras^i (f) (15)	نرسِ
zarUrI	(11)	ضروري	Acar^u (m)	(15)	آچر	gharavArI (f) (16)	گهرواري
maHAngO	(11)	مهانگو	arabA (f)	(15)	اربع	mistrI (m) (16)	مستري
miThO	(11)	مٺو	a$\tilde{g}$ArO (m)	(15)	اڱارو	mOcI (m) (16)	موچي
mumkin	(11)	ممڪن	jumO (m)	(15)	جمعو	darzI (m) (16)	درزي
garam	(12)	گرمُ	chanchar^u (m)	(15)	چنڇر	**Other Nouns**	
naram	(12)	نرمُ	KamIs^a (f)	(15)	خميس	afsOs (m) (9)	افسوس
naÕ	(12)	نئون	sUmar^u (m)	(15)	سومر	umId^a (f) (9)	اميد
parA$\tilde{R}$O	(12)	پراڻو				tap^u (m) (9)	تپ

Other Nouns	(cont)	Other Nouns	(cont)	Other Nouns	(cont)
thElHI (f) (9)	تيلهي	mAnI (f) (10)	ماني	ciThI (f) (12)	چٺي
HAl^u (m) (9)	حال	ijAzat^a (f) (11)	اجازت	daf'aO (m) (12)	دفعو
KErIat (f) (9)	خيريت	amb^u (m) (11)	انب	ddIH^u (m) (12)	ڏينهن
darjO (m) (9)	درجو	basar^u (m) (11)	بصر	rAt^i (f) (12)	رات
rupIyO (m) (9)	رپيو	bhAjjI (f) (11)	ڀاڄي	rAndIkO (m) (12)	رانديڪو
zamIn^a (f) (9)	زمين	taklIf^u (m) (11)	تڪليف	rOz^u (m) (12)	روزُ
sUr^u (m) (9)	سور	paTATO (m) (11)	پٽاٽو	sArI (f) (12)	ساڙي
Sukur^u (m) (9)	شڪر	paghAr^a (f) (11)	پگهار	sIArO (m) (12)	سيارو
qisim^u (m) (9)	قسم	cÃHi (f) (11)	چانهه	SAm^a (m) (12)	شامَ
khanD^u (f) (9)	کنڊ	sabaq^u (m) (11)	سبق	subuH^u (m) (12)	صبحُ
khIr^u (m) (9)	کير	salAmatI (f) (11)	سلامتي	kapaH^a (f) (12)	ڪپهَ
mathO (m) (9)	مٺو	sUf^u (m) (11)	صوف	gAddI (f) (12)	گاڏي
mizAj^u (m) (9)	مزاج	gudAm (m) (11)	گدام	gAH^u (m) (12)	گاهُ
maHarbAnI (9)	مهرباني	gajar^a (f) (11)	گجر	garamI (f) (12)	گرمي
vaqt^u (m) (9)	وقت	nArangI (f) (11)	نارنگي	manjhand^i (m) (12)	منجهندِ
Hath^u (m) (9)	هٿ	mÎHũ (m) (11)	مينهُن	maosam^a (f) (12)	موسمَ
pEsa (m.pl.) (10)	پيسا	HavA (f) (11)	هوا	maHInO (m) (12)	مهينو
thAv^a (m) (10)	ٺانو	UnHArO (m) (12)	اونهارو	vArO (m) (12)	وارو
SaI (f) (10)	شيء	bhErO (m) (12)	ڀيرو	HaftO (m) (12)	هفتو
qurAn SarIf^u (m) (10)	قرآن شريف	pOkh^i (f) (12)	پوک	agh^u (m) (13)	اڱهُ
ggAlH^i (f) (10)	ڳالھ	taraH^a (f) (12)	طرح	sEr^u (m) (13)	سيرُ
lifAfO (m) (10)	لفافو	cÃvar^a (m.pl) (12)	چانور	qImat^a (f) (13)	قيمت

Other Nouns	(cont)	Other Nouns	(cont)	Simple Verbs	
kAThI (f) (13)	کاٹھي	tafAvat^u (m) (15)	تفاوتُ	aca$\tilde{R}^u$ (10)	اچݨُ
kalAk^u (m) (13)	کلاکُ	TangO (m) (15)	ٹانگو	bbudha$\tilde{R}^u$ (10)	ٻڏݨ
kilO (m) (13)	کلو	jaHAn^u (m) (15)	جہانُ	bbudhAi$\tilde{R}^u$ (10)	ٻڌائݨ
gIH^u (m) (13)	گيہُ	darIAH^u (m) (15)	دَرياهُ	tarsa$\tilde{R}^u$ (10)	ترسݨ
maTar^a (m.pl) (13)	مَتَر	du'A (f) (15)	دُعا	paRHa$\tilde{R}^u$ (10)	پڑھݨ
fasal (m) (13)	فصل	dEr^i (f) (15)	ديرِ	caRHa$\tilde{R}^u$ (10)	چڑھݨ
mITar^u (m) (13)	ميٹرُ	KayAl (m) (15)	خيال	cava$\tilde{R}^u$ (10)	چوݨ
ma$\tilde{R}^u$ (m) (13)	مݨُ	SAdI (f) (15)	شادي	chadda$\tilde{R}^u$ (10)	چڏݨ
masjid^i (m) (13)	مسجدِ	SarU'^{u} (m) (15)	شُروع	dhOa$\tilde{R}^u$ (10)	ڈوئݨ
vAl^u (m) (13)	وال	mOkal^a (f) (15)	موکل	ddisa$\tilde{R}^u$ (10)	ڊسݨ
bAH^i (f) (14)	باہِ	vArO (m) (15)	وارو	ddIa$\tilde{R}^u$ (10)	ڊيݨ
bhARO (m) (14)	ڀاڙو	vAH^u (m) (15)	واهُ	rakha$\tilde{R}^u$ (10)	رکݨ
pakhI (m) (14)	پکِي	us^a (f) (16)	اُسَ	raHa$\tilde{R}^u$ (10)	رھݨُ
jAi (f) (14)	جاءِ	TapAl^a (f) (16)	ٹپالَ	samjha$\tilde{R}^u$ (10)	سمجھݨ
HAlat^a (f) (14)	حالتَ	jutI (f) (16)	جُتي	samjhAi$\tilde{R}^u$ (10)	سمجھائݨ
sAnjhI (f) (14)	سانجھي	khAdhO (m) (16)	کاڌو	kaDha$\tilde{R}^u$ (10)	کڍݨ
masvAR^a (f) (14)	مسواڙ	qamIs^a (f) (16)	قميص	kara$\tilde{R}^u$ (10)	کرݨ
lArI (f) (14)	لاري	sij^u (m) (16)	سجُ	khOla$\tilde{R}^u$ (10)	کولݨ
va$\tilde{R}^u$ (m) (14)	وݨُ	nEran^a (f) (16)	نيرنِ	ggAlHAi$\tilde{R}^u$ (10)	ڳالھائݨ
ibAdat^a (f) (15)	عبادت			likha$\tilde{R}^u$ (10)	لکݨ
imtIHAn (m) (15)	امتحانُ			mOkila$\tilde{R}^u$ (10)	موکلݨ
bbERI (f) (15)	ٻيڙي			vaTha$\tilde{R}^u$ (10)	وٺݨ

Simple Verbs	(cont)	Simple Verbs	(cont)	Simple Verbs	(cont)
vaÑaR̃ᵘ (10)	وِجݨ	khAiR̃ᵘ (12)	کائݨ	vikaR̃aR̃ᵘ (vikAmaR̃ᵘ) (14)	وکٹݨ وکامݨ
vijhaR̃ᵘ (10)	وِجھݨ	sumHaR̃ᵘ (12)	سمھݨ	vEHaR̃ᵘ (14)	ویہݨ
HalaR̃ᵘ (10)	ہلݨ	aR̃aR̃ᵘ (12)	آٹݨ	uthaR̃ᵘ (14)	اٹݨ
paHucaR̃ᵘ (11)	پہچݨ	uddAmaR̃ᵘ (12)	اذامݨ	ubharaR̃ᵘ (14)	ایرݨ
laggaR̃ᵘ (11)	لگݨ	bIHaR̃ᵘ (12)	بیہݨ	ThAHaR̃ᵘ (14)	ناہݨ
cAHaR̃ᵘ (11)	چاہݨ	pIaR̃ᵘ (12)	پیئݨ	khEddaR̃ᵘ (14)	کیڈݨ
pavaR̃ᵘ (11)	پوݨ	kamAiR̃ᵘ (14)	کمائݨ	sibaR̃ᵘ (14)	سبݨ
HujaR̃ᵘ (11)	ہجݨ	maraR̃ᵘ (14)	مرݨ	saghaR̃ᵘ (14)	سگھݨ
thIaR̃ᵘ (12)	تیݨ	nikaraR̃ᵘ (14)	نکرݨ	laHaR̃ᵘ (14)	لہݨ
paHaraR̃ᵘ (12)	پہرݨ	visAiR̃ᵘ (14)	وسائݨ	milaR̃ᵘ (14)	ملݨ

Compound Verbs		Compound Verbs	(cont)
arAm karaR̃ᵘ (11)	آرام کرݨ	madad karaR̃ᵘ (11)	مدد کرݨ
band karaR̃ᵘ (11)	بند کرݨ	mU'Af karaR̃ᵘ (11)	معاف کرݨ
tayAr karaR̃ᵘ (11)	تیار کرݨ	nimAzᵃ paRHaR̃ᵘ (11)	نماز پڑھݨ
KarIdᵃ karaR̃ᵘ (11)	خرید کرݨ	vApas karaR̃ᵘ (11)	واپس کرݨ
rangᵘ karaR̃ᵘ (11)	رنگ کرݨ	istrI karaR̃ᵘ (12)	استری کرݨ
rAndⁱ karaR̃ᵘ (11)	راند کرݨ	garam karaR̃ᵘ (12)	گرم کرݨ
rOzO rakhaR̃ᵘ (11)	روزو رکݨ	istimAl karaR̃ᵘ (13)	استعمال کرݨ
sAf karaR̃ᵘ (11)	صاف کرݨ	safar karaR̃ᵘ (13)	سفر کرݨ
kam karaR̃ᵘ (11)	کم کرݨ	ibAdat karaR̃ᵘ (13)	عبادت کرݨ

Compund Verbs	(cont)	Compund Verbs	(cont)
SarU' kara$\tilde{R}^u$ (15)	شروع کرڻ	imtiHAn ddIa$\tilde{R}^u$ (15)	امتحان ڏيڻ
fOtO kaDha$\tilde{R}^u$ (15)	فوٽو ڪڍڻ	imtiHAn vaTha$\tilde{R}^u$ (15)	امتحان وٺڻ
TapAl^a vijha$\tilde{R}^u$ (16)	ٽپال وجھڻ	pUrO kara$\tilde{R}^u$ (15)	پورو ڪرڻ
mOTI aca$\tilde{R}^u$ (16)	موتي اچڻ	du'A ghUra$\tilde{R}^u$ (15)	دعا گھرڻ

LESSON SEVENTEEN

17-A Pronunciation Drill

1. Contrasting /d/ and /D/   (12/17)

مَندي جو اِرادو
بادشاهُ سمندَ ڈانهن ڊوڙي ويو.
استاد ءِ مَندو مندرمِ وِينا هئا.

2. Contrasting /O/ and /Õ/   (58/89)

وڏو ڪُوئو ڊوڙي ٿو.
ماڻهُو گهوڙو وِني وَيو.
ماڻهوءَ چيو تَ ڊاڍو ڏُونهون آهي.

17-B Cardinal Numbers by "threes"

23	۲۳	ٽيويھ	73	۷۳	ٽيهتر
33	۳۳	ٽيتيھ	83	۸۳	ٽياسي
43	۴۳	ٽيتاليھ	93	۹۳	ٽيانوي
53	۵۳	ٽيونجاھ	103	۱۰۳	سوءَ ٽي
63	۶۳	ٽيھٺ			

## 17 -C	The Simple Past Tense of Intransitive Verbs

Masculine		مذكر	
Singular	Plural	جمع	واحد
I lived	We lived	آسين رَهياسين	مان رَهيس
You lived	You lived	اوهين رَهيا	تُون رَهينَ
He lived	They lived	اُهي رَهيا	هُو رهيو

Feminine		مؤنث	
Singular	Plural	جمع	واحد
I lived	We lived	آسين رَهيونسين	مان رَهيس
You lived	You lived	اوهين رَهيُون	تُون رَهينءَ
She lived	They lived	اُهي رَهيُون	هُو رهي

1. We have already been using both transitive and intransitive verbs. (see explanatory note on 10: B-1). However, as we begin to take up verb tenses based on the Perfect Participle, it is necessary at all times to distinguish them.

2. The Perfect Participle of a regular Sindhi verb is formed by adding ‎-يو to the root, after dropping the final short vowel. In the case of a verb, such as ‎-ﺗﻲُ ,‎ﺗﯿﭧ which ends in ‎-ي plus the short vowel, only ‎-و is added to form the perfect participle; for example, the perfect participle of ‎رهٽ (above) is ‎رهيو; that of ‎ﺗﯿﭧ, ‎ﺗﯿﻮ.

3. When used with a subject and personal endings, as charted above, the perfect participle forms the basis of the simple past tense. The endings in the case of <u>intransitive verbs</u>, agree with the subject in gender, number, and person. The formation of the simple past tense of transitive verbs is described in 17-E and F.

4. This tense describes simple, completed action or state/condition at a definite time in the past. The sentences in the following section illustrate this meaning.

5. The following transitive verbs, already introduced in the course, have irregular perfect participles.

اچڻ _ آيو	مرڻ _ مئو
اذامڻ _ اذاتو	نکرڻ _ نکتو
بيهڻ _ بينو	وڃڻ _ ويو

پوٹ ـ پيو		وکامٹ ـ وکاٹو	
پهچٹ ـ پهتو		وسامٹ ـ وسايو	
لڳٹ ـ لڳو		ويهٹ ـ وينو	
لهٹ ـ لتو		هئٹ ـ هو	

In future when a verb with an irregular perfect participle is given in the vocabulary list, its participle will be listed also.

17–D Statements, questions, and negatives in the simple past tense of intransitive verbs

Did he live in Shikarpur two years ago?	هو ٻه سال اڳي شڪارپور ۾ رهيو؟
No, he came to Shikarpur last year and left after six months.	نہ، هو گذريل سال شڪارپور آيو، ۽ ڇهن مهينن کان پوءِ ويو.
The girls sat behind the trees.	چوڪريون وڻن جي پٺيان وينيون.
Where did the boys sit?	چوڪرا ڪٿي وينا؟
Some boys sat in front of the house and the rest were inside.	ڪي چوڪرا گهر جي سامهون وينا ۽ باقي گهر جي اندر هئا.
Did you understand the teacher?	تون ماستر جون ڳالهيون سمجهينءَ ڇا؟
Yes, I understood well.	هائو، مان چڱي طرح سمجهيس.
Were you girls afraid of the teacher?	ڇا، توهين چوڪريون ماستر کان ڊنيون؟
No, we weren't afraid, but we sat quietly.	نہ، اسين نہ ڊنيونسين پَر خاموشي ۾ وينيون هيو سين.
What happened? Their father got sick.	ڇا ٿيو؟ هنن جو پيءُ بيمار ٿيو.
The little girl was sick too.	ننڍي چوڪري ٻہ بيمار هئي.
I learned Sindhi in six months.	مان سنڌي ٻولي ڇهن مهينن ۾ سکيس.
Did you come to my house yesterday?	توهين ڪلهہ منهنجي گهر آيا ڇا؟
Yes, but there was no one in the house.	هائو، پر گهر ۾ ڪو بہ ڪو نہ هو.
Why didn't you come early?	توهين سوير چو نہ آيا؟
I got up late.	مان دير سان اٺيس.
The baby was born last week.	ٻار گذريل هفتي ۾ ڄائو.

After the baby died, the mother cried very hard.	ٻارَ جي مرڻ کان پوءِ ماءُ ڏاڍي رُني.
My sister's dress was torn.	منھنجي ڀيڻ جي قميص ڦاٽي.
I met the teacher yesterday.	مان ڪالھہ استاد سان مليس.
Those boys fought with the gardener's son.	اھي ڇوڪرا مالھيءَ جي پُٽَ سان وڙھيا.
Did you bring my book?	ڇا توھين منھنجو ڪتاب ڪٿي آيا؟
Why didn't you bring my book?	اوھين منھنجو ڪتاب ڪٿي ڇو نہ آيا؟
I forgot it. (Lit: it was forgotten by me.)	اُھو مون کان وسري ويو.
Did you read the whole book?	توھين پورو ڪتاب پڙھيا ڇا.

1. A few words in Sindhi are used either transitively or intransitively. These are:

سکڻ - سکيو, to learn, study

پڙھڻ - پڙھيو, to read, study

سمجھڻ - سمجھيو, to understand

For transitive use of these verbs, see the examples in 17-F.

2. ڪو combined with نہ means "none" or "no one". The repetition of the ڪو gives added emphasis: "no one at all".

3. It is important to note the difference between ھو (was) and ٿيو (became). ھو indicates that something was or existed as such. ٿيو means that it became, or got to be. For example,

مان ڪلھہ بيمار ٿيس.   I got sick yesterday.

مان ڪلھہ بيمار ھوس.   I was sick yesterday.

The idea of the first sentence is that the sickness started yesterday. But in the second, we are told the state of the speaker yesterday, not when he got sick. He may have been sick before that time.

4. Some verbal ideas which have a transitive force in English, i.e. which may take an object, are used intransitively in Sindhi. Two of these used in the examples above are ملڻ (to meet) and وڙھڻ (to fight). Both verbs take the postposition سان with any expressed object.

5. The compound verbs previously introduced (with the exception of موٽي اچڻ) are all made up of a noun or adjective plus a verb. Here we are introduced to compound verbs made up of two verbs. In these compounds if the second verb is intransitive the whole compound will be treated as an intransitive verb. This is true even if the first verb is transitive and has an object. The first verb

will take the form of its conjunctive participle and will remain constant. The second verb will agree with the subject in person, number and gender.

The two examples above are وڃڻ وڃڻ (to take away) and کڻي اچڻ (to bring). The two verbs, وڃڻ (to take) and khaRaRu (to pick up, bring) may be combined with either vaNaR̃u or acaR̃u, the meaning then becomes, literally, as follows:

وڃي وڃڻ	–	to take away, to take and go
وڃي اچڻ	–	to take and come
کڻي وڃڻ	–	to take away, to pick up (something) and go
کڻي اچڻ	–	to bring, to pick up and come

In the examples above کڻي اچڻ is used for bringing a book. کڻي used with either اچڻ (to bring) or with وڃڻ (to take away) is used for small things with one can be said <u>to pick up</u> or carry. وڃي with اچڻ or وڃڻ is used for people or animals which one would take along or lead. This is illustrated as follows:

I took my brother	مان پنهنجي ڀاءُ کي وڃي ويس.
The landlord brought a horse.	زميندار گهوڙي کي وڃي آيو.
The girl brought her little brother.	ڇوڪري پنهنجي ننڍي ڀاءُ کي کڻي آئي.

This use of کڻي آئي tells us that the girl was carrying the child. If he was bigger and walking along the side, we would say,

The girl brought her little brother.	ڇوڪري پنهنجي ننڍي ڀاءُ کي وڃي آئي.

6. In verbal compounds made up of two verbs, the negative should be placed between the two verbs. In a question having both a question word and a negative as illustrated in the third from the last sentence, the word نه is placed before the final verb, and the question word just before that. The usual place for question word is just before the verb. When the sentence also contains a negative, the question word will be placed just before the negative. Only for special emphasis is the question word placed earlier in the sentence. An exception to this is ڇا when it is used as a sign of a question. ڇا in this case is normally placed at the beginning of the question, although it may be found at the end, after the verb.

17 –E The Simple Past Tense of Transitive Verbs

I)		We		آسان		مُون
You)	wrote	You	wrote	لکيو	لکيو	تو
He/She)		They		هُنن		هُنَ

1. When transitive verbs, those which expect an object, either stated or implied, occur in the simple past tense, the subject is put into the <u>oblique</u> form. This breaks the normal agreement of the subject as the doer or agent of the action with the verb. Attention is thus focused on the object.

Thus, "I wrote", whether "I" is a man or woman speaking becomes مُون لکيو.

2. The object will be found in the <u>nominative</u> form. The verb will then agree <u>with the object</u> according to the following principles:

   a) If no object is stated, the verb will remain in the masculine singular form of the perfect participle.

   b) If the object is stated, and is in the nominative form, the verb agrees with it in number and gender only.

The boys ate the bread.	چوکرن ماني کاڏي.
He/She opened the doors.	هُنَ دروازا کوليا.

Notice that the pronoun هُنَ does not tell us if it was "he" or "she".

   c) If the object is in the oblique form allowed by کي, the agreement between object and verb is broken, and the verb remains in the masculine singular form of the perfect participle. This rule also applies if the object is in the oblique form with any other postposition.

   d) The verb may have an indirect object followed by کي as well as an object in the nominative form. In this case the verb will agree with the object. For example:

The man gave the woman the scissors.	ماڻهو زال کي ڪينچي ڏني.

ڏني is the feminine form of ڏنو, the irregular perfect participle of ڏيڻ, "to give". It has the feminine ending in agreement with ڪينچي.

(Note: some Sindhi words are changing in their spelling. Scissors is alternatively spelled now ڪينچي or قينچي.)

17 –F Statements, questions and negatives in the Simple Past Tense of Transitive Verbs.

I learned Sindhi.	مون سنڌي سکي.
I read two books.	مون ٻه ڪتاب پڙهيا.
We didn't understand.	اسان نہ سمجهيو.
What did they show you?	هنن تو کي ڇا ڏيکاريو؟
They showed me their house.	هنن مون کي پنهنجو گهر ڏيکاريو.
What did you show your friends?	تو پنهنجن دوستن کي ڇا ڏيکاريو؟
I showed them all my books and pictures.	مون هنن کي پنهنجا سڀ ڪتابَ ۽ تصويرون ڏيکاريون.
Did you send the letter in the mail?	توهان ٽپال ۾ خط موڪليو؟
Yes, I sent it with my husband. (lit: Having given it to my husband, I sent it.)	هائو، مون پنهنجي مڙس کي ڏيئي موڪليو.
Did you hear anyone's voice?	ڇا توهان ڪنهن جو آواز ٻڌو؟
I heard someone's voice but didn't see anyone.	مون ڪنهن جو آواز ٻڌو پر ڪنهن کي بہ نہ ڏٺو.
Did you recognize the girl?	ڇا توهان ڇوڪريءَ کي سڃاتو؟
No, but her brother recognized us.	نہ، پر هن جي ڀاءُ اسان کي سڃاتو.
The washerman took the clothes last week.	ڌوٻي گذريل هفتي ڪپڙا کنيا.
Did, your daughter find the lamps?	ڇا توهان جي ڌيءَ بتيون لڌيون؟
No, (she) only found one candle.	نہ، رڳو هڪڙي موم بتي لڌي.
We bought vegetables yesterday.	اسان ڪالھ ڀاڄيون ڳڌيون.
Did you buy fruit too?	ڇا توهان ميوا بہ ڳڌا؟
My son put the clothes in that room.	منهنجي پٽَ هن ڪوٺيءَ ۾ ڪپڙا رکيا.
Did he put them in the box?	ڇا هن پيتيءَ ۾ وڌا؟
Perhaps he put them on the bed.	شايد هن کٽَ تي رکيا.
The men slaughtered the dogs.	ماڻهن ڪتن کي ڪُٺو.
The boys broke the key.	ڇوڪرن ڪنجي ڀڳي.

Lesson 17/ 219

| They broke the lock, too. | انهن ڪلف کي به ڀڳو. |
| The little girl combed her hair herself and put on her own clothes. | ننڍيءَ ڇوڪريءَ پاڻ وارن کي ڦڻي ڏني ۽ پنهنجا ڪپڙا پاتا. |

1. In sentence 4 notice that although ڪتاب (books) is masculine, the verb agrees with the object which is closest to it. Thus, it is feminine plural to agree with تصويرون (pictures). If the order were reversed, the sentence would be:

| I showed them all my books and pictures. | مون هنن کي پنهنجون سڀ تصويرون ۽ ڪتاب ڏيکاريا. |

2. رکڻ carries the idea of placing, putting or keeping, while وجهڻ means "to put in".

3. گنهڻ is an older word now being replaced by خريد ڪرڻ (see 17-G below).

4. The first three sentences illustrate the transitive use of سکڻ, پڙهڻ and سمجهڻ, as we pointed out in 17-D-6. These verbs may be correctly used either way, although you may find your locality prefers one way or the other.

5. موم بتي literally means a wax light or lamp. موم means wax. You will also hear a candle called a ميڻ بتي in some areas.

6. Most transitive verbs whose roots end in –i form their perfect participles regularly by adding يو to the root after dropping the short vowel.

The following are exceptions.

آڻڻ ـ آندو   ڪرڻ ـ ڪيو

Those transitive verbs which have roots ending in –u may have regular or irregular perfect participles. These must be learned by a great deal of practice and use in sentences. The following are the irregular perfect participles of verbs already learned.

ڏوئڻ ـ ڏوتو	بڌڻ ـ بڌو
ڏسڻ ـ ڏنو	پيئڻ ـ پيتو
ڏيڻ ـ ڏنو	چوڻ ـ چيو
وڻڻ ـ ورتو	ڪائڻ ـ ڪاڏو
وجهڻ ـ وڌو	ڪٽڻ ـ ڪنيو
	لهڻ ـ لڌو

17-G Compound Verbs in the Past Tense

The boy helped me.	چوڪري منھنجي مدد ڪئي.
The washerman did not iron the clothes well.	ڌوبيءَ ڪپڙن جي استري نہ ڪئي.
Did you "give" the exam yesterday?	توھان ڪالھ امتحان ڏنو؟
We prayed to God and he answered.	اسان خدا کان دعا گھري ۽ ھن جواب ڏنو.
The carpenter and the laborer worked the whole day.	واڍي ۽ مزور سڄو ڏينھن ڪم ڪيو.

1.   In the case of compound verbs formed from a noun and a verb, the gender of the noun determines the ending of the verb in the past tense. In fact this noun is the object of the verb. If the noun is feminine, as مدد, استري, and دعا, the verb ending will be feminine in agreement. When the noun is masculine as, امتحان, ڪم, and جواب, the verb ending will be masculine.

2.   Notice the new compound verb, جواب ڏيڻ, to answer, to give an answer. This compound may also mean "to refuse, to dismiss" (from employment).

17-H Vocabulary

Note: Since the roots of all intransitive verbs end in –u, and thus their conjunctive participles end in ي-, the roots of these verbs will no longer be given in the vocabulary lists. Irregular perfect participle will be listed for all the verbs.

English	Sindhi	English	Sindhi
to break	ڀڃڻ (ڀڄ) ڀڳو	to wear, put on	پائڻ (پاءِ) پاتو
to be torn	ڦاٽڻ ڦاٽو	scissors (f)	ڪينچي، قينچي
comb (f)	ڦڻي	to bring, take	کڻي اچڻ
to comb	ڦڻي ڏيڻ	to take away	کڻي وڃڻ
silence (f)	خاموشي	to buy	وٺڻ (اگھڻ)
answer	جواب	to find	لھڻ (لھ)
to answer	جواب ڏيڻ	candle (f)	موم بتي، ميڻ بتي

to be born	جمڻ جائو	carpenter (m)	واڍو
whole	سڄو	hair (m.pl)	وارَ
to learn, study	سکڻ	to take, or bring	وٺي اچڻ
to recognize, know	سڃاڻڻ (سڃاڻ) سڃاتو	to take or lead away	وٺي وڃڻ
to kill, slay	کُهڻ (کُه) کتو	to fight	وڙهڻ
room (f)	ڪوٺي		

This is the same verb, لهڻ which used intransitively means "to set (as the sun) or to get down. Used transitively it means "to find".

17-I Conversional Review

1. Repeat each of the following sentences after your teacher, then change the sentence to the simple past tense, changing time words where necessary, and/or any other necessary changes. For example:

T.	مان ايندڙ سال ڪينيڊا ويندس.
S.	مان گذريل سال ڪينيڊا ويس.
	مان سيئاٽي ايندس.
	مان آچر جي ڏينهن آرام ڪندس.
	ڇا تون رات جو درپون ڪوليندين؟
	هو اربع تي مون سان گالهائيندو.
	لاري اڄ شام ويندي.
	اسين ايندڙ هفتي هنن سان ملندا سين.
	ڇا توهين هنن کي ڏاڍائيندا؟
	اسين ڇا خريد ڪندا سين؟
	توهين ڪڍڻ چني لڪندا؟
	مستري اڄ هي ڪم ڪندو.

چوڪريون ٽوري ڊير ۾ ڪائيندِيون؟
ڪير تنهنجي مدد ڪندو؟

2. In your conversations with your teacher and other Sindhis concentrate on describing actions in the past, what you did yesterday or last week.

Ask questions of people using the past tense. Be sure to distinguish between the use of the past habitual and the simple past. By intensive practice and use of these structures the proper tense will become automatic. Listen carefully to Sindhis describing actions or states in the past, and observe and imitate their usage.

3. Use the following words and phrases in the dialogue given below. The teacher should correct your pronunciation and grammar when necessary.

ڳاڏي، گھوڙا، ٽي لاريون، نوان پردا

ٽپالي، هن جو مڙس، اهو گھر

ڇھ ڇوڪرا، گھٽيون موم بتيون ـــــــ

S. مون ـــــــــ ڏٺو. توهان به ـــــــــــ ڏٺو

T. هائو مون به ـــــــ ڏٺو. ڇا توهان ـــــــــ ڏٺو؟

LESSON EIGHTEEN

18-A   Pronunciation Drill

1. Contrasting   (48/49)   /ي/ ءِ /ين/

پيتيءَ مِر ڪينچي نَ آهي.
هو ڏونهين جي ڪري ڪمري مِر نَ وينو.
چوڪري گذريل مهيني ڪر ڪري ويئي.

2. Contrasting   (34/35)   /خ/ ءِ /غ/

اخبار مِر ڪا بَ خبر آهي ڇا؟
هن اخبار باغ مِر خريد ڪئي.
خبر آئي نَ غريب خان غالب ٿيو.

18-B   Cardinal Numbers by "fours"

24	۲۴	چوويهَ	74	۷۴	چوهتر
34	۳۴	چوتيهَ	84	۸۴	چوراسي
44	۴۴	چوئيتاليهَ	94	۹۴	چورانوي
54	۵۴	چونجاهَ	104	۱۰۴	سؤ چار
64	۶۴	چوهٺ			

18-C   More Postpositions with جي

They fought against their enemies.	هو پنهنجن دشمنن جي برخلاف وڙهيا.
That boy speaks against this matter.	اهو ڇوڪرو هن ڳالھ جي برخلاف ڳالهائيندو آهي.
Why are you opposed to this?	توهين هن جي برخلاف ڇو آهيو؟
This bucket is equal to that one.	هي بالٽي هن بالٽيءَ جي برابر آهي.
Both are equal.	ٻئي برابر آهن.
The wall is even with the window.	ڀِتِ دريءَ جي برابر آهي.
For safety it should be even with the roof.	اها حفاظت لاءِ ڇت جي برابر ٿيڻ گھرجي.
Instead of Thursday we'll go on Friday.	خميس جي بدران اسين جمعي جي ڏينهن وينداسين.
Give me water instead of tea.	چانھ جي بدران مون کي پاڻي ڏيو.
Why did the tailor do other work instead of sewing my shirt?	منهنجي قميص جي سبڻ جي بدران درزيءَ ٻيو ڪم ڇو ڪيو؟
Our relatives didn't come on account of the rain.	اسان جا مائٽ مينهن جي سببان نہ آيا.
It's cold today because there's no sunshine.	اڄ اُس نہ ٿيڻ جي سببان سيءُ لڳي ٿو.
On account of the extreme heat, the laborers didn't finish the work.	مزورن وڏيڪ گرمي جي ڪري ڪم پورو نہ ڪيو.
Because of his father's coming, the boy didn't go to school.	ڇوڪرو پنهنجي پيءُ جي اچڻ جي ڪري اسڪول نہ ويو.

1.   جي برخلاف is used in the sense of "against, in opposition to".

2.   جي برابر means "equal to, even with, level with". The جي may be omitted and in this case, برابر is used as an adjective or adverb meaning "equal, level, correct".

3.   جي بدران means "instead of, in the place of".

4.   جي سببان and جي ڪري are synonyms, and both mean "on account of, because of". Of the

two, جي ڪري is the more common.

5. Notice the use of the infinitive as a noun in the above sentences.

6. سبب used without جي is a masculine noun meaning "cause, reason". As,

What is his reason?	هن جو ڪهڙو سبب آهي؟

7. In the use of جي ڪري, جي may be omitted without changing the meaning.

18 - D Common conjunctions

نڪي (neither)

Neither he nor I drank water.	نڪي مون پاڻي پيتو نڪي هن.
I am neither rich nor poor.	آءُ نَڪي امير آهيان نڪي غريب آهيان.

بلڪ ، (but) مگر، ليڪن (but, rather, moreover)

The men came but I didn't meet them.	ماڻهو آيا ليڪن مان هنن سان نه مليس.
The child rested, but didn't sleep.	ٻار آرام ڪيو مگر نه سمهيو.
He will to the bazaar, moreover he will go happily!	هو بازار ويندو بلڪ خوشيءَ سان ويندو!
The workman completed the work, moreover, it was very good work.	مستري ڪم پورو ڪيو بلڪ تمام ستو ڪم.
Come again tomorrow, but rather come early.	سڀاڻي ڀيڻ اچجو بلڪ سوير اچجو.

تنهنڪري (تنهن ڪري) (therefore, so)

I was sick, so I didn't eat anything.	مان بيمار هوس، تنهنڪري مون ڪجهه نه کاڌو.
My son is about to come; therefore I won't go to the bazaar.	منهنجو پٽ اچڻ وارو آهي، تنهن ڪري مان بازار نه ويندس.

چا لاءِ جو، چا ڪاڻ تہ، چا لاءِ تہ، چو جو، چو تہ (because)

The boy didn't bring fish because it wasn't fresh.	ڇوڪري مڇي نه آندي چالاءِ جو اها تازي نه هئي.

These girls don't go to school because their father doesn't earn enough money.	ھي چوڪريون اسڪول نہ ٿيون وڃن چاڪاڻ تہ ھنن جو پيءُ ڪافي پيسا نہ ٿو ڪمائي.
That girl didn't pass the examination because she didn't work hard.	ھن چوڪري امتحان پاس نہ ڪيو چا لاءِ تہ ھن محنت نہ ڪئي.
That boy will succeed because he is hard-working.	ھو چوڪرو ڪامياب ٿيندو چو جو ھو محنتي آھي.

انھيءَ لاءِ تہ (so that, in order that)

You ought to send the children to school so they will learn good behaviour. (manners)	توھان کي ٻار اسڪول موڪلڻ گھرجن انھيءَ لاءِ تہ ھو اخلاق سکندا.
We are going to eat now so that we may arrive at the station early.	اسين ھاڻي ماني کائون ٿا انھي لاءِ تہ اسين اسٽيشن سوير پھچون.

1. نڪي...نڪي means "neither … nor", and as the illustrations show, may be used with nouns or pronouns as well as with adjectives. Note the sentence order when this phrase is used.

2. ليڪن and مگر (but) are both synonymous with پر. بلڪ carries a somewhat different shade of meaning with the idea of "moreover, rather".

3. Of the phrases meaning "because", چا لاءِ جو and چا ڪاڻ تہ are the most commonly used.

4. محنت is a noun meaning "hard work, diligence"; محنت ڪرڻ is the verb meaning "to work hard, diligently", and محنتي is an adjective meaning "hard-working, diligent, industrious".

5. اخلاق (m. pl) means "manners, morals, ethics", and is often used in the sense of good or proper behaviour. With the prefix bad – i.e., بداخلاق, it means "bad-mannered, rude". بداخلاقي is a noun meaning "bad manners".

O son! Don't be rude, always speak politely.	اي پٽ بداخلاق نہ ٿيو، ھميشہ اخلاق سان ڳالھايو.

18 –E The Present Perfect Tense of Intransitive Verbs

Masculine		مذكر	
Singular	Plural	جمع	واحد
I have come	We have come	اسين آيا آهيون	مان آيو آهيان
You have come	You have come	توهين آيا آهيو	تون آيو آهين
He has come	They have come	أهي آيا آهن	هو آيو آهي

Feminine		مؤنث	
Singular	Plural	جمع	واحد
I have come	We have come	اسين آيون آهيون	مان آئي آهيان
You have come	You have come	توهين آيون آهيون	تون آئي آهين
She has come	They have come	اُهي آيون آهن	هوءَ آئي آهي

1.   When the present auxiliary forms of the verb هئڻ (to be) are used with the perfect participle of a Sindhi verb, the <u>present perfect tense</u> is formed.

2.   In the case of intransitive verbs, the participle will agree with the subject in gender and number. The auxiliary will also agree with the subject.

3.   The present perfect tense indicates a past action or state / condition which in some way is relevant at the present time. In other words it links what happened before with a current situation. The action or state / condition may have occurred in the recent or remote past, but because of the use of the present auxiliary, that action or state is relevant to the situation at the present time.

18 –F The Present Perfect Tense of Transitive Verbs

Masculine & Feminine		مذكر ۽ مؤنث	
Singular	Plural	جمع	واحد
I	We	اسان	مون
You	You	توهان	تو
He	They	هنن	هن

(center columns: لکيو آهي)

1.   The meaning and usage of transitive verbs in the present perfect tense is the same as for intransitive verbs. (18-E-3)

2.   Transitive verbs in the present perfect tense, as in the simple past tense, have the subject in the oblique form. The agreement between subject and verb is thus cut off. Both the perfect participle and the form of the auxiliary verb هئڻ (to be) agree with the object as explained in 17-

E-2. In this agreement of the verb with the subject, the participle will agree with the object in number and gender, and the auxiliary will be found only in the singular آهي or plural آهن.

18 –G Statements, questions and negatives in the Present Perfect Tense.

Where have you put the chairs?	توهان ڪرسيون ڪٿي رکيون آهن؟
We have put all the chairs in front of the table.	اسان سڀ ڪرسيون ميز جي سامهون رکيون آهن.
Where have the girls put the clothes?	ڇوڪرين ڪپڙا ڪٿي رکيا آهن؟
They have put all the clothes in the box. (trunk)	هنن سڀ ڪپڙا پيتيءَ ۾ وڌا آهن.
I left my book here. Has anyone seen it?	مون پنهنجو ڪتاب هتي ڇڏيو. ڇا ڪنهن هن کي ڏٺو آهي؟
Your sister took it.	توهان جي ڀيڻ هن کي کڻي وئي.
Have you read today's paper?	ڇا توهان اڄ جي اخبار پڙهي آهي؟
No I haven't read it yet.	نه، مون اڃا نه پڙهي آهي.
Who has ironed the clothes?	ڪپڙن جي استري ڪنهن ڪئي آهي؟
The washerman's boy has ironed them.	ڌوٻيءَ جي ڇوڪري هنن جي استري ڪئي آهي.
How many times you have gone there.	تون هوڊي گهڻا ڀيرا ويو آهين؟
I have gone twice.	مان ٻه ڀيرا ويو آهيان.
What has his mother told him?	هن جي ماءُ هُن کي ڇا ٻڌايو آهي؟
The poor fellow hasn't been able to remember!	ويچارو ياد ڪري نه سگهيو آهي!

1. You have already had the words ويهڻ (to sit) and بيهڻ (to stand) in this tense. (15-D-3). They are most commonly used in this way. Even the English words "are sitting" or "is sitting" suggest an action which is completed, not in process. Note the in meaning of the following sentences:

The women are (just now in the act of) sitting (down) in the garden.	زالون باغ ۾ ويهي رهيون آهن.
The women usually sit in the garden.	زالون باغ ۾ ويهنديون آهن.
The women are seated (that is, have sat and are still sitting) in the garden.	زالون باغ ۾ ويٺيون آهن.
Where are the boys sitting?	ڇوڪرا ڪٿي ويٺا آهن؟
A man is sitting under the tree.	هڪُ ماڻهو وڻَ جي هيٺان ويٺو آهي.

His father is standing outside.	هن جو پيءُ ٻاهر بيٺو آهي.

2. It is often difficult for the language student to know when to use the simple past tense or the present perfect tense. The actual forms are not as confusing as the situations that call for one or the other. Since either form may be correct, it is the speaker's point of view that determines which to use. If the past action has relevance at the present time, or is still continuing on, the present perfect tense is called for. If the action was finished, completed at a past time, the simple past tense should be used.

3. ويچارو is an adjective meaning "miserable, wretched, unfortunate". It may be translated "poor", but in the sense of "unfortunate", not financially poor. غريب means "financially poor". Someone who has lost a loved one may, even though "rich" and therefore not غريب, be properly referred to as ويچارو. Occasionally the two may be used interchangeably but in the sense of "unfortunate", not "financially poor". Notice the following sentence using both غريب and ويچارو. Notice also that the noun is understood, and is not expressed.

Why has that woman asked you for a handout?	انھيءَ زال اوھان کان بخشش ڇو گھري آھي؟
The unfortunate woman is very poor.	ويچاري تمام گھڻي غريب آھي.

18 -H   Vocabulary

rich	امير	Thursday, the eve of Friday (f)	خميس
manner, morals, behaviour (m. pl)	اخلاق	because	ڇا ڪاڻ تَہ ڇا لاءِ تَہ ڇا لاءِ جو
station (f)	اسٽيشن	because	ڇو تَہ ڇو جو
bad mannered, rude (adj.)	بَد اخلاق	thirty-four	چوٽيھہ
rude or bad behaviour (f)	بَد اخلاقي	forty-four	چوئتاليھہ
equal to, even with	(جي) برابر	eighty-four	چوراسي
against, opposed to	(جي) برخلاف	ninety-four	چورانوي
gift, donation, grant (f)	بخشش	fifty-four	چونجاھہ

but, moreover	بلڪ	twenty-four	چوويھ
again	ٻيھر	seventy-four	چوھتر
therefore, on account of	تنھنڪري	sixty-four	چوھٺ
protection, safety (f)	حفاظت	but	مگر
reason (m)	سَبَبُ	fish (f)	مڇي
on account of	سببان (جي)	hard work (f)	محنَتَ
cold (m)	سِيءُ	to work hard	محنت ڪَرَڻُ
poor	غريبُ	neither	نڪي
on account of	ڪري (جي)	wretched, unfortunate, miserable	ويچارو
to earn	ڪمائڻ	but	ليڪن
to succeed	ڪامياب ٿيڻ	enemy	دشمن

18–I   Conversational Review.

1.   Do the following replacement drill without looking at the book. The teacher will read the sentence, and the student will repeat after him. The teacher will then give the word or phrase to be substituted in the sentence, and the student will repeat the sentence with the resulting change, and any other necessary changes. The second phrase or word will then be substituted in that sentence. For example:

T:	استاد: استاد صاحب اڳي ويٺو آھي.
S:	شاگرد: استاد صاحب اڳي ويٺو آھي.
T:	اُ: مان.
S:	ش: مان اڳي ويٺو آھيان /ويٺي آھيان.
T:	اُ: پنيان.
S:	ش: مان پنيان ويٺو آھيان.

(1) مان (2) پئنيان (3)هن جو دوست (4)هن جي ساهيڙي (5) آهن
(6) وهڻ (7) ڊاڪٽر صاحب (8) ڇو؟ (9) نَہ (10) اهي ٻہ شاگرد
(11) آهيو (12) هن جو پيٽون (پينرون) (13) ويهڻ (14) استاد صاحبُ

2. Using Exercise 1, 3, and 4 of Lesson 17-I, change each sentence to the present perfect tense.

3. Following the patterns given in Exercise 4 of 16-G, practice using the simple past and the present perfect tenses of سگهڻ.

4. Answer the following questions, trying to use the new vocabulary of the lesson where possible:

a.	ا. توهان اڄ پڙهڻ جي بدران ڇا ڪيو آهي؟
b.	ب. ڇوڪرا ڇا جي ڪري اسڪول نہ آيا؟
c.	ج. توهان هن ڳالھہ جي برخلاف ڇا پڌو آهي.
d.	د. هُن پنهنجو ڪم پورو ڇو نہ ڪيو آهي؟
e.	ھ. ڇوڪري سبق ڪهڙي سبب جي ڪري نہ سگهي.
f.	زالون اندر ڇو نہ آيون؟

5. Complete the following sentences:

a.	مان بازار وڃڻ تي هوس مگر.....
b.	هن کي انب پسند آهن بلڪ....
c.	ڇوڪريءَ کي چانھہ پسند آهي ليڪن...
d.	مان اڄ نڪي ماني کاڌي آهي نڪي.....
e.	مزمان آيا آهن تنھنڪري.....
f.	ڪالھہ مان اچي نہ سگهيس ڇا ڪاڻ تہ...

Ask your teacher to make up more sentences on this pattern for you to complete. Vary the vocabulary and verb tenses.

LESSON NINETEEN

19-A   Pronunciation Drill

1.   Contrasting   (21/25/34)   /ک/ ، /ڪ/ ءِ /خ/

هن اخبار ڪَٽ تي رکي ڪر ڪيو.
هن کي ڪپُ آهي. هن کي ڪپُ آهي.
مون کي ڪا بہ خبر نہ ملي.

2.   Contrasting   (22/26/35)   /گ/ ، /گھ/ ءِ /غ/

گھوڙي ءِ گانءِ باغ ۾ ڊوڙ ڪيو.
ڪاغذ باغ ۾ گم ٿي ويو.
گھر جي باغ ۾ گاھُ آهي.

Note: At this point, more than half through this course, the student may either be discouraged with sounds that are still difficult to pronounce or to distinguish between, or overconfident of his ability to be understood. In the first case he may be tempted to give up trying, and just "get by", or, on the other hand he may become careless about his pronunciation. This is a good time to take stock, and to make careful note on these sounds that are still giving trouble, and to work harder at mastering them.

19-B Cardinal Numbers by "sixes"

16	١٦	سورهن
26	٢٦	ڇويہہ
36	٣٦	ڇٽيہہ
46	٤٦	ڇائيتاليہہ
56	٥٦	ڇاونجاھ
66	٦٦	ڇاہٺ
76	٧٦	ڇاہتر
86	٨٦	ڇھاسي
96	٩٦	ڇھانوي
106	١٠٦	سؤ ڇھَ

19-C The Present Continuous Tense Transitive and Intransitive Verbs.

a) With the conjunctive principle plus رهڻ

Masculine		مذكر	
Singular	Plural	جمع	واحد
I was doing	We were doing	اسين كري رهيا هئاسين / هئاسون	مان كري رهيو هوس
You were doing	You were doing	توهين كري رهيا هئا	تون كري رهيو هئين
He was doing	They were doing	اُهي كري رهيا هئا	هو كري رهيو هو

Feminine		مؤنث	
Singular	Plural	جمع	واحد
I was doing	We were doing	اسين كري رهيون هيون سين	مان كري رهي هيس
You were doing	You were doing	توهين كري رهيون هيون	تون كري رهي هئين
She was doing	They were doing	اُهي كري رهيون هيون	هوءَ كري رهي هئي

1. This form of the past continuous tense uses the conjunctive participle of the principle verb

followed by the perfect participle of رهڻ and the past tense of the auxiliary verb هئڻ (to be).

2.   Since the conjunctive participle does not change and رهڻ is an intransitive verb, all verbs, both transitive and intransitive, follow the rule for intransitive verbs and agree with the subject in gender and number.

3.   This tense is parallel to the present continuous tense (Lesson 16). It is expressed in several different ways, but it always denotes and action that was in progress at a definite time in the past.

b) Using the indeclinable particle پئي

Intransitive Verbs:

Masculine		مذڪر	
Singular	Plural	جمع	واحد
I was walking	We were walking	اسين هليا سين پئي	مان هليس پئي
You were walking	You were walking	توهين هليا پئي	تون هليئن پئي
He was walking	They were walking	اُهي هليا پئي	هو هليو پئي

Feminine		مؤنث	
Singular	Plural	جمع	واحد
I was walking	We were walking	اسين هليون سين پئي	مان هليس پئي
You were walking	You were walking	توهين هليون پئي	تون هليئن پئي
She was walking	They were walking	اُهي هليون پئي	هوءَ هلي پئي

Transitive Verbs:

Masculine & Feminine				مذڪر ۽ مؤنث			
Singular		Plural		جمع		واحد	
I	was / were writing	We	were writing	اسان	لکيو پئي	مان	لکيو پئي
You		You		توهان		تو	
He		They		هنن		هن	

1.   A second way of expressing a continuous idea in the past uses the indeclinable particle پئي with the simple past tense of the verb.

2.   The meaning conveyed is the same as with رهڻ, that is, an action that was in progress at a definite time in the past.

3. As with all other transitive verbs based on the perfect participle the subject is in the oblique, and the verb agrees with the object if expressed, in gender and number.

c) With the indeclinable forms ويٺي and بيٺي

As in the Present Continuous Tense we are able to express action being done while sitting or standing, so the same distinction may be made in the past by using the indeclinable forms ويٺي (sitting) or بيٺي (standing). This form of the past continuous is the same as that shown in b) above, with ويٺي or بيٺي substituted for پئي. However when ويٺي or بيٺي is used, it <u>always precedes</u> the verb. For example:

I was (sitting) waiting.	مان ويٺي ترسيسُ / ترسيس
I was (standing) writing.	مون بيٺي لکيو

In English the idea of standing or sitting while doing the action is not necessarily expressed. In Sindhi as well as bringing a graphic description of the person as sitting or standing, it emphasizes that the action was being done at a specific time.

19 –D   Sentences Illustrating the Past Continuous Tense

What were the women doing?	عورتن چا پئي کيو؟
They were (standing) waiting.	هو بيٺي ترسيون.
The man was (sitting) eating.	ماٺهوءَ ماني ويٺي کاڌي.
The boys were drinking tea.	چوکرا چانھ پي رهيا هئا.
Where were you going?	تون ڪيڏانهن وڃي رهيو هئين؟
I was going to the Post Office.	مان ٽپال آفيس وڃي رهيو هوس.
What were the children doing?	ٻارن چا پئي کيو؟
They were playing in the garden.	هنن باغ ۾ کيڏيو پئي.
What were your sisters buying from the shop?	توهان جون ڀينرون هٽَ تان چا خريد ڪري رهيون هيون؟
They were buying some yellow cloth.	هو ڪجھ پيلا ڪپڙا خريد ڪري رهيون هيون.
What was the woman asking?	عورت چا پڇي رهي هئي؟
I don't know what she was asking.	مون ڪي خبر نہ هئي تہ هو چا پڇي رهي هئي.

Which page were you reading?	توهان ڪهڙو صفحو پڙهي رهيا هئا؟
I was reading the 176th page.	مان هڪ سؤ ڇاهترون صفحو پڙهي رهيو هوس / رهي هيس.
We were both learning Sindhi.	اسان ٻنهي سنڌي سکي پئي.
What was the farmer doing at the well?	هاري کوه تي ڇا ڪري رهيو هو؟
Who was plucking the roses?	گلابن کي ڪير توڙي رهيو هو؟
I don't know, but there some children running in the road.	مون کي خبر نه آهي، مگر ڪجھ ٻار رستي ۾ ڊوڙيا پئي.
They were not listening to me.	هنن منهنجي نه پئي ٻڌي.

1. Remember in distinguishing this tense from other past tense that its distinctive shade of meaning is that of a definite time in the past when the action was actually taking place.

2. With the compound verb مرمت ڪرڻ (to repair), the postposition جي is used. Thus it means literally "to do the repair of some thing".

3. توڙڻ means "to break", and when used with flowers as above, it means "to pick".

4. Negatives are not common in this tense, since one does not usually describe graphically what did not happen. However, the negative may occasionally be used.

19 –E   Causal Verbs

1. From nearly every Sindhi verb, a causal form may be derived. As the name "causal" implies, it gives the idea of "causing an action to be done". If the basic form of the verb is intransitive, the causal formed will be transitive. If the basic form is already transitive, the causal then implies getting or "causing" someone else to do the action. In English this would often require a different verb altogether.

2. By understanding this basic verb / causal verb relationship, the student will find it easier to expand his vocabulary, and to understand and remember new verbs by relating them to verbs he already knows.

3. You have already learned some casual verbs:

to hear	ٻڌڻ	to tell (lit: to cause to hear)	ٻڌائڻ
to understand	سمجھڻ	to explain (cause to understand)	سمجھائڻ
to see	ڏسڻ	to show (cause to see)	ڏيکارڻ

4. There are three basic ways in which causal verbs are formed. A few examples of each type are given here. You have already learned either the basic verb or the causal of each verb listed.

a) These causals are formed by lengthening the first syllable.

    Basic Verb   Causal Verb

to die	مرݨ	to beat, kill	مارݨ
to climb	چڑھݨ	to raise, offer up	چاڑھݨ
to be made	تھݨ	to make	تاھݨ

b) These are formed by adding –اء– to the root.

to go	وَڄݨ	to lose, waste	وِڄائݨ
to walk, go	ھَلݨ	to drive, to carry on	ھلائݨ
to wait	ترسُݨ	to detain	ترسائݨ
to do	کرݨ	to cause to do	کرائݨ
to read, study	پڑھݨ	to teach	پڑھائݨ

c) These causals are formed by adding – ار – to the root.

to get up	اٹھݨ	to raise	اٹھارݨ
to sleep	سمُھݨ	to put to sleep	سمھارݨ
to sit	ویھݨ	to seat	ویھارݨ
to stand	بیھݨ	to cause to stand	بیھارݨ
to drink	پیئݨ	to give or cause to drink	پیئارݨ

d) In addition some causal forms are irregular, but related to the root of the basic verb:

| to eat | کائݨ | to feed | کارائݨ |
| to be found | لبݨ | to find | لھݨ |

(The perfect principle of both is لڌو)

to see	ڏسڻ	to show	ڏيکارڻ
to learn, study	سکڻ	to teach	سيکارڻ

19 –F   Sentences illustrating causal verbs.

From whom have you heard this thing?	توهان هي ڳالھ ڪنهن کان ٻڌي آهي؟
My father has told me.	منهنجي پيءُ مون کي ٻڌايو آهي.
The boy didn't stand of his own accord, but the teacher made him stand.	ڇوڪرو پاڻ ڪين بيٺو، پَر ماستر هن کي بيهاريو.
Sit in the garden and seat the guests too.	باغ ۾ ويھي مزمان کي به هتي ويهاريو.
Don't make your children do too much work!	پنهنجي ٻارن کي تمام گهڻو ڪم نہ ڪرايو!
No one woke the baby. He woke up himself.	ڪنهن بہ ٻار کي نہ جاڳايو آهي، هو پاڻ جاڳيو.
The mother will give him milk, then she will put him to sleep.	ماءُ هن کي کير پياريندي. پوءِ هوءَ هن کي سمهاريندي.
The fire is burning here. Who lit it?	باھ هتي ٻري ٿي پئي. ڪنهن هن کي ٻاريو؟
I have gotten the tea ready. (meaning, I got someone else to do it)	مان چانھ تيار ڪرائي آهي.
Who prepared the tea?	ڪنهن چانھ تيار ڪئي؟
My son has learned this work.	منهنجي پُٽَ هي ڪم سکيو آهي.
His father has taught him.	هن جي پيءُ هن کي سيکاريو آهي.

19 –G   Telling Time.

Asking the time of day.

What time is it?	وقت گهڻو ٿيو آهي؟
(lit: What time has become?)	وقت ڇا ٿيو آهي؟

(lit: How many have struck?)	ڪيترا لڳا آهن؟
(lit: How many have struck)	گھٽا وڳا آهن؟
(lit: How much time has become?)	ٽائيم گھٽو ٿيو آهي؟

1. All of these forms are acceptable and common ways of asking the time. The word ٽائيم is more common than وقت.

2. لڳڻ and وڄڻ both mean here "to strike", as related to the striking of a clock or gong. لڳڻ has many other idiomatic uses, but both are commonly used to express the English idea "o'clock". They are used in the singular for one and fractions related to one, and in the plural for two through twelve.

3. In English we more often use the present tense, but in Sindhi the present perfect tense is used. For example,

What time has become? How many (hours) have struck?	وقت ڇا ٿيو آهي؟ ڪيترا لڳا آهن؟
It's 2 o'clock. (Two (hours) have struck)	ٻه لڳا آهن.

Answering questions about time.

12: 45	It's a quarter to one.	منو لڳو آهي يا منو هڪ لڳو آهن.
1: 00	It's one o'clock.	هڪ لڳو آهي.
1: 15	It's quarter past one.	سوا هڪ ٿيو آهي.
1: 30	It's half-past one.	ڏيڍ وڳو آهي.
1: 45	Now it's a quarter to two.	هاڻي پوڻا ٻه ٿيا آهن.
2: 00	It's two o'clock.	ٻه لڳا آهن.
2: 15	It's a quarter past two.	سوا ٻه وڳا آهن.
2: 30	It's two-thirty.	اڍائي لڳا آهن.
3: 00	It's three o'clock.	ٽي ٿيا آهن.
3: 15	According to my watch it's three-fifteen.	منهنجي واچ ۾ سوا ٽي ٿيا آهن.
3: 30	It's half past three.	ساڍا ٽي لڳا آهن.

4. The fractions used to express time by quarter and half hours are the same as those learned in Lesson 13 for weights and measures. The singular form of the verb is used for one and related

fractions. Notice however, that 1: 45 becomes "quarter to two", so the verb is in the plural.

5.   While all the above verbs are acceptable and proper in stating the time, certain localities may prefer one over the other. Observe the forms used most commonly in your area of Sindh.

Expressing time more exactly in minutes

It's 8:05 (lit: 8 having struck, 5 minutes have become)	اٺ لڳي پنج منٽ ٿيا آھن.
It's 23 minutes past 10.	ڏھ لڳي ٽيويھه منٽ ٿيا آھن.
It's 6: 35.	ڇھ لڳي پنجٽيھه منٽ ٿيا آھن.
It's 25 to 7. (lit: In 7, 25 minutes are left)	ستن ۾ پنجويھه باقي آھن.
It's 10 to 9.	نون ۾ ڏھ منٽ باقي آھن.

6.   To express time after the hour, the present perfect tense of ٿيڻ is used with the conjunctive participle of لڳڻ. Time after the half-hour may be expressed in this way, as in the third sentence above. However, generally time before the hour is stated as in the last two examples above.

19-H   Mentioning Time in statements and questions

My watch is wrong. It's not working / running properly.	منھنجي واچ غلط آھي. اھا ٺيڪ نٿي ھلي.
What's the time now?	ھاڻي وقت ڇا ٿيو آھي؟
It will soon be 5 o'clock.	جلدي پنج لڳندا.
What is the time by your watch?	توھان جي واچ ۾ ڪيترا وڳا آھن؟
What time does the bus go from Sukkur?	لاري سکر کان ڪائين بجي ويندي آھي؟
Sir, it goes at exactly 4 o'clock.	سائين اھا پوري چئين بجي ھلندي آھي.
And what time does it arrive?	۽ گھٽي بجي پھچندي آھي؟
It arrives in 3 and 3/4 hours, that is at 7: 45.	اھا پوٽن چئن ڪلاڪن ۾، يعني پوٽي انين بجي پھچندي آھي.
How many hours does the train take?	ريل گاڏي ڪيترن ڪلاڪن ۾ پھچندي آھي؟
It arrives in just 2 and 3/4 hours.	اھا رڳو پوٽن ٻن ڪلاڪن ۾ پھچندي آھي.

What time does your husband go to work?	توهان جو مڙس ڪهڙي وقت تي ڪم تي ويندو آهي؟
My husband goes to work at 8:30 in the morning.	منهنجو مڙس صبح جو ساڍي اٺين بجي ڪم تي ويندو آهي.
He comes at 2 in the afternoon.	هو ٻه بجي منجھند جو ايندو آهي.
We usually eat our evening meal at 7:30.	اسين اڪثر شام جي ماني ساڍي ستين بجي کائيندا آهيون.
What time may I come?	مان ڪائين بجي اچان؟
Come at 5 pm.	سوا پنجين بجي شام جو اچجو.
What time is it now?	هاڻي ڪيترا لڳا آهن؟
By my watch it's 3:05.	منهنجي واچ ۾ ٽي لڳي پنج منٽ ٿيا آهن.
Your watch is fast. It's 5 to 3.	توهان جي واچ اڳتي هلي ٿي. ٽن ۾ پنج منٽ باقي آهن.
Perhaps your watch is slow (behind).	شايد توهان جي واچ پوئتي هلي ٿي.
When did the guests come?	مزمان ڪڏهن آيا؟
They came at 10 last night.	هو رات جو ڏهين بجي پهتا.
The train will come at (exactly) 6:05.	گاڏي ڇهه لڳي پنجن منٽن تي ايندي.
It goes at (exactly) 6:35.	اها ڇهه لڳي پنجٽيهن منٽن تي هلندي آهي.

1. "Time at which" something happened or will happen is expressed by the oblique form of the cardinal form of the number with بجي, the inflected form of بجو (hour). It is used commonly only in this way. The usual word for "hour" is ڪلاڪ. (cf. 11-C for the oblique form of cardinals).

2. To express the general time of day, as we use AM and PM in English, شام جو, صبح جو, etc. are used. Notice in the examples above when the general time of day is stated before the examples above when the general time of day is stated before the hour جو is inflected to its oblique form جي. If the general time is after the hour it is uninflected. See the sentences above for illustrations.

3. When stating that something happened or will happen at an exact time, the postposition تي (on, at) is used. This is illustrated in the last two sentences above.

4. غلط is an adjective meaning mistaken. The noun غلطي (mistake) is formed from it.

5. ڪائين (what, which) is the oblique form of ڪائون. It is used almost exclusively in questions about time with بجي. It is never used except in relation to numbers.

6. يعني is an adverb meaning "namely, that is" and is used when one is explaining, or elaborating on something. Although it is from the Arabic and has Arabic spelling in Sindhi, it is often pronounced yAnE, or yanE.

7. اڳتي and پوئتي are adverbs meaning "ahead" and "behind", in the context here they refer to the running of a watch which may be "ahead", i.e. "fast" or "behind", "slow". They may also be used of people walking ahead or behind, as,

| They boys are walking behind. | ڇوڪرا پوئتي هلن ٿا. |
| Walk ahead. (or, in front) | اڳتي هلو. |

19- I   Vocabulary

To raise	اُٿارڻ (اُٿار)	To ask	پچڻ
before, ahead	اڳتي	To teach	پڙهائڻ
Fire (f)	باھ	To cause, give to drink	پيئارڻ
To burn	برڻ	Behind	پوئتي
To light	ٻارڻ (ٻار)	To detain	ترسائڻ
To cause to stand	بيهارڻ (بيهار)	To break, to pluck (flowers)	توڙڻ
To wake up	جاڳڻ	What, which (with numbers)	ڪائون
To cause to wake up	جاڳائڻ	To cause to do, to get it done	ڪرائڻ
To raise up, offer	چاڙھڻ	To feed, give or cause to eat	کارائڻ
fifty-six	ڇاونجاھ	Well (m)	کوہُ

seventy-six	ڇاهتر	Rose (m)	گلاب
Sixty-six	ڇاهٺ	To beat, kill	مارڻ (مار)
Forty-six	چوئيتاليھ	Repair (f)	مرمت
Thirty-six	ڇٽيھ	To repair	مرمت ڪرڻ
Twenty-six	ڇويھ	Guest (m)	مزمانُ
Eighty-six	ڇھاسي	To lose	وڃائڻ
Ninety-six	ڇھانوي	To seat	وھارڻ
To run	ڊوڙڻُ	Farmer (m)	ھاري
Sukkur	سکرُ	To drive, cause to go	ھلائڻ
To teach	سيکارڻ	Namely, that is	يعني
Mistaken	غلط	Mistake (f)	غلطي

19-J   Conversational Review.

1. Practice asking and telling the time with your teacher, and with other Sindhi friends. Use a clock during your class. Let the teacher move the hands around, and ask you the time.

2. Converse about the time at which certain events happen, happened or will happen. Ask your teacher to pretend to be a station master while you inquire about trains to certain places in Sindh. You can talk about trips you have taken or plan to take by train or bus. In this exercise you should practice the proper pronunciation of cities and towns in your immediate area and all the large and important cities of Sindh. Listen carefully to the correct pronunciation. Don't fall into the habit of using incorrect Anglicized pronunciations of places.

3. Repeat each of the following sentences after your teacher, and then change to the Past Continuous Tense using رھڻ. For example,

T:	اُ: مان بازار وڃان ٿو /ٿي.
S:	ش: مان بازار وڃي رھيو ھوس /رھي ھيس.
	معاف ڪجو آءُ آرام ڪريان ٿو.
	توھين منھنجي ٻڌو ٿا؟

هوءَ سمهي ٿي.
لاري لاهور وڃي ٿي.
اسين هن هٽ تان ڪپڙا خريد ڪريون ٿا.
تون ڪجھ وڙيڪ پاڇيون آڌين ٿو؟
توهين ڪوھ جي مرمت ڪريو ٿا.
شاگرد پندرهون سبق پڙهن ٿا.
ڇوڪرو گلابن کي ٽوڙي ٿو.

4. Repeat the exercise above using the form of the Past Continuous Tense with پئي and the Past Tense of the verb.

LESSON TWENTY

20-A Pronunciation Drill

1. Contrasting /D/ and /dd/   (17/13/)   /ڏ/ ، /ڊ/

هن ڊوهُ ڪيو آهي.	هن ڏوهُ ڪيو آهي.
ماٺهوءَ ڊوهي ڏني.	ماٺهو ڏوهي آهي.
ڏوهي ماٺهو ڊوهي ڏني.	ڏوهي ماٺهو جي ڊوهي.

2. Contrasting /R/ and /D/   (43/17)

هو روڊ تي ڊوڙي ٿو.
هو روڊ تي رڙيون ڪري ٿو.
ڊگٽرُ رڙ جهڙو آهي.

20-B Cardinal Numbers by "sevens"

17	۱۷	سترهن
27	۲۷	ستاويهه
37	۳۷	ستتيهه
47	۴۷	ستيتاليهه
57	۵۷	ستونجاهه
67	۶۷	ستهٺ

77	٧٧	ستهتر
87	٨٧	ستاسي
97	٩٧	ستانوي
107	١٠٧	هڪ سؤ ست

20 –C   Pronominal Suffixes as used with postpositions.

In the place of the regular pronouns which you have already learned, Sindhi uses a series of pronominal suffixes. These may be added to postpositions, nouns and verbs. These abbreviated pronoun forms are a notable feature of the Sindhi language, and reflect Semitic influence transmitted through Persian. The use of pronominal suffixes makes for brevity. Sindhi spoken or written in this way is sometimes referred to as "nanDhI Sindhi" (i.e. short Sindhi). They add grace to the language by removing ambiguity and relieving the monotony of recurring identical pronouns. To the beginning student, however, they may be confusing and difficult. These notes will help the student to identify and understand the more common pronominal suffixes, and to begin to use them.

Recognition and understanding of the use of these forms is very important, since in colloquial spoken Sindhi, they are almost universally used. This is true especially of village people. The more common pronominal suffixes are used in literature, school primers and the Bible. In order to understand Sindhi, and to speak it as Sindhis speak it, you must learn to use them.

Note: southern Sindhis were not in the habit of using these forms, but recent migration of southerners to Hyderabad and Karachi has meant that these forms are becoming more widespread.

Note: As this is not "regular" grammar, the pronunciation of various forms is open to much variation. Listen carefully to how the forms are used in your area.

Tell him today.	اچ کيس ٻڌايو. اچ هن کي ٻڌايو.
Give me his book.	مون کي سندس ڪتاب ڏي. مون کي هن جو ڪتاب ڏي.
We will go along with him.	اسين ساٽس گڏ هلنداسين. اسين هن سان گڏ هلنداسين.
I found out from him.	مون کائنس معلوم ڪيو. مون هن کان معلوم ڪيو.
He had many books.	وٽس گھڻا ڪتاب آهن. هن وٽ گھڻا ڪتاب آهن.

I gave them the news.	مون کين خبر ڏني. مون هنن کي خبر ڏني.

1. Generally with postpositions only the third person, singular and plural pronominal suffixes are used, that is suffixes which stand for "him" or "them". These suffixes are:

-s^i : 3rd person singular, standing for "هُن", him, her.

-n^i : 3rd person plural, standing for "هُنن", them.

2. The most common postpositions which may take a pronominal suffix are those illustrated above. They are simple postpositions کي, وٽ, کان, سان, and سندو. (The use of سندو and سندس was introduced in 10-F. Here you see that the –s^i ending on سندس is really a pronominal suffix).

3. When the pronominal suffix is added to کان, -u is added before the ending. Thus, it becomes کائنس (from him / her) and کائن (from them).

When the pronominal suffix is added to سان, -R̃a is added before the ending. Thus سان becomes ساڻس (with him / her) and ساڻن (with them).

20 –D   Pronominal Suffixes used with nouns of relationship.

His son is coming.	پُٽس اچي رهيو آهي.
He saw his (someone else's) father.	هن پيئس کي ڏٺو.
His / her mother was talking with me.	ماٽس مون سان گالهايو پئي.
His / her brother has done very good work.	ڀاٽس تمام سٺو ڪم ڪيو آهي.
Both their sons are studying.	ٻئي پٽ پڙهندا آهن.
His sister's wedding will be next week.	ڀيڻس جي شادي ايندڙ هفتي ۾ ٿيندي.
Their fathers will decide about this matter.	پيئرن هن گالهه بابت فيصلو ڪندا.
I gave an invitation to all their mothers.	مون سيئني مائرن کي دعوت ڏني.
His brother can't come today.	ڀاٽس اڄ اچي نہ ٿو سگهي.
All their brothers have gone to Karachi.	سڀ ڀائرن ڪراچي ويا آهن.
How old is his daughter?	ڏيٽس جي ڪيتري عمر آهي؟
He has two daughters. His elder daughter is six years old his younger daughter is two.	ڪيس ٻہ ڌيئرون آهن. وڏي ڏيٽس جي عمر ڇہ سال آهي ۽ ننڍي ڏيٽس ٻن سالن جي آهي.

All their daughters are still small.	سڀ ڌيئرون اڃا ننڍيون آهن.

4. The same third person pronominal suffixes are commonly added to certain nouns, mainly those denoting relationship. When used in this way they indicate relationship, that is, his, her and their.

The following are regular in the way they add the suffix:

His son	پُٽس	His sons	پُٽس
Their son	پُٽن	Their sons	پُٽن
His sister	پيئٽس	Their sister	پينرن

The others are slightly irregular, adding –Ra or ra to the simple form before adding the suffix.

His father	پٽس	Their fathers	پيئرن
Their father	پٽھن	His mother	ماٽس
Their mother	ماٽن	Their mothers	مائرن
His brother	ياٽس	Their brothers	يائرن
His daughter	ڊيٽس	Their daughters	ڊيئرن

Note: The forms for "their brother" and "their daughter" using pronominal suffixes are not used.

20 –E   Pronominal Suffixes as used with the verb "to be", هجڻ.

5. The chart of pronominal suffixes as used with the verb "to be" in the construction which means "to have" is as follows:

I have	We have	اٿئون	اٿم
You have	You have	اٿَو	اٿيئي
He / she has	They have	اٿن	اٿس

Notice that the pronominal ending could also stand for وٽ، مون وٽ، کي، وٽن، ڪيس آهي etc.

Do you have a radio?	ريڊيو اٿئي ڇا؟
We have two children.	ٻه ٻار اٿئون.
Do you have any fresh news?	ڪا تازي خبر اَٿَوَ.

I know that the fever has gone down.	.خبر اٿم تہ تپُ ڍرو اٿس
How many children do they have?	کيترا ٻار اٿن؟
(if) You have money, (so) get a ticket.	.پيسا اَٿَوَ تہ ٽکيٽ وٺو
Congratulations!	.(مبارڪ هجيوَ (اوهان کي مبارڪ هجي
I hope he will come back.	.اميد اٿم تہ ھو موٽي ايندو
They have some doubt that the matter is true or not.	.شڪ اٿن تہ هي ڳالھ سچ آهي يا نہ
I'm sorry that his father is sick.	.ڏاڍو افسوس اٿم تہ پٽس بيمار آهي

6. When a pronominal suffix is added to the verb "to be" as above, the form is irregular. The pronominal ending is added to ath– rather than آهي.

Notice also that the suffix added stands for a pronoun <u>plus</u> the postposition کي or وٽ.

7. The last group of sentences illustrates the use of abstract nouns with the verb "to be". It was pointed out in Lesson 9-F-3-d that the postposition کي is used with abstract nouns and the verb "to be". To say "I know", "I hope", "I am sorry", "I doubt" in Sindhi, this impersonal or indirect construction is used. Often the person is not named, as أُميد آهي, (It is hoped …). If the person is named it is with the use of أُميد اٿم .هن کي or مون کي أُميد: کي (lit: to me hope is) or شڪ آهي تہ … (He doubts that … / lit: to him doubt is that …)

20 –F Relative and co-relative words and their use in compound sentences

1. A compound sentence is one in which there are two main parts or clauses. One of the clauses may be less important, or subordinate to the other. In Sindhi the less important, or subordinate clause will normally come first in the sentence. The only reason for changing the order would be to place the emphasis on that clause. In Sindhi emphasis may be shown by placing something at the end of the sentence rather than in its normal place.

The student should be aware at this point of the problems that the deeply entrenched thought patterns of his first language bring to bear on learning the second language. In English the more important clause in a compound sentence comes first and this way of thinking will interfere with learning the Sindhi way of thinking and thus speaking. Being aware of the interference and contamination from the first language will help a great deal in changing the thought patterns so that one can begin to think the way the Sindhi does.

In English we would say "<u>Show me the book</u> / which is in your hand". The first part of the sentence is the main clause: <u>Show me the book</u> /. The second clause, the subordinate clause is: "which is in your hand". This tells us which book and where it is. In Sindhi this sentence would be said in this way:

.جو ڪتاب تنهنجي هٿ ۾ آهي سو مون کي ڏيکاريو

The book which is in your hand, that one show me.

جو is called the <u>relative word</u>, in this case an adjective because it describes 'book'. سو is its <u>co-relative</u>, and may <u>not</u> be omitted. جو may also function as a pronoun:

جو تنهنجي هٿ ۾ آهي سو مون کي ڏيکاريو.

Whatever is in your hand, show me that.

جيڪو is another word used exactly as is جو. It is synonymous with جو and also uses سو as co-relative. جو or جيڪو agree with the noun qualified as follows:

	Nominative		Oblique	
	Singular	Plural	Singular	Plural
Masculine:	جيڪو، جو ... سو	جيڪي، جي ... سي	جنهن ... تنهن	جن ... تن
Feminine	جيڪا، جا ... سا	جيڪي، جي ... سي	جنهن ... تنهن	جن ... تن

Who was the man who came yesterday?	جيڪو ماڻهو ڪالھ آيو سو ڪير هو؟
The man who came yesterday was my teacher.	اهو ماڻهو جو ڪالھ آيو سو منهنجو استاد هو.
The woman you saw is his wife.	جيڪا عورت توهان ڏٺي سا سندس زال آهي.
The fruit you brought was very expensive.	جو ميوو توهان آندو سو تمام مهانگو هو.
I didn't understand the things he told me.	جيڪي ڳالهيون هن ٻڌايون سي مون نہ سمجهيون.
I don't know anything about the thing you mentioned.	جيڪا ڳالھ توهان ذڪر ڪئي تنهن بابت مون کي خبر ڪانهي.
The students I saw were all big.	جن شاگردن کي مون ڏٺو سي سڀ وڏا آهن.
The question I'm talking about is the fifth one.	اهو سوال جنهن بابت مان ڳالهائي رهيو آهيان سو پنجون سوال آهي.
I have answered the men who questioned me.	جن ماڻهن مون کان سوال پڇيا تن مون کي جواب ڏنو.

You should put more lights in those rooms which don't have enough light.	جن ڪوٺين ۾ ڪافي روشني نہ آهي، تن ۾ توهان کي وڌيڪ بتيون لڳائڻ کپن.
The way (road) he showed you was very difficult.	جا واٽ هن توکي ڏيکاري سا تمام مشڪل هئي.
The man who saw you yesterday is here.	جنهن ماڻهو توکي ڪالھ ڏٺو سو هتي آهي.
The man you saw yesterday is here.	جنهن ماڻهو کي تو ڪالھ ڏٺو سو هتي آهي.
Do what I tell you. (or, whatever)	جيڪي مان توکي چوان ٿو سو ڪر.

2. In nearly all the sentences above, جو, or جيڪو (or one of the inflected forms) functions as an adjective, qualifying a noun. In most of the sentences the noun could be omitted and the relative <u>adjective</u> would then become a pronoun. Sentence one would be:

جيڪو ڪلھ آيو سو ڪير هو؟ Who was it who came yesterday?

3. ذڪر ڪرڻ is a compound verb meaning "to mention". ذڪر is a masculine noun meaning "saying, mention, remembrance". Since the noun part of the compound is masculine, the verb should normally be in a masculine form in the past tense to agree with ذڪر, its object within the compound. However since the logical object of "to mention" is ڳالھ a feminine noun, the agreement is with that word, thus, ڳالھ ذڪر ڪئي.

4. In the last sentence above, جيڪي is an indeclinable pronoun related to جو and جيڪو. It has the meaning of "Whatever".

5. There are three more relative adjectives each with its correlatives. You have already learned the question words related to two of them.

جهڙو..... تهڙو, اهڙو   like, just like - used for description.

ڪهڙو؟ - Which

جيترو... تيترو, ايترو   as many as, as much as - used for quantity.

ڪيترو؟ How many?

جيڏو.... تيڏو, ايڏو   as big as - used for size.

ڪيڏو؟ How big as?

These are all used as adjectives and agree with the noun that they qualify in gender and number. They are inflected in the oblique after a postposition.

I want a pen just like the one you have.	جهڙو قلم توهان وٽ آهي اهڙو (تهڙو) مون کي کپي.
There are no shoes in this shop like the ones I saw yesterday.	جهڙيون جتيون مون ڪالهه ڏٺيون تهڙيون هن دڪان تي نه آهن.
I'll order the kind of books you want.	جهڙا ڪتابَ توهان کي کپن تهڙا مان توهان لاءِ گهرندس.
Cook as much meet as there is.	جيترو گوشت آهي تيترو پچايو.
Answer as many questions as there are.	جيترا سوال هجن تيترن جا جواب ڏيو.
I'll bring as much wood as you need.	جيتري ڪاٺي اوهان کي کپي ايتري مان ڪٿي ايندس.
There are not as much windows in our room as in their room.	جيتريون دريون هنن جي ڪوٺيءَ ۾ آهن تيتريون اسان جي ڪوٺي ۾ نه آهن.
I'll try to bring the fruit as cheap as I can (get it).	مان ڪوشش ڪندس ته ميوو جيترو سستو ملي ڪٿي ايندس.
My son is as big as this boy.	جيڏو هي چوڪرو آهي تيڏو منهنجو پٽ به آهي.
How big is your daughter? She is so big.	توهان جي ڌيءُ ڪيڏي آهي؟ هوءَ ايڏي آهي.
Bring as big apples as you can get.	جيڏا صوفَ توهان کي ملي سگهن تا ايڏا ڪٿي اچو.

6.   As with جو, each of these relative adjectives must be used with its co-relative word. This co-relative although not expressed in English must be included in Sindhi. ايڏو, ايترو, and اهڙو as well as being used as co-relative words in compound sentences may also be used as simple adjectives, as,

I want a pen like that.	مون کي اهڙو قلم کپي.

I can't eat that much food.   مان ايترو ڪاڏو ڪائي نٿو سگھان.

I never saw such a big mango!   مون ايڏو انب ڪڏهن نہ ڊٺو.

7. In 16-B-7 the use of ملڻ with سان meaning "to meet" was explained. Above it is used to mean "to get, to obtain". In this use it is expressed in an indirect construction. For example,

You won't get mangoes nowadays.   توهان ڪي اڄڪالھ انب نہ ملندا.

I got a letter today.   مون ڪي اڄ هڪڙو خط مليو.

He got a notebook.   هن ڪي ڪاپي ملي.

In this use of ملڻ, the subject is in the oblique with ڪي, and the verb agrees with the thing gotten or obtained. Thus the literal translation of the first sentence above is "Mangoes won't be gotten to / by you nowadays".

There is another use of ملڻ with سان for <u>things</u>. In this case it means "to match, resemble". For example,

This color doesn't match the other.   هي رنگ ٻئي رنگ سان نٿو ملي.

8. There are also a number of adverbs which are used as relative words with their co-relatives. You are already familiar with the related questions words.

Relative	Co-relative	Question	Denotes:
جيئن in the same way, as, like	تيئن ايئن	ڪيئن How?	manner
جڏهن when … then	تڏهن	ڪڏهن When?	time
جتي Where … here, there	اتي, ِاتي, تتي هتي, هُتي	ڪتي Where?	location
جتان From where	اتان تتان اِتان هُتان هِتان from here, there	ڪتان from where?	direction from

			direction towards	ڪيڏانهن
جيڏانهن	تيڏانهن			
هوڏانهن هيڏانهن				

towards where ... towards here, there   Towards where?

I did just as you said.	جيئن توهان چيو تيئن (ايئن) مون ڪيو.
We're not going the same way they went.	جيئن هو ويا ايئن (تيئن) اسين نه وينداسين.
When our neighbor came, we were eating.	جڏهن اسان جو پاڙيسري آيو تڏهن اسان ماني کائي پئي.
Please tell me when he comes.	جڏهن هو اچي تڏهن مون کي ٻڌائج
Where we live there isn't a paved road.	جتي اسان رهندا آهيون هتي پڪو رستو نه آهي.
He / she likes it where there's a lot of excitement. (or, a lot going on)	جتي رونق آهي تتي هن جي دل لڳي ٿي.
Where we got this cloth, we can get more.	جتان اسان کي هي ڪپڙو مليو، تتان (هتان) اسين وڌيڪ وٺي سگهون ٿا.
The little boy goes wherever his brother goes.	جيڏانهن ڀاڻس وڃي تيڏانهن ننڍو چوڪرو به وڃي ٿو.
When I go, I will shut the door.	جڏهن مان ويندس تڏهن دروازو بند ڪندس.
When you have finished this work, you may leave.	جڏهن توَ هي ڪم پورو ڪيو آهي تڏهن توکي اجازت آهي.

9. Notice that while the word order may vary in English, the normal word order does not change in Sindhi. The relative word will come at the beginning of the compound sentence.

10. دل لڳڻ is another idiomatic use of لڳڻ. It means "to like". It is used for things and places, not for people. Another example:

He / she doesn't like it here.	هتي هن جي دل نٿي لڳي.
Do you like it here?	ڇا توهان جي دل هتي لڳي ٿي؟

Why aren't you eating?			توهان ڪاڏو چو نٿا ڪائو؟
I don't feel like it, or, I don't like it.			دل نہ ٿي لڳي۔

20 –G   Vocabulary.

neighbor (f)	پاڙيسري	to set one's heart, to like	دل لڳڻ
to cook	پچائڻ	excitement, activity (f)	رونق
ticket, postage stamp (f)	ٽڪيٽ	eighty-seven	ستاسي
When ... then	جڏهن تڏهن	forty-seven	ستيتاليہہ
Where ... there	جتان تتان	thirty-seven	ستڙيہہ
shoe (f)	جُتي	twenty-seven	ستاويہہ
Where ... there	جيڏانهن تيڏانهن	ninety-seven	ستانوي
As big as ... so big as	جيڏو تيڏو	fifty-seven	ستونجاهہ
as ... so	جتي ... تتي	seventy-seven	ستهٺ
as ... like	جيترو ... تيترو	attempt (f)	ڪوشش
as many, as much as ... so many, so much	جيترو تيترو	to try	ڪوشش ڪرڻ
whoever, whatever... that one	جيڪو، جو، سو	decision (f)	فيصلو
whatever	جيڪي	to decide	فيصلو ڪرڻ
to find out	معلوم ڪرڻ	invitation (f)	دعوت
thus	ائين	to descend, come down	ڍرڻ
like, this kind of	اهڙو	mention, saying (f)	ذڪر

so much	ايترو	to mention	ذڪر ڪرڻ
so big	ايڏو	doubt	شڪ

20-H   Conversational Review.

1. Say each of the following phrases in a different way using a pronominal suffix: For example,

Teacher: استاد: هن جو پُٽُ

Student: شاگرد: پُٽّس

هن جا، هن جي ماءُ، هن جون ڌيئر،

هن جو پيءُ، هن جي ڌيءَ، هن جا پُٽَ،

هن کي، هن وٽ، هنن کان، هن سان،

هنن وٽ، هنن کان، هنن سان، هنن کي

2. Change each of the following sentences, using pronominal suffixes. Say the sentence in two different ways where possible.

Teacher: استاد: اسان وٽ ھہ ھار آھن۔

Student: شاگرد: وٽس ھہ ھار آھن۔

ھہ ھار اٿس۔

مون کي خبر ڪانهي۔

ڇا توهان کي هن جي لاءِ ڪا اميد آهي؟

هنن کي ڇھ پُٽَ آهن۔

هن کي وڏو گهر آهي۔

تو وٽ منهنجو ڪتابُ آهي ڇا؟

اسان کي هاڻي وقت ڪونهي۔

Repeat this exercise changing the pronoun in each sentence.

3. Substitute each of the following nouns in the first phrase of the sentence, and an adjective in the second phrase, changing the second phrase freely.

Nouns: اسمَ: پٽاٽا، آنا، ڪنڊُ، ڪيرُ، گجرُ، گوشت،

جُتي، ڪتاب، ميوو

Lesson 20/ 257

Adjectives: صفتون: مهانگو، سستو، وڏو، ننڍو، ستو
وغيره
جو /جيڪو... مون ڊٺو سو تمام ... هو

4. Substitute each of the following words in the sentence given below, choosing the proper inflected form. Repeat, using plural nouns.

ماڻهو، ڊاڪٽر، ٽپالي، ڌوٻي، هٽ وارو
بورچي، هاري، ڇوڪرا، مالي، استادُ
جنهن/جن.. توهان ڊٺو سو .... هو / هئا

5. Substitute each of the following phrases in the sentence below, inflecting where necessary. Fill in the second clause freely.

جون ڇوڪريون،   منهنجي پيٽ، اسان
منهنجو پي ءُ، منهنجو يا ءُ، منهنجي ماءُ،
اسان جا مائٽ، استاد صاحب، اهو ماڻهو،
اها عورت،   منهنجو پاڙيسري
جيئن... چوي/چيو تيئن..

6. Substitute each of the following verbs in the sentence given below, choosing the proper ending. Use the same verb in the last clause. Vary the tense of the verb. Repeat, changing the pronouns.

موڪلڻ، بيهارڻ، ڊوڙڻ، کر کرڻ،
ماني پچائڻ، ڪيڏڻ، سفر ڪرڻ،
وڃڻ، اچڻ، سيکارڻ، دل لڳڻ.

(جتي)   (تتي)
(جتان)   توهين... (تتان)   اسين ٻـ....
(جيڏانهن)   (تيڏانهن)

7. Substitute each of the following nouns in the sentence given below, remembering to properly inflect the form.

پاڄي، چانھ، ڪنڊُ، دوا، ڪيرُ
گوشت، قلمَ، ڪتابَ، ڪاپيون،
ڪاٺي، پينسل، چانور، ڪپھ

جيترو......... اسان وٽ آھي تيترو ڪافي نہ آھي.

8. Repeat Exercise 7, substituting جھڙو...تھڙو, as in the following sentence, making whatever inflections are necessary. Change the verb in the last clause freely.

جڏھن مون .... ڪي ڏٺو تڏھن ......

LESSON TWENTY-ONE

21-A Pronunciation Drill

1. Contrasting /jh/ and /j/ plus /H/   (31/29+41)   /جھ/ ۽ /ج/ + /ھ/

جھڙو جھاڙو ملي اھڙو جھليو.
جھاز تي جھڳڙو ھو.
جھان ۾ جَھاز جھجھا آھن.

2. Contrasting /c/ and /j/   (28/29)   /ج/ ۽ /چ/

موچي چڱيءَ طرح جتيون جوڙي ٿو.
اھي ٻہ چورَ جوڙو آھن.
جنگ چڱي نہ آھي.

21-B Compound Postpositions with كان (from).

My relatives are coming from Larkana today.	منھنجا مائٽ اڄ لاڙڪاڻي کان اچن ٿا.
Who did you hear this news from?	توھان ھي خبر ڪنھن کان ٻڌي؟
My uncle told me.	منھنجي چاچي مون کي ٻڌايو.
I asked that man for a book.	مون ڪتاب ھن ماڻھوءَ کان گھريو.
The teacher asked me for the letter.	استاد صاحب مون کان چٺي گھري.

1. The postposition كان means "from". Notice that as illustrated in the last two sentences above, in Sindhi we do not request the man for the book, rather we request of ask the book from the man. Thus the item requested is the object of the verb, and in the past tense, the verb agrees with its object.

2. The postposition کان may also be compounded with other postpositions as illustrated in the sentences below.

Take the girl's clothes from (out of) the cupboard.	چوڪريءَ جا ڪپڙا ڪٻٽ مان ڪڍو۔
The boys took all of the books out of the box.	ڇوڪرن سڀ ڪتاب پيتيءَ مان ڪڍيا۔
The man came out from the crowd.	ماڻھو ميڙ منجھان نڪتو۔

3. مان and منجھان give the idea that the thing or person was "in" or "inside" and came or was taken out from inside something. مان may be described as being formed from مِ (in) and کان (from). منجھان comes from منجھ, a noun meaning "the inside, a secret". منجھ may also be used as a postposition meaning "inside", but it's most common use is as illustrated above, meaning "from inside of".

The girl took the fruit from the table.	چوڪريءَ ميوو ميز تان ورتو۔
You will get good cloth from this shop.	توھان کي سٺو ڪپڙو ھن دڪان تان ملندو۔

4. تان is formed from تي (on) and کان (from). Thus wherever the postposition تي would be used to describe the position of an object, تان would be used to describe where it is coming from.

The children passed by the shop.	ٻار دڪان وٽان لنگھيا۔
The marriage procession will pass by this house.	ڄڃ ھن گھر وٽان لنگھندي۔

5. وٽان expresses the idea of "nearby", and is used with verbs of motion. It must be differentiated from وٽ which can mean "near" or "to", as in this sentence:

The children came near / to the shop.	ٻار دڪان وٽ آيا۔
Are there any other chairs besides these?	ھنن ڪرسين کان سواءِ ٻيون ڪرسيون آھن ڇا؟
I didn't see anyone besides this boy.	مون ھن ڇوڪري کان سواءِ ڪنھن کي نه ڏٺو۔
What should we do without his help?	اسين ھن جي مدد کان سواءِ ڇا ڪريون؟

6. In the first two sentences above, کان سواءِ means "besides", "in addition to". It can also mean "without" as in the last sentence.

My father has been sick for two days.	منھنجو پيءُ ٻن ڏينھن کان بيمار آھي۔
The guests came yesterday (since yesterday) and will stay till tomorrow.	مزمان ڪالھ کان وٽي سڀاڻي تائين ٽڪندا۔

| Rain has been falling steadily since last week. | مينهن گذريل هفتي کان وٽي لڳاتار پئي رهيو آهي. |
| My brother has been alright since yesterday. | منهنجو ڀاءُ ڪالھ کان (وٽي) ٺيڪ آهي. |

7. When speaking about time since, کان وٽي may be properly used. However, as in the last sentence above وٽي may be omitted and کان used alone.

21-C The formation of the Past Perfect Tense.

Intransitive Verbs.

Singular	Plural	جمع	واحد
Masculine		مذکر	
I had walked	We had walked	اسين هليا هئا سين / هئا سون	مان هليو هوس
You had walked	You had walked	توهين هليا هئا	تون هليو هئين
He had walked	They had walked	اُهي هليا هئا	هُو هليو هو / هيو
Feminine		مؤنث	
I had walked	We had walked	اسين هَليوُن هُيُونسين	مان هلي هُيَس
You had walked	You had walked	توهين هليون هيون	تون هلي هُئين
She had walked	They had walked	اُهي هليون هُيون	هُوءَ هلي هُئي

Transitive Verbs.

Singular		Plural		جمع		واحد	
I	had written	We	had written	اسان	لکيو هو	مون	لکيو هو
You		You		توهان		تو	
He / she		They		هنن		هن	

1. When the past auxiliary forms of the verb هئڻ (to be) are used with the Perfect Participle of a Sindhi verb, the Past Perfect Tense is formed. (See lesson 17-C-2)

2. If the main verb is intransitive, the participle and the auxiliary verb will agree with the subject. If the main verb is intransitive, the subject will be in the oblique form. As in other past forms of the verb, there is no agreement with the subject, and agreement is with the object, as detailed in Lesson 17-E-2.

3. The Past Perfect Tense indicates a past action or state/condition which was completed or relevant in the more remote past. This contrasts with the Present Perfect which indicates action complete in the very recent past, or continuing in the present.

4. You will notice the sentences in the section following that in Sindhi the Past Perfect Tense is often used where the English speaker would expect a simple past tense.

21 –D   Statements, questions, and negatives in the Past Perfect Tense.

Who was the man who came (lit: had come) yesterday?	جيڪو ماڻهو ڪالھ آيو هو سو ڪير هو؟
The woman you saw was his wife.	جيڪا عورت توهان ڏني هئي سا سندس زال هئي.
We had bought the books.	اسان ڪتاب خريد ڪيا.
I had seen the teacher.	مون استاد کي ڏٺو هو.
The meat you cooked yesterday was very good.	جو گوشت تو ڪالھ پچايو هو سو تمام سٺو هو.
What had the teacher described?	استاد صاحب ڪھڙي ڳالھ جو بيان ڪيو هو؟
He described Moenjodaro.	هن موئن جي دڙي جو بيان ڪيو هو.
Did you turn on the light in front, too?	توهان سامهون جي بتي بہ لڳائي هئي؟
Yes, I turned on all the lights.	هائو مون سڀ بتيون لڳايون هيون.
The cook prepared (cooked) local / indigenous food.	بورچي ديسي ڪاڏو پچايو هو.
Did anyone not like it?	ڇا ڪنهن کي پسند نہ هو؟
No, the foreigners liked it very much, too.	نہ، پرديسي ماڻهن بہ اهو تمام پسند ڪيو هو.
Didn't you like that color?	ڇا اهو رنگ توهان کي پسند نہ هو؟
My wife didn't like it.	منهنجي گهر واري کي اهو پسند نہ آيو هو.
Had you returned by five o'clock?	توهين پنجين بجي تائين موٽي آيا هئا؟
Yes, I had come, but the teacher had already gone.	هائو مان آيو هوس پر استاد صاحب اڳ ۾ ويو هو.

هنن جا مزمان ڪوٽي ۾ ويٺا هئا.	There guests were sitting in the room.
نوڪرياڻيءَ ڪين ويھاريو ھو.	The (lady) servant has seated them.
جڏھن ھو بيمار ٿيو ھو تڏھن مان ھن سان مليس.	When he was sick, (lit: had become sick) I met (or saw) him.

1. The word پسند is an adjective meaning "approved, chosen". It is used with the verb "to be", هئڻ or the verb "to come", اچڻ as an intransitive compound verb meaning "to like", "to be pleased with". In this case it is used impersonally with the subject inflected with کي. The thing "liked" thus becomes the subject of the verb, and the verb must agree with it. Thus,

مون کي ھي رنگ پسند آھي

means literally, "This color is pleasing to me".

2. پسند may also combine with ڪرڻ to form a transitive compound verb. Its use is illustrated above.

3. بتي لڳائڻ means "to turn on a light". This is another idiomatic use of لڳائڻ (to apply, attach).

4. Two compound verbs are used in the sentences above, خريد ڪرڻ "to buy" and بيان ڪرڻ "to describe". Most compound verbs made up of a noun and a verb are treated as transitive in Sindhi, even if they are intransitive in English. The noun with which the verb is compounded is the object, and thus in the past tenses based on the perfect participle, the verb will agree with this noun, even if there is some other external object. In the sentence above:

استاد صاحب کهڙي ڳالھ جو بيان ڪيو ھو.

بيان is the object of ڪرڻ, thus making the verb masculine in the past perfect tense. Even though ڳالھ is the logical object, and feminine, بيان has the closer and stronger effect on the verb. (Note: not every language helper will agree with this rule, meaning it is not a clear-cut rule in everyday usage. It will be helpful for you to continue trying compound verbs in the past tense as you learn them in order to discover how your language helper understands their usage.)

There are a few exceptions to this rule, and خريد ڪرڻ is one of them. خريد is feminine, and thus one would expect the verb to be in the feminine in the past perfect tense. However, in this case the verb must agree with the external object. Thus:

اسان ڪتاب خريد ڪيا ھئا، ھن ڪتاب خريد ڪيو ھو.

5. شروع ڪرڻ is another exception also. It will agree with the external object rather than with شروع, the internal object. For example, ھن چني شروع ڪئي. (He began the letter).

21 –E   Intensifying Verbs.

Idiomatic Sindhi makes extensive use of another type of verbal compound called <u>intensives</u>. A verb is intensified by joining its conjunctive participle with one of a limited group of verbs called <u>intensifiers</u>.

The compound verb takes its meaning from the root verb in the conjunctive participle. The intensifying verb will change to indicate the tense and person, following either transitive or intransitive rules, as the case may be. Both the intensifiers introduced here are intransitive.

In these compound verbs the intensive verb loses all or most of its original significance, and has no distinct meaning of its own. Its function is to strengthen, emphasize or slightly alter the force of the root verb. However you will find as you observe the use of intensives in Sindhi that in many cases there is no real difference between the verb used alone and used with an intensifying verb added. Sindhi speakers use these forms a great deal especially in the tenses formed from the perfect participle, and in commands. Intensive compounds may be used in other tenses as well, but never in negatives.

1.   Sentences illustrating the use of وڃڻ and پوڻ as intensifiers.

My hat was left behind.	منهنجي ٽوپي پوئتي رهجي وئي.
When his parents left, the son was left behind.	جڏهن هن جا ماءُ پيءُ هليا ويا تڏهن پٽ پوئتي رهجي ويو.
Five houses burned down.	پنج گهر سڙي ويا.
Today the bus came late.	اڄ بس دير سان اچي وئي.
Did you understand well?	چا توهان چڱي طرح سمجهي ويا؟
I completely forgot.	مون کان صفا وسري ويو.
The man who was sick died.	جيڪو ماڻهو بيمار هو سو مري ويو.

a.   وڃڻ when used as an intensifier expresses the idea of <u>completeness thoroughness</u>, or <u>finality</u> of action.

b.   It is necessary to judge by the context whether the verb وڃڻ is being used as an intensifier, or in its simple meaning "to go". The fourth sentence above could mean, "The bus came and went". However the usual law of expressing this idea in the past is with the use of وڃڻ as an intensive. Another example of this usage,

Have your relatives come?	چا توهان جا مائٽ اچي ويا.

Note well, that this does <u>not</u> mean they have gone, since the original meaning of وڃڻ is lost in the intensive compound.

c. To say in Sindhi "I forgot ..." one says "It was forgotten by me". In this indirect construction, the verb agrees with the object if expressed.

| I forgot that matter. | مون کان اها ڳالھ وسري وئي. |

d. هلڻ is one of a few verbs which have a continuous conjunctive participle. It is the only one commonly used, and the only one which is declined. This continuous conjunctive participle is formed by adding – و to the regular from. In intensive compounds it is inflected to agree with the subject in gender and number. For example,

Boy, go away!	چوکرا هليو وڃ!
Boys, go away!	چوکرؤ هليا وڃو!
All the women went away.	سڀ عورتون هليون ويون.

e. The following sentences illustrate the use of پوڻ in intensive compounds.

He burst out laughing.	هو کلي پيو.
Lie down.	سمهي پؤ.
Yesterday she got sick / fell sick.	ڪالھ هوء بيمار ٿي پئي.
When the boys fell off the wall, their father got very angry.	جڏهن چوکرا پٽ تان ڪري پيا تڏهن پٽن تمام ڪاوڙجي پيو.
My car got stuck in the mud.	منهنجي موٽر گپ ۾ ڦاسي پئي.
I got confused because I was alone.	مان منجهي پيس ڇا لاءِ جو مان اڪيلو هوس.
I was in the middle of the road when the tonga suddenly came upon me.	مان رستي جي وچ ۾ هوس ت بگي منهنجي مٿان اچي پئي.
On account of walking so far we all got very tired.	ايترو پري پنڌ ڪرڻ ڪري اسين سڀ ٿڪجي پيا سين.
After arriving home, the children quickly fell asleep.	گهرءَ پهچي ٻار جلدي سمهي پيا.
Why did the lady get so angry?	بيگم صاحبءَ ڇو ڪاوڙجي پئي؟

Because so many glasses fell down.

They all broke.

چا کاڻ تہ گھڻا گلاس ڪري پيا.
سڀ ڀڃي پيا.

f. پوڻ when used as an intensifier expresses the idea of suddenness. It is often used with certain verbs which express feeling or emotion, such as "to be tired" and "to be, or get, angry".

g. Grammatically one could say چوڪرا ڪِريا (the boys fell) or چوڪري بيمار ٿي (the girl got sick), but the idiomatic way of expressing illustrated in the sentences above with پوڻ.

h. This use of پوڻ must not be confused with the continuous tense with پئي. (Lesson 19-C-b)

i. مُنجھي پوڻ is an intransitive verb meaning "to be confused, to be in a fix, to be at a loss, not to know what to do".

21–F   Vocabulary.

alone	اڪيلو	approved, pleasing	پسند
horse-drawn vehicle, tonga (f)	بگي	to like	پسند اچڻ پسند ڪرڻ پسند هئڻ
description (m)	بَيانُ	distance (m)	پنڌ
to describe	بيان ڪرڻ	to walk	پنڌ ڪرڻ
to be tired	ٿَڪَجڻ	uncle, father's brother	چاچو
foreign, foreigner	پرديسي	thief	چور
local, indigenous	ديسي	to pass by	لنگھڻ
marriage procession (f)	جَڃَ	continuously	لڳاتار
to be left behind	رھجڻ	out of	مان، منجھان
to be angry	ڪاوڙجڻ	to be confused, to be in a fix, to not know what to do.	منجھي پوڻ
to fall	ڪِرڻ	crowd (m)	ميڙُ
from	کان	nearby	وٽان

except, besides without	کان سواءِ	to be forgotten	وسارڻ
since	کان وٺي	to be stuck, entangled	ڦاسڻ
to laugh	کلڻ	mud (f)	ڳٻ
from off of	تان		

21-G   Conversational Review.

1. In your conversations this week notice how your Sindhi friends use intensives, particularly وڃڻ and پوڻ. Make a point of using them in your conversations. If your teacher or someone else corrects your usage or tells you not to use it in that way, make a note of this. Only by very close observation, and careful listening will you master the use of intensives as Sindhis use them.

2. Ask your teacher to read out each of the following verbal compounds. Make up sentences using each one. Ask him to make up a sentence using each one. He may ask a question which should have an intensive compound in the answer.

رھجي وڃڻ،	ھليو وڃڻ،	سڙي وڃڻ
اچي وڃڻ،	سمجهي وڃڻ،	وسري وڃڻ
مري وڃڻ،	کلي پوڻ،	سمهي پوڻ
بيمار پوڻ،	ڪري پوڻ،	ڦاسي پوڻ
منجهي پوڻ،	ٿڪجي پوڻ،	ڪاوڙجي پوڻ
يڃي پوڻ،	جاڳي پوڻ	

3. Use the patterns given in 16-C-4 changing the tense to the past perfect tense of سگهڻ.

4. Use the drills in 17-I-1 and 3, changing the form of the verb to the past perfect.

5. Do the replacement drill in 18-I-1, changing the first sentence to the Past Perfect, that is:

استاد صاحب اڳي ڀڻو ھو۔

Continue through the drill, carrying the Past Perfect tense throughout the drill.

6. Make up sentences using the following postpositions. Ask your teacher to do a dialogue with you using them.

مان، منجهان، کان، تان، وٽان، وَٽِ، کان وٽي، کانسواءِ

For example:

Teacher:

| استاد: ڪتابُ ڪيٽ ۾ آهن. هنن کي ڪيٽ مان ڪڍو. |

Student:

| شاگرد: مان ڪتاب ڪيٽ مان ڪڍي رهيو آهيان. |

or,

| يا، مون ڪتاب ڪيٽ مان ڪڍيا هئا. |

LESSON TWENTY-TWO

22-A Pronunciation Drill

1. Contrasting /g̃/ and /n/ plus /g/   (4/2+22)   /ڳ/ ۽ /ن/ + /گ/

ڇا ڇوڪري جو سنگتي ڊنگو آهي يا ڇڳو؟
مينهن جو سڱُ ڊنگو آهي.
ھار جي آڳر جو رنگ خراب ٿي ويو.

2. Contrasting /H/ and /K/   (41/25)   /ح/ + /خ/

هي حصو هن خالي خاني ۾ وجهو.
هُن خادم خدا جي حُڪُرَ جي خبر ڏني.
حڪومت جي خاص خبر اخبار ۾ هئي.

22-B Cardinal Numbers by "Eights"

18	۱۸	ارڙھن
28	۲۸	اڻاويھ
38	۳۸	اڻتيھ
48	۴۸	اڻتاليھ
58	۵۸	اڻونجاھ
68	۶۸	اٺھٺ
78	۷۸	اٺھتر
88	۸۸	اڻاسي
98	۹۸	اڻانوي
108	۱۰۸	ھڪ سؤائ

22 –C   The infinitive with ڏيڻ (to give) to indicate permission.

Let him come in.	هن کي اندر اچڻ ڏنو ويو.
The girl is sick today. Her father didn't let her go to school.	اڄ چوڪري بيمار آهي. هن جي پيءُ کيس اسڪول وڃڻ نہ ڏنو.
The teacher let me recite the lesson first.	استاد صاحب مون کي پهريائين سبق پڙهائڻ ڏنو.
I will let you read my book.	مان توهان کي پنهنجو ڪتاب پڙهڻ ڏيندس.
Who let the dog come into the house?	ڪنهن ڪُتي کي گهر ۾ اچڻ ڏنو؟
These days we let our son drive the car.	اڄڪالھ اسين پنهنجي چوڪري کي ڪار هلائڻ ڏيون ٿا.
Next year we'll let our daughter drive too.	ايندڙ سال اسين چوڪريءَ کي بہ هلائڻ ڏينداسين.
Should I call them again?	مان وري هنن کي سڏ ڪريان ڇا؟
No, forget it. (Lit: let it go)	نہ، رهڻ ڏيو (ڇڏي ڏيو).
The teacher doesn't let me speak English in class.	استادياڻي مون کي ڪلاس ۾ انگريزي ڳالهائڻ نہ ٿي ڏي.
They let us take pictures.	هنن اسان کي تصويرون ڪڍڻ ڏنيون.

1.   When any tense of ڏيڻ follows the infinitive of a verb, the resulting sentence shows permission to do something. The one who is given permission is indicated by کي, the postposition.

2.   When the infinitive is followed by a form of the verb ڏيڻ to indicate permission, it is inflected, the final short vowel –u becoming –a.

3.   Since ڏيڻ is a transitive verb, it will agree with any expressed object in those tenses based on the perfective participle. See the last sentence above as an example. If we use the word فوٽو instead of تصوير, it would be as follows:

They let us take pictures.	هنن اسان کي فوٽا ڪڍڻ ڏنا.

4. رھڻ ڏيو is a common idiom meaning "let it go", "forget it", "don't bother". This same thought may be expressed by ڇڏڻ. That is, ڇڏي ڏيو.

22–D   More Postpositions.

Bring a notebook like that one.	ھڪ ڪاپي ھن جھڙي ڪٽي اچو.
This cloth isn't like that cloth.	ھي ڪپڙو ھن ڪپڙي جھڙو نہ آھي.
Tailor, why didn't you make my shirt like the pattern?	درزي، تون منھنجي قميص نموني وانگر چو نہ ٺاھي؟
The Hyderabad fort is worth seeing.	حيدرآباد جو قلعو ڏسڻ جھڙو آھي.

1. جھڙو and وانگر are interchangeable when used as postpositions. Be sure to distinguish the use of جھڙو as a postposition from its use as a relative word. (20-E-5) جھڙو and وانگر mean "like, similar to".

2. جھڙو as used in the last sentence above means "worthy of".

Why didn't you do as I said? (lit: according to my saying)	تو منھنجي چوڻ موجب چو نہ ڪيو؟
We ought to act according to the law.	اسان کي قانون موجب ھلڻ کپي.
According to God's commands we ought to show love to each other.	خدا جي حڪمن موجب اسان کي ھڪ ٻئي ڏانھن پيار ڏيکارڻ گھرجي.
The judge will bring judgment according to the new law.	جج صاحب قانون موجب عدالت ڪندو.

3. موجب means "according to", "as". It may be used with or without جي as,

خدا جي حڪمن جي موجب.

4. حڪم means "command" or "order", while قانون means "law".

The doctor made every effort for the sake of this patient. (lit: tried very hard)	ڊاڪٽر ھن مريض جي واسطي ڏاڍي ڪوشش ڪئي.
According to the Christian faith, Jesus Christ gave his life on the cross for us sinners.	مسيحي ايمان جي موجب عيسیٰ مسيح اسان گنھگارن جي واسطي پنھنجي جان صليب تي ڏني.

5. جي واسطي means "for the sake of". There is a shade of difference in meaning between لاءِ meaning simply "for", and لاءِ (or جي لاءِ). واسطي (جي) is more general and may be used impersonally or for people whereas واسطي (جي) is stronger, and usually used with people.

22 –E   Reported Speech.

In English when we report what someone says or thinks or what they said or thought, we often use indirect speech or quotation. This involves a complicated change of tense, pronouns and other words such as adverbs. For example, if the person actually said, "Meet me here tomorrow at 5 o'clock", it would be reported as, "He said to meet him there at 5 o'clock the next day".

In Sindhi the indirect form of speech is seldom, in fact, almost never used. When reporting what others said or thought, the actual words are used without change. Since quotations are not used in written Sindhi, the sign or reported speech or a quotation is the particle تہ.

The man said that his brother has come, and so he is not able to come.	ماٹھوءَ چيو تہ منھنجو ڀاءُ آيو آھي. تنھنڪري آءُ اچي نہ ٿو سگھان.
The servant said that his brother has come, so he can't come.	نوڪر چيو تہ ھن جو ڀاءُ آيو آھي، تنھنڪري ھو اچي نہ ٿو سگھي.
They said they had come from Dadu.	ھنن چيو تہ اسين دادو ڪان آيا آھيون.
She said she was going to Jacobabad.	ھن چيو تہ مان جيڪب آباد وڃان ٿي.
The lady doctor said to take this medicine three times a day.	ڊاڪٽرياڻي چيو تہ ھي دوا ھر روز ٽي ڀيرا کائو.
The girl says she will come tomorrow.	چوڪري چوي ٿي تہ مان سڀاڻي ايندس.
They were asking where that road goes.	ھو پڇي رھيا ھئا تہ ھي رستو ڪيڏانھن ٿو وڃي.
I thought that surely the guests would come today.	مون خيال ڪيو تہ مزمان اڄ ضرور ايندا.
The man told the workmen that the door wasn't straight but crooked.	ماٹھو مستريءَ ڪي ٻڌايو تہ دُر سڌو ناھي مگر اھو ڏنگو آھي.
I have heard that that boy is very bad.	مون ٻڌو آھي تہ اھو چوڪرو تمام ڏنگو آھي.

1. In sentence two above, the servant is talking about someone else's brother, not his own. Generally there is no confusion in this type of sentence. However at times when pronouns are used, one must judge by the context just who is being talked. It will help the student to understand

reported speech as the equivalent of a direct quotation in English in which the exact words of the speaker are repeated.

2.   In reporting what was said the gender of the speaker must be retained where appropriate, as in sentence four above.

3.   ڏنگو is an adjective meaning "crooked, bent, awry". It is commonly used to describe a naughty child.

22-F The inflected infinitive plus لاءِ with چوڻ to give an order or to instruct.

I said to make coffee, not tea.	مون ڪافي بنائڻ لاءِ چيو، چانھ نہ.
Have you told anyone to repair the wall?	ڇا توھان ڪنھن ڪي ڀت جي مرمت ڪرڻ لاءِ چيو آھي؟
The mother-in-law told her daughter-in-law to boil four eggs.	سَسُ نُنھن ڪي چار آنا ابارڻ لاءِ چيو.
Who did they tell to search for it?	ھنن ڪنھن ڪي ڳولڻ لاءِ چيو؟
Tell the washerman to take the clothes on Wednesday.	ڌوبي ڪي اربع جي ڏينھن ڪپڙا کڻ لاءِ چئو.

1.   When the inflected infinitive plus لاءِ is followed by the verb چوڻ (to say, tell), it means to tell or instruct someone to do something. If the person thus requested or told is mentioned, the noun or pronoun will be inflected and followed by ڪي.

22-G Vocabulary.

English	Sindhi	English	Sindhi
eighty-eight	اٺاسي	fifty-eight	اٺونجاھُ
ninety-eight	اٺانوي	forty-eight	اٺيتاليھَ
twenty-eight	اٺاويھہ	judgment (f)	عدالت
thirty-eight	اٺتيھہ	to judge	عدالت ڪرڻ
seventy-eight	اٺھتر	Jesus Christ	عيسيٰ مسيح
sixty-eight	اٺھٺ	Faith (m)	ايمان
to make	بڻائڻ	fort (m)	قلعو
love (m)	پيارُ	law (m)	قانون
life (f)	جان	sinner (m)	گنھگارُ

judge(m)	جَجُ	to search	گولݨ
like	جهڙو	according to	(جي) موجب
Order, command (m)	حڪم	sick person, patient (m)	مريض
bent, crooked, naughty	ڏنگو	Christian	مسيحي
to call	سڏ ڪرڻ	pattern, example	نمونو
mother-in-law(f)	سسُ	daughter-in-law(f)	نُنهَن
cross(m)	صليب	like	وانگر

22 -H   Conversational Review.

1. Develop a conversation with your teacher about things permitted by your parents when you were a child and a teen-ager. Ask about what Pakistani parents permit their children to do. Use this as a theme with some of your friends to learn about this aspect of Pakistani culture.

2. From the above theme go into a conversation using reported speech, talking about what he, she, they say, said, think, thought, are, were asking.

3. Use the following adjectives with nouns given in this lesson. Make up sentences using each noun with the adjective in the singular and the plural where possible. Then change the sentence by adding a postposition, changing the tense of the verb, etc. Where possible use the postpositions introduced in this lesson.

چڱو   ڏنگو   وڏو   ننڍو تلهو   سنهو   سچو   پورو

For Example:

چڱو نمونو   هي چڱو نمونو آهي.

هي قميص جو چڱو نمونو آهي.

مان درزي کي هي چڱو نمونو ڏيندس. وغيره، وغيره

REVIEW THREE

1. One of the main purposes of the four review lessons in this course is to allow the student to stop and evaluate his/her progress without having any new material to cope with. The aim of this review is to cover in depth the patterns and structures introduced in Lessons 17 to 22. It is also good at this point to go back to any previous lessons to review anything that has proven difficult or about which you have any questions. How much of this is done will depend on the needs of the individual student and on the time available. It should be emphasized however that this is not time for the teacher to introduce new material which involves vocabulary or structures not yet taught. To <u>master</u> all the structures and vocabulary thus far is quite enough to keep the student occupied. It is expected that through his/her reading and personal contacts the student has added vocabulary and is perhaps able to understand and use some of those items not yet taught in this course. While we encourage this, there is a danger of going ahead without fully grasping the use of some basic forms and patterns. So this is time to find the weak points, and pick up anything you are not quite sure of.

2. Pronunciation is still very important. If, however, the teacher has been faithful in correcting the student in class and in drilling, there should not be any serious difficulties. This is the time for checking up and doing extra drill on those sounds or individual words that may still be a problem. Review all the pronunciation drills from the beginning. Mark those where extra drill is needed, and concentrate on them. Do this with the book closed, using ears and tongue. Use your eyes not to "read" the drills while your teacher pronounces them, but to watch his face and mouth. Mimicry is vital to your correct Sindhi pronunciation.

    By this time you should not be groping through drills and pattern sentences. Intonation and voice inflection are a vital part of gaining fluency. Mimic your teacher in every way – pronunciation, speed, the rise and fall of his/her voice. Allowing for natural differences – some people are slower speakers in their own language – the student should not be content to stumble cautiously through a sentence.

3. Ask your teacher to go back over each section in Lessons 17-22, choosing representative sentences or combinations of sentences illustrating each grammar pattern. Practice the sentences, substituting from a wide variety of vocabulary. Utilize the list on the following pages, as well as the lists of words in the two previous review lessons. With the help of your teacher you should be able to think up many substitutions. Have your teacher pick out those sentences in the form of questions. Make a game of answering a question in different ways.

4. In the sections under review, the tenses based on the perfect participle have been introduced. A thorough grasp of these tenses in both transitive and intransitive verbs is absolutely essential to a practical use of Sindhi; so much time can be profitably spent on them.

5. You have already realized that one purpose of the Conversational review at the end of each lesson is to teach the student to think in Sindhi. When new structures and vocabulary are introduced, the English translation has to be used. In many cases, at best, the English rendering is awkward. Always keep in mind that in this course our aim is not to be able to accurately translate from English to Sindhi what we want to communicate. Rather the student needs to learn in Sindhi what to say in given situation, to comprehend what s/he hears and to respond appropriately. Progress in this area will not necessarily be dramatic, but should be steady.

Use the conversational reviews as a framework for preparation for this review evaluation. Don't let the teacher give explanations or words for substitution in English. Use Sindhi entirely. Practice conversing on different topics, using the grammar patterns you have learned. If you find it difficult to remember any particular word or words, make up some sentences that you can use them in so as to be able to remember them.

6. A very useful drill is the "Progressive Replacement Drill". Take any pattern sentences and replace the various parts at random: subject, object, negative / positive, verb tense, location, time etc.

Questions Words		Postpositions		Relative / co-relatives	
chO (18)	چو	(jE) badarÃ (18)	(جي) بدران	jaddaHi ... taddaHi (20)	جڏهن تڏهن
kÃÕ? (19)	ڪائون	(jE) barAbar[i] (18)	(جي) برابر	jitÃ ... titÃ	جتان تتان
		(jE) bariKlAf (18)	(جي) برخلاف	jitE ... titE	جتي .. تتي
Conjunctions		(jE) sababÃ (18)	(جي) سببان	jEddÃHã ... tEddÃHã	جيڏانهن تيڏانهن
balki (18)	بلڪ	(jE) karE (18)	(جي) ڪري	jEddO ... tEddO	جيڏو تيڏو
tãHinkarE (18)	تنهنڪري	tÃ (21)	تان	jEtrO ... tEtrO	جيترو تيترو
chA kARa ta (18)	چا ڪاڻ ت	khÃ (21)	ڪان	jEkO, jO, jEkI, sO	جيڪو، جو، جيڪي، سو
chA lAi ta (18)	چا لاءِ ت	khÃ savAi (21)	ڪانسواءِ	jaHaRO ... taHaRO	جهڙو تهڙو
chA lAi jO (18)	چا لاءِ جو	khÃ vaThI (21)	ڪان وٽي	jIã ... tIã	جيئن تيئن
chO ta (18)	چو ت	mÃ (21)	مان	**Numbers**	
chO jO (18)	چو جو	manjhÃ (21)	منجهان	cOTIHa (18)	چوٽيہ
lEkin (18)	ليڪن	vaTÃ (21)	وٽان	cOrAsI (18)	چوراسي
magar (18)	مگر	jaHiRO (22)	جهڙو	cOrAnavE (18)	چورانوي
nakI (18)	نڪي	(jE) mUjib (22)	(جي) موجب	cOvanjAH[u] (18)	چوونجاهُ
ya'nE (19)	يعني	vAngUr (22)	وانگر	cOvIHa (18)	چوويہ

Numbers	(cont)		Numbers	(cont)		Adverbs		
cOHatar^i	(18)	چوهتر	aThaTIHa	(22)	انتيهَ	bbIHar	(18)	بيهر
cOHaTh^i	(18)	چوهٺ	aThaHatar^i	(22)	انهتر	aggitE	(19)	اڳتي
cOEtAlIHa	(18)	چوئيتاليهَ	aThaHaTh^i	(22)	انهٺ	poitE	(19)	پوئتي
chAvanjAH^u	(19)	چاونجاهُ	aThavanjAH^u	(22)	انونجاهُ	Iã	(20)	ايئن
chAHatar^i	(19)	چاهتر	aThEtAlIHa	(22)	انيتاليهَ	laggAtAr	(21)	لڳاتار
chAHaTh^i	(19)	چاهٺ	**Adjectives**			**Nouns – People**		
chAEtAlIHa	(19)	چائيتاليهَ	sajjO	(17)	سڄو	vADhO (m) (17)		وادو
chaTIHa	(19)	چتيهَ	amIr^u	(18)	اميرُ	duSman m (18)		دشمن
chavIHa	(19)	چويهَ	badiKlAq^a	(18)	بداخلاق	mizmAn^u m (18)		مزمانُ
chaHAsI	(19)	ڇھاسي	GarIb^u	(18)	غريبُ	HArI (m) (18)		هاري
chaHAnavE	(19)	ڇھانوي	vEcArO	(18)	ويچارو	pAREsarI (m) (20)		پاڙيسري
satAsI	(20)	ستاسي	Galat^i	(19)	غلطِ	cAcO (m) (21)		چاچو
satEtAlIH^i	(20)	ستيتاليهَ	aHaRO	(20)	اهڙو	cOr^u (m) (21)		چورُ
sataTIHa	(20)	ستتيهَ	EtrO	(20)	ايترو	mER^u (m) (21)		ميڙُ
satAvIHa	(20)	ستاويهَ	EddO	(20)	ايڏو	IsA masIH^u (22)		عيسيٰ مسيحُ
satAnavE	(20)	ستانوي	akElO	(21)	اڪيلو	jaj^u (m) (22)		جڄ
satavanjAH^u	(20)	ستونجاهُ	pardEsI	(21)	پرديسي	sas^u (f) (22)		سسُ
sataHatar^i	(20)	ستهتر	pasand^u	(21)	پسندُ	gunaHagAr^u (m) (22)		ڳنھگار
sataHath^i	(20)	ستهٺ	dEsI	(21)	ديسي	marIz^u (m) (22)		مَريضُ
aThAsI	(22)	اناسي	ddingO	(22)	ڏنگو	masIHI (m) (22)		مَسيحي
aThAnavE	(22)	انانوي	masIHI	(22)	مسيحي	nūHã (f) (22)		نُنھَن
aThAvIha	(22)	اناويهَ						

Nouns - Places		Abstract Nouns	(cont)	Other Nouns	(cont)
sakharu (m) (19)	سکر	Hukumu (m) (22)	حُكمُ	bagI (f) (21)	بَگِي
jEkababAd (m) (19)	جيکب آباد	qAnUnu (m) (22)	قانونُ	jjaÑa (f) (21)	جَجَ
dAdU (m) (19)	دادو	**Other Nouns**		gapu (m) (21)	گَپُ
HaiderabAdi (m) (19)	حيدرآباد	phaR̃I (f) (17)	ڦُٽِي	sallbu (m) (22)	صَلِيبُ
		javAbu (m) (17)	جوابُ	qilO (m) (22)	قِلعو
		kOThI (f) (17)	ڪوٺي	namUnO (m) (22)	نَمُونو
Abstract Nouns		kaĩcI (f) (17)	ڪينچِي	**Simple Verbs**	
KAmOSI (f) (17)	خاموشِي	mUmbatI (f) (17)	موم بَتِي	bhaÑaR̃u (17)	ڀِڄَڻُ
iKlAqa (m.pl) (17)	اخلاق	vAra (m.pl) (17)	وارَ	pAiR̃u (17)	پائِڻُ
badiKlAqI (f) (17)	بداخلاقِي	isTESan (f) (18)	اِستيشَنَ	phATaR̃u (17)	ڦاٽَڻُ
HifAzata (f) (17)	حِفاظَتَ	baKSiS (f) (18)	بخشِشِ	jjamaR̃u (17)	جَمَڻُ
GalatI (f) (19)	غلطي	jumErAti (f) (18)	جمعراتِ	sikhaR̃u (17)	سِکَڻُ
raonaqa (f) (20)	رونق	sIu (m) (18)	سِيءُ	suÑaR̃aR̃u (17)	سِڄاٽَڻُ
kOSiSi (f) (20)	ڪوشِشِ	sababu (m) (18)	سَبَبُ	kamAiR̃u (17)	ڪمائَڻُ
faisalO (m) (20)	فيصلو	machI (f) (18)	مَڇِي	kuHaR̃u (17)	ڪُهَڻُ
dAvata (f) (20)	دعوتَ	miHinata (f) (18)	مِحنتَ	gginHaR̃u (17)	ڳِنهَڻُ
zikuru (m) (20)	ذکرُ	bAHi (f) (19)	باهِ	laHaR̃u (17)	لَهَڻُ
bayAnu (m) (21)	بيانُ	khUHu (m) (19)	کُوهُ	vIRHaR̃u (17)	وِڙهَڻُ
pandhu (m) (21)	پنڌُ	gulAbu (m) (19)	گُلابُ	uthAraR̃u (19)	اُتارَڻُ
adAlata (f) (22)	عدالتَ	marimata (f) (19)	مرمتَ	bbAraR̃u (19)	ڀارَڻُ
ImAnu (m) (22)	ايمانُ	TikETa (f) (20)	ٽِڪيٽَ	bbaraR̃u (19)	ڀَرَڻُ
pIAru (m) (22)	پيارُ	jutI (f) (20)	جُتِي	bIHaraR̃u (19)	بِيهارَڻُ
jAni (f) (22)	جانِ				

Simple Verbs	(cont)	Simple Verbs	(cont)	Simple Verbs	(cont)
puchaR̃u (19)	پچڻ	sEkhAraR̃u (19)	سيکارڻ	raHijaR̃u (21)	رھجڻ
paRHaiR̃u (19)	پڙھائڻ	karAiR̃u (19)	ڪرائڻ	kAviRijaR̃u (21)	ڪاوڙجڻ
pIaraR̃u (19)	پيئارڻ	khArAiR̃u (19)	ڪارائڻ	kiraR̃u (21)	ڪرڻ
tarsAiR̃u (19)	ترسائڻ	mAraR̃u (19)	مارڻ	khilaR̃u (21)	کلڻ
TORaR̃u (19)	توڙڻ	viÑAiR̃u (19)	وڃائڻ	langhaR̃u (21)	لنگھڻ
jAggaR̃u (19)	جاڳڻ	vEHAraR̃u (19)	ويھارڻ	visaraR̃u (21)	وسرڻ
jAggAiR̃u (19)	جاڳائڻ	HalAiR̃u (19)	ھلائڻ	phAsaR̃u (21)	ڦاسڻ
chARHaR̃u (19)	چاڙھڻ	pacAiR̃u (20)	پچائڻ	baR̃AiR̃u (22)	ٻائڻ
DORaR̃u 19)	ڊوڙڻ	DharaR̃u (20)	ڌرڻ	ggOlaR̃u (22)	ڳولڻ
sumHAraR̃u (19)	سمھارڻ	thakijaR̃u (21)	ٿڪجڻ		

		Compound	Verbs		
phaR̃I ddIaR̃u (17)	ڦٽي ڏيڻ	mAlUm karaR̃u (20)	معلوم ڪرڻ		
javAb ddIaR̃u (17)	جواب ڏيڻ	zikur karaR̃u (20)	ذڪر ڪرڻ		
khaR̃I acaR̃u (17)	ڪٽي اچڻ	dil laggaR̃u (20)	دل لڳڻ		
khaR̃I vaÑaR̃u (17)	ڪٽي وڃڻ	bayAn karaR̃u (21)	بيان ڪرڻ		
vaThI acaR̃u (17)	وٽي اچڻ	pasand[u] acaR̃u (21)	پسند اچڻ		
vaThI vaÑaR̃u (17)	وٽي وڃڻ	pasand[u] karaR̃u (21)	پسند ڪرڻ		
miHinat[a] karaR̃u (18)	محنت ڪرڻ	pasand[u] HUaR̃u (21)	پسند ھئڻ		
kAmIAb thIaR̃u (18)	ڪامياب ٿيڻ	mūjhI pavaR̃u (21)	منجھي پوڻ		
marimat[a] karaR̃u (19)	مرمت ڪرڻ	pand[u] karaR̃u (21)	پنڊ ڪرڻ		
kOSiS[i] karaR̃u (20)	ڪوشش ڪرڻ	adAlat[a] karaR̃u (22)	عدالت ڪرڻ		
faisalO karaR̃u (20)	فيصلو ڪرڻ	sadd[u] karaR̃u (22)	سڏ ڪرڻ		

LESSON TWENTY-THREE

23 - A Pronunciation Drill

In these last six lessons in place of the drills you have been accustomed to, you will be using difficult or tongue-twister type of sentences in Sindhi. Your aim should be to be able to recite each one after your teacher up-to-speed, pronouncing the sequences of sounds correctly. Take it as a game and see how well you can "twist" your tongue around these sentences.

هڪڙو ڏيڍر ڏيڍ ڏوڏو ڏينهن ۾ کائي ٿو.
ڏينيُن منهنجي چنگهن ۾ ڏنگ هنيا.

23 - B Expressing Probability or Presumption

Of a Present State or Condition.

Where is her husband?	هُن جو مڙس ڪٿي آهي؟
He must be in his office.	هُو پنهنجي آفيس ۾ هُوندو.
What time is it?	وقَت ڇا آهي؟
I don't for sure, but it must be 2:30.	مون کي پڪي خبر نہ آهي، پر اڍائي وڳا هوندا.
Where is my letter?	مُنهنجي چٺي ڪٿي آهي؟
It must be on the table / desk.	اُها ميز تي هوندي.
Be careful! This job must be dangerous.	خبردار! هي ڪم خطرناڪ هوندو.
When will that girl's wedding be?	هُن ڇوڪريءَ جي شادي ڪڏهن هُوندي؟
There's no definite decision yet, but it will probably be next month.	اڃا پڪو فيصلو نہ آهي پر ايندڙ مَهيني ۾ هُوندي.
Where will be the wedding ceremony be?	جَڄَ ڪٿي هُوندي؟

The ceremony will be in the bridegroom's village.	جَيَ گھوٽ جي ڳوٺ ۾ ٿيندي.

1.   The simple future tense of هئڻ, without another verb may be used to describe a state or condition which is <u>presumed</u> to be true, or <u>probably</u> true.

    Notice that when هوندو is used, there is a shade of uncertainty even though the probability or presumption is there that it will happen. When the future of ٿيڻ, ٿيندو (to be, become) is used, there is just a shade more certainty expressed. Observe carefully how people use these forms, so that you will know which to use in a given context.

Of a Present Action.

The teacher must have a class (must teaching a lesson) at 10 o'clock.	استاد صاحب ڏهين بجي سبقُ پڙهائيندو هوندو.
That student must be studying his lessons very well, because he always gives the right answer.	اُهو طالب علم پنهنجو سبق خُوب پڙهندو هوندو چاڪاڻ تہ هُو هميشہ دُرست جواب ڏئي ٿو.
I'm sure she must be writing to her parents every week.	مون کي يقين آهي تہ هوءَ پنهنجي ماءُ پيءُ کي هَر هفتي خط لکندي هُوندي.
You must be having some doubt about what he / she said. (lit: you must be doubting)	تُون هن جي ڳالهہ تي شڪ ڪندين هوندين.
The lady must not be coming today.	بيگم صاحبہ اڄ نہ ايندي هُوندي.
You must be afraid of dogs.	تُوهين ڪُتن ڪان ڊڄندا هُوندا.

2.   The Imperfect participle plus the future tense of هئڻ is used to describe an action which is presumed to be true, either generally or true at the moment. This is often called the <u>Present Presumptive</u> tense. Both the principal verb and هوندو change to agree with the subject.

3.   Notice that with the verb ڊڄڻ (to be afraid, to fear) the postposition ڪان (from) is used. Thus, the English idea "to be afraid <u>of</u>" something is expressed in Sindhi ...

ڪان ڊڄڻ , literally, "to be afraid <u>from</u> ..."

Of a Past Action or State / Condition.

The girls must have gotten very tired.	چوڪريون تمام ٿڪجي پيون هُونديون.
The boys must have prepared for today's lesson.	چوڪرن اڄ جي سبقُ لاءِ تياري ڪئي هوندي.
He / she must not have recognized me.	هُن مون کي سُڃاتو نہ هوندو.
Yesterday it was rather cold. It must have rained somewhere or other.	ڪالھ ڪجھ سيءُ هو. ڪٿي نہ ڪٿي مينهن پيو هوندو.
They must not have said anything.	هُنن ڪجھ چيو نہ هوندو.
The result of the examination must have been published (come out) just today.	امتحان جو نتيجو اڄ ئي نڪتو هُوندو.
You must not have believed him / her.	تو هُن تي يقين ڪيو نہ هوندو.
The cook must have put in too much pepper for the children.	بورچي ٻارن جي لاءِ زياده مرچ وڌا هُوندا.
It's very hot today. You must have really gotten very thirsty.	اڄ ڏاڍي گرمي آهي. توهان کي سچ پچ ڏاڍي اُڃ لڳي هوندي.
The bridegroom's family, according to the custom, must have given a ring and other jewelry besides to the bride.	گھوٽ جي خاندان رسم موجب ڪنوار کي مُنڊي ۽ ٻيا ٻہ زيور ڏنا هوندا.
Would the jewelry be gold or silver?	زيور سونَ جا هوندا يا چانديءَ جا؟
They are important people, so they must have given gold.	هو وڏا ماڻھو آهن. تنهنڪري هُنن سون ڏنو هوندو.

4. When the future tense of هئڻ is added to the perfect participle of a verb, the combination refers to an action or a state / condition which is <u>presumed</u> to have taken place <u>in the past</u>. This tense is sometimes is called the <u>Past Presumptive</u>.

5. Just as with any verb form based on the perfect participle (cf. 17-E & 18-G) special attention must be given to transitive verbs. The verb will agree with any expressed object, and the subject will be in the oblique when used with tenses based on the perfect participle.

23 –C   Expressing Possibility or Doubt / Uncertainty.

Of a Present State / Condition.

Where is his / her brother?	هن جو ڀاءُ ڪٿي آهي؟
I don't know. Perhaps he may be in the office.	خبر نہ آهي. شايد هو آفيس ۾ هجي.
Be careful! Perhaps this job may be dangerous.	خبردار! شايد هي ڪم خطرناڪ هجي.
Perhaps they may not be willing / pleased to go.	شايد هو وڃڻ لاءِ راضي نہ هجي.
See who's at the door. It's possible it may be the mailman.	ڏسو تہ دَرَ تي ڪير آهي. ممڪن آهي تہ ٽپالي هجي.

1.   The simple subjunctive of هئڻ can be used to describe a state or condition about which there is some doubt, but which is possibly true. (cf. 11-F & G). Note that when this form is used, there is a greater degree of doubt than when the future of هئڻ is used. In either case, it is not <u>known</u> to be true. However, when the simple subjunctive is used, as in the above examples, there is a greater doubt. Thus this tense is sometimes called the <u>Present Dubious</u>.

Of a Present Action.

Suppose they don't live at that place anymore.	فرض ڪريو تہ هو هاڻي هُن جاءِ تي نہ رهندا هجن.
It's possible that the lady doctor may eat at this time.	ممڪن آهي تہ ڊاڪٽرياڻي هن وقت ماني کائيندي هجي.
Perhaps the teacher sleeps in the afternoon.	شايد استاد صاحب منجهند ڪان پوءِ سمهندو هجي.
Perhaps the girls are afraid of the dog.	ڇوڪريون شايد ڪتي ڪان ڊڄنديون هجن.
Don't bother them. Perhaps they take a rest this time.	هُنن کي تڪليف نہ ڏي. شايد هُو هن وقت آرام ڪندا هجن.

2.   The imperfect participle plus the subjunctive of هئڻ is used to describe an action which may be generally true, or even occasionally true. In the sentences above, the context tells this. However one is not absolutely sure and it is not even <u>presumed</u> to be true. Rather this form clearly expresses doubt and uncertainty. Thus this tense may be called the <u>Present Habitual Dubious</u>.

3. فرض ڪرڻ (to suppose) is idiomatically used of an assumption or a conjecture. Any logical conclusion can follow the assumption or supposition, or it may be taken as rhetorical, not expecting an answer. فرض by itself means "duty".

Of a Past Action or State / Condition.

Perhaps the gardener has gone to the bazaar.	شايد مالهي بازار ويو هجي.
It's cloudy today. It's possible that it has rained in Quetta.	اڄ جُهڙُ آهي. ٿي سگهي ٿو ته ڪوئٽا ۾ مينهن پيو هجي.
It's possible that they didn't try.	مُمڪن آهي ن هنن ڪوشش ن ڪئي هُجي.
Suppose that they didn't make any arrangements.	فرض ڪريو ته هنن بندوبست ن ڪيو هجي.
Perhaps the electricity is off from the city.	شايد بجلي شهَر کان بند ٿي هُجي.
It seems (appears) that you might not have put in the salt.	ايئن لڳي ٿو ته تو لُوڻ ن وڌو هُجي.
Maybe I forgot.	شايد مُون کان وسري ويو هجي.
But I was afraid lest I might have put in too much.	پر مون کي ڀوُ ٿيو متان مون زيادهه وڌو هجي.

4. By adding the subjunctive of هئڻ to the perfect participle of a verb, the resulting combination refers to a state / condition or action which <u>may have been true</u> in the past. Since there is an element of doubt or uncertainty, this tense is often called the <u>Past Dubious</u>.

5. As with the other tenses formed from the perfect participle, it is important to remember the rules of agreement with the object when the verb is transitive. (see 17-E, 18-G, & 23-B-5)

6. ڀوُ is a masculine noun meaning "fear, dread". It is commonly used with ٿيڻ (to become, to be) to express the idea of being afraid.

7. متان is a negative or prohibitive participle used frequently with the subjunctive tenses. Another example,

O child, be careful lest the glass fall.	اي پٽ، خبردار متان گلاس ڪري پوي.

23 –D Completion as shown by چڪڻ.

Has the postman already come?	ٽپالي اچي چڪو آهي؟
Yes, He's already come.	ها، اچي چڪو آهي.
Washerman, have you finished washing the clothes?	چا ڌوٻي، تون ڪپڙا ڌوئي چڪو آهين؟
Yes, I have finished the work.	ها، مان ڪم ختم ڪري چڪو آهيان.
Has the boys' holiday finished?	ڇوڪرن جي موڪل پوري ٿي چڪي آهي؟
No, it will be finished by next Sunday.	نه، ايندڙ آچر تائين ختم ٿيندي.
Have you already done the eleventh lesson?	اوهين يارهن سبق ڪي پڙهي چڪا آهيو؟
Yes, and I've read three lessons in addition to that.	ها، بلڪ هن کان مٿي ٽي سبق پڙهي چڪو /چڪي آهيان.
When I saw him, he had already gotten sick.	جڏهن مون هن کي ڏٺو تڏهن هو بيمار ٿي چڪو هو.

1. The <u>conjunctive participle</u> of any verb <u>plus</u> the appropriate tense of چڪڻ (to finish, to have already done) results in a kind of "completive compound".

2. چڪڻ is used in a way that parallels the use of سگھڻ. That is, the conjunctive participle of the main verb remains unchanged while چڪڻ is conjugated as required. Like سگھڻ it is an intransitive verb, so agrees with its subject in gender and number, even if used with a transitive verb.

3. Since the basic meaning of the verb چڪڻ is "to have finished, or to have already done" something, it usually occurs only in past or perfect tenses.

4. In compound verbs used with چڪڻ to denote completion, both the nonverbal part of the compound and the verb in its conjunctive participle remain unchanged. Thus,

When you have finished your work, tell me.	جڏهن تون پنهنجو ڪم ختم ڪري چڪين تڏهن مون کي ٻڌاء.

5. چڪڻ is never used alone, but only with the conjunctive participle of another verb. Thus, the pronoun, or other subject may be omitted in the answer but never the verb. See the following examples.

Has the postman already taken the mail?	چا ٽپالي ٽپال کڻي چڪو آهي؟

Yes, (he) has already taken it.	ها, كڍي چُكو آهي.
Is (has) the marriage ceremony already finished?	نكاح ٿي چُكو آهي؟
(It's) finished.	ٿي چُكو آهي.

23 –E Vocabulary for lesson 23.

thirst (f)	اُڃَ	to finish, to have already done	چُڪڻُ
electricity (f)	بِجلي	dangerous	خَطرناڪ
arrangement (m)	بندوبست	thoroughly, well	خُوبُ
to arrange, to make arrangements	بَندوبَست ڪرڻ	correct	دُرُست
fear, dread (m)	ڀَوءُ	custom (f)	رَسمَ
to be afraid	ڀَوءُ ٿيڻ	pleased, agreed, glad	راضي
certainty (f)	پَڪَ	jewel, ornament (m) (m.pl jewelry)	زيور
cloudiness (m)	جُهڙُ	truth, true (m)	سَچُ
silver (f)	چاندي	gold (m)	سونُ
doubt (m)	شَڪُ	pepper (m. pl)	مرچ
city (m)	شهر	ring (f)	منڊي
duty	فرض	result (m)	نتيجو
bride (f)	ڪنوار	wedding ceremony (m)	نڪاح
Quetta	ڪوئيٽا	to strike	وِڄڻُ (وڄڻ)
bridegroom (m)	گهوٽُ	belief, confidence (m)	يَقينُ
lest, not, perhaps	متان		

23-F Conversational Review.

1. Carry on conversation with your teacher about wedding customs in Pakistan. If your teacher is a Muslim, you will be discussing Muslim customs. Try to find an opportunity to talk with a Hindu about their wedding customs, keeping in mind that there will be certain differences between the customs of tribal Hindus and other Hindus. Bring into the conversation wedding customs of your home country. Your vocabulary on the subject of weddings will be expanded beyond the words in this lesson. Keep a list and learn to use these new words. Practice using the new verb forms from this lesson expressing doubt / uncertainty and probability / presumption.

2. Answer each of the following questions, using <u>presumptive</u> forms in your answer.

استاد: هاڻي وقت ڇا آهي؟

شاگرد: خبر نہ آهي پر..... هوندو / هوندا

ڊاڪٽر صاحب ڪٿي آهي؟

ڇوڪرا هن وقت ڇا ٿا ڪن؟

ڪير پاڻ ۾ ڳالهائن ٿا؟

ڪنهن ڪاڏو تيار ڪيو؟

توهان جي پيئڻ اڄ ڇا خريد ڪئي؟

3. Complete the following sentences, using <u>dubious</u> forms.

هن جو ڇوڪرو اڄ نہ آيو. ممڪن آهي تہ ....

مان هنن کي تڪليف نہ ڏيندس. ڇا ڪاڻ تہ هو شايد .....

نوڪرياڻي هتي نہ آهي. شايد هوءَ ...

ٽي سگھي ٿو تہ هن جا ماءُ پيءُ ....

شايد گھوٽ جي ڳوٺ ۾ ....

4. Use the drill in the lesson 16-G-4, using the proper form of چڪڻ in place of سگھڻ. Substitute other verbs from the list of verbs in Review Three in order to practice using a variety of verbs with چڪڻ.

LESSON TWENTY-FOUR

24 -A	**Pronunciation Drill**

پُٽَ، پَٽَ تان پَٽي ڪٽي پُٽيءَ ڪي ٻڍي.
گهوڙي جي چنگهه تي ڳوڙهي آهي. هن ڪي گوري ڏي.

24 -B	**Cardinal Numbers by "Nines"**

9	٩	نَوَ
19	١٩	اٽويهه
29	٢٩	اُنٽيهه
39	٣٩	اُنيتاليهه
49	٤٩	اُنونجاهه
59	٥٩	اُٺهٺ
69	٦٩	اُٺهتر
79	٧٩	اُٺاسي
89	٨٩	اُٺانوي
99	٩٩	نوانوي
109	١٠٩	(هڪ) سؤ نَوَ

24 –C	**Ages of People and Things**

How old is your brother?

My brother is fifteen years old.

How old is this little girl?

توهان جي ڀاءُ جي ڪيتري عمر آهي؟
منهنجو ڀاءُ پندرهن سالن جو آهي.
هن ننڍيءَ چوڪريءَ جي ڪيتري عمر آهي؟

She is exactly one year.	هوءَ پوري سال جي آهي.
I have heard that your daughter's birthday was yesterday.	مون ٻڌو آهي تہ ڪالهہ توهان جي ڌيءَ جو جنر ڏينهن هو.
How old is that old man?	هن ٻڍي جي عمر گهٹي آهي؟
I don't know but his age must be about seventy-five.	خبر نہ آهي پر هن جي عمر اٽڪل پنجهتر هوندي.
They have a 10-days old baby at their house.	هن جي گهر ۾ ڏهن ڏينهن جو ٻار آهي.
How old is the well in (at) this place?	هيءُ کوهہ هن جاءِ تي گهٹن سالن کان آهي؟
I think it must be about ten years old. (lit: from about ten years)	منهنجو خيال آهي تہ اهو اٽڪل ڏهن سالن کان آهي.
Is your pen new?	توهان جو قلم نئون آهي ڇا؟
No, I've had it for six months.	نہ، هيءُ مون وٽ ڇهن مهينن کان آهي.
How old is your watch?	توهان جي واچ گهٹن سالن جي آهي؟
It's about four years old.	اها تہ اٽڪل چئن سالن جي آهي.
Are these curtains old?	ڇا هي پردا پراڻا آهن؟
Yes, they are about five years old.	هائو اٽڪل پنجن سالن جا آهن.
When was that window broken?	اها دري ڪڏهن ڀڄي پئي؟
This happened three days ago. (lit: this is a three days old affair).	هي تہ ھاڻي ٽن ڏينهن جي ڳالهہ آهي.

1. The word عمر (age) is used for expressing the ages of people. When we say in Sindhi توهان جي ڀاءُ جي ڪيتري عمر آهي؟ We are literally saying, "Your brother's age is how much?" The possessive adjective جي is in the feminine form to agree with عمر. An alternate way of saying the same thing is illustrated in sentence three above. The sentence we are using here would be as follows: توهان جو ڀاءُ گهٹن (ڪيترن) سالن جو آهي؟ In this case جو is in the masculine because it refers to ڀاءُ (brother). In sentence three above جو is in the feminine form جي because it must agree with ڌيءُ (daughter). In the latter way of expressing age we are

saying literally, "Your brother is a how-many-years (boy / brother)" or "Your brother is of how many years". In either case جو (of) agrees with the word understood, boy / brother.

2. In speaking of age, ڪيتري or گهٽي may be used interchangeably with عمر. Whichever is used may precede or follow عمر. For example,

How old is he?	هن جي ڪيتري عمر آهي؟
How old is he?	هن جي عمر گهٽي آهي؟

3. One way of expressing the age of things, but not people, is illustrated in the sentences above using ڪان (from such and such a time). Another way is with the interrogative word ڪڏهن (when). For example,

When did they buy a car?	هنن ڪار ڪڏهن خريد ڪئي؟
They bought it last month.	هنن گذريل مهيني خريد ڪئي.
When was your house built?	توهان جو گهر ڪڏهن جڙيو؟
I don't know when it was built.	مون کي خبر نه آهي تي ڪڏهن جڙيو.

24 –D   More Postpositions

لائق (worthy of), جي ذريعي, جي وسيلي (through, by means of) جي معرفت (through, care of).

The girl is fine, but the boy isn't worthy of her.	چوڪري سٺي آهي پر چوڪرو هن جي لائق نه آهي.
Their family is worthy of (or deserves) a great deal of respect. (of honor)	هنن جو خاندان ڏاڍي عزت جي لائق آهي.
May I help you? (Any service for me?)	منهنجي لائق ڪا خدمت آهي ڇا؟
He is a very fine (worthy) man.	هو تمام لائق ماڻهو آهي.

1. جي لائق is a postposition meaning "worthy of", "suitable for". جي may be omitted. لائق may also be used without جي as an adjective. This is illustrated in the last example above.

2. Sentence three illustrates a very idiomatic way of offering one's services خدمت. The literal meaning, "Is there any service of which I am worthy?" reveals something of the culture, in that it expresses a certain humility and deference toward another. Its usage is often merely a courtesy,

and the person does not expect any particular response. It may also be an indirect way of asking for a gratuity. In either case the proper response, would be a polite negative, as,

No thank you, sir.	نَه سائين مهرباني.
Send this letter through mail. (i.e. by post)	هيءُ خط ٽپال جي ذريعي موڪليو.
You'll get well from (by means of) this medicine.	تون هن دوا جي ذريعي چاق ٿي ويندين.
The young man got the service through a recommendation. (or, influence)	نوجوان کي سفارش جي وسيلي نوڪري ملي.
According to the Gospel we receive forgiveness through the death of Jesus Christ.	پاڪ انجيل جي موجب اسان کي عيسىٰ مسيح جي موت جي وسيلي معافي ملي ٿي.
Send my mail in care of my husband.	منهنجي ٽپال منهنجي مڙس جي معرفت موڪليو.

1. Although by definition these postpositions are nearly synonymous, each has a slightly different usage and shade of meaning. جي ذريعي comes from the noun ذريعو meaning "means, medium, agency". The meaning of the postposition جي ذريعي is "by means of".

جي وسيلي is derived from the noun وسيلو (m), "means, mediation, interest". In common usage they are often interchanged. However, جي ذريعي is more often applied to something concrete or tangible, while جي وسيلي is related to more abstract concepts. جي وسيلي is sometimes used with the addition of سان, that is:

هن کي سفارش جي وسيلي سان نوڪري ملِي.

2. جي معرفت is ordinarily used as we would use "care of, in care of" in English, that is, when mail is not sent directly, but through some other person or address. جي is very often omitted in using معرفت.

24 –E Fulfillable Conditions

Future / Present Possibility

If I go there, I'll tell him.	جيڪڏهن مان هوڏي وڃان تہ مان کيس ٻڌائيندس.
If he comes, I will see him.	جيڪڏهن هو اچي تہ مان هن کي ڏسندس.
If the old woman comes, call me.	جيڪڏهن ٻڍي زال اچي تہ مون کي سڏ ڪريو.
If they are reading a story, let them carry on. (i.e. with reading)	جيڪڏهن هو آکاڻي پڙهندا هوندا تہ پڙهڻ ڏيو.

1. The simple subjunctive (see 11-F) is commonly used with جيڪڏهن (if) when the condition is possible, or carries the condition of fulfillment. The degree of doubt or presumption may vary, but the <u>possibility</u> of fulfillment is there. This is in contrast to the kind of conditions explained in section 24-F where the conditions are contrary-to-fact, or impossible.

2. The dubious and presumptive tenses which are really a kind of subjunctive may also be used in this sense. The last sentence illustrates this.

3. تہ as the correlative of جيڪڏهن usually introduces the second clause of the sentence, but it is not translated into English.

Future Certainty

If he comes, we'll finish this work.	جيڪڏهن هو آيو، تہ اسين هي ڪم پورو ڪنداسين.
If Uncle gives (you) (some) money, then bring it along.	جيڪڏهن چاچي پيسا ڏنا تہ ڪٽي اچو.

4. If there is <u>no doubt</u> at all that the condition will be fulfilled, then the simple past tense is used in the "if" clause. It is almost the same as saying "when" instead of "if". This use of the past tense in a future sense is also used in another way.

Come here, boy! I have come.	اي چوڪرا، هيڏي اچ. آيو آهيان.

5. The idea rendered here is that (even though the boy may not have moved!) the thing is as good as done.

Past Probability

If they did go, I didn't know anything about it.	جيڪڏهن هو ويا هئا تہ مون کي انهيءَ جي ڪا خبر نہ هئي.
If the young girls came yesterday, why didn't I see them?	جيڪڏهن جوان چوڪريون ڪالهہ آيون هيون تہ مون هنن کي ڇو نہ ڏٺو؟
If you really had prepared well, why did you get a low score in the exam?	جيڪڏهن تو خوب تياري ڪئي هئي تہ تو کي امتحان ۾ گهٽ نمبر ڇو مليو؟

6.   When, for the sake of argument, conditions are presumed to have been met in the past, the past perfect tense may be used with جيڪڏهن. However, there is some doubt in the speaker's mind! We might paraphrase the meaning thus:

   If they did go (which I doubt), I didn't know anything about it.

Future Probability

If you are going, then I'll go with you.	جيڪڏهن توهين ويندا، تہ مان بہ توهان سان گڏ ويندس / ويندياس.
If the old man comes, I will meet him.	جيڪڏهن ڪراڙو ايندو، تہ مان هن سان ملندس / ملنديس.
If he is telling the truth, why don't you believe him?	جيڪڏهن هو سچ ڳالهائي ٿو تہ تون هن جو يقين ڇو نہ ٿو ڪرين؟
If children learn good habits from childhood, there will be good consequences for life.	جيڪڏهن ٻار ننڍپڻ ۾ چڱيون عادتون سکن ٿا، تہ عمر ڀر سٺو نتيجو ٿيندو.

7.   The present or the future tenses, as illustrated above, can be used with جيڪڏهن to indicate a future probability. Although there may be an element of doubt, the assumption is that the condition will be fulfilled.

8.   يقين (certainty, confidence) combines with ڪرڻ to form a compound verb meaning "to believe, to have confidence". Notice that it is used with the postposition جو.

9.   ننڍپڻ means "childhood, youth, the time of youth". Its root is the adjective ننڍو (small) which also can mean young.

10.   عمرڀر is an adverb meaning "for life". It comes from the word for age, عمر, plus ڀر, from ڀرڻ "to fill", thus, "a full or complete life".

24 –F Unfulfilled Conditions in the Past.

If he had gone, I would have given him the money.	جيڪڏھن ھو ويجي ھا تہ مان ھن کي پئسا ڏيان ھا.
I you had written, I wouldn't have written.	جيڪڏھن توھين لکو ھا تہ مان نہ لکان ھا.
If the old woman had come, I would have recognized her.	جيڪڏھن ڪراڙي اچي ھا تہ مان ڪيس سڃاڻان ھا.
If the old man had taken the medicine, he would be well by now.	جيڪڏھن ڪراڙو دوا کائي ھا تہ ھائي ھو چاق ٿئي ھا.
If the old man had learned good habits in his childhood, he wouldn't be doing immoral deeds in old age.	جيڪڏھن پيڊو ننڍپڻ ۾ چڱيون عادتون سکي ھا، تہ ھو پيڊاپي ۾ بدڪاري نہ ڪري ھا.
If the boys hadn't quarreled, they would have finished the work.	جيڪڏھن نوجوان ڇوڪرا نہ وڙھن ھا، تہ ھو ڪم پورو ڪن ھا.

1. Where both the condition and the resulting clause show conditions which were not fulfilled, or contrary to fact, the subjunctive tense plus an inflected particle ھا is used. The same form will be used in both clauses. This is called the <u>Past Conditional Tense</u>.

2. The contrary to fact, or unfulfilled condition in the past may be seen more clearly if we paraphrase the above sentences in this way:

   If you had written (which you didn't), then I would not have written (which I did).

3. ڪراڙو and پيڊو are adjectives meaning "old". They are only applied to people, not things. Like some other Sindhi adjectives, they may be used alone with the noun omitted and understood. In the sentences above we could say, ڪراڙو ماڻھو and ڪراڙي عورت, but more often the adjective is used alone, meaning, "old woman" or "old man". غريب (poor) and شاھوڪار (rich) which are also adjectives are often used alone to mean "poor people" and "rich people".

4. پيڊاپي is a feminine noun meaning old age, or the period of life when a person is old.

24 –G   Vocabulary for Lesson 24

English	Sindhi	English	Sindhi
habit (f)	عادت	seventy-nine	اٺاسي
eighty-nine	اٺانوي	service (f)	خدمت
twenty-nine	اٺتيھ	through, by means of	ذريعي (جي)
Gospel, New Testament (m)	انجيل	respect, honor (f)	عزت
forty-nine	اٽونجاھ	age (f)	عمر
nineteen	اٽويھ	for life	عمر ڀر
thirty-nine	اٽتاليھ	recommendation, influence (f)	سفارش
sixty-nine	اٺهتر	to know (a person), to recognize	سڃاڻڻ (سڃاتو)
evil, immorality (f)	بد ڪاري	motor car (f)	ڪار
old	ٻڍو	old (person)	ڪراڙو
old age (f)	ٻڍاپي	worthy (of)	لائق (جي)
to make	جوڙڻ	forgiveness (f)	معافي
birth (m)	جنم	in care of	معرفت (جي)
youth, adolescent soldier (m)	جوان	death (m)	موت
well	چاق	result (m)	نتيجو
uncle, father's brother (m)	چاچو	Childhood (m)	ننڍپڻ
young man, adolescent	نوجوان	through, be means of	وسيلي (جي)
ninety-nine	نوانوي	to believe, have confidence in	يقين ڪرڻ

24 -H   Conversational Review

1. Converse with your teacher, and with other Sindhi friends about the members of his family, and your own immediate and extended family. Discuss their ages, along with customs and interesting facts about childhood and old age. Discuss similarities and differences between Pakistani life and life in your home country.

2. Talk about the ages of things in the room, asking and answering questions about them.

3. In the following sentence, substitute from the list of words to fill the blanks.

جيڪڏهن آءُ (تي) وڃان تہ اوهين بہ ويندا؟

ڪار، بگي، لاري، ريل گاڏي، گهوڙو گڏه، بازار، شادي، سکر، ڪراچي

4. Using the same sentence, change the subjects of both clauses, using the following words:

ڪراڙا، ٻڍو، ٻڍي، جوان ڇوڪريون، نوجوان ڇوڪرو، ڇوڪرا، ماءُ، پيءُ

5. Substitute freely from the list of verbs in Review Three, changing the verbs in both clauses.

6. Using the same model, and a variety of verbs, practice using forms of the verb to express Future certainty, Past Probability, Future Probability and Past Unfulfilled conditions.

7. Look for opportunities in your daily conversations with neighbors, friends and your teacher to use the postpositions introduced in this lesson.

LESSON TWENTY-FIVE

25-A Pronunciation Drill

پڙهيل ماڻهو پڙهيل آهي.
ٻڍي ٻوڙي ٻڍي وئي.

25-B Some Uses of the Imperfect Participle

As an adjective

Never run in front of a mov<u>ing</u> car.	هلندي۽ موٽر جي سامهون ڪڏهن نه ڊوڙو.
Make the tea with boil<u>ing</u> water.	چانهه ابرندڙ پاڻي۽ سان ٺاهيو.
The boil<u>ing</u> water is finished now.	ابرندو پاڻي هاڻي ختم ٿي ويو.
Turn out the light that is burn<u>ing</u>.	ٻرندڙ بتي۽ کي وسايو.

1. The imperfect participle is essentially a verbal adjective. When it immediately precedes a noun, it describes or qualifies it, like any adjective.

2. The imperfect participle describes an action that is, was, or will be in process at the same time as the main verb. It is not yet completed, or perfected at that time, but still going on. This participle was introduced before in Lessons 12-C, 14-C and E. In those cases, it was used in the formation of the habitual and future tenses.

3. When used as an adjective, there are two ways of forming the imperfect participle. It may end in –و, and will inflect to agree with the noun. See sentences one and three above. Or it may end in –ڙ, as in sentences two and four. In this case it is not inflected.

Sentences one and three could be as follows:

هلندڙ موٽر جي سامهون ڪڏهن نه ڊوڙو.
ابرندڙ پاڻي سان چانهه ٺاهيو.

As a Predicate Adjective

The girl came crying.	ڇوڪري روئيندي آئي.
The boy came crying.	ڇوڪرو روئيندو آيو.

The boy was laughing while beating the dog.	چوڪرو کلندي کلندي ڪتي ڪي ماري رهيو آهي.
I got tired from continuously writing letters.	مان خط لکندي لکندي ٿڪجي پيس.
The gardener will go running to the bazaar.	مالهي ڊڪندو بازار ويندو.
The women are coming, talking among themselves.	زالون پاڻ ۾ ڳالهيون ڪندي اچي رهيون آهن.

4. When the imperfect participle is used in this way, it describes the subject of the sentence in terms of some state, condition or action which is or was happening at the same time as the main verb.

5. The participle may inflect to agree with the subject, as in sentences one and five above. More often it takes an uninflected form, e.g. روئيندي, کلندي, لکندي, as in the other sentences above.

Did you see my cook going to the bazaar?	توهان منهنجو بورچي بازار ويندي ڏنو؟
I saw him drinking tea.	مون هن کي چانھ پيئندي ڏنو.
My son saw the men shaking hands.	منهنجي پٽ ماڻهن کي هٿ ملائيندي ڏنو.
I was seeing the women while cooking the meal.	مان زالن کي ماني پچائيندي ڏسي رهيو هوس / هيس.
Watch him burning the waste paper.	ڪيس ردي ڪاغذ ڪي جلائيندي ڏس.
Did you hear the girl crying?	توهان چوڪريءَ جو روئڻ ٻڌو؟
Yes, she came crying very hard.	هائو، هو ڏاڍو روئيندي آئي.

6. When the imperfect participle is used predicatively, that is, in close relationship to the verb, rather than the subject, it may have its own object. That object may take ڪي or not. However the participle will take the uninflected form ending in ‑ي.

7. هٿ ملائڻ (to shake hands) means literally "to cause hands to meet".

8. In the last pair of sentence above, we could technically use the imperfect participle in the first sentence, i.e. توهان چوڪريءَ ڪي روئيندي ٻڌو . But it is more idiomatic to think of "crying" as the object of the verb "to hear". Thus the infinitive is used. In the last sentence, it is obvious that the girl was crying while coming, so the imperfect participle gives the right meaning. Notice that ڏاڍو modifies "crying", not the girl, so it is in the masculine form.

To Show Concurrent State or Action

On the way back I forgot the way.	موٽندي وقت مون کان رستو وسري ويو.
While the teacher was talking, the boy fell asleep a little.	ماستر جي ڳالھائيندي وقت ڇوڪرو ٿورو سمھي پيو.
While the woman was reading the letter, she burst out crying.	زال چٺي پڙھندي وقت روئي پئي.

9. The imperfect participle may be followed by وقت (time) to indicate or emphasize that the action took place at exactly the same time as the main verb.

As soon as he saw his mother, the little child was (became) very happy.	پنھنجي ماءُ کي ڏسندي ئي ننڍو ٻار تمام خوش ٿي ويو.
I got up from the chair as soon as I heard your voice.	توھان جي آواز کي ٻڌندي ئي مان ڪرسيءَ تان اٿيس.
As soon as his sister took the medicine, she got better.	دوا کائيندي ئي ھن جي ڀيڻ ٺيڪ ٿي وئي.
As soon as I wrote the note, I sent it to him / her.	چٺي لکندي ئي مون ڪيس موڪلي.

10. The imperfect participle followed by the particle ي- for added emphasis, indicates an action occuring immediately after another action or state, or at the same time as the action of the main verb. This idea is often expressed by the use of a conjunctive participle instead of the imperfect participle with –I. For example, the last sentence could be said thus,

چٺي لکي مون ڪيس موڪلي (I wrote the note and sent it to him.) This use of the imperfect participle emphasizes the idea that the action of the main verb happened immediately after, if not at the same time, as the principle verb.

To Show Gradual or Repeated Action or State

I am tired of explaining over and over again. (lit: Explaining explaining I have gotten tired).	مان سمجھائيندي سمجھائيندي ٿڪجي پيو آھيان.
The student fell asleep from studying so long.	شاگرد پڙھندي پڙھندي سمھي پيو.

In spite of knocking the door again and again we couldn't wake anyone.	اسين در کڙڪائيندي کڙڪائيندي کنهن کي جاڳائي نہ سگھياسين.
The poor fellow went to the hospital in fear and trembling.	ويچارو ڏجندي ڏجندي اسپتال ويو.

11.   Repetition of the imperfect participle shows a gradual, repeated or continual action or state. Used in this way it is always found in its uninflected form ending in ي‎–.

As a Noun

Don't wake the sleeping (one).	سمھندڙ کي نہ جاڳايو.
Tell the ones (men, boys) who are fighting not to fight.	وڙھندڙن کي سمجھايو تہ نہ وڙھو.
May I give some money to the person who is begging?	پنندڙ کي ڪجھ پيسا ڏيان؟

12.   The imperfect participle may also function as a noun. The context will usually indicate whether it is a man or woman, or more than one. It is inflected as any noun ending in a short vowel.

25 –C   The Infinitive with چاھڻ to show desired state or action

I want to learn Sindhi.	مان سنڌي سکڻ چاھيان ٿو / ٿي.
That boy wants to become a doctor.	اھو ڇوڪرو ڊاڪٽر ٿيڻ چاھي ٿو.
The girls want to go to the bazaar at three o'clock.	ڇوڪريون ٽين بجي بازار وڃڻ چاھن ٿيون.
We didn't want to come yesterday.	اسان ڪالھ اچڻ نہ چاھيو.
We don't want to trouble you.	اسين توھان کي تڪليف ڏيڻ نہ ٿا چاھيون.
The girl doesn't want to go alone.	ڇوڪري اڪيلي وڃڻ نہ ٿي چاھي.
She wants to go with someone.	ھوءَ ڪنھن سان گڏ وڃڻ چاھي ٿي.
Heat the water. Perhaps our guest wants to take a bath.	پاڻيءَ کي گرم ڪر. شايد اسان جو مزمان تڙ ڪرڻ چاھي.
I didn't want to write a note.	مون چٽي لکڻ نہ چاھي.
I wanted to talk with him face-to-face.	مون ھن جي روبرو ڳالھائڻ چاھيو.

If I get the chance, (lit: if a chance is gotten) I want to meet him.	جيڪڏهن موقعو ملي تہ مان هن سان ملڻ چاهيان ٿو / ٿي.
The children only want to eat sweets.	ٻار فقط مٺائي کائڻ چاهن ٿا.

1. Desire (to wish, want or like to do / be something) may be expressed in Sindhi by the infinitive of a verb plus the appropriate tense of چاهڻ.

2. The infinitive is used as a noun. That is, it is really the object of wanting. In the last sentence above it is seen that "eating sweets", i.e. مٺائي کائڻ is the object of "want", i.e. چاهن ٿا. In English we might say, "The children only want sweets". But in Sindhi it is more idiomatic when using چاهڻ to use the infinitive. This infinitive is used impersonally. چاهڻ is transitive, and in tenses based on the perfect participle will agree with any stated object. The object, for example, مٺائي is really the object of کائڻ (to eat), but in the past tense چاهڻ will agree with that object. Thus,

Yesterday the children only wanted to eat sweets.	ٻارن ڪالھ فقط مٺائي کائڻ چاهي.

3. As is stated above چاهڻ should be used with another verb. If you want to express the need or desire for a thing, it is better to use کپي or گھرجي. <u>Never</u> use چاهڻ to say that you want a person, as this would give the idea of sexual desire. You may say,

I want to meet the teacher.	مان استاد صاحب سان ملڻ چاهيان ٿو.
I want to talk with the gardener.	مان مالهي سان ڳالهائڻ چاهيان ٿو.

Do <u>not</u> say "I want the teacher", as that would give a very wrong idea.

25 –D   The infinitive plus اچڻ / ڄاڻڻ to express knowing how to do something

So far he doesn't know how to write Sindhi.	اڃا تائين هو سنڌي لکڻ نہ ٿو ڄاڻي.
But I know how to write Sindhi.	پر مان سنڌي لکڻ ڄاڻان ٿو.
His / her aunt knows how to cook both English and indigenous food very well.	هن جي چاچي چڱي طرح انگريزي ۽ ديسي ڪاڍو ٻئي پچائڻ ڄاڻي ٿي.
Do you know the counting from one to a hundred?	توهين هڪ کان سو تائين ڳڻڻ ڄاڻو ٿا ڇا؟

As yet he doesn't know how to write Sindhi.	اڃا تائين هن کي سنڌي لکڻ نه ٿي اچي.
I don't know how to speak Urdu.	مون کي اردو ڳالهائڻ نه ٿي اچي.
Both boys know how to play cricket.	ٻئي ڇوڪرا ڪرڪيٽ کيڏڻ ڄاڻن ٿا.
The girl doesn't know how to make bread.	ڇوڪريءَ کي ماني پچائڻ نه ٿي اچي.
They don't know how to speak Sindhi.	هنن کي سنڌي ڳالهائڻ نه ٿي اچي.
But I know Sindhi.	پر مون کي سنڌي اچي ٿي.

1. "To know how to" do something may be expressed in two ways in Sindhi:

a) actively, with the infinitive of a verb plus ڄاڻڻ (to know). ڄاڻڻ is a transitive verb with an irregular perfect participle, ڄاتو. It is most often used in the present tense, and not too commonly on the past tenses based on the perfect participle.

b) impersonally, with the subject in the oblique followed by کي, and the verb اچڻ. In this case اچڻ may or may not be inflected to agree with the object. In the last three sentences اچڻ is feminine to agree with ماني or سنڌي. Some Sindhis would disagree with this, and would consider the infinitive to be the real object of اچڻ. In this case we would say it in this way:

ڇوڪري کي ماني پچائڻ نه ٿو اچي. The girl doesn't know how to make bread.

هنن کي سنڌي ڳالهائڻ نه ٿو اچي. They don't know how to speak Sindhi.

If the verb in the infinitive is omitted, which it may be, it is easy to see how the agreement between سنڌي and اچڻ comes about:

هنن کي سنڌي نه ٿي اچي. They don't know Sindhi.

Colloquially it is more commonly understood that the agreement will be with the object of the verb in the infinitive, thus اچڻ will take a feminine form if this object is feminine.

2. When this idea of knowing how to do something as expressed with اچڻ is used in the negative, it conveys the meaning of inability to do it. For example:

I'm not able to open the box.	مون کي پيتي کولڻ نه ٿي اچي.
We can't do this work. (or, we don't know how to …)	اسان کي هي ڪم ڪرڻ نه ٿو اچي.
But the laborers know it.	پر مزورن کي اچي ٿو.

3. The meaning expressed may be either one of inability, or of not knowing how to do it. Notice that the infinitive may be omitted, as illustrated in the last sentence above.

25 –E The Infinitive plus سکڻ to express learning how to do some thing

I'll learn to cook Sindhi food.	مان سنڌي کاڌو پچائڻ سکندس.
Where did you learn to speak Sindhi?	توھان ڪٿان سنڌي ڳالھائڻ سکي؟
I learned (how to speak) Sindhi, after coming to Sindh.	مون سنڌ اچڻ کان پوءِ سنڌي سکي.

1. "Learning how to …" is expressed in Sindhi by using the infinitive of a verb plus سکڻ (to learn) in the appropriate tense. Thus one may learn something, using a noun as an object, as for example, to learn Sindhi. Or an infinitive may be used, as to learn how to speak Sindhi. This use of the infinitive with سکڻ is another example of the use of an infinitive as a noun.

2. سکڻ is a transitive verb, and will agree with any expresses object in the past tenses based on the perfect participle. Thus it will be inflected to agree with an object of the verb in the infinitive form. The infinitive is also inflected to agree with any object which is feminine.

25 –F Vocabulary

yet, as yet	اڃا، اڃا تائين	to run, race	ڊڪڻ
to burn, to be burning	ٻرڻ	waste, rejected	ردي
to beg	پنڻ	to cry, weep	روئڻ (رنو)
bathing, a bath (m)	تڙ	The game of cricket (f)	ڪرڪيٽ
to bathe	تڙ ڪرڻ	to knock	کڙڪائڻ
to burn, to light	جلائڻ	to count, reckon reflect, consider	ڳڻڻ
to know, know how	ڄاڻڻ (ڄاڻو)	opportunity (f)	موقعو
aunt, wife of father's brother	چاچي	to shake hands	ھٿ ملائڻ
to fear, be afraid	ڊڄڻ (ڊِنو)		

25 -G   Conversational Review

1. Complete the following sentences using the correct form of the imperfect participle of one of the verbs in the list. There may be more than one possible form. You may also be able to substitute more than one verb in some sentences,

كلڻ، جلائڻ، پارڻ، هلڻ، ڳالهائڻ، روئڻ، كمائڻ، وڃڻ، اچڻ،
كم كرڻ، ڊڪڻ، كرڪائڻ، ڍڄڻ، پڙهڻ، تڙ كرڻ

For example:

زالون، ..... وڃي رهيون هيون.

زالون كلندي وڃي رهيون هيون.

..... بتيءَ كي وسائڻ كپي.

پار ..... موٹر جي سامهون ڊڪي رهيو آهي.

مان توكي سنڌي ... ٻڌڻ چاهيان ٿو/ ٿي.

..... چوكري سمهي پئي.

..... ماٹهو ڊڪي ويو.

مون كالھ اوهان كي گهر وٹان .... ڊٺو.

ويچارو سڄي رات .... بيمار ٿي پيو.

2. Using the following model, change the introductory phrase as many different ways you can think of. Also change the object in the second part of the sentence.

..... مون .... ٻڌو / ڊٺو

موٹندي وقت مون استاد صاحب كي ڊٺو.

3. Using the following model with your teacher substitute for the infinitive given from the list of phrases given. Substitute freely in answering.

هتي ويهڻ، خط/ چٹي لكڻ، ماني پچائڻ، سوال چئڻ، تڙ كرڻ،
ڊڪڻ، وڃڻ

هو هتي ويهڻ چاهي ٿو.

كير هتي ويهڻ چاهي ٿو؟

اهو ماٺهو هتي ويهڻ چاهي ٿو.

Now change the pattern, making a negative statement. Then go through the exercise again changing the pronoun freely.

4. Use the following pattern substituting the words / phrases given for the blank space.

مان، هو، منهنجي ماءُ، هنجي پيئُ،
اهي زالون، چاچي، ڇوڪرا، اسين، اوهين

ڪنهن کي ديسي ڪاڌو پچائڻ اچي ٿو؟

مون کي ديسي ڪاڌو پچائڻ اچي ٿو.

5. Using the same pattern, change the form of اچڻ to the proper form of جاڻڻ. Then do the same using سکڻ.

6. Repeat the exercises above in 4 and 5, substituting a variety of verbs from those you now know. Use negatives too, in your substitutions.

7. Converse with your teacher and with other friends about Muslim holidays. Depending on the season of the year, one or the other holidays may be being celebrated. Make your own list of new words which you learn from such conversations, and try to use them so as to learn them well.

LESSON TWENTY-SIX

26-A   Pronunciation Drill

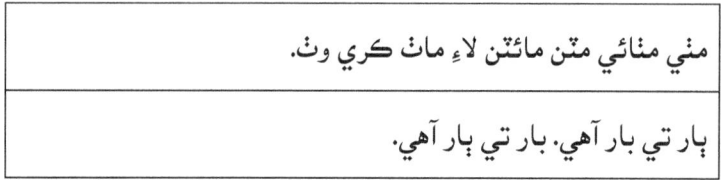

26-B   The Imperfect Participle used with رهڻ

She keeps on studying Sindhi.	هوءَ سنڌي پڙهندي رهندي آهي.
The man kept on laughing a long time.	ماڻهو گهڻي دير تائين کلندو رهيو.
The young men kept on fighting.	نوجوان ڇوڪرا وڙهندا رهيا.
Keep on singing! I like it.	ڳائيندا رهو! مون کي هي پسند آهي.
The meat isn't tender yet. Keep on cooking it.	گوشت اڃا نہ ڳريو آهي. ڪيس رڌيندا رهو.
Does the watchman stay awake the whole night?	ڇا چوڪيدار سڄي رات جاڳندو رهندو آهي؟
Don't turn off the stove. Let the water keep on boiling.	چلهو بند نہ ڪر. پاڻي ٻرندو رهي.
Against the Doctor's orders grandmother kept on eating too much cooking oil.	ڊاڪٽر جي حڪم جي برخلاف ناني زياده گيھہ کائيندي رهي.
Keep on writing. There is still time.	لکندا رهو. اڃا وقت آهي.

1.   When the imperfect participle of a verb is combined with any tense of the verb رهڻ (to remain, stay), it expresses the idea of continuing or keeping on with the action.

2.   رهڻ is intransitive, thus it will agree with the subject in all tenses. Even though the main verb may be transitive, it will lose its transitive character in the compound with رهڻ. The imperfect participle will be inflected to agree with the subject in gender and number.

3.   It will be useful here for the student to review the Present and Past Continuous tenses (16-C and 19-E). It is important to understand the differences in formation and meaning.

4.   ڳرڻ is an intransitive verb meaning "to melt, as ice melts, to dissolve, to soften in cooking". In this last use, it may be used for meat, vegetables, or anything that becomes tender of soft in

cooking. ڳرڻ can also mean "to waste away, to become emaciated" when applied to people.

5. چلهو is a masculine noun meaning "fireplace", particularly the small mud or cement enclosure used commonly in Sindhi courtyards or kitchens for cooking with wood or charcoal. By extension it is used for a gas burner or any cooking stove.

26 –C   Showing Progression by the use of اچڻ and وڃڻ

His condition went from bad to worse. (i.e. went on becoming bad)	هن جو حال خراب ٿيندو ويو.
We need to go on writing and speaking Sindhi.	اسان کي کپي ته سنڌي لکندا ۽ ڳالهائيندا وڃون.
Keep on giving grandfather the medicine.	ناني کي دوا پياريندا وڃو.
He will get better by taking the medicine. (lit: to him benefit will keep on becoming)	دوا پيئڻ کان هن کي فائدو ٿيندو ويندو.
Nowadays the price of everything keeps going up. (lit: keeps on becoming great, more)	اڄ ڪالھ هر شيءِ جي قيمت زياده ٿيندي وڃي ٿي.
Grandfather's condition is improving daily.	ڏاڏي جو حال ڏينهون ڏينهن ٺيڪ ٿيندو وڃي ٿو.
This nation keeps on making progress.	هي قوم ترقي ڪندي اچي ٿي.

1. When the imperfect participle of any verb is combined with a form of اچڻ or وڃڻ, it gives a continuous idea that is similar to the use of رهڻ in the previous section. However while the use of رهڻ implies a simple continuation of the action, the use of اچڻ or وڃڻ with the imperfect participle suggests a progression, either for the better, or from bad to worse. The English translations do not do justice to the subtle difference in the Sindhi meaning.

2. Since both اچڻ and وڃڻ are intransitive verbs, the compound will function as an intransitive verb even if the verb in the imperfect participle is transitive. The participle will inflect to agree with the subject in gender and number.

3. نانو, ناني and ڏاڏو, ڏاڏي mean grandfather and grandmother. The precise relationship is clearly shown in the Sindhi terms, since نانو and ناني refer to one's mother's parents. ڏاڏو and ڏاڏي are used for paternal grandparents. Each relationship in Sindhi has its own name. This can be confusing for the newcomer, and it may be helpful to list the common ones and practice using them with your teacher and with other Sindhi friends. This is a cultural phenomenon necessitated by the joint family system, and by the fact that first names are almost never used to address older family members or relatives.

4. ڏينهون ڏينهن is another way of saying "daily".

26–D   Expressing Necessity by the use of ضروري, ضرورت, and ضرور

That much cooking oil isn't necessary. We aren't going to fry the meat.	ايتري گيھ جي ضرورت ناهي. اسين گوشت نہ ترينداسين.
This is a small frying pan. A big one is necessary for frying so much meat.	هي ڪڙاهي آهي. ايتري گوشت ڪي ترڻ لاءِ ڪڙاهو ضروري آهي.
I need a ladle and a wooden spoon, too.	مون ڪي ڪيوي ۽ ڏوئي بہ ضروري آهن.
It's necessary that we boil the drinking water.	ضروري آهي تہ اسين پيئڻ جو پاڻي اُباريندا آهيون.
We don't need such a big earthen jar. A small one or a long-necked clay jar is big enough.	ايڏي مٽ جي ضرورت نہ آهي. مٽڪو يا صراحي ڪافي وڏي آهي.
Spoons, forks and knives are all necessary.	چمچا، ڪانٽا ۽ ڇريون سڀ ضروري آهن.
So many things aren't necessary. Bring only cups and plates.	ايترين شين جي ضرورت ناهي. فقط پيالا ۽ بسيون ڪڍي اچو.
Do you wash dishes in hot water?	توهان ٿانو گرم پاڻي ۾ ڌوئيندا آهيو چا؟
Certainly, it should always be done that way!	ضرور، هميشہ ائين ڪرڻ گهرجي!
Do you want this cauldron?	چا توکي هي ديگ / ديگ ڪپي.
No, only this small one is needed.	نہ، رڳو هن ننڍي ديگچي / ديگچي جي ضرورت آهي.
Is the meat tender yet?	چا گوشت اڃا ڳري ويو؟
No, it needs more cooking.	نہ، وڌيڪ رڌڻ ضروري آهي.
Will you peel the guavas?	توهين هن زيتون ڪي ڇلندا؟
Yes, we'll certainly peel them.	هائو اسين ضرور هن ڪي ڇلينداسين.
There is no need to throw the peelings on the floor.	ڇلن (ڪلن) ڪي فرش تي اڇلڻ جي ضرورت ناهي.
Please throw them into that bucket.	هن بالٽي ۾ ڦٽي ڪريو.

1.   ضروري (necessary) was introduced in Lesson 11, and ضرور (certainly) in 14. They are both illustrated here with ضرورت (necessity) in order to help you to distinguish the difference in usage between them.

2. ضرورت is a feminine noun meaning "need, necessity". It is preceded by the possessive جي and a noun or verb in the infinitive. The first sentence above would literally mean, "There is no need / necessity <u>of</u> so much cooking oil". The last would mean, "There is no need / necessity <u>of</u> throwing the peelings on the floor".

3. ضروري, the adjective meaning "necessary" may be interchanged with ضرورت جي. For example,

وڃڻ ضروري ناآهي	or,	وڃڻ جي ضروري ناآهي.
It's not necessary to go,	or,	There is no need of going.

4. ضرور functions as an adverb meaning, "certainly", "surely", "of course".

26 –E   Repetition of Words

Give the boys one rupee each.	ڇوڪرن کي هڪ هڪ رپيو ڏيو.
Each student has two books.	شاگرد کي ٻه ٻه ڪتاب آهن.
There is a half seer of milk in each of these bowls.	هنن پيالن ۾ اڌ اڌ سير کير آهي.
The buses go every two and a half hours.	لارين ادائي ادائي ڪلاڪن کان پوءِ وينديون آهن.
The girls have rupees 2.75 each.	ڇوڪرين وٽ پوٽا ٽي ٽي رپيا آهن.
You'll get these books for 5.50 each.	هي ڪتاب سادي پنجين پنجين رپئي ۾ ملندا.

1. When numbers are repeated, a <u>distributive</u> idea is expressed. The equivalent meaning in English would be "each, every, apiece".

2. Fraction words which are used alone, such as, اَڌُ (a half), ڏيڍُ (one and a half), ادائي (two and a half) may be repeated in this way. However, those fractions which are added to whole numbers are never repeated. These are پوٽا (a quarter less), سادِا (and a half), and سوا (and a quarter). Instead the whole number is repeated. See the last two sentences above for examples.

Repetition of Nouns

The student came by turns to the teacher.	طالب علم واري واري سان ماسٽر وٽ آيا.
Ask each of the boys.	ڇوڪري ڇوڪري کان پڇيو.
In that shop there are different kinds of teapots.	هن دڪان تي طرح طرح جا چانهه دان آهن.

There are different kinds of dishes in the kitchen.	بورچي خاني ۾ قسم قسم جا ٿانو آهن.

3.   Nouns may be repeated with a distributive force or they may suggest variety. The idea of variety is inherent in the words قسم (kind, sort) and طرح (manner, way sort).

4.   بورچي خانو is a compound made up of بورچي (cook) and خانو meaning "compartment". Thus it means the compartment, or place of the cook. خانو is also used for a drawer in a chest of drawers.

Repetition of Adjectives

Drink hot tea! (heard on railway stations)	گرم گرم چانھ پيو!
Small children can't understand this.	ننڍا ننڍا ٻار هن کي سمجهي نَ ٿا سگهن.
There are very few trees on high mountains.	وڏن وڏن جبلن تي وڻ ٿورا آهن.

5.   Adjectives may be repeated before a noun in order to show that all or each of the items is included, thus a distributive force. The repetition itself does not imply intensity. For instance, the tea may be very, very hot, but repeating گرم means that it is all, every bit of it, hot.

Repetition of Pronouns

Only a few go to school from this village.	هن ڳوٺ مان ڪو ڪو اسڪول ويندو آهي.
There was no one at all in the house.	گهر ۾ ڪو ڪو نَ آهي.
Who all will come?	ڪير ڪير ايندو؟

6.   When the pronouns ڪو and ڪير are repeated, it gives a distributive idea or a selective sense. ڪو when repeated with a negative means "no one at all".

7.   Note that ڪو ڪو meaning "a few" is treated as a singular in Sindhi.

Repetition of Adverbs

Please speak slowly so that I can understand.	آهستي آهستي ڳالهايو انهي لاءِ تہ مان سمجهين سگهان.
She answers very quickly.	هو جلدي جلدي جواب ڏي ٿي.
We go to his / her house sometimes.	اسين ڪڏهن ڪڏهن هن جي گهر وڃون ٿا.

26 –F The use of the Perfect Participle as an Adjective

He is an educated man.	هو پڙهيل ماڻهو آهي.
But his wife is illiterate.	ليڪن هن جي گهر واري اڻ پڙهيل آهي.
The boy's clothes are completely torn.	ڇوڪري جا ڪپڙا خوب ڦاٽل آهن.
Last year I went to Murree.	گذريل سال مان ڪوهه مري ويس.
Will the bazaar be open at this time?	ڇا هن رات بازار کليل هوندي؟
Be careful! There's broken glass on the road.	خبردار! ڀڳل شيشو رستي تي آهي.
Put the boiled water in the clay jar.	ابريل پاڻي مٽڪي ۾ وجهو.
Do you drink only boiled water?	ڇا اوهين فقط ابريل پاڻي پيئندا آهيو؟
There's water mixed with / in the milk.	کير ۾ پاڻي گڏيل آهي.
There's a lock on their door. (lit: … applied to their door)	هنن جي در تي ڪلف لڳل آهي.
Today I saw it written in the newspaper.	مون اڄ هن ڳالهه بابت اخبار ۾ لکيل ڏٺو.
Close every window that you see open.	هر هڪ در ڪي جا تون کليل ڏسين تو/ تي بند ڪر.

1. When the perfect participle is used as an adjective, it ends in –يل after dropping the usual –و ending. Some times, as with پڙهڻ and گذرڻ the –ئيل ending is elided to –يل. In those verbs which do not have the –يو ending in the perfect participle, the ending of this adjective form will be –يل.

2. The sense of this usage is a <u>statical</u> one. That is, it expresses a <u>state</u> of having been boiled, broken, opened, etc.

3. This statical form of the perfect participle functions as an indeclinable adjective.

26 –G Vocabulary

to throw	اڇلڻ	kitchen (m)	بورچي خانو
saucer, plate (f)	بسي	to fry	ترڻ
to throw away	ڪٽي ڪرڻ	need, necessity (f)	ضرورت
cup, bowl (m)	پيالو	guava (m)	زيتون

dish, utensil (m)	ٹانو	much, more, excessive	زياده
to cook, boil, stew	رنڊڻ (رڌو)	benefit (m)	فائدو
tea pot (m)	چانھ دان	nation (f)	قوم
peeling (m)	چل	small frying pan (f)	ڪڙاھي
to peel	چلڻ	large frying pan (m)	ڪڙاھو
stove (m)	چلھو	fork (m)	ڪانٽو
spoon (m)	چمچو	ladle (f)	ڪيوي
knife (f)	ڇُري	to sing	ڳائڻ
shop (m)	دڪان	to melt, dissolve, become tender	ڳارڻ
cauldron (f)	ديڳ، ديڳ	large earthen jar (m)	مٽ
small cauldron (f)	ديڳچي، ديڳچي	small earthen jar (m)	مٽڪو
paternal grandfather (m)	ڏاڏو	maternal grandfather (m)	نانو
paternal grandmother (f)	ڏاڏي	maternal grandmother (f)	ناني
wooden spoon (f)	ڏوئي	mountain (m)	جبل
long-necked clay jug (f)	صراحي	mountain (m)	ڪوهُ

26-H Conversational Review

1. Practice conversing about the kitchen and food preparation. Take your teacher into the kitchen, and practice using the proper names for the various items there. If you have a servant or cook, spend time talking with him or her about these things. Add these words in addition to those given in the lesson. Don't be satisfied with a limited vocabulary in this aspect of everyday living. This can be especially interesting for a woman student. When you are visiting with close friends, ask to see the kitchen, and don't be afraid to ask questions. Your friends will be interested to see your kitchen, too. Talk about the differences, and find out if the things in your kitchen are really

the same as what a Sindhi woman will use. For instance, is your European or American frying pan or skillet called a كڙاهي, or is a كڙاهي something different.

2. Using the following patterns complete the sentences in a variety of ways. Use the imperfect participle of any verb with رهڻ.

چوڪرا
اسين   گهٽي دير تائين
توهين
زالون
ڊاڪٽر جي حڪم جي برخلاف

Using the same patterns, ask your teacher to ask questions using ڇو؟ The student may answer freely.

3. Practice the repetition of numbers using the following pattern:

چوڪرين کي .... ڏيو
چوڪرين کي .... آهن

4. Fill in ضروري or ضرورت جي in each of the following sentences and complete the sentence in a variety of ways.

ڊاڏي جو اڃُ .... آهي ليڪن .....
ايترو/ي ..... ناهي پا ڪاڻ ته
اوهان کي ..... بـ ... آهي /آهن
مون کي هي /هن .... آهي

LESSON TWENTY-SEVEN

27-A   Pronunciation Drill

مَينهن مينهَن مِ يڃي پئي.
ڏيڏر جو مطلب آهي ڏي بہ، ڏر بہ.

27-B   The Use of Pronominal Suffixes with Verbs

In Lesson 20-D and E a set of pronominal suffixes was taught along with its use when added to postpositions, nouns of relationship, and with the verb هئڻ. A slightly different set of pronominal suffixes may be used to replace the pronoun subject of other verbs.

Note: In northern Sindh, village men and especially women can hardly speak without using this grammar. Pronominal suffixes are however, used far less by southern Sindhis, and even regarded by them as an uneducated way of speaking. Among teachers not used to using this grammar you may find a great deal of disagreement about exact pronunciations, and some teachers may tell you that these forms are no longer used. Even among those who commonly use this grammar disagree on the exact pronunciation, and so you will need to personally whether or not to use the grammar, and if so, then how to pronounce the forms.

	Singular	Plural		
1st person	I	We	‑ سِين، سُون	‑مِ
2nd person	You	You	‑ وَ	‑ ءِ، ئي
3rd person	He/She	They	‑ آئون	‑ آئين، ئين

The simple past tense of the verb لکڻ (to write) with pronominal suffixes replacing the subject would be as follows:

I wrote	We wrote		
I wrote	We wrote	لکيوسين	لکيم
You wrote	You wrote	لکيوَ	لکيئي
He / She wrote	They wrote	لکيائون	لکيائين

27 –C Sentences illustrating the use of Pronominal Suffixes as the subject of verbs

I wrote for two hours.	ٻن ڪلاڪن تائين لکيم.
Did you write the tenth class examination last year?	چا گذريل سال ڏهين ڪلاس جو امتحان لکيئي؟
No, but I'll write it this year.	نه، پر هن سال لکندم.
Did you write a letter to your mother this week?	چا هن هفتي ۾ پنهنجي ماءُ کي خط لکيو؟
Yes I wrote to her this morning.	هائو، اڄ صبح جو ڪيس لکيم.
They wrote long letters to their friends.	پنهنجي دوستن کي ڊگھا خط لکيائون.
I'll tell him that I'll come tomorrow.	ڪيس ٻڌائيندم ته سياڻي ايندم.
Today I'll go with them to the bazaar.	اڄ ساڻن گڏجي بازار ويندم.
He said to me that he was unable to come.	مون کي چيائين ته مان اچي نه ٿو سگهان.
What did they say to you?	توهان کي چا چيائون؟
They said they would come on Tuesday.	چيائون ته اڱاري تي اينداسين.
What did you say to them?	ڪين چا چيوَ؟
I said not to come on Tuesday because I'll go to Sukkur.	چيم ته اڱاري تي نه اچو چاڪاڻ ته سکر ويندم.
What did he say to them?	هنن کي چا چيائين؟

1.   Sentence seven above would read as follows without the use of pronominal suffixes:

مان هن کي ٻڌائيندس ته مان سياڻي ايندس.

It is easy to see why Sindhis call this way of speaking with pronominal suffixes "nanDhI sindhI", i.e. "short Sindhi".

In spoken Sindhi however, the pronoun may be included along with a pronominal suffix. This is grammatically redundant, and would not be found in literary Sindhi. Thus, you may hear this sentence as follows:

مان ڪين ٻڌائيندم ته مان سياڻي ايندم.

2.   Pronominal suffixes are more commonly used in the past tenses. However they are occasionally used in the present and future tenses.

3.   اچڻ (to come) and وڃڻ (to go) are the only intransitive verbs commonly used with pronominal suffixes. When used, it will often be in a compound with transitive verb.

4. Although theoretically any pronominal suffix could be used with any verb to replace a pronoun, in actual practice some combinations would be awkward and thus are not used. By observation and careful listening the student will learn first to recognize the commonly used ones, and then to use them. By those he will also learn which verbs are not used with pronominal suffixes.

27 –D Pronominal Suffixes used in the Present and Past Perfect Tenses.

I have written to my brother.	پنهنجي ڀاءُ کي لکيو اٿم.
He / she has read many books.	گهڻا ڪتاب پڙهيا اٿس.
We have told him many times that he may come.	گهڻا ڀيرا چيو اٿئون ته هو اچي.
They had written before this.	هن کان اڳ ۾ لکيو هئائون.
What did you say to them?	کين ڇا چيو اٿوَ؟
Have you (sing.) done the work?	ڪم ڪيو اٿئي؟
Has he already finished the work?	ڇا ڪم ڪري چڪو آهي؟
I have given her books.	ڪيس ڪتاب ڏنا اٿم.
When did you write to him?	ڪيس ڪڏهن لکيو هُوَ؟
I wrote him a note last month.	ڪيس گذريل مهيني چني لکي هومِ.
They had spoken to me about taking leave.	مون کان موڪل وٺڻ لاءِ چيو هئائون.
He had given to me the pictures.	مون کي تصويرون ڏنيون هئائين.

1. In the Present and Past Perfect Tense the pronominal suffix is added to the auxiliary verb to replace the pronoun subject, <u>not</u> to the Perfect Participle.

2. Notice that the suffixes added to the past auxiliary verb are irregular except in the first person singular and the second person plural. This may cause some confusion since the same suffix, –AŪ is used to replace "we" in the Present Perfect, and "they" in the Past Perfect. Note sentences three and four above, and the chart which follows.

3. The following chart shows the pronominal suffixes used to replace the <u>subjects</u> with the verb لکڻ (to write) in the Present and Past Perfect Tenses.

Present Perfect Tense		Past Perfect Tense	
I have written	لکيو اٿم	I had written	لکيو هومِ
You have written	لکيو اٿئي	You had written	لکيو هوءِ
He has written	لکيو اٿسِ	He had written	لکيو هئائين
We have written	لکيو اٿئونِ	We had written	لکيو هوسين
You have written	لکيو اٿوَ	You had written	لکيو هُوَ
They have written	لکيو اٿنِ	They had written	لکيو هئائون

27 –E Double Pronominal Suffixes to express both Subject and Object.

1. Two pronominal suffixes may be added to the Perfect Participle pf transitive verbs in the Simple Past Tense. The first will replace the pronoun subject and the second will replace the pronoun object.

The suffixes used for the subject will follow the form given in the chart in 27-B and those used for the object will be according to the chart in 27-D-3.

2. The following examples illustrate the wide variety Sindhi offers for expression through the use of these pronominal suffixes.

"He said to me" may be expressed in the following ways:

"They said to him" could be as follows:

1.	هنن هن کي چيو.
2.	هنن کيس چيو.
3.	هنن چيسِ.
4.	کيس چيائون.
5.	چيائونس.

3. When the first person singular suffix –m^i is followed by another suffix, it is changed to –مان-. The final –O of the Perfect Participle which was shortened to –u- before –m^i is lengthened again to –O-. For example,

I wrote	لکيم	I wrote to him.	لکيوماس
I said	چيم	I said to you.	چيومانوَ
I left	ڇڏيم	I left them.	ڇڏيومان

In the last example above, چڍيومان, the nasalization of –Ã- is dropped before –n[i], the third person plural suffix.

4. Double pronominal suffixes are sometimes used in other tenses, although not as commonly. See the following examples:

I will give him the money.	پيسا ڏيندو مانس.
I will tell them tomorrow.	سڀاڻي ٻڌائيندو مان.

Sentences Illustrating Double Pronominal Suffixes.

I'll tell him I'll come tomorrow.	ٻڌائيندو مانس ته سڀاڻي ايندم.
I'll write him / her this morning.	اڄ صبح جو لکندو مانس.
What did he say to you?	اوهان کي چا چيائين؟ / چا چيائينوَ؟
He told me that he couldn't come.	چيائينم ته مان اچي نه ٿو سگهان.
What did they say to you?	چا چيائونوَ؟
They said that they gave me the money last week.	چيائونم ته گذريل هفتي پيسا ڏنم.
What did he say to them?	چا چيائين؟
He said he would surely go.	چيائين ته ضرور ويندم.

This treatment of pronominal suffixes is far from complete. Indeed this aspect of Sindhi is far too complex for the first year student should be able to recognize and understand these commonly used forms. He has been and will continue to hear them. They are also used in written Sindhi, particularly in narrative, as in the Sindhi New Testament. He should also begin to use the simple and more common pronominal suffixes. As the student further progresses in Sindhi he will need to study in greater depth this important and very idiomatic pattern of the language. Some of the older grammars[1] have extensive lists of verbs with various combinations of pronominal suffixes which may be of interest to the student. The best source of modern usage will be your

---

[1] A Grammar of the Sindhi Language, by the Rev. C. W. Haskell (out of print)
A Manual of Sindhi, by Dulamal Bulchand (Sindh Language Authority)

teacher and other educated Sindhi friends, and reading.

27 –F   Inherently Passive Forms of Verbs.

Only a transitive verb can be used in a passive form (or voice). As soon as it is changed from active to passive in form, it is treated as intransitive. In Sindhi there are two types of inherently passive verbs.

With ٿي وڃڻ /ٿيڻ **instead of** ڪرڻ.

Active		Passive	
to prepare, get ready	تيار ڪرڻ	to be prepared, gotten ready	تيار ٿيڻ
to close	بند ڪرڻ	to be closed	بند ٿيڻ
to begin	شروع ڪرڻ	to begin	شروع ٿيڻ
to fix, to set right	ٺيڪ ڪرڻ	to be fixed, right	ٺيڪ ٿيڻ
to please	خوش ڪرڻ	to be happy	خوش ٿيڻ
to make a mistake	غلطي ڪرڻ	to be mistaken	غلطي ٿيڻ

1.   Many of the compound verbs commonly used in Sindhi may be used with either ڪرڻ or ٿيڻ (or its intensive form ٿي وڃڻ). Those listed above are representative. Any compound verb using ٿيڻ will be <u>inherently passive</u>. Those using ڪرڻ will be <u>inherently active</u>. Such inherently passive verbs are always intransitive.

The following illustrate such verbs.

When will the cook prepare dinner?	بورچي سانجهي جي ماني ڪڏهن تيار ڪندو؟
When will dinner be ready?	سانجهيءَ جي ماني ڪڏهن تيار ٿيندي؟
We start our class at 8 : 30.	اسين ساڍي اٺين بجي پنهنجو ڪلاس شروع ڪندا آهيون.
Our class starts at 8 : 30.	اسان جو ڪلاس ساڍي اٺين بجي شروع ٿيندو آهي.
I made a mistake, please forgive / excuse me.	مون غلطي ڪئي، معاف ڪجو.
A mistake was made (by me). Please excuse / forgive me.	(مون کان) غلطي ٿي وئي، معاف ڪجو.

The children are trying to please the teacher.	ٻار ڪوشش ڪن ٿا ته ماسٽر کي خوش ڪن.
The teacher will be pleased.	ماسٽر خوش ٿيندو.
Now the tool is alright.	هاڻي اوزار نيڪ ٿي ويو.
Who fixed it?	ڪنهن هن کي ٺيڪ ڪيو؟
Almighty God created the whole world.	خدا تعاليٰ سڄي دنيا کي پيدا ڪيو.
All things were made by him.	سيئي شيون هن جي وسيلي پيدا ٿيون آهن.
When was this little child born?	هي ننڍو ٻار ڪڏهن پيدا ٿيو؟

2. Note that the <u>object</u> of the active form becomes the subject when the verb is put into passive form. The real subject or doer of the action is not usually mentioned in a passive form of a verb.

3. It is significant that actions which are felt to be blameworthy are usually put into a passive form. In other words the Sindhi speaker, on making a mistake, rarely takes the kind of responsibility that an active verb implies. The examples in sentences five and six above are given for contrast. One is not likely to hear مون غلطي ڪئي, as in sentence five. Rather,

غلطي ٿي وئي (a mistake happened) is the common way in which this idea is expressed. The passive form seems to bring out the haplessness of the speaker who is portrayed as a victim of circumstances beyond his control. Compare the English expression "Something went wrong", which also skirts the blame and leaves unsaid who or what exactly was to blame.

4. If the person responsible is mentioned at all, he is spoken of indirectly using a postposition like کان, (by, through, from) to indicate who did the action.

5. پيدا ٿيڻ is a compound verb which may mean either "to be created", or "to be born". Its active counterpart پيدا ڪرڻ means "to create".

With some basic verbs instead of their causals

Active / causal			
to make	ٺاهڻ	to be made	ٺَهَڻ
to burn (something)	ٻارڻ	to burn, to be burned	بَرَڻ
to open	کولڻ	to be opened	کُلڻ
to beat, kill	مارڻ	to die	مَرَڻ
to break	ڀَڃڻ	to be broken	ڀِڄڻ

6. Some, but not all active / causal verbs have a basic form that is inherently passive. The above is only a representative list.

Following are some sentences illustrating this type of passive verb.

I have lit the fire.	مون باهه ٻاري آهي.
The fire is burning nicely.	باهه چڱيءَ طرح ٻري ٿي.
Who opened the door?	ڪنهن در کوليو؟
The windows are open, too.	دريون بہ کليل آهن.
Who broke the glass?	هي گلاس ڪنهن ڀڳو؟
How did this glass happen to get broken?	هي گلاس ڪيئن ڀڄي پيو؟
Well, this was broken by me.	هي تہ مون کان ڀڄي پيو.

7.   These examples also illustrate the fact the object of an active verb becomes the subject when the verb is in its passive form, while the real subject or doer is not usually named.

8.   The last pair of sentences above is another illustration of the way in which mishaps are described in Sindhi. The passive, less direct form of expression is preferred.

9.   These are only a few examples of inherently passive verbs which are very common in Sindhi. You have been using many of them without realizing that they are indeed a kind of passive form. This explanation will help you to recognize more of them.

27 –G   Derived Passive Forms of Verbs.

Simple Construction.

He learns what is taught him.	جيڪي هن کي سيکاريجي ٿو سو سکي ٿو.
He doesn't learn more than what is taught him.	جيڪي هن کي سيکاريجي ٿو تنهن کان وڌيڪ نہ ٿو سگهي.
The letter is being written right now.	خط هينئر لکجي ٿو پيو.
The letter will be written tomorrow.	سڀاڻي خط لکبو.
What is this called in Sindhi? (lit: What will be said to this in Sindhi?)	سنڌيءَ ۾ هن کي ڇا چئبو آهي؟
We will meet on the way.	رستيءَ ۾ اسين گڏباسين / گڏ ٿينداسين.
The little boys will get tired after a long walk.	ايترو پري پنڌ ڪري ننڍا ٻار ٿڪبا / ٿڪجي پوندا.

If his mother sees him, she will be very angry.	جيڪڏهن هن جي ماءُ ڏسندي ته هوءَ تمام ڪاوڙبي / ڪاوڙجي ويندي.

1. A passive infinitive may be formed from an active verb by adding –j– before the infinitive ending –ڻ. For example, سيکارجڻ, "to be taught"; لکجڻ, "to be written"; چوجڻ, "to be said".

2. The Imperfect participle of such passive verbs will be formed by adding –بو to the root, e.g. لکبو, چئبو, سيکاربو, etc.

3. گڏجڻ (to meet, mix), ٿڪجڻ(to be, get tired), ڪاوڙجڻ(to be or get angry) take the form of passive verbs, even though they are not the passive forms of any active verbs. Because of this passive form, the imperfect participle is formed in the same way as the imperfect participles of other passive verbs, i.e. ڪاوڙبو, ٿڪبو, گڏبو. However the alternate form, as illustrated above will be more commonly used in speech.

4. It is grammatically possible to form all the tenses based on the root and the imperfect participle in this way. However they will seldom be found in spoken Sindhi. Because of their occasional usage in speech, and quite frequent use in literature and newspapers, it is sufficient for the student to recognize and understand them.

Using the Perfect Participle of Transitive Verbs with وڃڻ.

The table has been set.	ميز لڳائي وئي هئي.
Don't worry. Your note was sent yesterday.	فڪر نه ڪجو. توهان جي چٽي ڪالهه موڪلي وئي.
That much food won't be eaten.	ايترو کاڌو کاڌو نه ويندو.
Can (will) fish be caught in this place?	هن جاءِ مڇيون پڪڙيون وينديون ڇا؟
This work should be finished this very day.	گهرجي ته هي ڪم اڄ ئي ختم ڪيو ويندو.
Sure, (truly) the window was opened, but who opened it?	سچ پچ دري کولي وئي، ليڪن ڪنهن هن کي کوليو؟
This book was prepared so that you might learn Sindhi quickly!	هي ڪتاب تيار ڪيو ويو انهي لاءِ ته اوهين هن جي ذريعي سنڌي جلدي سکو!
Arrangements are not made for so many people.	ايترن ماڻهن لاءِ بندوبست ڪيو نه ٿو وڃي.

I have some doubt that perhaps a lie has been told.	مون کي شڪ آهي ته شايد ڪو ڪوڙ ڳالهايو ويو آهي.
It will be seen. (i.e. wait and see).	ڏٺو ويندو.
If this note is written with a pen it will be better.	جيڪڏهن هي چٺي قلم سان لکي ويندي ته وڌيڪ سٺو ٿيندو.
This invitation was sent by (the hand of) a servant.	هي دعوت نوڪر جي هٿ سان موڪلي وئي.
Many people were killed in the fight.	لڙائي ۾ گھڻا ماڻهو ماريا ويا.

5. Transitive verbs may be made passive by using the perfect participle with any tense of وڃڻ. The combination then becomes intransitive and both parts of the verb inflect to agree with the subject in gender, number and person.

6. The negative when required may close before the main verb, or it may be placed between the participle and the main verb.

7. Since passive verbs are used quite infrequently in Sindhi, we have not put great emphasis on them. It is necessary to understand them, and also to distinguish the form with وڃڻ. There are times when the passive is needed. When the emphasis is not directed to the doer of the action, either because it is unknown or not emphasized, the passive is appropriate. In most cases if the agent is known, the sentence may be said in an active form.

8. مارڻ (to beat, hit, kill) is used above in its passive form with وڃڻ, thus, ماريا ويا (were killed). While this could be said using مرڻ (to die) ماريو وڃڻ is more descriptive of how they died, i.e. they were killed.

9. سچ پچ is typical of the use of "rhyming words" in Sindhi. پچ has no meaning of its own. You will hear many such words used.

10. Sentence eight above is an illustration of the passive used with نه وڃڻ to express the idea of inability or impossibility.

27-H Vocabulary.

tool, instrument (m)	اوزار	to make a mistake	غلطي ڪرڻ
to be fixed, right, alright	ٺيڪ ٿيڻ	to be mistaken	غلطي ٿيڻ
to fix, make right	ٺيڪ ڪرڻ	lie (m)	ڪوڙ
to be created, to be born	پيدا ٿيڻ	to meet, mix	گڏجڻ
to create	پيدا ڪرڻ	to forgive, to excuse	معاف ڪرڻ
to seize, catch	پڪڙڻ	now, just now	هينئر
to walk, go by foot	پنڌ ڪرڻ	fight, battle, war (f)	لڙائي
truth (m)	سچ	to be pleased, happy	خوش ٿيڻ
to please, make happy	خوش ڪرڻ		

27-I Conversational Review.

1. Listen carefully for pronominal suffixes as you listen to Sindhis converse among themselves. Check yourself to see if you are understanding them properly. The teacher should make up sentences using a pronoun as subject with one of the following verbs. The student should then repeat the sentence replacing the pronoun with a pronominal suffix.

Verbs:

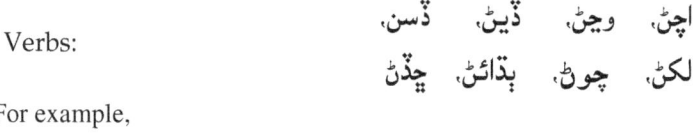

For example,

T:	استاد: مان سيݨاٽي ايندس.
S:	شاگرد: سيݨاٽي ايندم وغيره.

Continue the exercise using the verbs above, and a variety of other verbs from the list in Review 3. After you feel you have a grasp of pronominal suffixes used to replace the pronoun subject, go through it again with only transitive verbs replacing pronoun subject and object with the correct pronominal suffixes. For example:

T:	استاد: مون هن کي خط لکيو.
S:	شاگرد: خط لکيو مانس.

2. Ask your teacher to make up sentences using pronominal suffixes. Repeat the sentence replacing the suffixes with the proper nouns.

3. In your reading be aware of the passive forms, taking special note of them.

4. Use the following verbs to make up sentences. The teacher should make up a sentence using the active form. The student should then respond with the same sentence in the passive form.

تيار ڪرڻ، بند ڪرڻ، شروع ڪرڻ، ٺيڪ ڪرڻ، خوش ڪرڻ، گرم ڪرڻ غلطي ڪرڻ، پورو ڪرڻ

For example,

T:	ا: توهان چانھ تيار ڪئي آهي؟
S:	ش: چانھ تيار ٿي وئي آهي.

5. The teacher should ask the following questions, with the student giving a suitable reply.

توهان جي چٽي ڪڏهن ڪڍڻ موڪلي ويندي.
هي ڪتاب ڪنهن جي لاءِ تيار ڪيو ويو آهي.
هي سبق ڪيستائين ختم ڪيو ويندو؟
مڇي چو ڪاڏي نہ ويندي؟
لڙائي ۾ گهٽا ماڻهو ماريا ويا؟
ٻار چو ايترا ٿڪجي پيا؟

LESSON TWENTY-EIGHT

28 - A   Pronunciation Drill

> هن بيٽ تي بيت جي پيٽ کئي.
>
> چوڪري جي چنيءَ تي اها چني ملي.

28 -B   The use of the Infinitive with لڳڻ meaning "to begin"

Their daughter started to cry.	هنن جي چوڪري روئڻ لڳي.
The blind man began to see.	انڌو ماڻهو ڏسڻ وائسڻ لڳو.
The students have started to study the 27th lesson.	شاگرد ستاويهون سبق پڙهڻ لڳا آهن.
The train departed at exactly four o'clock.	گاڏي ٺيڪ چئين بجي هلڻ لڳي.
The girls started to cook dinner early.	چوڪريون شام جو ڪاڌو جلدي پچائڻ لڳيون.
The workman has started to make my table.	مستري منهنجي ميز بنائڻ لڳو آهي.
Let's not make a lot of noise. The little girl might wake up and cry.	اسين شور نه ڪريون. شايد ننڍي چوڪري جاڳي روئڻ لڳي.

1. لڳڻ in the use illustrated here is never used alone. It must always occur with a verb in the infinitive form. In Sindhi we may not say "He began yesterday". We must say <u>what</u> he began to do.

2. When the infinitive is used with لڳڻ, it is inflected, the ending changing from –u to –a.

3. It is possible to use لڳڻ in this way in any tense, but it is more commonly used in the simple past or the present perfect tense. The idea of "began" implies an origin in the past.

4. In the future tense and some other tenses, it is more idiomatic to use the compound verb

شروع ڪرڻ with the infinitive to express the idea of beginning.

We will start studying lesson eighteen next week.	اسين ايندڙ هفتي ارڙهون سبق پڙهڻ شروع ڪنداسين.

5. لڳڻ is an intransitive verb, so it will agree with its subject in all tenses.

6. In sentence two above the word وائسڻ has no meaning of its own. It is another example of a rhyming word, and is included purely for its pleasant sound. Another example is,

They are conversing.	هو ڳالھ ٻولھ ڪن ٿا پيا.

In this case ٻولھ has a nearly synonymous meaning, but is included for its rhyming quality. Such reiteration is very common in spoken Sindhi and is found with many nouns and adjectives.

28 –C   Some Idiomatic Uses of لڳڻ

Why are/ were you so late?	توهان کي ايتري دير ڇو لڳي؟
Because the bus was so slow.	ڇاڪاڻ ت لاري تمام آهستي آئي.
How long does it take to get to the hospital?	اسپتال وڃڻ ۾ ڪيتري دير ٿي؟
It will take only fifteen minutes.	رڳو پندرهن منٽ لڳندا.
This fruit tastes very sweet.	هي ميوو تمام مٺو لڳي ٿو.
People like what children say.	ٻارن جون ڳالهيون ماڻهن کي مڻيون لڳن ٿيون.
This key doesn't fit the lock.	ڪلف ۾ هي ڪنجي نہ ٿي لڳي.
This lesson will take three days.	هن سبق تي ٽي ڏينهن لڳندا.
I like Pakistan very much.	منهنجي دل پاڪستان ۾ ڏاڍي لڳي ٿي.
Don't you like it here?	ڇا، تنهنجي دل هتي نہ ٿي لڳي؟
Are you hungry?	توهان کي بک لڳي آهي؟
Yes, I'm very hungry.	هائو مون کي ڏاڍي بک لڳي آهي.
Why is the child crying?	ٻار ڇو ٿو روئي؟
He's thirsty.	هن کي اڃ لڳي آهي.
Yesterday his house caught fire.	ڪالھ هن جي گهر کي باھ لڳي هئي.
What relationship is he to you?	هو توهان جو ڇا ٿو لڳي؟
He is my brother.	هو منهنجو ڀاءُ آهي.

In the beginning of April there will be a fair in that city.	اپريل جي شروع ۾ هن شهر ۾ ميلو لڳندو.
I am very surprised!	مون کي ڏاڍو عجب تو لڳي!
Was his father angry?	ڇا هن جي پيءُ کي ڪاوڙ لڳي هئي؟
The girl was struck on the head.	ڇوڪريءَ کي مٿي تي ڏک لڳو.

1. The verb لڳڻ is intransitive with an inherently passive meaning. Its basic meaning is "to be applied, attached, stuck, or fixed to something or someone". It cannot and should not be translated literally. All of the above sentences are very common and idiomatic ways of expressing everyday feelings and happenings. It is essential that the student learn them and be able to use them correctly.

2. In sentence three above اسپتال وڃڻ ۾ illustrates another example of the infinitive used as a noun. It may be understood as literally, "in going to the hospital, how much delay is applied?"

3. The example in asking about a relationship (sentence sixteen) is a very useful and idiomatic expression. The literal meaning is "He is fixed/applied to you as your what?"

4. لڳڻ is often used to express emotions as well as hunger and thirst. Notice that the idea rendered by the present tense in English is often expressed by the present perfect in Sindhi. Similarly where in English, we would use a simple past, the past perfect is used.

جيستائين تيستا.ين

28 –D   More Correlatives: تيستا.ين ... جيستائين (as long as, until)

As long as our guests are here we won't go.	جيستائين اسان جا مزمان هتي آهن تيستائين اسين نہ وينداسين.
As long as your mother is sick, she should take this medicine.	جيستائين اوهان جي ماءُ بيمار آهي، تيستائين هن کي هي دوا کائڻ گهرجي.
So long as we don't call him, he won't come.	جيستائين اسين هن کي سڏ نہ ڪريون تيستائين هو نہ ايندو.
Until he learns Sindhi (as long as he doesn't…) he won't feel at home here.	جيستائين هو سنڌي نہ سکي تيستائين هن جي دل هتي نہ لڳندي.

1. Both the English ideas "as long as" and "until" may be expressed in Sindhi by جيستائين with its correlative تيستا.ين. This is a bit difficult to grasp since it is not possible to translate literally the English word "until" as we use it. The idiomatic English rendering of sentence three above is "He won't come until we call him." In Sindhi the idiomatic way of expressing this is with جيستائين and a negative with the verb in the subjunctive. Thus literally we say in Sindhi, "So long as we may not call him that long he won't come". It may help in understanding this use of the negative if we remember that the "un-" in "until" is really a negative.

2. Although تيستا.ين is not usually expressed in English, and there is no real equivalent, it may not normally be omitted in Sindhi.

3. The interrogative ڪيستائين is often used to mean "How long?" as,

| How long will the guests stay? | مزمان ڪيستائين ٽڪندا؟ |

4. تيستا.ين is sometimes shortened to ايستا.ين. In this form it may be used alone, as,

| Fill the cooking pot so much. | ديڳچي ايستائين ڀريو. |

جيتوٽيڪ... تہ ڀہ (although, nevertheless)

Although the boy was wrong, (nevertheless) he didn't admit his mistake.	جيتوٽيڪ چوڪري غلطي ڪئي، تہ ڀہ هن پنهنجي غلطي نہ مڃي.
Even though it's raining, (nevertheless) I'm sure the teacher will come.	جيتوٽيڪ مينهن پوي ٿو پيو، تڏهن ڀہ مون کي پڪ آهي تہ استاد صاحب ايندو.
Although he said so, I still don't believe him.	جيتوٽيڪ هن ائين چيو تہ ڀہ مان هن جو يقين نہ ٿو ڪريان.
Although the food is very tasty, I can't eat anymore.	جيتوٽيڪ کاڌو تمام مزيدار آهي تہ ڀہ مان وڌيڪ ڪائي نہ ٿو سگهان.
Although the cloth is quite expensive, I bought it any way.	جيتوٽيڪ اهو ڪپڙو ڪافي مهانگو آهي تہ ڀہ مون خريد ڪيو.

5. To express a concessive idea (although, even though, notwithstanding, in spite of the fact that) in Sindhi we use جيتوٽيڪ in the first clause and تہ ڀہ, or less commonly تڏهن ڀہ in the second clause.

6. The correlative idea may be expressed in English by "nevertheless, still, anyway", or it may not be expressed at all. It is not usually omitted in Sindhi. As with other relative words, good Sindhi requires the correlative word to be expressed.

28 –E   The use of وٽڻ (to like), اوڌر ونڻ (to borrow); اوڌر ڏيڻ (to lend); لهڻ (to have due)

| I like mangoes. | مون کي انب وٽن ٿا. |
| I like the cold weather, but I don't think anyone likes hot weather. | مون کي سيارو وٽندو آهي، پر منهنجو خيال آهي تہ گرميءَ جي موسم ڪنهن کي ڪين وٽندي آهي. |

In Canada I like summer.	ڪينڊا ۾ مون کي اونھارو وڻي ٿو.
I like the girl but I don't like her brother.	مون کي چوڪري وڻي ٿي پر ھن جو ڀاءُ نہ ٿو وڻي.

1. We may express the idea of liking by using the verb وڻڻ. It is used impersonally with the subject in the oblique followed by کي. The verb will agree with the subject in gender and number. A more literal meaning for وڻڻ is "to be pleasing" or "to be pleased". Thus in Sindhi we are really saying, "mangoes are pleasing to me", "That girl is pleasing to me".

Borrowing is a very bad thing.	اوڌر وٺڻ تمام خراب آھي.
Giving loans isn't good either.	اوڌر ڏيڻ بہ سٺي ڳالھ ناھي.
Who did he borrow so much money from?	ھن ڪنھن کان ايترا پيسا اوڌر ورتي؟
We won't give a loan to anyone.	اسين ڪنھن کي اوڌر نہ ڏينداسين.
Please lend me the book.	مون کي ڪتاب اڌارو ڏيو.
He lent me a hundred rupees.	ھن مون کي سئو رپيو اڌارو ڏنو.

2. اوڌر is a feminine noun meaning "credit". In Sindhi when one borrows he "takes a loan/credit", اوڌر وٺڻ. To lend one "gives a loan/credit", اوڌر ڏيڻ.

3. اڌارو may be used in the same way, but it is used as an adjective or adverb meaning "on loan, lent, borrowed".

I owe the gardener ten rupees.	مالھي مون کي ڏھ رپيا لھي.
We owe the workman fifty rupees.	مستري اسان کي پنجاھ رپيا لھي.
What does she owe you?	توھين ھن کي ڇا لھو؟
She doesn't owe us anything now.	ھاڻي اسين ھن کي ڪجھ بہ نہ لھون.
But her brother owes me ten rupees.	پر مان ھن جي ڀاءُ کي رڳو ڏھ رپيا لھان.

4. The verb لھڻ means "to have due". The one to whom something is owed is the subject of the verb. The one who owes is in the oblique form followed by the postposition کي. Thus we may translate the first sentence literally as, "The gardener has ten rupees due from me".

5. The verb is used in the subjunctive where the present tense would be used in English.

28 –F The use of وَنڊ as an Intensifier, to indicate quickness

I read the letter quickly.	مون چٺي پڙهي ورتي.
The traveler drank the cold water.	مسافر ٿڌو پاڻي پي ورتو.
I'll write quickly.	مان لکي ونندس.
Do this work quickly.	هي ڪم ڪري وَنڊُ.

1. The conjunctive participle of a verb may be used with an appropriate tense of وَنڊ as an intensifier. وَنڊ is used in this way only with transitive verbs, and it indicates urgency or quickness.

2. Since وَنڊ is a transitive verb, it will agree with any stated object in tenses based on the perfect participle.

3. The perfect participle of وَنڊ is irregularly formed as ورتو or وتو.

28 –G Some Prefixes and suffixes

بي - (without); لا - (without); اڻ – (not, un-).

Of course, I didn't see it with my own eyes!	بيشڪ مون پنهنجي اکين سان نَہ ڏٺو!
There is a great deal of injustice in this world.	هن دنيا ۾ ڏاڍي بي انصافي آهي.
What can the poor thing do before (an) unjust judge?	ويچاري بي انصافي جج جي سامهون ڇا ڪري؟
This patient is completely without hope/hopeless.	هي مريض بلڪل لاعلاج آهي.
That man is illiterate/ uneducated.	اهو ماڻهو اڻپڙهيل آهي.
The stars in the sky countless.	تارا آسمان ۾ اڻ ڳڻت آهن.

1. بي -, لا-, and اڻ- are all negative prefixes. بي - (without) plus شڪ (doubt) means "without doubt, doubtless". لا - (without) plus اميد (hope) means "without hope, hopeless". اڻ- means the same as the negative prefix un- in English.

The suffix -ي to turn an adjective into a noun

2. Many adjectives may add the suffix -ي and thus become nouns. These nouns would always be feminine. You are already familiar with many of them.

sick	illness	بيماري	بيمار
hot	heat	گرمي	گرم
happy	happiness	خوشي	خوش

3. Some nouns may add the suffix ي– in order to become adjectives. Such adjectives are not inflected.

Pakistan	Pakistani	پاكستاني	پاكستان
foreign country	foreigner	پرديسي	پرديس
person	personal	شخصي	شخص

‑ڙو as a Diminutive Suffix

Put in very little pepper. Foreigners will be eating the food.	تورڙو مرچ وجهو. پرديسي ماڻهو كاڏو كائيندا.
The little girl is very sweet.	ننڍڙي چوكري تمام پياري آهي.
Give the tiny baby only boiled water.	ٻارڙي كي فقط ابريل پاڻي ڏيو.
Whose is this booklet?	هي كتابڙو كنهن جو آهي؟

4. The suffix ڙو– , ‑ڙي, may be added to nouns or adjectives as a diminutive, meaning very small, very little. The ending will be inflected according to the gender of the original verb.

Sindhi has been influenced by many languages, particularly Persian and Arabic. As a result many common Sindhi words are compounds made with prefixes and suffixes, only a few of which are given here. This is only a sampling, based mainly on words you have already had in this course. The purpose is to make the student aware of the way in which words are formed, and to help in vocabulary- building.

28 –H   Vocabulary

April	اپريل	star (m)	تارو
surprise (m)	عجب	so long as, until	جيستائين... تيستائين ايستائين
sky, heaven (m)	آسمان	blow, injury (m)	ڌڪ
on loan, credit	اڌارو	noise, disturbance (m)	شور

to loan	اڌارو ڏيڻ	person (m)	شخص
to borrow	اڌارو وٺڻ	personal	شخصي
credit, money lent or borrowed (f)	اوڌر	How long, how far?	ڪيستائين
to lend	اوڌر ڏيڻ	head (m)	مٿو
to borrow	اوڌر وٺڻ	traveler (m)	مسافر
thirst (f)	اُڃَ	to accept, obey admit	مڃڻ
hunger (f)	بک	minute (m)	منٽ
foreigner	پرديسي	to be pleasing	وڻڻ
beloved, sweet	پياري	to have due	لهڻ
remedy, cure (f)	علاج		

28–I Conversational Review

1. Practice using each of the patterns in 28-C both in conversation with your teacher and with other Sindhi friends. Substitute freely on each one so that each pattern will become natural and automatic.

2. With your teacher make up sentences using words from the following list of subjects and verbs. End each sentence with a form of لڳڻ.

Subjects: ڇوڪريون، منهنجو پاءُ، تون،
زال، مان، اسين، ڇوڪرا، توهين،
ماني کائڻ، ڪلڻ، روئڻ،

Verbs: ڪتاب پڙهڻ، شور ڪرڻ، گاريون ڏيڻ،
در تي کڙڪائڻ، يوءُ ٽيٽ

For example: ڇوڪريون ڪلڻ لڳيون.

3. Complete the following sentences from the list of verbs given below.

جيتوٽيڪ مان .... تہ ہ.............

Verbs:

جيستائين اهو ماٿهو...... تيستائين ......

اوڏر وڃُ، اوڏر ڍيڻ

مچڻ، لهٽڻ، وڃڻ، پنڌ ڪرڻ

Substitute freely from recently acquired nouns and verbs.

4. Practice listening for rhyming words and diminutive and other suffixes and prefixes. Make note of the ones you hear commonly and learn to use them as your Sindhi friends use them.

5. Make up sentences with your teacher using the following words:

بيمار، بيماري، گرم، گرمي

خوش، خوشي، غلط، غلطي

پاڪستان، پاڪستاني

پرديس، پرديسي، شخص، شخصي

REVIEW FOUR

Having come to this final review lesson, it is a good time to look back and see how far you have come since beginning with Lesson 1 of this course. You have seen a great deal of progress in your ability to understand and to communicate in your daily work and life with the Sindhis around you. Review the areas mentioned in the course Introduction. The important elements to be acquired in your study of Sindhi were:

i) pronunciation, ii) structure, iii) vocabulary, iv) fluency, and v) culture.

a) The sounds of Sindhi are still basic. If you are still having any problems with difficult sounds, it is essential that you continue to work on these. Even though you are coming to the end of this basic course, you have not stopped learning Sindhi! You have only laid the foundation for your continued study and learning, whether formal or informal.

b) In this final review lesson go back over the basic patterns of Lesson 23-28. Some of these are complicated, and you should drill them over with a variety of words, using those on the following pages, and the previous word lists following lessons, 8, 16, and 22. It is necessary to repeat/drill a pattern so many times, while varying the subject, object, adjectives, time words, verb tenses, etc. that it will be natural to you to say it correctly. This cannot be emphasized too much.

c) You have been encouraged throughout this course to begin building your own vocabulary to meet your particular needs. The words included in the course are limited. You need to plan to systematically build your vocabulary so as to learn what you need for your present and future needs. Words have to be put into context if you are to understand them fully, and to be able to use them correctly. When you write down a new word, make the effort to use it in a number of sentences and contexts so that you know how use it correctly.

The same holds true of reviewing the words on the following pages. If you feel the need of this type of review, please do not use them as words in isolation for which you can give an English meaning. Put them into sentences with your teacher. In this way he can be sure that you are using them correctly as to gender, if you can use the verbs correctly in the past tenses, if you know which postposition to use, etc.

d) As you use these words in sentences, be sure that you are imitating Sindhi patterns of intonation. Proper pronunciation, good speed and rhythm within a correct sentence are all elements that make up fluency.

e) During your year or more in Sindh, you have come along way in your understanding of how to behave, what to do in many situations, and what not to do. This understanding has grown as your language proficiency has developed. You will continue to learn in the area of culture as long as you are in Sindh.

Adjectives		Numbers (cont)		Adverbs (cont)	
durust$^{u;}$ (23)	درست	uR̃aHaTh^i (24)	اٺهت	zIAdAh^a (26)	زيادھ
rAzI (23)	راضي	navAnavE (24)	نوانوي	HIara (27)	هينئر
KatarnAk^u (23)	خطرناڪ	**Postpositions**		**Nouns – people**	
Kub (23)	خُب	(jE) zarI'E (24)	(جي) ذريعي	tAlib ilm (23)	طالب علم
bbuDhO (24)	ٻڍو	(jE) lAiq (24)	(جي) لائق	kũvAr (23)	ڪنوار
kurARO (24)	ڪراڙو	(jE) m'Arafat (24)	(جي) معرفت	ghOT^u (23)	گھوٽ
radI (25)	ردي	(jE) vasIlE (24)	(جي) وسيلي	javAn (24)	جوان
udhArO (28)	اڌارو			chAchO (24)	چاچو
pIArI (28)	پياري	**Relative-Correlatives**		naojavAn (24)	نوجوان
SaKsI (28)	شخصي	jEstAĩ .... tEstAĩ (28)	جيستائين تيستائين	chAchI (25)	چاچي
pardEsI (28)	پرديسي	jEtOR̃Ek.... ta bi (28)	جيتوٽيڪتہ بہ	ddAddO (26)	ڏاڏو
AR̃apaRHEL (28)	اٽپڙهيل	**Question Words**		ddAddI (26)	ڏاڏي
Numbers		kEstAĩ (28)	ڪيستائين	nAnO (26)	نانو
uR̃AsI (24)	اٺاسي	**Conjunctions**		nAnI (26)	ناني
uR̃AnavE (24)	اٺانوي	matã (23)	متان	SaKs (28)	شخص
uR̃aTIh^a (24)	اٺتيھ	**Adverbs**		musAfir^u (28)	مسافر
uR̃avanjAH^u (24)	اٺونجاھ	cAk^u (24)	چاڪ	**Nouns - places**	
uR̃avIH^a (24)	اوٺيھ	umarbhar^i (24)	عمر ڀر	kOETA (23)	ڪوئيٽا
uR̃EtAlIH^a (24)	اٺيتاليھ	aÑA, aÑA tAĩ (25)	اڃا، اڃا تائين	bOrcIKAnO (26)	بورچي خانو
uR̃aHatar^i (24)	اٺهتر			dukAn^u (26)	دڪان

Nouns abstract			Nouns abstract		(cont)	Other Nouns		(cont)
uÑa	(23)	أڃَ	maoq'O	(25)	موقعو	karikEt^i	(25)	ڪرڪيٽ
bhaO	(23)	ڀَوُ	zarUrat^a	(26)	ضرورت	basI	(26)	بسي
pak^a	(23)	پڪ	fAidO	(26)	فائدو	pIAlO	(26)	پيالو
rasam^u	(23)	رسم	kUr^u	(27)	ڪوڙ	cÃHidAnI	(26)	ڇانھ داني
sac^u	(23)	سچ	ajab^u	(28)	عجب	chil^u	(26)	ڇل
Sak^u	(23)	شڪ	bukh^a	(28)	بک	culHO	(26)	چلھو
faraz^u	(23)	فرض	SOr^u	(28)	شور	camcO	(26)	چمچو
yaqIn^u	(23)	يقين	**Other Nouns**			chUrI	(26)	ڇري
natIjO	(23)	نتيجو	bijilI	(23)	بجلي	dEgg^i dEg^i	(26)	ديگ ديگ
Adat^a	(24)	عادت	bandObast^u	(23)	بندوبست	dEggcI dEgcI	(26)	ديگچي ديگچي
badkArI	(24)	بدڪاري	jhuR^u	(23)	جھڙ	ddOI	(26)	ڊوئي
bbuDhApI	(24)	ٻڊاپي	cAndI	(23)	چاندي	sarAHI	(26)	صراحي
janam^u	(24)	جنم	zEvar^u	(23)	زيور	zEtUn	(26)	زيتون
Kidmat^a	(24)	خدمت	sOn^u	(23)	سون	qaom^a	(26)	قوم
izat^a	(24)	عزت	nikAH^u	(23)	نڪاحُ	kaRAHI	(26)	ڪڙاهي
umar^i	(24)	عمر	mUnDI	(23)	منڊي	kaRAHO	(26)	ڪڙاهو
safArIS^i	(24)	سفارش	mIrc^a	(23)	مرچ	kAnTO	(26)	ڪانٽو
mu'AfI	(24)	معافي	InjIl^u	(24)	انجيل	kEvI	(26)	ڪيوي
mOt^u	(24)	موت	kAr^i	(24)	ڪار	maT^u	(26)	مٽ
natIjO	(24)	نتيجو	nambar^u	(24)	نمبر	maTkO	(26)	مٽڪو
nanDhapIR̃^{u}	(24)	ننڊيپڙ	taR^u	(25)	تڙ	jabal^u	(26)	جبل

Other Nouns	(cont)		Simple Verbs			Simple Verbs		(cont)
kOH^u	(26)	کوہُ	vaggaR̃^{u}	(23)	وَڳٹ	uchalAiR̃^{u}	(26)	اُچلائٹ
aozAr^u	(27)	اوزار	cukaR̃^{u}	(23)	چُڪٹ	taraR̃u	(26)	ترٹ
laRAI	(27)	لڑائي	juRaR̃^{u}	(24)	جڙٹ	randhaR̃^{u}	(26)	رنڌٹ
aprEl	(28)	اپريل	suÑARaR̃^{u} (24)		سڄاڙٹ	chilaR̃^{u}	(26)	چلٹ
AsmAn^u	(28)	آسمانُ	pinaR̃^{u}	(25)	پنٹ	ggAiR̃^{u}	(26)	ڳائٹ
Odhar^i	(28)	اوڌر	jalAiR̃^{u}	(25)	جلائٹ	ggaraR̃^{u}	(26)	ڳرٹ
ilAj^a	(28)	علاج	jjAR̃aR̃^{u}	(25)	ڄاڙٹ	pakiRaR̃^{u}	(27)	پڪڙٹ
tArO	(28)	تارو	DijjaR̃^{u}	(25)	ڏڄٹ	gaddijaR̃^{u}	(27)	گڏجٹ
dhak^u	(28)	ڍڪ	DukaR̃^{u}	(25)	ڏڪٹ	maÑaR̃^{u}	(28)	مڃٹ
mathO	(28)	متو	rOaR^u	(25)	روئٹ	vaR̃aR̃^{u}	(28)	وڙٹ
minT^u	(28)	منٽ	khaRkAiR̃^{u}	(25)	کڙڪائٹ	laHaR̃aR̃^{u}	(28)	لهٹٹ
			ggaR̃aR̃^{u}	(25)	ڳڻٹ			

Compound Verbs			Compound Verbs		(cont)
bandObast karaR̃^{u}	(23)	بندوبست ڪرٹ	KuS thIaR̃^{u}	(27)	خوش ٿيٹ
bhaO thIaR̃^{u}	(23)	ڀوُ ٿيٹ	KuS karaR̃^{u}	(27)	خوش ڪرٹ
yakIn karaR̃^{u}	(24)	يقين ڪرٹ	GalatI thIaR̃^{u}	(27)	غلطي ٿيٹ
taR^u karaR̃^{u}	(25)	تڙ ڪرٹ	GalatI karaR̃^{u}	(27)	غلطي ڪرٹ
Hath^a milAiR̃^{u}	(25)	هٿ ملائٹ	mu'Af thIaR̃^{u}	(27)	معاف ٿيٹ
phiTI karaR̃u	(26)	ڦٽي ڪرٹ	mu'Af karaR̃^{u}	(27)	معاف ڪرٹ
ThIk^u thIaR̃^{u}	(26)	ٺيڪ ٿيٹ	udhArO ddIaR̃^{u}	(28)	اڌارو ڏيٹ
ThIk^u karaR̃^{u} (26)		ٺيڪ ڪرٹ	udhArO vaThaR̃^{u}	(28)	اڌارو وٺٹ

paida thIa $\tilde{R}^u$ (27)	پیدا تیݨ	Odhar^i ddIa $\tilde{R}^u$ (28)	اودّر ڈیݨ
paidA kara $\tilde{R}^u$ (27)	پیدا کرݨ	Odhar^i vaTha $\tilde{R}^u$ (28)	اودّر وٹݨ
pand^u kara $\tilde{R}^u$ (27)	پنڈ کرݨ		

APPENDIX I – Summary of the Verb Forms used in this course

This summary will be useful for review of the verbs, and as a basis for practicing substitutions with a variety of other verbs, in every possible form, changing the tense, subject, using with objects, etc. The verb likhaR̃ᵘ is used because it is completely regular. These are not complete sentences, but only the verb, in most cases with the third person singular subject, HU. They are grouped according to the form of the verb which is the basis of the tense. Following each verb is the number of the lesson and page where it is first introduced and explained.

I. Based on the Root

1.	Write 10/107 likhᵘ, likhO		لِکُ، لِکو
2.	Please write 10/107, 14/181 likhO, likhijO, likhijÃi		لِکو، لِکجو، لکجانءِ
3.	He writes 10/111 HU likhE thO		هو لِکي ٿو.
4.	He may write 11/131 Let him write HU likhE		هو لِکي
5.	If he writes, I may write 11/131 JekaddaHĨ HU likhE ta mÃ likhÃ		جيڪڏهن هو لِکي تہ مان لکان
6.	It is necessary that he write 11/131 zarUrI AHE ta HU likhE		ضروري آهي تہ هو لِکي
7.	He is writing (in the act of) 16/204 HU likhE thO payO		هو لِکي ٿو پيو
8.	He is writing (while sitting) 16/205 HU vEThO likhE		هو ويٺو لِکي
9.	He is writing (while standing) 16/205 HU bIThO likhE		هو بيٺو لِکي
10.	If he had written, I would not have written 24/313 JekaddaHĨ HU likhE Ha ta mÃ na likhÃ HA		جيڪڏهن هو لِکي ها تہ مان نہ لکان ها
11.	It is written 27/347 likhijE thO		لکجي ٿو

II. Based on the Conjunctive Participle

12.	Having written 16/200 likhI		لِکي
13.	He wrote before going 16/201 He wrote and went away HU likhI HalIO vIO		هو لِکي هليو ويو
14.	He is writing (in the act of 16/203 HU likhI raHIO AHE		هو لِکي رهيو آهي
15.	He was in the act of writing 19/242 HU likhI raHIO HO		هو لِکي رهيو هو
16.	He is able to write 16/207 HU likhI saghE thO		هو لِکي سگهي ٿو
17.	He has already written 23/303 He has finished writing HU likhI cukO AHE		هو لِکي چُڪو آهي

III. Based on the Imperfect Participle

18.	He writes (regularly, habitually) 12/147 HU likhandO AHE		هو لکندو آهي
19.	He used to write 14/178 HU likhandO HO		هو لکندو هو
20.	He will write 14/175 HU likhandO		هو لکندو
21.	He keeps on writing 26/328 HU likhandO raHandO AHE		هو لکندو رهندو آهي
22.	He kept on writing 26/328 HU likhandO raHIO		هو لکندو رهيو
23.	Keep on writing 26/328 likhandA raHO		لکندا رهو
24.	He keeps on writing 26/329 HU likhandO vaÑE thO HU likhandO acE thO		هو لکندو وڃي ٿو هو لکندو اچي ٿو
25.	He must be writing 23/298 HU likhandO HUndO		هو لکندو هوندو
26.	He may/ might be writing 23/301 HU likhandO HujE		هو لکندو هجي
27.	If he writes, I will write 24/313 jEkaddHĪ HU likhandO ta mĀ likhandus		جيڪڏهن هو لکندو تہ مان لکندس

28.	He got tired from writing continuously 25/318 HU likhandE likhandE thakajI payO		هو لكندي لكندي ٿڪجي پيو
29.	I saw him writing 25/318 mŨ Huna khE likhandE ddiThO		مون هن کي لکندي ڏٺو
30.	He fell asleep while writing 25/319 HU likhandE vaqt sumHI payO		هو لکندي وقت سمهي پيو
31.	As soon as he wrote, he left 25/320 likhandE –I HU HalIO vIO		لکندي ئي هو هليو ويو
32.	Don't talk to the one who is writing 25/321 likhandaRª sÃ na ggAlHAIO		لکندڙ سان نه ڳالهايو

IV. Based on the Perfect Participle

33.	He wrote 17/222 Huna likhIO		هن لِکيو
34.	He has written 18/235 Huna likhIO AHE		هن لکيو آهي
35.	He was writing (in the act of) 19/243 Huna likhIO paE		هن لکيو پئي
36.	He was (sitting) writing 19/244 Huna vEThE likhIO		هن ويٺي لکيو
37.	He was (standing) writing 19/244 Huna bIThE likhIO		هن بيٺي لکيو
38.	He got it written (caused it to be) 19/246 Huna likhAIO		هن لکايو
39.	He had written 21/275 Huna likhIO HO		هن لکيو هو
40.	He must/might have written 23/299 Huna likhIO HundO		هن لکيو هوندو
41.	Perhaps he may have written 23/301 SAyad Huna likhIO HujE		شايد هن لکيو هجي
42.	If he writes, we'll write, too 24/312 JekaddaHĨ Huna likhIO ta asĨ bi likhandAsĨ		جيڪڏهن هن لکيو ته اسين به لکنداسين
43.	If he wrote, I didn't receive it 24/312 jEkaddaHĨ Huna likhIO HO ta mŨ khE na milIO		جيڪڏهن هن لکيو هو ته مون کي نه مليو

V. Based on the Infinitive

44.	He needs to write 12/153 Huna khE likha R̃ª khapE		هن کي لکڻ کپي
45.	He ought to write 14/191 Huna khE likha R̃ᵘ ghurjE		هن کي لکڻ گهرجي
46.	He is about to write 15/190,191 HU likha R̃ª varO AHE		هو لکڻ وارو آهي
47.	HU likha R̃ª tE AHE.		هو لکڻ تي آهي
48.	Let him write 22/285 Huna khE likha R̃ᵘ ddEO		هن کي لکڻ ڏيو
49.	He told me to write 22/289 Huna mŨ khE likha R̃a lAi cayO		هن مون کي لکڻ لاءِ چيو
50.	He knows how to write 25/321 Huna khE likha R̃ᵘ acE thO		هن کي لکڻ اچي ٿو
51.	HU likha R̃ᵘ jja R̃E thO		هو لکڻ ڄاڻي ٿو
52.	He wants to write 25/321 HU likha R̃ᵘ cAHE thO		هو لکڻ چاهي ٿو
53.	He learns how to write 25/324 HU likha R̃ᵘ sikhE thO		هو لکڻ سکي ٿو
54.	He likes to write 28/357 Huna khE likha R̃ᵘ va R̃E thO		هن کي لکڻ وڻي ٿو
55.	He began to write 28/352 HU likha R̃ª laggO		هو لکڻ لڳو
56.	He has to write 15/193 Huna khE likha R̃O AHE		هن کي لکڻو آهي
57.	He has to write 15/193 Huna khE likha R̃O pavE thO		هن کي لکڻو پوي ٿو

Appendix 2

Tense Paradigms:

6-D The present tense of the verb HuaR̃ᵘ (to be)

Person	Singular		Plural	
1st	(AŨ) AHIÃ (I am)	آءٌ آهيان	(asĨ) AHIŨ (We are)	(اسين) آهيون
2nd	(tŨ) AHĨ (You are)	(تُون) آهين	(tavHĨ) AHIO (You are)	(توهين) آهيو
3rd	(HU) AHE (He/she/it is)	(هُو) آهي	(HU) AHin (They are)	(هُو) آهِن

10-D The formation of the present tense

Infinitive: acaR̃ᵘ	root: acᵘ	اچ	اچُ
mÃ acÃ thO/thI I come	asĨ acŨ thA/thIŨ We come	مان اچان ٿو/ٿي	اسين اچون ٿا/ٿيون
tŨ acĨ thO/thI You come (sing.)	tavHĨ acO thA/thIŨ You come (pl.)	تون اچين ٿو/ٿي	توهين اچو ٿا/ٿيون
HU acE thO/thI He comes	HU acan thA/thIŨ They come	هو اچي ٿو/ٿي	اُهي اچن ٿا/ٿيون
Infinitive: khOlaR̃ᵘ	Root: khOlⁱ	کول	کولُ
mÃ khOlIÃ thO/thI I open	asĨ khOlIŨ thA/thIŨ We open	مان کوليان ٿو/ٿي	اسين کوليون ٿا/ٿيون
tŨ khOlĨ thO/thI You open	tavHĨ khOlIO thA/thIŨ You open	تون کولين ٿو/ٿي	توهين کوليو ٿا/ٿيون
HU khOlE thO/thI He opens	HU khOlin thA/thIŨ They open	هو کولي ٿو/ٿي	هو کولن ٿا/ٿيون

11-F The formation of the subjunctive tense

mÃ vaÑÃ I may go	asĪ vaÑU we may go	اسين وڃون	مان وڃان
tŨ vaÑĪ you may go	tavHĪ vaÑO you may go	توهين وڃو	تون وڃين
HU vaÑE He may go	HU vaÑan They may go	هو وڃن	هو وڃي
mÃ mOkilIÃ I may send	asĪ mOkilIŨ We may send	اسين موڪليون	مان موڪليان
tŨ mOkilĪ you may send	tavHĪ mOkilIO You may send	توهين موڪليو	تون موڪلين
HU mOkilE He may send	HU mOkilIan They may send	هو موڪلين	هو موڪلي

12-C The formation of the present habitual tense

tarsaR̃ᵘ root: tars(u)-plus -andO with the present tense of HuaR̃ᵘ (to be)

mÃ tarsandO AHIÃ I wait	asĪ tarsandA AI IIŨ We wait	اسين ترسندا آهيون	مان ترسندو آهيان
tŨ tarsandO AHĪ You wait	avHĪ tarsandA AHIO you wait	اوهين ترسندا آهيو	تون ترسندو آهين
HU tarsandO AHE He waits	HU tarsandA AHin They wait	هو ترسندا آهن.	هو ترسندو آهي

khOlaR̃ᵘ root: khOl (i) – plus – IndO with the present tense of HuaR̃ᵘ (to be)

mÃ khOlIndO AHIÃ I open	asĪ khOlIndA AHIŨ We open	اسين ڪوليندا آهيون	مان ڪوليندو آهيان
tŨ khOlIndO AHĪ You open	avHĪ khOlIndA AHIO You open	اوهين ڪوليندا آهيو	تون ڪوليندو آهين
HU khOlIndO AHE He opens	HU khOlIndA AHin They open	هو ڪوليندا آهن	هو ڪوليندو آهي

13-E The past tense of the verb Hua R̃ ᵘ (to be)

The past tense of Hua R̃ᵘ has separate masculine and feminine forms:

	Masculine	Feminine	Feminine	Masculine
Sing:	mÃ HOs I was	mÃ HuIas	مان هُيَس	مان هوس
	tŨ HuI you were	tŨ HuIᵃ	تون هُئِينَ	تون هُئِين
	HU HO, HuIO he was	HUᵃ HuI she was	هُوَءَ هئي	هُو هو، هيو
Pl:	asĨ HuAsĨ or, HuAsŨ we were	asĨ HuIŨsĨ	اسين هيونسين	اسين هئاسين
	tavHĨ HuA you were	tavHĨ HuIŨ	توهين هُيُون	توهين هئا
	HU HuA they were	HU HuIŨ	هو هُيُون	هو هُئا

14-C The Formation of the Simple Future Tense

tarsa R̃ᵘ   (tarsᵘ-)   Imperfect participle: tarsand- plus personal endings

MASCULINE		مذكر	
Singular	Plural	جمع	واحد
mÃ tarsandus I shall wait	asĨ tarsandAsĨ (or, tarsandAsŨ) we shall wait	اسين ترسنداسين	مان ترسندس
tŨ tarsandẼ you will wait	tavHĨ tarsandA You will wait	توهين ترسندا	تون ترسندين
HU tarsandO He will wait	HU tarsandA They will wait	هو ترسندا	هو ترسندو

FEMININE		مؤنث	
Singular	Plural	جمع	واحد
mÃ tarsandIas I shall wait	asĨ tarsandIŨsĨ we shall wait	اسين ترسنديونسين	مان ترسنديس
tŨ tarsandĨᵃ You will wait	tavHĨ tarsandIŨ You will wait	توهين ترسنديون.	تون ترسندينءَ
HUᵃ tarsandI She will wait	HU tarsandIŨ They will wait	هو ترسنديون	هو ترسندي

14 -E The Formation of the past Habitual Tense

kholaR̃ᵘ   (kholⁱ-)   Imperfect participle: khOlindO/I/A/IŨ plus the past tense of HuaR̃ᵘ (to be)

MASCULINE		مذكر	
Singular	Plural	جمع	واحد
mÃ khOlindO HOs I used to open	asĨ khOlindA HuAsĨ We used to open	اسين کوليندا ہئاسين	مان کوليندوہوس
tŨ khOlindO HuĨ You used to open	tavHĨ khOlindA HuA You used to open	توہين کوليندا ہئا	تون کوليندو ہئين
HU khOlindO HO He used to open	HU khOlindA HuA They used to open	ہو کوليندا ہئا	ہو کوليندو ہو
FEMININE		مؤنث	
mÃ khOlindI HuIas I used to open	asĨ khOlindIŨ HuIŨsĨ We used to open	اسين کوليندیون ہيوسين	مان کوليندي ہيس
tŨ khOlindI HuĨᵃ You used to open	tavHĨ khOlindIŨ HuIŨ You used to open	توہين کوليندیون ہيون	تون کوليندي ہئينءَ
HUᵃ khOlindI HuI She used to open	HU khOlindIŨ HuIŨ They used to open	ہو کوليندیون ہئي	ہوءَ کوليندي ہئي

16 -C The Formation of the Present Continuous Tense

The use of raHIO plus the conjunctive participle.

Masculine		مذكر	
Singular	Plural	جمع	واحد
mÃ karE raHIO AHIÃ I am doing (in the act of, now)	asĨ karE raHIA AHĨU We are doing	اَسين کري رہيا آہيون.	مان کري رہيو آہيان.
tŨ karE raHIO AHĨ Your are doing	tavHĨ karE raHIA AHIO You are doing	توہين کري رہيا آہيو.	تون کري رہيو آہين.
HU karE raHIO AHE He is doing	UHE karE raHIA AHin They are doing	اہي کَري رہيا آہن.	هُو کَري رہيو آهي.

Feminine		مؤنث	
mÃ karE raHI AHIÃ I am doing	asĨ karE raHIŨ AHĨU We are doing	آسين ڪري رهيون آهيون.	مان ڪري رهي آهيان.
tŨ karE raHI AHĨ Your are doing	tavHĨ karE raHIŨ AHIO You are doing	توهين ڪري رهيون آهيو.	تُون ڪري رهي آهين.
HU karE raHI AHE She is doing	UHE karE raHIŨ AHin They are doing	اُهي ڪري رهيون آهن.	هُو ڪري رهي آهي.

17-C   The Simple Past Tense of Intransitive Verbs

Masculine		مذڪر	
Singular	Plural	جمع	واحد
mÃ raHIus I lived	asĨ raHIAsĨ (raHIAsŨ) We lived	آسين رهياسين	مان رَهيس
tŨ raHĨ^a You lived	avHĨ raHIA You lived	اوهين رَهيا	تُون رَهِينَ
HU raHIO He lived	UHE raHIA They lived	اُهي رَهيا	هُو رهيو

Feminine		مؤنث	
Singular	Plural	جمع	واحد
mÃ raHIasⁱ I lived	asĨ raHIŨsĨ We lived	آسين رَهيونسين	مان رَهيس
tŨ raHI^a You lived	avHĨ raHIŨ You lived	اوهين رَهيون	تُون رَهِينءَ
HU^a raHI She lived	UHE raHIŨ They lived	اُهي رَهيون	هُو رهي

17-E   The Simple Past Tense of Transitive Verbs

mŨ) I)		likhIO wrote	asÃ We		likhIO wrote	آسان	مون
tO) You)			avHÃ You			توهان	تو
Huna) He/She)			Hunan They			هُنن	هُنَ

18 –E The Present Perfect Tense of Intransitive Verbs

Masculine		مذكر	
Singular	Plural	جمع	واحد
mÃ AIO AHIÃ I have come	asĨ AIA AHIŨ We have come	اسين آيا آهيون	مان آيو آهيان
tŨ AIO AHĨ You have come	tavHĨ AIA AHIO You have come	توهين آيا آهيو	تون آيو آهين
HU AIO AHE He has come	UHE AIA AHin They have come	اُهي آيا آهن	هو آيو آهي

Feminine		مؤنث	
Singular	Plural	جمع	واحد
mÃ AI AHIÃ I have come	asĨ AIŨ AHIŨ We have come	اسين آيون آهيون	مان آئي آهيان
tŨ AI AHĨ You have come	tavHĨ AIŨ AHIO You have come	توهين آيون آهيون	تون آئي آهين
HUª AI AHE She has come	UHE AIŨ AHin They have come	اُهي آيون آهن	هوءَ آئي آهي

18 –F The Present Perfect Tense of Transitive Verbs

Masculine & Feminine				مذكر ۽ مؤنث	
Singular		Plural		جمع	واحد
mŨ I	likhIO AHE	asÃ We	likhIO AHE	اسان	مون
tO You		tavHÃ You		توهان	تو
Huna He		Hunan They		هنن	هن
				لکيو آهي	لکيو آهي

19 –C The Present Continuous Tense Transitive & Intransitive Verbs.

a) With the conjunctive principle plus raHa R̃ᵘ

Masculine		مذكر	
Singular	Plural	جمع	واحد
mÃ karE raHIO HOs I was doing	asĨ karE raHIA HuAsĨ / HuAsŨ We were doing	اسين كري رهيا هئاسين / هئاسون	مان كري رهيو هوس
tŨ karE raHIO HUĨ You were doing	tavHĨ karE raHIA HuA You were doing	توهين كري رهيا هئا	تون كري رهيو هئين
HU karE raHIO HO He was doing	UHE karE raHIA HuA They were doing	اُهي كري رهيا هئا	هو كري رهيو هو

Feminine		مؤنث	
Singular	Plural	جمع	واحد
mÃ karE raHI HuIasᵃ I was doing	asĨ karE raHIŨ HuIŨsĨ We were doing	اسين كري رهيون هيون سين	مان كري رهي هيس
tŨ karE raHI HuĨᵃ You were doing	tavHĨ karE raHIŨ HuIŨ You were doing	توهين كري رهيون هيون	تون كري رهي هئين
HUᵃ karE raHI HuI She was doing	UHE karE raHIŨ HuIŨ They were doing	اُهي كري رهيون هيون	هوء كري رهي هئي

21 –C The formation of the Past Perfect Tense.

Intransitive Verbs.

Singular	Plural	جمع	واحد
Masculine		مذكر	
mÃ HalIO HOs I had walked	asĨ HalIA HuAsĨ / HuAsŨ We had walked	اسين هليا هئا سين / هئا سون	مان هليو هوس
tŨ HalIO HuĨ You had walked	tavHĨ HalIA HuA You had walked	توهين هليا هئا	تون هليو هئين
HU HalIO HO / HuIO He had walked	UHE HalIA HuA They had walked	أهي هليا هئا	هُو هليو هو / هيو
Feminine		مؤنث	
mÃ HalI HuIas I had walked	asĨ HalIŨ HuIŨsĨ We had walked	اسين هَليُون هُيُونسين	مان هلي هُيَس
tŨ HalI HuĨa You had walked	tavHĨ HalIŨ HuIŨ You had walked	توهين هليون هيون	تون هلي هُئين
HUa HalI HuI She had walked	UHE HalIŨ HuIŨ They had walked	أهي هليُون هُيون	هُوَ هلي هُئي

Transitive Verbs.

Singular		Plural		جمع		واحد	
mŨ I	likhIO HO had written	asÃ We	likhIO HO had written	اسين	لكيو هو	مون	لكيو هو
tO You		tavHÃ You		توهان		تون	
Huna He / she		Hunan They		هنن		هن	

Appendix Three Combined Vocabulary List/

Alif – آ ا

ubharaR̃ᵘ (14)	ايرڙ	acaR̃ᵘ (10)	اچڻُ	AsmAnᵘ (28)	آسمانُ
uthAraR̃ᵘ (19)	اٹارڻُ	achO (7)	اچو	asI (12)	اسي
uthaR̃ᵘ (14)	اٹڻُ	uchalAiR̃ᵘ (26)	اچلائڻُ	asĨ (6)	اسين
aTkal (13)	اتڪل	aKbArᵃ (8)	اخبار	afsOs (m) (9)	افسوس
aThᵃ (6)	اٺ	iKlAqᵃ (m.pl) (17)	اخلاق	akElO (13)	اڪيلو
uThᵘ (5)	اٺ	adhᵘ (13)	اڌُ	aghᵘ (m) (13)	اڳُھ
aThAsI (22)	اٺاسي	udhArO (28)	اڌارو	aggitE (19)	اڳِتي
aThAnavE (22)	اٺانوي	udhArO ddIaR̃ᵘ (28)	اڌارو ڏيڻ	aggᵘm̃Ẽ (16)	اڳ مِ
aThAvIha (22)	اٺاويھَ	udhArO vaThaR̃ᵘ (28)	اڌارو وٺڻُ	(jE) aggIÃ (8)	(جي) اڳيان
aThaTIha (22)	اٺٽيھَ	aDhAI (13)	اڍائي	ag̃ArO (m) (15)	اڳارو
aThavanjAHᵘ(22)	اٺونجاھُ	uddAmaR̃ᵘ (12)	اڏامڻ	asalAm 'alEkum (9)	السلام عليكم
aThaHatarⁱ (22)	اٺھترِ	arAm karaR̃ᵘ (11)	آرام ڪرڻ	AlO (16)	آلو
aThaHaThⁱ (22)	اٺھٺِ	arabA (f) (15)	اربع	imtIHAn (m) (15)	امتحانُ
aThEtAlIha (22)	اٺيتاليھَ	araRaHã (11)	اررھن	imtIHAn ddIaR̃ᵘ (15)	امتحان ڏيڻ
aprEl (28)	اپريل	usᵃ (f) (16)	اسَ	imtIHAn vaThaR̃ᵘ (15)	امتحان وٺڻ
ijAzatᵃ (f) (11)	اجازت	ustAdᵘ (4)	استاد	umIdᵃ (f) (9)	اميد
ajjᵘ (10)	اج	istrI karaR̃ᵘ (12)	استري ڪرڻ	amIrᵘ (18)	اَميرُ
ajjᵘ kAlHᵃ (11)	اڃڪلھ	istimAl karaR̃ᵘ (13)	استعمال ڪرڻ	ambᵘ (m) (11)	انب
uÑa (23)	اُڃ	isTESan (f) (18)	اسٽيشڻ	InjIlᵘ (24)	انجيل
aÑA, aÑA taĨ (25)	اڃا، اڃا تائين	ispatAlᵃ (8)	اسپتال	andar (16)	اندر
Acarᵘ (m) (15)	آچر	iskUlᵘ (8)	اسڪول	(jE) andar (8)	(جي) اندر

Appendix Three Combined Vocabulary List/ 72

andhO (16)	انڌو	Odhar^j ddIa$\tilde{R}^u$ (28)	اوڌر ڏيڙ	EddO (20)	ايڏو
u$\tilde{R}$AsI (24)	اٺاسي	Odhar^j vaTha$\tilde{R}^u$ (28)	اوڌر وٺڙ	EkAsI (14)	ايڪاسي
u$\tilde{R}$AnavE (24)	اٺانوي	aozAr^u (27)	اوزار	EkAnavE (14)	ايڪانوي
u$\tilde{R}$aTIh^a (24)	اٺتيہ	UnHArO (m) (12)	اونھارو	EkaTIHa (14)	ايڪتيہ
A$\tilde{R}$apaRHEL (28)	اٽپڙھيل	avHĨ (6)	اوھين	EkavanjAH^u 14	ايڪونجاھ
a$\tilde{R}$a$\tilde{R}^u$ (12)	آٽڙ	aHaRO (20)	اھڙو	EkavIHa, EkIha (14)	ايڪويہ ايڪيہ
u$\tilde{R}$avanjAH^u (24)	اٽونجاھ	AHistE (15)	آھستي	EkaHatar^j (14)	ايڪھتر
u$\tilde{R}$avIHa (11, 24)	اٽويہ	iHO/iHA (4/5)	اِھو/ اِھا	EkaHaTh^i (14)	ايڪھٺ
u$\tilde{R}$aHatar^j (24)	اٽھتر	uHO/uHA (4/5)	اُھو/اُھا	EkEtAlIHa (14)	ايڪيتاليہ
u$\tilde{R}$aHaTh^i (24)	اٽھٺ	iHE (4/5)	اِھي	ImAn^u (m) (22)	ايمائن
u$\tilde{R}$EtAlIH^a (24)	اٽيتاليہ	uHE (4/5)	اُھي	IndaR^a (14)	ايندڙ
UcO (15)	اوچو	AŨ (6)	آءٌ	Iã (20)	اِيئن
Odhar^j (28)	اوڌر	EtrO (20)	ايترو		

b - ب

bi, b^u (6)	بِہ	badiKlAq^a (18)	بداخلاق	bukh^a (28)	بک
bAzAr^j (8)	بازار	badiklAqI (f) (17)	بداخلاقي	bagI (f) (21)	بڳي
bAqI (13)	باقي	badkArI (24)	بدڪاري	balki (18)	بلڪ
bAlTI (8)	بالٽي	(jE) badarĂ (18)	(جي) بدران	bilkul (9)	بلڪل
bAH^i (f) (14, 19)	باھِ	(jE) barAbar^j (18)	(جي) برابر	band kara$\tilde{R}^u$ (11)	بند ڪرڻ
batI (5)	بتي	(jE) bariKlAf (18)	(جي) برخلاف	bandObast^u (23)	بندوبست
bijilI (23)	بجلي	basI (26)	بسي	bandObast kara$\tilde{R}^u$ (23)	بندوبست ڪرڻ
baKSiS (f) (18)	بخشِش	basar^u (m) (11)	بصر	ba$\tilde{R}$Ai$\tilde{R}^u$ (22)	بٽائڻ

Appendix Three Combined Vocabulary List/ 73

bOrcI	(6)	بورچي	bayAn karaR̃ᵘ (21)		بيان كرڻ	bImArᵘ	(8)		بيمار
bOrcIKAnO (26)		بورچي خانو	bIThO	(15)	بيٺو	bIHAraR̃ᵘ (19)			بيهارڻ
bayAnᵘ (m) (21)		بيانُ	bEgum	(8)	بيگم	bIHaR̃ᵘ (12)			بيهڻ

bh - ڀ								
bhARO (m) (14)		ڀاڙو	(jE) bharsÃ (8)		(جي) ڀرسان	bhaO thIaR̃ᵘ (23)		ڀيؤ ٿيڻ
bhAjjI (f) (11)		ڀاڄي	bhaÑaR̃ᵘ (17)		ڀڄڻُ	bhErO (m) (12)		ڀيرو
bhAᵘ (m) (9)		ڀاءُ	bhaO	(23)	ڀيؤ	bhER̃ᵘ (f) (9)		ڀيڻ
bhitⁱ	(5)	ڀت						

bb - ٻ								
bba	(4)	ٻہ	(jE) bbAHirÃ (8)		(جي) ٻاهران	bbilI	(5)	ٻلي
bbarᵘ	(7)	ٻار	bbaEtAlIHa (15)		ٻائيتاليه	bbIAsI	(15)	ٻياسي
bbArabbacA (m.pl.) (9)		ٻار ٻچا	bbaTIHa	(15)	ٻٽيه	bbIAnavE	(15)	ٻيانوي
bbAraR̃ᵘ (19)		ٻارڻ	bbacO (m)	(9)	ٻچو	bbERI (f)	(15)	ٻيڙي
bbAraHã (9)		ٻارهن	bbudhAiR̃ᵘ	(10)	ٻڌائڻ	bbIO	(12)	ٻيو
bbavanjAHᵘ (15)		ٻاونجاهُ	bbudhaR̃ᵘ	(10)	ٻُڌڻ	bbIHar	(18)	ٻيهر
bbAvIHa (15)		ٻاويه	bbuDhApI	(24)	ٻڍاپي	bbaI	(11)	ٻئي
bbaHatari (15)		ٻاهتر	bbuDhO	(24)	ٻڍو			
bbaHaThⁱ (15)		ٻاهٽ	bbaraR̃ᵘ	(19)	ٻرڻ			

Appendix Three Combined Vocabulary List/ 74

t - ت					
tArO (28)	تارو	taR^u karaR̃^{u} (25)	تڙ ڪرڻ	tāHinkarE (18)	تنهنڪري
tÃ (21)	تان	tasvIr^a (5)	تصوير	tŨ (6)	تون
tAĨ (13)	تائين	tafAvat^u (m) (15)	تفاوت	tavHĨ (6)	توهين
tap^u (m) (9)	تپ	takiRO (15)	تڪڙو	tE (8)	تي
tarsAiR̃^{u} (19)	ترسائڻ	taklIf^a (f) (11)	تڪليف	tayAr karaR̃^{u} (11)	تيار ڪرڻ
tarsaR̃^{u} (10)	ترسڻ	tikhO (11)	تکو	tEraHā (9)	تيرهن
taraR̃u (26)	ترڻ	tamAm^u (7)	تمام	tEz^u (11)	تيز
taR^u (25)	تڙ	tambU (4)	تنبو		

th - ٿ					
thÃv^a (m) (10)	ٿانو	thulHO (7)	ٿلهو	thElHI (f) (9)	ٿيلهي
thadhO (11)	ٿڌو	thOrO (9)	ٿورو	thIaR̃^{u} (12)	ٿيڻ
thakijaR̃^{u} (21)	ٿڪجڻ				

T - ٽ					
TangO (m) (15)	ٽانگو	TapAlI (6)	ٽپالي	TE (4)	ٽي
TapAl^a (f) (16)	ٽپال	TikET^a (f) (20)	ٽڪيٽ	TIÕ	ٽيون
TapAl AfIs (8)	ٽپال آفيس	TOpI (6)	ٽوپي	TIHa (12)	ٽيھ
TapAl^a vijhaR̃^{u} (16)	ٽپال وجهڻ	TORaR̃^{u} (19)	ٽوڙڻ		

Th - ٺ					
ThAHaR̃^{u} (14)	ٺاهڻ	ThIk^u thIaR̃^{u} (26)	ٺيڪ ٿيڻ	ThIk^u karaR̃^{u} (26)	ٺيڪ ڪرڻ

p - پ

(jE) pAr^i (15)	(جي) پار	pakiRaR̃^u (27)	پڪڙݨ	pOkh^i (f) (12)	پوک
pAREsarI (m) (20)	پاڙيسري	pakO (9)	پڪو	pavaR̃^u (11)	پوݨ
pAR̃^a (10)	پاݨ	pakhI (m) (14)	پڪي	pOR̃A (13)	پوٽا
pAR̃I (5)	پاݨي	paghAr^a (f) (11)	پگهار	poitE (19)	پوئتي
pAu (13)	پاءُ	panj^a (4)	پنج	paHucaR̃^u (11)	پهچݨ
pAiR̃^u (17)	پائݨُ	panjAsI (13)	پنجاسي	paHaraR̃^u (12)	پهرݨ
paTATO (m) (11)	پٽاٽو	panjAnavE (13)	پنجانوي	paHarIÕ	پهريون
(jE) puThIÃ (8)	(جي) پنهيان	panjAH^u (12)	پنجاهه	pIAr^u (m) (22)	پيارُ
pacAiR̃^u (20)	پچائݨُ	panjaTIH^a (13)	پنجتيهه	pIArI (28)	پياري
puchaR̃^u (19)	پچݨُ	panjavanjAH^u (13)	پنجونجاهه	pIAlO (26)	پيالو
par^a (7)	پر	panjavIH^a (13)	پنجويهه	pEtI (6)	پيتي
parAR̃O (12)	پراݨو	panjaHatar^i (13)	پنجهتر	paida thIaR̃^u (27)	پيدا ٿيݨ
pardO (4)	پردو	panjaHaTh^i (13)	پنجهٺ	paidA karaR̃^u (27)	پيدا ڪرݨ
pardEsI (21, 28)	پرديسي	panjEtAlIH^a (13)	پنجيتاليهه	pEsa (m.pl.) (10)	پيسا
paRHAiR̃^u (19)	پڙهائݨُ	pandaraHā (9)	پندرهن	pILO (6)	پيلو
paRHaR̃^u (10)	پڙهݨ	pandh^u (m) (21)	پنڌُ	pEnsil^i (5)	پينسل
pasand^u (21)	پسنڊ	pandh^u karaR̃^u (21, 27)	پنڌ ڪرݨ	pIu (m) (9)	پيءُ
pasand^u acaR̃^u (21)	پسند اچݨ	pinaR̃^u (25)	پنݨ	pIAraR̃^u (19)	پيئارݨ
pasand^u karaR̃^u (21)	پسند ڪرݨ	panO (4)	پنو	pIaR̃^u (12)	پيئݨ
pasand^u HUaR̃^u (21)	پسند هئݨ	pUrO (13)	پورو		
pak^a (23)	پڪ	pUrO karaR̃^u (15)	پورو ڪرݨ		

Appendix Three Combined Vocabulary List/ 76

ج - j

jAggaR̃ᵘ (19)	جاڳڙ	javAn (24)	جوان	(jE) rUbarU (15)	(جي) روبرو
jAggaiR̃ᵘ (19)	جاڳائڙ	jaHanᵘ (m) (15)	جھانُ	(jE) sAmHŨ (8)	(جي) سامھون
jAnⁱ (f) (22)	جانِ	jaHiRO (22)	جھڙو	(jE) sababÃ (18)	(جي) سببان
jAnvarᵘ (5)	جانور	jaHaRO ... taHaRO	جھڙو تھڙو	jEstAĨ .... tEstAĨ (28)	جيستائين تيستائين
jAi (f) (14)	جاءِ	(jE) aggIÃ (8)	(جي) اڳيان	jEkababAd (m) (19)	جيڪب آباد
jabalᵘ (26)	جبل	(jE) andar (8)	(جي) اندر	jEkaddaHĨ ta (11)	جيڪڏھن ت
jitÃ ... titÃ	جتان تتان	(jE) badarÃ (18)	(جي) بدران	(jE) karE (18)	(جي) ڪري
jutI (f) (16, 20)	جُتي	(jE) barAbarⁱ (18)	(جي) برابر	jEkO, jO, jEkI, sO	جيڪو، جو جيڪي، سو
jitE ... titE	جتي .. تتي	(jE) bariKlAf (18)	(جي) برخلاف	(jE) lAiq (24)	(جي) لائق
jajᵘ (m) (22)	جُج	(jE) bharsÃ (8)	(جي) پرسان	(jE) mathÃ (8)	(جي) مٿان
juRaR̃ᵘ (24)	جڙڙ	(jE) bbAHirÃ (8)	(جي) ٻاھران	(jE) m'Arafat (24)	(جي) معرفت
jaddaHi ... taddaHi (20)	جڏھن تڏھن	(jE) pArⁱ (15)	(جي) پار	(jE) mUjib (22)	(جي) موجب
jalAiR̃ᵘ (25)	جلائڙ	(jE) puThIÃ (8)	(جي) پنيان	(jE) HEThÃ (8)	(جي) ھيٺان
jaldI (14)	جلدي	jEtrO ... tEtrO	جيترو تيترو	(jE) vicamẼ (15)	(جي) وچ ۾
jumErAtⁱ (f) (18)	جمعراتِ	jEtOR̃Ek.... ta bi (28)	جيتوٽيڪت ب	(jE) vEjhO (8)	(جي) ويجھو
jumO (m) (15)	جمعو	(jE) cOdhArI (15)	(جي) چوڌاري	(jE) vasIlE (24)	(جي) وسيلي
janamᵘ (24)	جنم	jEddÃHã ... tEddÃHã	جيڏانھن تيڏانھن	jIã ... tIã	جيئن تيئن
javAbᵘ (m) (17)	جوابُ	jEddO ... tEddO	جيڏو تيڏو		
javAb ddIaR̃ᵘ (17)	جواب ڏيڙ	(jE) zarI'E (24)	(جي) ذريعي		

Appendix Three Combined Vocabulary List/ 77

jh - جھ					
jhuR^u (23)	جھڙ				

jj - ج					
jjAR̃aR̃^{u} (25)	جاٽڙ	jjaÑa (f) (21)	جَجَ	jjamaR̃^{u} (17)	جمڙ

c -					
cAcO (m) (21)	چاچو	cukaR̃^{u} (23)	چُڪڙ	cOr^u (m) (21)	چور
cAr^j (4)	چار	cag̃O (6)	چڳو	cOrAsI (18)	چوراسي
cAk^u (24)	چاق	cag̃O bhalO (9)	چڳو ڀلو	cOrAnavE (18)	چورانوي
cAndI (23)	چاندي	culHO (26)	چلهو	cavaR̃^{u} (10)	چوڙ
cÃvar^a (m.pl) (12)	چانور	camcO (26)	چمچو	cOvIHa (18)	چوويهَ
cÃHi (f) (11)	چانهَ	cOvanjAH^u (18)	چوونجاهُ	cOHatar^i (18)	چوهتر
cÃHidAnI (26)	چانهَ داني	cOthÕ	چوٿون	cOHaTh^i (18)	چوهٺ
cAHaR̃^{u} (11)	چاهڙ	cOTIHa (18)	چوتيهَ	cOEtAlIHa (18)	چوئيتاليهَ
ciThI (f) (12)	چني	(jE) cOdhArI (15)	جي چوڌاري		
caRHaR̃^{u} (10)	چڙهڻ	cOddaHã (9)	چوڏهن		

ch - چھ					
chA (4)	چا	chA lAi ta (18)	چا لاءِ تَہ	chAEtAlIHa (19)	چائيتاليهَ
chAchO (24)	چاچو	chA lAi jO (18)	چا لاءِ جو	chat^i (5)	چت
chAchI (25)	چاچي	chAHatar^i (19)	چاهتر	chaTIHa (19)	چتيهَ
chARHaR̃^{u} (19)	چاڙهڙ	chAHaTh^i (19)	چاهٺ	chaddaR̃^{u} (10)	چڏڙ
chA kAR̃^{a} ta (18)	چا ڪاڻ	chAvanjAH^u (19)	چاونجاهُ	chUrI (26)	چري

Appendix Three Combined Vocabulary List/ 78

chil^u (26)	چِل	chO ta (18)	چوتہ	chavIHa (19)	چویہہ	
chilaR̃^u (26)	چِلٹ	chO jO (18)	چوجو	chaH^a (6)	چھ	
chanchar^u (m) (15)	چِنچر	chOkirO (5)	چوکرو	chaHAsI (19)	چھاسي	
chO (18)	چو	chOkirI (5)	چوکري	chaHAnavE (19)	چھانوي	

K - خ						
KAs (14)	خاصُ	Kidmat^a (24)	خدمت	KuS^i (9)	خوش	
KAlI (6)	خالي	KarAb^u (11)	خرابُ	KuS thIaR̃^u (27)	خوش تیٹھ	
KAmOSI (f) (17)	خاموشي	KarId^a karaR̃^u (11)	خرید کرڻ	KuS karaR̃^u (27)	خوش کرڻ	
Kub (23)	خُب	Kat^u (4)	خط	KEr (9)	خیر	
Kabar^a (8)	خبر	KatA (5)	خطا	KErIat (f) (9)	خیریت	
KabardAr (12)	خبردار	KatarnAk^u (23)	خطرناک	KayAl (m) (15)	خیال	
KudA (m) (9)	خدا	KamIs^a (f) (15)	خمیس			

H - ح						
HAl^u (m) (9)	حال	HifAzat^a (f) (17)	حفاظت	HaiderabAd^i (m) (19)	حیدرآباد	
Halat^a (f) (14)	حالت	Hukum^u (m) (22)	حکمُ			

d - د						
dAdU (m) (19)	دادُو	darivAzO (4)	دروازو	dAvat^a (f) (20)	دعوت	
darjO (m) (9)	درجو	darIAH^u (m) (15)	دریاہُ	daf'O (m) (12)	دفعو	
darzI (m) (16)	درزي	duSman m (18)	دشمن	dukAn^u (26)	دکان	
darI (7)	دري	du'A (f) (15)	دُعا	dilcasp^u (7)	دلچسپ	
durust^u (23)	درست	du'A ghUraR̃^u (15)	دعا گھرڻ	dil laggaR̃^u (20)	دل لگڻ	

Appendix Three Combined Vocabulary List/ 79

davA (5)	دوا	dEr^i (f) (15)	دیرِ	dEgg^i (26) deg^i	دیگ دیگ
dOst^u (m) (12)	دوست	dEsI (21)	دیسي	dEggcI (26) dEgcI	دیگچي دیگچي

dh - ڌ					
dhak^u (28) dhObI (6)	ڌک ڌوبي	dhOaR̃^{u} (10)	ڌوئڙ	dhI^a (f) (9)	ڌيءَ

D - ڊ					
DakTar^u (6)	ڊاڪٽر	DukaR̃^{u} (25)	ڊڪٽ	DORaR̃^{u} (19)	ڊوڙٽ
DijjaR̃^{u} (25)	ڊجٽ	DighO (7)	ڊگھو		

Dh - ڊھ					
DharaR̃^{u} (20)	ڊھرٽ				

dd - ڏ					
ddADhO (13)	ڏاڍو	ddingO (22)	ڏنگو	ddiHARI (12)	ڏھاڙي
ddAddO (26)	ڏاڏو	ddisaR̃^{u} (10)	ڏسٽ	ddEDh^u (13)	ڏيڍُ
ddAddI (26)	ڏاڏي	ddOI (26)	ڏوئي	ddIH^u (m) (12)	ڏينھن
ddÃH^a (10)	ڏانھن	ddaHa (6)	ڏھ	ddIaR̃^{u} (10)	ڏيٽ

z - ذ					
(jE) zarI'E (24)	(جي ذريعي)	zikur^u (m) (20)	ذڪرُ	zikur karaR̃^{u} (20)	ذڪر ڪرٽ

Appendix Three Combined Vocabulary List/ 80

r - ر					
rAt^i (f) (12)	رات	rastO (8)	رستو	rOz^u (m) (12)	روزُ
rAzI (23)	راضي	rasam^u (23)	رسم	rOzAnO (12)	روزانو
rAnd^i karaR̃^{u} (11)	راند كرڻ	rakhaR̃^{u} (10)	رکڻ	rOzO rakhaR̃^{u} (11)	روزو رکڻ
rAndIkO (m)(12)	رانديكو	ruggO (8)	رڳو	raonaq^a (f) (20)	رونق
rabbaR^u (5)	ربڙ	randhaR̃^{u} (26)	رنڌڻ	rOaR^u (25)	روئڻ
rupIyO (m) (9)	رپيو	rãng^u (7)	رنگ	raHijaR̃^{u} (21)	رهجڻ
radI (25)	ردي	rang^u karaR̃^{u} (11)	رنگ كرڻ	raHaR̃^{u} (10)	رهڻ
risAlO (8)	رسالو	(jE) rUbarU (15)	(جي) روبرو		

z - ز					
zAl (5)	زال	zanAnO (8)	زنانو	zEtUn (26)	زيتون
zamIn^a (f) (9)	زمين	zIAdaH^a (13, 26)	زياده	zEvar^u (23)	زيور
zamIndAr^u (m) (9)	زميندار				

s - س					
sADha (13)	ساديا	sabaq^u (m) (11)	سبق	satar^i (12)	ستر
sArI (f) (12)	ساري	sibaR̃^{u} (14)	سبڻ	sataraHã (11)	سترهن
(jE) sAmHŨ (8)	(جي) سامهون	sabh^u (9)	سڀ	satavanjAH^u (20)	ستونجاهُ
sÃ (10)	سان	subhAR̃E (11)	سڀاڻي	sataHatar^i (20)	ستهتر
sAnjhI (f) (14)	سانجهي	sat^a (6)	ست	sataHathi (20)	ستهٺ
sAHERI (f) (12)	ساهيڙي	satAsI (20)	ستاسي	satEtAlIH^i (20)	ستيتاليهَ
sAĨ (6)	سائين	satAnavE (20)	ستانوي	sATh^i (12)	سٺ
sabab^u (m) (18)	سببُ	satAvIHa (20)	ستاويهَ	suThO (9)	سٿو
(jE) sababÃ (18)	(جي) سببان	sataTIHa (20)	ستتيهَ	sij^u (m) (16)	سجُ

sajjO (17)	سجو	saghaR̃u (14)	سگھڙ	sOraHā (9)	سورھن
suÑARaR̃u (17, 24)	سڃاڻڻُ	salAmatI (f) (11)	سلامتي	sOlO (14)	سولو
sacu (23)	سچ	samjhAiR̃u (10)	سمجھائڻ	sUmaru (m) (15)	سومر
saddu karaR̃u (22)	سڏ ڪرڻ	samjhaR̃u (10)	سمجھڻ	sOnu (23)	سون
sasu (f) (22)	سُس	sumHaraR̃u (19)	سمھارڻ	savEra (15, 16)	سوير
sustu (7)	سست	sumHaR̃u (12)	سمھڻ	suHiR̃O (6)	سھڻو
sastO (11)	سستو	sandasu (10)	سندس	sIArO (m) (12)	سيارو
safArISi (24)	سفارش	sanHO (7)	سنھو	sEru (m) (13)	سيرُ
safar karaR̃u (13)	سفر ڪرڻ	sao (12)	سو	sIu (m) (18)	سيُء
sakharu (m) (19)	سکر	savA (13)	سوا	sEkhAraR̃u (19)	سيکارڻ
sikhaR̃u (17)	سکڻُ	sUru (m) (9)	سور		

ش - S

SAdI (f) (15)	شادي	SaKsI (28)	شخصي	SOru (28)	شور
SAgirdu (4)	شاگرد	SarU'u (m) (15)	شروع	SaHaru (8)	شھر
SAma (m) (12)	شامَ	SarU' karaR̃u (15)	شروع ڪرڻ	SISO (4)	شيشو
SAyadi (11)	شايد	Saku (23)	شڪ	SaI (f) (10)	شيء
SaKs (28)	شخص	Sukuru (m) (9)	شڪر		

ص - s

sAfu (10)	صاف	subuHu (m) (12)	صبحُ	sallIbu (m) (22)	صَلِيبُ
sAf karaR̃u (11)	صاف ڪرڻ	sarAHI (26)	صراحي	sUfu (m) (11)	صوف
sAHibu (6)	صاحب				

z - ض

| zarUr (14) | ضرور | zarUrI (11) | ضروري | zarUrat^a (26) | ضرورت |

a - ع

Adat^a (24)	عادت	adAlat^a (f) (22)	عدالت	umar^i (24)	عمر
ibAdat^a (f) (15)	عبادت	adAlat^a karaR̃^{u} (22)	عدالت کرڻ	umarbhar^i (24)	عمر ڀر
ibAdat karaR̃^{u} (13)	عبادت کرڻ	izat^a (24)	عزت	aorat^a (5)	عورت
ajab^u (28)	عجب	ilAj^a (28)	علاج	IsA masIH^u (22)	عيسىٰ مسيحُ

G - غ

| Galat^i (19) | غلط | GalatI thIaR̃^{u} (27) | غلطي ٿيڻ | GarIb^u (18) | غريبُ |
| GalatI (f) (19) | غلطي | GalatI karaR̃^{u} (27) | غلطي کرڻ | | |

t - ط

| tAlib ilm (23) | طالب علم | taraH^a (f) (12) | طرح | | |

f - ف

fAidO (26)	فائدو	faraz^u (23)	فرض	fOtO kaDhaR̃^{u} (15)	فوٽو کڍڻ
farAsI (5)	فراسي	fasal (m) (13)	فصل	faisalO (m) (20)	فيصلو
faraS^u (4)	فرش	faqat^i (9)	فقط	faisalO karaR̃^{u} (20)	فيصلو کرڻ

ph - ق

| phATaR̃^{u} (17) | قاتڻُ | phaR̃I (f) (17) | قڻي | phaR̃I ddIaR̃^{u} (17) | قڻي ڏيڻ |
| phAsaR̃^{u} (21) | قاسڻ | | | | |

Appendix Three Combined Vocabulary List/ 83

ق - q					
qAnUn^u (m) (22)	قانونُ	phiTI karaR̃u (26)	ڦٽي ڪرڻ	qaom^a (26)	قوم
qurAn SarIf^u (m) (10)	قرآن شريف	qalam^u (4)	قلم	qImat^a (f) (13)	قيمت
qisim^u (m) (9)	قسم	qamIs^a (f) (16)	قميص	qImtI (13)	قيمتي

ڪ - k					
kAThI (f) (13)	ڪاني	kujh^u (8)	ڪجھ	kalH^a (13)	ڪلھ، ڪالھ
kApI (5)	ڪاپي	kacO (9)	ڪچو	kam^u (7)	ڪم
kAr^i (24)	ڪار	kaDhaR̃^{u} (10)	ڪيڊ	kamAiR̃^{u} (14, 17)	ڪمائڻ
kArO (7)	ڪارو	kaddaHI (14)	ڪڌھن	kamarO (4)	ڪمرو
kAGaz^u (4)	ڪاغذ	kurARO (24)	ڪراڙو	kam karaR̃^{u} (11)	ڪم ڪرڻ
kAfI (13)	ڪافي	kaRAHO (26)	ڪڙاهو	kunjI (5)	ڪنجي
kAmIAb thiaR̃^{u} (18)	ڪامياب ٿيڻ	kaRAHI (26)	ڪڙاهي	kũvAr (23)	ڪنوار
kAnTO (26)	ڪانٽو	karAiR̃^{u} (19)	ڪرائڻ	kO (8)	ڪو
kAviRijaR̃^{u} (21)	ڪاوڙجڻ	kursI (5)	ڪرسي	kOThI (f) (17)	ڪوٺي
kÃÕ? (19)	ڪائون	karikEt^i (25)	ڪرڪيٽ	kUr^u (27)	ڪوڙ
kabbaT^u (4)	ڪبٽ	karaR̃^{u} (10)	ڪرڻ	kOSiSi (f) (20)	ڪوشش
kitAb^u (4)	ڪتاب	kiraR̃^{u} (21)	ڪرڻ	kOSiSi karaR̃^{u} (20)	ڪوشش ڪرڻ
kutO (4)	ڪتو	kirOR^u (12)	ڪروڙ	kOH^u (26)	ڪوھ
kithÃ? (10)	ڪٿان	(jE) karE (18)	(جي) ڪري	kOETA (23)	ڪوئيٽا
kithE (8)	ڪٿي	kukuR^u (5)	ڪڪڙ	kaHiRO (7)	ڪھڙو
kapRA (4)	ڪپڙا	kalAk^u (m) (13)	ڪلاڪُ	kuHaR̃^{u} (17)	ڪُھڻ
kapRO (4)	ڪپڙو	kulf^u (5)	ڪلف	kEtrO (9)	ڪيترو
kapaH^a (f) (12)	ڪپهَ	kilO (m) (13)	ڪلو	kEddÃha? (10)	ڪيڏانهن

Appendix Three Combined Vocabulary List/

kEr^u (4)	کیر	kaĩcI (f) (17)	کَینچي	kĨa (9)	کَیئن			
kEstA Ĩ (28)	کیستائین	kEvI (26)	کیوي					

kh - ک						
khArAiR̃^{u} (19)	کارائٹ	khAiR̃^{u} (12)	کائٹ	khOlaR̃^{u} (10)	کولٹ
khAdhO (m) (16)	کاڈو	khaRkAiR̃^{u} (25)	کڑکائٹ	khUH^u (m) (19)	کُوہ
khÃ (10, 21)	کان	khilaR̃^{u} (21)	کِلٹ	khE (9)	کي
khÃ aggE (15)	کان اگِي	khanD^u (f) (9)	کنڈ	khEddaR̃^{u} (14)	کیڈٹ
khÃ pOi (15)	کان پوءِ	khaR̃I acaR̃^{u} (17)	کٹي اچٹ	khIr^u (m) (9)	کیر
khÃ savAi (21)	کانسواءِ	khaR̃I vaÑaR̃^{u} (17)	کٹي وِجٹ	khIsO (8)	کیسو
khÃ vaThI (21)	کان وٹي				

g - گ						
gAddI (f) (12)	گاڈِي	gaddijaR̃^{u} (27)	گڈِجٹ	gul^u (4)	گل
gAH^u (m) (12)	گاہُ	guzrEl^u (13)	گذریل	gulAb^u (m) (19)	گلابُ
gap^u (m) (21)	گپُ	garam (12)	گرمُ	gilAs^u (4)	گلاس
gajar^a (f) (11)	گجر	garam karaR̃^{u} (12)	گرم کرٹ	gunaHagAr^u (m) (22)	گنہگارُ
gudAm (m) (11)	گدام	garamI (f) (12)	گرمي	gIH^u (m) (13)	گیہُ
gadd^u (11)	گڈ				

gh - گھ						
ghaT^i (13)	گھٹِ	ghaRIAI^u (8)	گھڑیال	ghORO (5)	گھوڑو
ghar^u (7)	گھر	ghaR̃O (8, 9)	گھٹو		
gharavArI (f) (16)	گھرواري	ghOT^u (23)	گھوت		

Appendix Three Combined Vocabulary List/

gg - گ					
ggARHO (7)	گاڑھو	ggAlHAiR̃ᵘ (10)	گالھائٹ	ggaR̃aR̃ᵘ (25)	گٹڑ
ggAiR̃ᵘ (26)	گائٹ	ggaraR̃ᵘ (26)	گرڑ	ggOThᵘ (8)	گوٹھ
ggAlHⁱ (f) (10)	گالھ	gginHaR̃ᵘ (17)	گنھڑ	ggOlaR̃ᵘ (22)	گولڑ

l - ل					
lArI (f) (14)	لاري	laggAtAr (21)	لگاتار	langhaR̃ᵘ (21)	لنگھڑ
lAi (11)	لاءِ	laggaR̃ᵘ (11)	لگڑ	laHaR̃ᵘ (14, 17)	لھڑ
(jE) lAiq (24)	(جي) لائق	lakhᵘ (12)	لک	laHaR̃aR̃ᵘ (28)	لھڑڑ
laRAI (27)	لڑائي	likhaR̃ᵘ (10)	لکڑ	lEkin (18)	ليکن
lifAfO (m) (10)	لفافو				

m - م					
mAraR̃ᵘ (19)	مارڑ	maTᵘ (26)	مٹ	maradAR̃O (8)	مرداڑو
mAlHI, mAlI (6)	مالھي، مالي	maTarᵃ (m.pl) (13)	مٽَر	marimatᵃ (f) (19)	مرمتَ
mÃ (10, 21)	مان	maTkO (26)	مٽڪو	marimatᵃ karaR̃ᵘ (19)	مرمت ڪرڑ
mÃ (6)	مان	miThO (11)	مٺو	maraR̃ᵘ (14)	مرڑ
mAnI (f) (10)	ماني	machI (f) (18)	مڇي	marIzᵘ (m) (22)	مَريضُ
mAR̃HU (4)	ماڑھو	miHinatᵃ (f) (18)	محنتَ	mURasᵘ (m) (9)	مڑس
mAᵘ (f) (9)	ماءُ	miHinatᵃ karaR̃ᵘ (18)	محنت ڪرڑ	mizAjᵘ (m) (9)	مزاج
mAᵘ pIᵘ (m.Pl) (10)	ماءُ پيءُ	miHinatI (7)	محنتي	mazdUrᵘ (6)	مزدور
matÃ (23)	متان	maÑaR̃ᵘ (28)	مڃڑ	mizmAnᵘ m (18)	مزمانُ
(jE) mathÃ (8)	(جي) مٿان	madad karaR̃ᵘ (11)	مدد ڪرڑ	mazUrᵘ (6)	مزور
mathO (m)(9, 28)	مٿو	mIrcᵃ (23)	مرچ	masᵘ (5)	مس

Appendix Three Combined Vocabulary List/ 86

musAfir[u] (28)	مسافر	milaR̃[u] (14)	ملڻ	mOkal[a] (f) (15)	موکل
mistrI (m) (16)	مستري	mumkin (11)	ممکن	mOkilaR̃[u] (10)	موکلڻ
misTar (8)	مسٹر	minT[u] (28)	منٽ	mOlvI (6)	مولوي
masjid[i] (m) (13)	مسجدِ	manjhÃ (21)	منجهان	mUmbatI (f) (17)	موم بتّي
misaz (8)	مسز	manjhand[i] (m) (12)	منجهندِ	maHAngO (11)	مهانگو
masvAR[a] (f) (14)	مسواڙ	mũjhI pavaR̃[u] (21)	منجهي پوڻ	maHarbAnI (9)	مهرباني
masIHI (22)	مسيحي	mUnDI (23)	مندي	maHarbAnI karE (16)	مهرباني کري
muSkil (14)	مشکل	munO (13)	مُنو	maHInO (m) (12)	مهينو
mazbUt[u] (6)	مضبوط	maR̃[u] (m) (13)	مڻُ	mẼ (8)	مُ
mu'AfI (24)	معافي	mOt[u] (24)	موت	mITar[u] (m) (13)	ميٽرُ
mu'Af thIaR̃[u] (27)	معاف ٿيڻ	mOTI acaR̃[u] (16)	موٽي اچڻ	mER[u] (m) (21)	ميڙُ
mu'Af karaR̃[u] (11, 27)	معاف کرڻ	(jE) mUjib (22)	(جي) موجب	mEz[a] (5)	ميز
(jE) m'Arafat (24)	(جي) معرفت	mOcI (m) (16)	موچي	mĨHũ (m) (11)	مينهُن
mAlUm karaR̃[u] (20)	معلوم کرڻ	maosam[a] (f) (12)	موسمَ	mEvO (4)	ميوو
magar (18)	مگر	maoq'O (25)	موقعو		

n - ن						
na (4)	نَ	nAnI (26)	ناني	nikAH[u] (23)	نڪاح
nArangI (f) (11)	نارنگي	natIjO (23, 24)	نتيجو	nikaraR̃[u] (14)	نڪرڻ
nAlO (7)	نالو	naras[i] (f) (15)	نرسِ	nakI (18)	نَڪي
nAnO (26)	نانو	naram (12)	نرمُ	nimAz[a] paRHaR̃[u] (11)	نماز پڙهڻ

Appendix Three Combined Vocabulary List/ 87

nambar^u (24)	نمبر	nava (6)	نَو	navE (12)	نوي
namUnO (m) (22)	نَمُونو	navAnavE (24)	نواڻوي	naõ (12)	نئون
nanDhapIR̃^{u} (24)	نندپيڙ	naojavAn (24)	نوجوان	nEran^a (f) (16)	نيرنِ
nanDhO (6)	نندو	nOkar^u (6)	نوڪر	nIrO (6)	نيرو
nũHã (f) (22)	نُنهَن	nOkarIaR̃I (6)	نوڪرياڻي		

H - ھ					
HAO, HA (4)	هائو، ها	HujaR̃^{u} (11)	هجڻ	HavA (f) (11)	هوا
HArI (m) (18)	هاري	Har^i (12)	هرِ	HOddÃHã (10)	هوڏانهن
HAR̃E (10)	هاڻي	HazAr^u (12)	هزار	HOSIAr (7)	هوشيار
HitE (8)	هِتي	HaftO (m) (12)	هفتو	(jE) HEThÃ (8)	(جي) هيٺان
HutE (8)	هُتي	Hik^u, HikaRO	هڪ/هڪڙو	HEddÃHã (10)	هيڏانهن
Hath^u (m) (9)	هٿ	HalAiR̃^{u} (19)	هلائڻ	HĨara (27)	هينئر
Hath^a milAiR̃^{u} (25)	هٿ ملائڻ	HalaR̃^{u} (10)	هلڻ	HI^u/HI^a (4/5)	هِيءُ/هِيءَ
Hat^u (8)	هٿ	HU/HU^a (4/5)	هُو/هوءَ		

v - و					
vApas karaR̃^{u} (11)	واپس ڪرڻ	vaT^i (9)	وٽ	(jE) vicamẼ (15)	(جي) وچمِ
vADhO (m) (17)	واڍو	vaTÃ (21)	وٽان	vadhIk^a (11)	وڌيڪ
vAra (m.pl) (17)	وارَ	vaThaR̃^{u} (10)	وٺڻ	vaddO (6)	وڏو
vArO (m) (12)	وارو	vaThI acaR̃^{u} (17)	وٺي اچڻ	varI (10)	وري
-vArO (m) (15)	وارو	vaThI vaÑaR̃^{u} (17)	وٺي وڃڻ	vIRHaR̃^{u} (17)	وڙهڻ
vAl^u (m) (13)	وال	vijhaR̃^{u} (10)	وجهڻ	visAiR̃^{u} (14)	وسائڻ
vAngUr (22)	وانگر	viÑAiR̃^{u} (19)	وڃائڻ	visaraR̃^{u} (21)	وسرڻ
vAH^u (m) (15)	واهُ	vaÑaR̃^{u} (10)	وڃڻ	(jE) vasIlE (24)	(جي) وسيلي

Appendix Three Combined Vocabulary List/ 88

va 'alEkum asalAm (9)	وعلیکم السلام	vaR̃ᵘ (m) (14)	وڻُ	vEcArO (18)	ویچارو
vaqtᵘ (m) (9)	وقت	vaR̃aR̃ᵘ (28)	وڻڻُ	vIHa (11)	ویھ
vikaR̃aR̃ᵘ (vikAmaR̃ᵘ) (14)	وکڻڻُ وکامڻُ	vEThO (15)	ویٺو	vEHaraR̃ᵘ (19)	ویھارڻ
vaggaR̃ᵘ (23)	وڳڻُ	(jE) vEjhO (8)	(جي) ویجھو	vEHaR̃ᵘ (14)	ویھڻ

a - ء					
aĨ (7)	ء				

y - ي					
yA (11)	یا	ya'nE, yAnE (13, 19)	یعني	yakIn karaR̃ᵘ (24)	یقین کرڻ
yAraH ã (9)	یارھن	yaqInᵘ (23)	یقین		

APPENDIX 4 – SUBJECT INDEX

Note 1: the page numbers are given as 109.4 (10) meaning page 109, point #4, lesson 10.

Note 2: Most Sindhi words can be located by looking them up in the Reviews or in Appendix 3 where their lesson number is given. However, a few words have special explanations in the text and some of those explanations are given here.

acaR̃ᵘ 301 , 307 , 315.3

Adjective: ... 47
- comparison ... 120
- demonstrative ... 55
- imperfect part. as ... 297
- possessive ... 61
- repetition ... 309
- statical ... 311.2
- superlative ... 120

Adverb: ... 159.10-11 , 169.4 , 242.7
- correlatives ... 253.8
- repetition ... 310

Age - of people and things ... 288

bayAnᵘ karaR̃ᵘ ...263.4

bbIO ... 145.5, 159.15

bi ... 47.5-6, 86.3

bIhAR̃ᵘ 181.3 , bIThO 197 , bIThE 235.c

caHaR̃ᵘ 300

cavaR̃ᵘ 103.4

chA ... 31-33, 61.4

chaddaR̃ᵘ 103.4 , chaddE ddEO 271.4

Comparison: ... 120

Conditions:
- Fulfillable ... 292
- Unfulfillable ... 292

Conjunctions: ... 225

Conjunctive participles: ... 193 , 234.2 , 285.1 , 331.1

Correlatives/Relatives: ... 249 , 328

cukaR̃ᵘ 285

Days of the Week: ... 179

ddEkhAraR̃ᵘ 103.4

ddIaR̃ᵘ 103.4, 270

dOst ... 143.3

Each/every: ... 309.1

Fractions: ... 156 , 333.2

Future tense ... 167

Future Imperative ... 173.4

garamI ... 141.3

ggAlhAiR̃ᵘ 101.1

ghÃRO ... 84, 85.2

ghuraR̃ᵘ 185

Greetings: ... 83

HA ... 294.1

halaR̃ᵘ 145.3, 172.6, 195.6, 215.3, 265

HitE/HutE ... 72

HuaR̃ᵘ 45, 160, 172.4

HujaR̃ᵘ 126

I ... 70.6, 299.10

Iã ... 253.8

Imperfect participles: ... defined 138.2, 281.2, 283.2, 297, 306, 307.1, 322

Imperative ... 99

Indefinite/definite articles: ... 31.4

Intensifiers: ... 264 , 331

Interjections: ... see Vocatives

jEkeddaHĨ ... 124, 294

jEkI ... 251.4

jEkO ... 250

jjAraR̃ᵘ 301

jO ... 51, 62, 249

kaddahi ... 169.1

kA Ẽ (bajE) ... 242

KarId^a karaR̃^u ...263.4

KayAl ... 180.6

kEddAha ... 107.6

keHiRO ... 57, 61.4, 82

kEr^u ... 31, 57

kestaĨ ... 329

kEtrO ... 84

khÃ ... 107.5, 121.1, 259, 281.3

khapE ... 144

khE ... 86, 102

kIã ... 84

kithÃ ... 107.7

kithE ... 66

kO ... 68

kucO/pakO ... 83.3

Kinship: ... 88 , 107.4 , 307

luggaR̃^u 126.8, 141.3, 239, 254.10, 263, 326.7

matÃ ... 284.7

m Ẽ ... 68

milaR̃^u 196.7, 253.7

Monetary Units: ... 155

nAO ... 142.9

Necessity: ... 143 , 184-186 , 308

Nouns:
- Feminine: ... 37 , 59
- imperfect participles as nouns: ... 300
- infinitives as nouns: ... 181
- masculine: ... 29 , 41.5 , 46.1 , 59
- oblique forms: ... 53-55
- repetition of nouns: ... 309

Numbers
- 1-5 ... 29
- 6-10 ... 43
- 11-16 ... 81
- 17-20 ... 118
- Cardinal numbers by ones ... 166
- Cardinal numbers by twos ... 178
- Cardinal numbers by threes ... 212
- Cardinal numbers by fours ... 223
- Cardinal numbers by fives ... 152
- Cardinal numbers by sixes ... 232
- Cardinal numbers by sevens ... 245
- Cardinal numbers by eights ... 269
- Cardinal numbers by nines ... 288
- Cardinal numbers by tens ... 137
- Chart of numbers ... 135
- Fractions ... 156
- One thousand and greater ... 137
- Ordinal numbers
  - oblique form ... 147
  - use of ... 145
- repetition of numbers ... 309

Object/subject: ... 68, 103, 144.1, 217, 227.8, 298.4-6, 320.2

Oblique Forms
- masculine and feminine words ... 53 , 59
- kEr^u and kaHiRO ... 57
- demonstratives ... 57
- personal pronouns ... 59
- of jO ... 62
- kO ... 68
- pAR̃^a ... 108
- sandas^u ...110
- cardinal numbers ... 119 , 155.3
- nAO ... 142.9
- monetary units ... 155.4-6
- reflexive ... 109.4
- subjects in past tense ... 227.2
- time telling ... 241.1
- correlatives and relative words ... 252

OdhaR̃^u 329

paE ... 234

pAR̃^a ... 108

Particles:

- HA ... 294.1
- I ... 299.10
- matÃ ... 284.7
- paE ... 234
- payO ... 197.2

pasand ... 263

Past Tense (Simple) ... 160, 213

Past Continuous Tense ... 196

Past Habitual Tense ... 170

Past Perfect Tense ... 261

pavaR̃ᵘ 187.2-3, 264

payO ... 197.2

Perfect participle: defined 213.2, exceptions 219.6, 311, 322

Permission: ... 270, 273

Postpositions: ... 72, 180, 224, 271, 246, 259, 290

Prefixes/suffixes: ... 57.4, 226.5, 331

Present (simple) Tense ... 45, 104

Present Continuous Tense ... 233

Present Habitual Tense ... 138

Present Perfect Tense ... 227

Possibility/uncertainty: ... 283

Prices/cost: ... 153

Probability/presumption: ... 280

Progression: ... 307

Pronominal suffixes: 246, 314

Pronouns:
- personal: ... 40.2 (5), 44 (6), 59.5 (7)
- pronouns: ... 30 (4), 38 (5), 40 (5), 55-56 (7)
- reflexive: ... 108 (10)
- repetition: ... 310 (26)

Questions
- chA ... 31-33, 61.4
- ghARÕ ... 84, 85.2
- kaddahi ... 169.1
- kAẼ (bajE) ... 242
- kEddAha ... 107.6
- keHiRO ... 57, 61.4, 82
- kEr ... 31, 57
- kestaĨ ... 329
- kEtrO ... 84
- kIã ... 84
- kithÃ ... 107.7
- kithE ... 66

raHaR̃ᵘ ... 196, 213, 233, 306

Relatives/correlatives – see above on correlatives

Relatives (family) – see Kinship

Repetition of words ... 309

Reported speech ... 272

Rhyming words: ... 327.6

sabhᵘ ... 107.8

saghaR̃ᵘ 200

samjhAiR̃ᵘ 101.1

sandasᵘ ... 110

sikhaR̃ᵘ 303

Sentence order: ... 31.5, 32.4, 33.2, 47.5, 48.2, 68.3, 82.2, 107.1, 187.4

Sentence types
- compound sentences ... 249
- fulfillable conditions ... 292
- negative ... 105, 139, 160, 170, 198, 214, 216.6, 218, 228, 236.4, 262, 264
- probability/presumption ... 280
- uncertainty/possibility ... 283
- unfulfillable conditions ... 294

Subject – see above object/subject

Subjunctive Tense ... 124

Suffixes – see above on Prefixes

tE ... 68, 184, 241.3

thIaR̃ᵘ 215.3

Time
- telling time ... 238
- time of day ... 141.2,4,6; 169.3;
- seasons ... 142.10

To Know How to ... 301

To Learn How to ... 303

vaÑaR̃ᵘ 264

vaRaR̃ᵘ 329

vArO ... 182

vaThaR̃ᵘ ... 331

vaTⁱ ... 86

vEHaR̃ᵘ ... 181.3, vEThE 197, vEThO 235.c,

Verbs
- active verbs ... 320
- causal verbs ... 236
- compound verbs ... 120, 141.7, 215.5, 319.1
- conjunctive participles ... 193
- infinitive ... 45.1-3, 101.1-3, 181, 184, 186, 270, 273, 300, 301, 303, 322.1, 326
- intransitive/transitive ... defined 108 (footnotes), 213-220, 227, 261, 282.5, 284.5, 322
- passive verbs ... 317, 321
- roots ... 101
- transitive – see above - intransitive

Verb Tenses (see also Appendix 2)
- future ... 167
- future imperative ... 173.4
- imperative ... 99
- past (simple) ... 160, 213
- past habitual ... 170
- past continuous ... 196
- past perfect ... 261
- present (simple) ... 45, 104
- present habitual ... 138
- present continuous ... 233
- present perfect ... 227
- subjunctive ...124

Vocative ... 142

Weight ... units of – 156.11

Writing ... ا 93, ب etc. (ن + ي) 93, د etc. 95, ر etc. 95, و 96, ه 96, ج etc. 114, س etc. 115, ک 115, ك etc. 115, ل etc. 116, م 116, ص etc. 131, ط etc. 131, ع etc. 132, ق etc. 133, ء 133, diacritical markings 134, numbers 135

zarUr ... 308

zikur karaR̃ᵘ ... 251.3

www.ingramcontent.com/pod-product-compliance
Lightning Source LLC
Chambersburg PA
CBHW080723300426
44114CB00019B/2474